XENOTRANSPLANTATION

This book is dedicated with love to the memory of
Bill and Judy

The authors are grateful to the Department of Health for research support. However, the book does not represent the views of the Department, and the themes and conclusions in the book are solely those of the authors.

Xenotransplantation

Law and Ethics

SHEILA A.M. McLEAN and LAURA WILLIAMSON
University of Glasgow, UK

Routledge
Taylor & Francis Group
LONDON AND NEW YORK

First published 2005 by Ashgate Publishing

Reissued 2019 by Routledge
2 Park Square, Milton Park, Abingdon, Oxon, OX14 4RN
52 Vanderbilt Avenue, New York, NY 10017

Routledge is an imprint of the Taylor & Francis Group, an informa business

A Library of Congress record exists under LC control number:

ISBN 13: 978-0-8153-9916-2 (hbk)
ISBN 13: 978-1-138-35865-2 (pbk)
ISBN 13: 978-1-351-14272-4 (ebk)

Contents

Preface

It is always risky writing a book in areas of law where things can change very rapidly. It has been our fate that, since this manuscript was submitted, some very significant changes have been made in law; changes to which it is impossible for us to do justice. We have, with the kind tolerance of Ashgate, been able to make brief reference to the Human Tissue Act 2004, the Mental Capacity Act 2005 and the Human Tissue (Scotland) Bill 2005, but our consideration of these legal reforms is necessarily short and descriptive. In part, this is to accommodate the fact that the manuscript had already been paginated, but it also arises from the fact that the impact of the new laws remain currently unclear.

Second, since the manuscript was submitted, the case of *Chester* v *Ashfar*[1] has been reported. As there is considerable emphasis on consent to treatment in this book, it is unfortunate that no consideration of this case is possible within the narrative of the book itself. However, as this case seems likely to have a major impact on the law of consent, we will discuss it briefly here. Despite our critique of the *Bolam Test*[2] in later chapters, *Chester* v *Ashfar* seems to have moved UK law away from a rigid application of this test, and indeed can be said to go further than the cases which succeeded *Bolam* in recent years[3] and to have modified its apparently simplistic commitment to the professional test, which has traditionally informed UK law in this area.

Although not a unanimous decision, *Chester* seems to give weight more heavily than in the past to the rights of the individual to make decisions based on the disclosure of risks, even if they are small. *Chester*, then, seems to challenge the decision in *Sidaway* v *Board of Governors of the Bethlem Royal Hospital and the Maudsley Hospital*[4] and seems to enhance patients' rights. Its particular relevance for this book lies in the extent to which the House of Lords – by majority – was willing to accept what could be seen as a modification of the general rules of causation in order, as Lord Steyn put it, to 'right wrongs'[5] and reflect 'the reasonable expectations of the public in contemporary society'.[6]

The issue under consideration was whether or not Ms Chester would have avoided the surgery for all time had she been warned of the risk which eventuated. As the court noted, she was honest enough to say that she couldn't guarantee this,

---

1 [2005] Lloyd's Rep Med 109 (HL).

2 Derived from the case of *Bolam* v *Friern Hospital Management Committee* [1957] 2 All ER 118.

3 Cf *Bolitho* v *City and Hackney Health Authority* [1997] 4 All ER 771; *Pearce* v *United Bristol Healthcare NHS Trust* [1999] 48 BMLR 118.

4 [1985] 1 All ER 643.

5 At p. 114.

6 *Ibid.*

but that she would certainly have postponed it so that she could give the matter more consideration. In Lord Hope's opinion:

> To leave the patient who would find the decision difficult without a remedy, as the normal approach to causation would indicate, would render the duty [to disclose] useless in the cases where it may be needed most.[7]

Thus, even if the direct link in causation as traditionally understood is not unequivocal, nonetheless in this case '[t]he injury was intimately involved with the duty to warn'.[8]

Given our argument that the risks of xenotransplantation are currently unknown, and may even be unknowable, the decision in *Chester* v *Ashfar* seems, by linking the disclosure of risk with the harm, even where it is not certain that the patient would ultimately have chosen to avoid the harm, to raise the barrier, situating potential innovators of xenotransplantation within the context of a duty of care which has apparently been rendered more stringent.

---

7 At p. 125.

8 Per Lord Hope, at p. 125.

Chapter 1

Human Organ Transplantation: An Overview

Introduction

In 1991, the World Health Organization (WHO) had this to say:

> Over the past 30 years, organ transplantation has become a worldwide practice and has saved many thousands of lives. It has also improved the quality of life of countless other persons ... A feature of organ transplantation since its commencement has been the shortage of available organs. Supply has never satisfied demand, and this has led to the continuous development in many countries of procedures and systems to increase supply.[1]

Since then, organ transplantation continues to save many lives every year, and associated advances, particularly in respect of rejection of organs, have developed apace, to make organ donation an increasingly successful form of medical treatment. Indeed, in 2003, the WHO stated that:

> The transplantation of organs, cells and tissue has become the treatment of choice for a wide range of both fatal and non-fatal diseases, resulting in high levels of demand for transplantation services, particularly in high- and middle-income countries.[2]

Despite, or perhaps because of, this, numbers on waiting lists continue to grow and people who could be saved die before an organ is made available for them. In 2000, the British Medical Association (BMA) noted that:

> In 1998 7% fewer transplants were carried out in the UK than in 1997; in the same period the waiting list increased by 3%. This increasing gap between supply and demand appears to be a continuing trend. The statistics for 1999 compared with 1998 show no change to the number of transplants and an increase of 3% in the waiting list.[3]

In response to the problems of organ procurement, the National Health Service Organ Donor Register was launched in the UK in 1994, in an effort to recruit more, identifiable potential donors. By 2003, more than 10 million people were registered as donors,[4] which according to some commentators should be sufficient 'to have a significant impact on donation', although 'ideally nearly one third of the population [about 20

---

1 WHO (1991), *Human Organ Transplantation*, WHO: Geneva.

2 WHO (2003), *Human Organ and Tissue Transplantation*, EB113/14, 27 November.

3 BMA (2000), *Organ Donation in the 21st Century*, BMA: London, June, p. 2.

4 UKTransplant website, http://www.uktransplant.org.uk, accessed on 09/02/04.

million people] need to be on the register'.[5] Figures relating to the number of transplants carried out between 1 April 2002 and 31 March 2003 showed the highest rate of donations for six years: 2,777, and, encouragingly, 'more than 1.2 million people added their names to the NHS Organ Donor Register – the biggest increase for three years'.[6] In February 2004, UKTransplant indicated that the total numbers on the active and suspended waiting list at the end of December 2002 were 7,072, a three per cent increase on the previous year.[7] By February 2004, the total number registered for a transplant (excluding those suspended for health, personal or other reasons) stood at 5,825, with by far the largest number awaiting kidney transplants (5,159).[8] On 29 October 2004, UKTransplant confirmed that 11,716,823 people in total had joined the Register. Since 1 April 2004, 443 people had donated organs and 1,324 people had received transplants.[9]

Although the existence of the Register is expected to continue to improve the numbers of organs available for transplantation – a campaign that has enthusiastically been taken up by a number of newspapers – it has been said that:

> Whilst, in theory, a central organ donor register should improve the efficiency of an organ donation programme, it is a matter of great concern that the current system in the UK is ineffective and has serious flaws. Most people who add their name to the register assume that in doing so, their wishes will be known if they die in a situation which would make their organs suitable for donation. In fact, the register is not routinely checked when a potential donor is identified and the onus rests with the family to make the patient's wishes known or to guess what the patient would have wanted ...[10]

Despite the increasing numbers of registrants, and a UK Government initiative launched on 6 October 2004 to add a further one million names to the list, the shortage of organs continues to predict premature, unnecessary deaths every year. This problem is, of course, not unique to the United Kingdom,[11] and sadly it seems likely that even the known figures do not represent the full scale of the human tragedy caused by the shortfall between supply and demand for organs for transplantation. Not everyone who is in need of an organ will appear on waiting lists, as those who are thought unlikely to be well enough to receive one will generally be excluded.[12] What is clear is that 'a critical shortage of donor organs is the single greatest impediment facing transplant programmes around the world'.[13] Paradoxically, the shortage of available organs continues to impede the programme at the same time as survival post transplant is increasing.[14]

---

5 Royal College of Surgeons of England (1999), *The Report of the Working Party to Review Organ Transplantation*, Royal College of Surgeons: London, para. 135, p. 40.

6 http://www,uktransplant.org.uk/statistics/statistics.htm, accessed on 06/02/04.

7 http://www.uktransplant.org.uk/statistics/general, accessed on 09/02/04.

8 http://www.uktransplant.org.uk, accessed on 09/02/04.

9 http://www.uktransplant.org.uk/ukt/default.jsp, accessed on 29/10/04.

10 BMA (2000), p. 7.

11 WHO (1991).

12 BMA (2002), p. 2.

13 Wight, C. et al. (1998), 'Donor Action: A Systematic Approach to Organ Donation', *Transplantation Proceedings*, **30**, p. 2253.

14 See British Transplantation Society Ethics Committee Response to the Consultation on Human Bodies: Human Choices, 13/10/02, available at http://www.bts.org.uk/humanbodies.htm, accessed 20/01/04.

A number of reasons have been postulated which might explain the shortfall in organs for transplantation. Most certainly, it is the case that fewer people are dying in circumstances in which their organs would be of use. For example, the dramatic fall in the numbers of people dying in road traffic accidents has significantly reduced the pool of potential cadaveric donors. Additionally, there is a perceived shortage of beds in intensive care units (ICUs), meaning that some potential donors will be unable to be maintained until the point at which their organs could be used. Equally, historically at least, it was alleged that doctors were reluctant to ask families about the possibility of donating organs. However, Gentleman, et al., found that, in fact, request rates were reasonably high and argued that '[t]he belief that the main reason for losing potential donors is the failure to ask relatives to consent is no longer sustainable'.[15] It is also thought that some groups whose organs might have been viable for transplantation purposes (those, for example, in older age groups) are discounted on the basis of their age.[16] However, over recent years the need for organ procurement has become so acute that there can be few who are unaware of its potential benefits, and increasingly medical staff may be willing to raise the subject, and to consider as possible donors those who might otherwise have been discounted. Mason, McCall Smith and Laurie note that the viable limit on the age of donors 'is higher than might be expected – 70 in the case of kidneys, 50 for livers and 40 for donors of hearts'.[17] They continue that these ages 'may be extended as the general health of the aged steadily improves'.[18] Finally, some may object to organ donation on religious grounds, although religious objections may not be so clear as some might initially believe. For example, UKTransplant makes the point that it knows of no Asian religion which outlaws donation.[19]

For whatever reason, it remains the case that many potentially viable organs are lost to the transplantation programme, and the BMA's view is that medical practices may still be a fundamental contributor to the problem. Commenting on an audit carried out in intensive care units in England and Wales in 1989 and 1990, they note that, although in almost 14 per cent of the deaths in these units the patients might have possibly been diagnosed as brain dead (and therefore suitable for donation), fewer than 40 per cent of them actually became donors.[20] By far the largest apparent reason for not considering donation was that the tests for brain stem death were not carried out. As the BMA says:

> Timely and routine referral is crucial to the overall success of any organ donation service. For example, in 24.4% of potential donors (797) ... brain stem tests were not carried out. There may be good reasons why the test was not appropriate in each of these

---

15 Gentleman, D., Easton, J. and Jennet, B. (1990), 'Brain Death and Organ Donation in a Neurological Unit: Audit of Recent Practice', *British Medical Journal*, **301**, 24 November, at pp. 1203, 1205–1206.

16 Salih, M.A.M. et al. (1991), 'Potential Availability of Cadaveric Organs for Transplantation', *British Medical Journal*, **302**, 4 May, pp. 1053 and 1055.

17 Mason, J.K., McCall Smith, R.A. and Laurie, G.T. (2002), *Law and Medical Ethics*, (6th Ed.), Butterworths: London, at p. 426.

18 Ibid.

19 http://www.uktransplant.org.uk, accessed on 09/02/04.

20 BMA (2000), at p. 5.

> cases, for example there may have been clear contra-indications to donation, but it is also possible that at least some of them would have provided suitable organs for donation.[21]

Nonetheless, and despite the establishment of transplant co-ordinators throughout the United Kingdom, combined recently with a recent advertising campaign which was endorsed by the BMA, it is clear that much remains to be done to achieve parity of supply and demand – if indeed this is ever possible. Additionally, recent research (albeit on a relatively small scale) suggests that next of kin refusal rates had risen to 49 per cent throughout the period of the research (1 April 2003 to 30 June 2003) – a figure that 'was higher than expected.'[22] This study notes that the main reasons given for refusal were 'that they were not sure whether the patient would have agreed to donation (22 per cent), they did not want surgery to the body (21 per cent), the patient "had suffered enough" (18 per cent) or the next of kin were divided over the decision (12 per cent)'.[23] It may be that these figures, obtained after the publicity surrounding events at Bristol Royal Infirmary[24] and Alder Hey Hospital,[25] will prove to be a short-lived phenomenon, but they do represent a significant increase on the 30 per cent refusal rate recorded in the late 1980s and early 1990s,[26] and must be cause for concern.

Particular concern is also raised by the even more substantial shortage of organs in certain groups within UK society. Black people are reported to be three times more likely to need a kidney transplant, yet only one per cent of organ donors are black.[27] Additionally, UKTransplant reports that the potential need for organs in the South Asian community is three times greater than in the general population, yet this group is also underrepresented on the donor register.[28] These statistics are significant, as a donation from the same ethnic group is more likely to be successful.

Law reform in respect of organ transplantation (and other uses of human organs and tissue) has recently taken place in England, Wales and Northern Ireland, and a draft Bill has now been produced in Scotland. The terms of these legislative reforms will be analysed next, before consideration is given to alternative strategies which will either be impossible under the new legislation or which may co-exist with it. Throughout the UK jurisdictions, it is clear that those who proposed radical reform of the basis of organ donation have lost the argument. However, as we will see, some more radical schemes survive by not being directly outlawed in the revised legislative regime.

---

21 BMA (2000), at p. 23.

22 British Transplantation Society, http://www.bts.org.uk, accessed on 06/02/04.

23 Ibid.

24 HMSO (2001a), *Learning from Bristol: the report of the public inquiry into children's heart surgery at the Bristol Royal Infirmary 1984–1995*, CM 5207, HMSO: London.

25 HMSO (2001b), *The Royal Liverpool Children's Inquiry Report*, HMSO: London, HC 12.

26 BMA (2000).

27 http://www.uktransplant.org.uk, accessed on 09/03/04.

28 Ibid.

Regulating Transplantation

The History

Before looking at the new legislation in England, Wales and Northern Ireland and the proposed legislation in Scotland, it is instructive to evaluate the previous legal regime, not least to explicate why law reform was necessary. As we have seen, the use of human material was forcefully brought to the attention of the public by the events at Bristol Royal Infirmary and elsewhere. The impetus to review the lawful use of organs and tissue spread beyond the removal and retention of tissue and organs for research or educational purposes, because the same law governed this and organ transplantation and it became obvious that it was – as many had argued before – inadequately clear.

Live Organ Donation

Much of the debate in this area has focused on the use of cadaveric organs, not least because – given an adequate regulatory system – it is likely that the deceased will provide the largest supply of organs with the least risk to the donor. Nonetheless, the incidence of live donation is increasing, and represents a potentially valuable resource. In 1998, for example:

> [d]ata ... show a large increase (40%) in the number of live kidney donations from healthy donors compared with the previous year, representing 14% of the total kidney transplant programme for that year. This increase continued during 1999, with a further 8% increase in the number of live kidney donations, representing 16% of the total kidney transplant programme for 1999. Some people within the transplant community have called for serious consideration to be given to encouraging more live donations as a way of overcoming the shortfall of kidneys for donation. They argue that whilst, traditionally, attitudes toward living kidney donors in the UK has been, understandably, cautious, evidence from other countries indicates that the procedure is generally very safe, with few risks for the donor and a high chance of success for the recipient. Major complications for the donor are rare and the mortality rate is about 0.03%.[29]

Recent figures show that '[a] total of 1,783 received a kidney transplant of which 475 (27%) were given their kidney by a friend or relative – the highest number of living kidney transplants ever recorded in the UK'.[30]

The regulation of live organ transplantation was covered by the terms of the Human Organ Transplants Act 1989. This Act has now been overtaken in England, Wales and Northern Ireland by the terms of the Human Tissue Act 2004, which will be discussed briefly below, and will be repealed by the Human Tissue (Scotland) Bill 2005 should it become law. It is, however, worth reminding ourselves briefly why legislation in this area was felt to be necessary.

---

29 BMA (2000), at p. 10.

30 Information taken from UKTransplant website http://www.uktransplant.org.uk/ukt/default.jsp, accessed on 28/06/05.

Until 1989, the common law would have been the only legal resource in the event of concerns about live organ donation, and the only source for its vindication. However, in that year, it emerged that impoverished individuals from Turkey had been brought to the United Kingdom and were paid to donate their kidneys. This provoked considerable public concern and resulted in the passing of the 1989 Act, which is described in its preamble as:

> An Act to prohibit commercial dealings in human organs intended for transplanting; to restrict the transplanting of such organs between persons who are not genetically related; and for supplementary purposes connected with those matters.[31]

The legislation did not confine itself to the question of organ sales or the coercion of needy individuals, but took the opportunity to regulate the entire field of live organ donation. Briefly, the law imposed the following conditions on live donation. It created a criminal offence for any financial (including payment in money's worth) transactions involving organs intended for transplantation, whether or not the person from whom the organ was removed was dead or alive.[32] The law also regulated those who could donate and receive organs by making it an offence to remove or transplant an organ unless the people involved were genetically related.[33] Interestingly, the definition of who is genetically related for these purposes was rather wider than might have been anticipated, including as it does half brothers and sisters and aunts and uncles of the half blood.[34] Mason et al. noted that this definition was so wide as to 'raise the suspicion that family loyalties are preferred to genetic niceties',[35] while at the same time commenting on the arguably paradoxical situation that, if family loyalties are the driving factor here, spouses were precluded from donating to the their partner.

Non-genetically related transplants were not completely excluded, however.[36] Regulations made under the Act also set up a supervising organization, the Unrelated Live Transplants Regulatory Authority (ULTRA), which had responsibility for determining the acceptability of non-genetically related transplants.[37]

Cadaveric Donation

Despite the increased use of live donation, by far the most fruitful source of organs for donation is likely to be people who have died. Assuming that organs can be kept in a condition which allows them to be used, it would technically be possible to go some way towards meeting the demand for organs for donation by utilizing the

[31] Human Organ Transplants Act 1989, chapter 31

[32] S. 1 (1).

[33] S. 2 (1).

[34] S. 2 (2).

[35] Mason et al. at p. 428.

[36] Human Organ Transplants (Unrelated persons) Regulations 1989, SI 1989/2480.

[37] Human Organ Transplants (Establishment of Relationship) Regulations 1989, SI 1989/2107 and Human Organ Transplants (Unrelated Persons) Regulations 1989, SI 1989/2480.

organs of everyone who dies in appropriate situations and from particular conditions. Leaving aside for the moment the difficult question of using non-heart beating donors, or the possibility of elective ventilation, Gentleman et al. found in their experience that '... most donors are patients who die while being ventilated in intensive care units, about half come from neurosurgical units, and about half of all donors are head injured'.[38]

The possibility of using cadaveric organs for transplantation has widespread public support. The BMA notes, for example, that about 70 per cent of the UK population express their support for organ donation,[39] and a legislative framework has been in place since 1961. However, it is clear that the anticipated benefit of cadaveric donation has not yet materialized. Recent figures show that there are (as at 28 June 2005) 6,135 people awaiting transplants, despite the fact that 12,356,033 people – representing 20 per cent of the population – have now signed up to the donor register.[40] Despite this significant level of registration, the number of people waiting for a transplant is high. This may, of course, reflect a failure to consider donation or to consult the donor register at the appropriate time. However, it is also possible that there may still be a reluctance on the part of healthcare workers to ask recently bereaved families for a donation;[41] some potential donors may be unused because of age;[42] a shortage of ICU facilities may preclude maintaining the body in a condition which would preserve the organs; not all organs made available will be used;[43] the definition of brain stem death remains controversial for some, who fear being pronounced dead before their time so that their organs can be used; and, of course, some families will have religious or other objections to removal of organs for any purpose including transplantation. In respect of this last group, the Council of Europe has said that '[n]o removal must take place when there is an open or presumed objection on the part of the deceased, in particular, taking into account his religious and philosophical convictions'.[44]

A number of factors, therefore, may combine to reduce the number of organs available from cadavers.

In the UK, there was one further – and arguably major – reason for concern in this area; the relevant legislation itself. The Human Tissue Act 1961 was passed at a time when organ transplantation was in its infancy, and its terms were sufficiently ambiguous and outdated to have placed barriers in the way of facilitation of a successful programme. Although those charged with the responsibility of co-

---

38 Gentleman et al. (1990).

39 BMA (2000), note 2, at p. 4.

40 UKTransplant website http://www.uktransplant.org.uk/ukt/default.jsp, accessed on 28/06/05.

41 But see Gentleman et al. (1990).

42 Ibid.

43 In their survey, Gentleman et al. (1990), at p. 1204 say: 'Transplant surgeons complain about failure to obtain consent, but transplant teams sometimes fail to use offered organs. In Glasgow, 16 of 24 consents in 1989 were for donation of multiple organs, but in only half of these were organs other than kidneys used. The reasons were either that hypotension had developed before the transplant team arrived or that resource constraints in recipient units led to offers being declined.'

44 Council of Europe (1980), 'Removal, Grafting and Transplantation of Human Substances', *The International Journal of Medicine and Law*, **1** (4), pp. 385–402, at p. 387.

ordinating organ transplantation throughout the UK have done an excellent job, their task can scarcely have been rendered easier by an Act which has been subject to repeated criticism as being 'unsatisfactory and in need of reform'.[45]

The legacy of this Act has contributed to the impetus for law reform, and a critique of its provisions will explain why. Before considering the problems of the Act, it is worth outlining its terms. The relevant sections of the Act are reproduced here for convenience:

Section 1: Removal of parts of bodies for medical purposes

(1) If any person, either in writing at any time or orally in the presence of two or more witnesses during his last illness, has expressed a request that his body or any specified part of his body be used after his death for therapeutic purposes or for purposes of medical education or research, the person lawfully in possession of his body after his death may, unless he has reason to believe that the request was subsequently withdrawn, authorise the removal from the body of any part or, as the case may be, the specified part, for use in accordance with the request.

(2) Without prejudice to the foregoing subsection, the person lawfully in possession of the body of a deceased person may authorise the removal of any part from the body for use for the said purposes if, having made such reasonable enquiry as may be practicable, he has no reason to believe –

(a) that the deceased had expressed an objection to his body being so dealt with after his death, and had not withdrawn it; or

(b) that the surviving spouse or any surviving relative of the deceased objects to the body being so dealt with.

S. 1 (1) of the Act roughly equates to what is generally referred to as an 'opting in' system; namely, the individual him or herself can express his or her views in advance of death. Closer examination of this section, however, immediately highlights its relative lack of specificity. First, the Act provides no definition of who is the person 'lawfully in possession of the body'. Although it is generally believed that this is the hospital authority, there is no legislative provision that this is so. Second, a verbal intention to donate is only legally valid when it is made in the course of a last illness. A recent Scottish Report on the Removal and Retention of Organs at Post-Mortem[46] has queried this requirement as being an unreasonable restriction on the rights of the individual to dispose of his or her body, and recommended that this provision be re-addressed following a repeal of the legislation and the enactment of a dedicated organ transplantation statute.[47]

What this section does appear at first sight to do, however, is to give priority to the wishes of the deceased person, as expressed in writing before his/her death. The

---

45 BMA (2000), at p. 3.

46 Independent Review group on Retention of Organs at Post-Mortem (2001), Scottish Executive, November (also available at http://www.show.scot.nhs.uk/scotorgrev). Although this Report was not directed at transplantation, but rather at the removal and retention of organs for other purposes, its recommendations have a clear and direct impact on the law on organ transplantation as both are covered by the same legislation.

47 Recommendation 29, p. 21.

obligation is merely to satisfy the person lawfully in possession of the body that the person had not changed their mind. As was noted as long ago as 1983, '[i]f a patient carries a signed donor card or has otherwise recorded his wishes there is no legal requirement to establish lack of objection on the part of relatives ...'.[48] However, this reflection of the law's content was often modified or ignored in practice by the doctors involved, who would usually, and in line with what has been described as 'good practice',[49] seek the views of close relatives. In these circumstances, an objection by a relative would often serve as a direct veto on the wishes of the deceased, even though it was legally irrelevant. Again, the Report of the Review Group previously referred to recommends that, although the current legal requirement that it should be established that the person has not withdrawn their request should remain, the wishes of the deceased should be respected irrespective of the wishes of the relatives.[50]

S. 1 (2) of the 1961 Act, on the other hand, can be described as a weak 'opting out' scheme, and applied where the deceased had left no recorded expression of his/her wishes. In this case, the person lawfully in possession of the body was authorized to remove organs for transplantation purposes if they were satisfied, after reasonable enquiry, that the deceased did not object in life to organ removal, or that the surviving spouse or 'any surviving relative'[51] had no objection to the use of the organ(s). Again, the problems with this section are manifest. The law provided no definition of what is a reasonable enquiry, although some commentators have suggested that this should be interpreted as an enquiry which is not so protracted as to result in the loss of viability of the organ.[52]

Equally, although it is fairly evident why a spouse should be invited to express their views, this does not reflect the reality of the situation in which many adults now live.[53] Additionally, there was an obligation, irrespective of the views of the spouse, to consult 'any surviving relative'. It is not clear on what basis the views of the surviving relatives should be deemed of equal significance to those of the person living most closely with the deceased individual.[54] In all, it can be seen that there were many reasons to believe that the pre-existing legislation was more of a hindrance to an effective transplantation programme than it was an assistance.

The question was: how would law reform tackle these problems, and to what extent would the value of transplantation itself inform the regime proposed. In

---

48 *Cadaveric Organs for Transplantation*, Health Departments of Great Britain and Northern Ireland, (1983), London.

49 Ibid.

50 Independent Review Group on Retention of Organs at Post-Mortem (2001), recommendation 27, p. 21.

51 Human Tissue Act 1961, s. 1 (2) (b).

52 See Skegg, P.D.G. (1984), *Law, Ethics and Medicine*, Clarendon Press: Oxford.

53 The Review Group, note 25, above, recommended that this proviso should be modified to take account of those who live in non-married or same sex relationships; recommendation 31, p. 22. See also the (failed) attempts at reform in the Transplant of Human Organs Bill 2001, which sought to substitute for 'surviving spouse' the words 'cohabiting partner, or in the absence of any surviving spouse or partner, any parent or child'. S. 3.

54 Again, the Independent Review Group (2001) recommended that this requirement be repealed; recommendation 31.

considering the new and proposed law reform from the Parliaments in London and Edinburgh, it is necessary to bear in mind the context within which reform was contemplated. Seldom – probably since Burke and Hare were systematically robbing graves in Edinburgh – had the focus on the human body and its parts been more intense. Revelations about the unauthorized removal and retention of organs and tissue from children without their parents' knowledge or agreement raised the profile of our interest in our own bodies and those of our loved ones. Although these events did not engage directly with the transplantation programme, the general concern that third parties (in this case doctors) were assuming unwarranted authority over the bodies of the dead extended indirectly into the transplantation programme. Indeed, the Government has chosen to combine transplantation and other uses of human organs and tissue in the same piece of legislation, although it might have been preferable to consider them separately because each has a different goal, and arguably different considerations can or should inform their underpinning principles. For example, the use of organs and tissue from the dead for educational, research or audit purposes may provide a benefit in the future; organ donation can save a life immediately. Equally, people may be less inclined to provide organs and tissue for research purposes, when they cannot control the kind of research that is done, than they are to give the gift of life to an existing person. However, as we will see, these considerations were not taken on board by the governments in London and Edinburgh; presumably because of a lack of parliamentary time. The outcome of this, however, is that it was impossible in developing transplantation legislation to take serious account of some of the major alternative strategies which have a certain amount of endorsement in the public, such as an opting out regime, which will be discussed below. The perceived need to react to Bristol, Alder Hey and the Scottish Inquiry located the use of organs and tissue firmly within the opting in system; that is, people – in all uses of organs and tissue – would need to volunteer rather than there being a presumption that they were available for legitimate uses.

The Human Tissue Act 2004

Although alternatives were available, the Westminster Government was unimpressed by, for example, the option of presumed consent.[55] The regime is deeply rooted in the notion of donation as a gift relationship and the conscious and deliberate altruism that is said to characterize such systems. Appropriate consent in respect of children or adults is defined in the Act,[56] and is the trigger for the lawful use of human organs and tissue. Where the individual is unable to give consent, or has not left behind details of their wishes, following death those in a qualifying relationship with the deceased can authorize organ removal. Unlike the previous situation, the qualifying relationship is hierarchical; that is, consent from the person highest up the list is sufficient and it is not necessary to consult every surviving relative. The hierarchy is contained in s. 27 of the Act and is as follows:

---

[55] For further discussion, see below.

[56] Ss. 2 and 3.

(4) (a) spouse or partner;
(b) parent or child;
(c) brother or sister;
(d) grandparent or grandchild;
(e) child of a person falling within paragraph (c);
(f) stepfather or stepmother;
(g) half-brother or half-sister;
(h) friend of longstanding.

It is also provided that '[r]elationships in the same paragraph of subsection (4) should be accorded equal ranking'[57] and that '[c]onsent should be obtained from the person whose relationship to the person concerned is accorded the highest ranking in accordance with subsections (4) and (5)'.[58] Finally, for the avoidance of doubt, it is provided that '[if] the relationship of each of two or more persons to the person concerned is accorded equal highest ranking in accordance with subsections (4) and (5), it is sufficient to obtain the consent of any of them'.[59]

The legislation also creates a new body, the Human Tissue Authority,[60] with responsibility for overseeing the uses of human material removed from the body, maintaining a 'statement of the general principles which it considers should be followed'[61] and developing codes of practice for the future. Donation from living people is prohibited unless:

(a) the Authority is satisfied –
(i) that no reward has been or is to be given in contravention of section 32, and
(ii) that such other conditions as are specified in the regulations are satisfied, and
(b) such other requirements as are specified in the regulations are complied with.[62]

Furthermore, it is provided that:

(1) Where part of a body lying in a hospital, nursing home or other institution is or may be suitable for use for transplantation, it shall be lawful for the person having the control and management of the institution –
(a) to take steps for the purpose of preserving the part for use for transplantation, and
(b) to retain the body for that purpose.[63]

This provision would seem directly and clearly to endorse the potential of non-heart beating donors (NHBDs), whose potential is discussed below.

---

57 S. 27 (5).
58 S. 27 (6).
59 S. 27 (7).
60 S. 13.
61 S. 15.
62 S. 33 (3).
63 S. 43.

Human Tissue (Scotland) Bill 2005

The Scottish Parliament was provoked into action by the Report of The Independent Review Group on the Retention of Organs at Post-Mortem,[64] which, like its English counterparts, exposed the scale of non-consensual removal and retention of organs and tissue. The opportunity to revise transplantation legislation was taken at the same time as, and for similar reasons to those which informed, the Westminster Government. Although it has already been suggested that it might have been beneficial to separate out retention and use of organs and tissue for non-transplantation purposes from those which are for transplantation, the Edinburgh Parliament took the same route as the London one, presumably for similar reasons. Again, therefore, the regime which covers removal and retention of organs for education, research and audit is to be the same as that which covers removal for transplantation. The fundamental ideology underpinning transplantation law reform in Scotland is explicitly based in the value of transplantation programmes. The Bill begins with the clear statement that:

> It is the duty of the Scottish Ministers to –
> (a) promote, support and develop programmes of transplantation;
> (b) promote information and awareness about the donation for transplantation of parts of a human body;
> (c) promote the taking of any necessary measures relating to the quality and safety, storage and use of any such part donated for that purpose.[65]

Like its English counterpart, the Scottish Bill is firmly rooted in the need for donation to be voluntary, although the Scottish Bill, on the recommendation of the Independent Review Group, eschewed the language of consent, preferring instead the concept of authorization. The rationale for this related specifically to children, in that the Review Group was concerned that the traditional concept of consent was inapplicable when a parent is asked to agree to the use of organs or tissue from their child. Parental rights to consent on behalf of a child are constrained by the need to act in the child's best interests. How, the Review Group asked, could it be said to be in the child's best interests to have organs removed from its body after death? Moreover, authorization also allows agreement to participate without requiring the level of information disclosure generally assumed to be necessary to obtain an 'informed' consent. In other words, parents who wish their child's body to be used for research, education or transplantation would be permitted to authorize this without being forced to receive information that they would not wish. Adults can authorize the use of parts of their body following death for audit, research, education and transplantation if they have either in writing or verbally in the presence of two witnesses specifically done so.[66] Where no such authorization exists, removal and use may be authorized by the nearest relative.[67] Authorization from anyone over the age of 12, if properly executed, is to be taken as evidence of their wishes, and is to

[64] Supra cit.

[65] S. 1.

[66] S. 6.

[67] S. 7.

be respected.[68] In the case of live donation, the provisions echo those in the Human Tissue Act 2004,[69] and both exclude trafficking in human body parts.

This consideration of the new and the proposed law is necessarily brief, since there has been no time to evaluate any impact. What does seem clear, however, is that the grounding in consent or authorization of the new law will mean that some of the alternatives discussed below will be unacceptable. Others, however, may be able to operate in parallel with the new legislation, including – of course – xenotransplantation.

Alternative Strategies

Although the UK situation is firmly based on consent or authorization, reforms which have been put in place in other jurisdictions have almost inevitably removed or reduced the commitment to 'pure' donation. In balancing the interests of society in preserving life against the interests or rights of the deceased, the most common alternative strategies pay less attention to the latter, although they do not necessarily ignore it altogether.

Presumed Consent

What is now virtually uniformly referred to as presumed consent was also in the past known as 'opting out'. Under this system, a presumption of willingness to donate is made. Thus, individuals would be expected to declare their *objection* to the use of their organs for donation, rather than being required to express their *willingness* to donate. The presumption is that this would increase the number of organs available, perhaps because of the evidence suggesting that the majority of people are willing to donate but don't take the necessary steps to record this. The popularity of presumed consent also rests on the view that the deceased's interests are less relevant or important than those of the needy living. Harris, for example, argues that:

> ... it seems clear that the benefits from cadaver transplants are so great, and the reasons for objecting so transparently selfish or superstitious, that we should remove altogether the habit of seeking the consent of either the deceased or relatives.[70]

In an historical shift from all of its previous pronouncements on this subject, the BMA has endorsed a move towards the presumed consent system.[71] The rationale given was as follows:

68 S. 9.

69 S. 15.

70 Harris, J. (1998), *Clones, Genes and Immortality*, Oxford University Press: New York, at p. 125.

71 BMA (2000), note 2, at pp. 13–17. At p. 16 the Report says: 'The BMA supports a system of presumed consent in which close relatives' views are also taken into account ... accompanied by adequate safeguards to ensure that those who do not wish to donate are given a genuine opportunity to opt out.'

- It is reasonable and appropriate to assume that most people would wish to act in an altruistic manner and help others by donating their organs after death.
- Studies show that the majority of people would be willing to donate but only a small number of these are on the NHS Organ Donor Register or carry a donor card. While this level of apathy exists, people will continue to die waiting for organ donors.
- Given that the majority of people would be willing to donate, there are good reasons for presuming consent and requiring those who object to donation to register their views.
- A shift to presumed consent would prompt more discussion within families about organ donation.
- It is more efficient and cost-effective to maintain a register of the small number who wish to opt out of donation than of the majority who are willing to be donors.
- With such a shift, organ donation becomes the default position. This represents a more positive view of organ donation which is to be encouraged.

Despite the acknowledged difficulties of obtaining meaningful data about the success of presumed consent in other countries, the BMA believes that, as one part of a broader strategy, a shift to presumed consent is likely to have a positive effect on donation rates.[72]

The thrust of the BMA's proposals can be divided into three parts. First, the BMA takes account of evidence that people are by and large willing to donate. Were donation the 'default position', then presumably the unexpressed, but real, intentions of those who are positive about donation, but do nothing to record this, would be more likely to be vindicated. In this way, both personal and social utility would be maximized. Thus, from an individual basis, the presumed consent model represents a reinforcement of respect for the individual, and an acknowledgement of their silent altruism. From a consequentialist point of view, it may maximize the health of others, reduce societal costs and enhance social existence. As Chadwick, for example, says:

> From a consequentialist point of view it might seem to be clear that it is desirable, if not a moral requirement, to use recyclable corpses to prolong the lives of those who are desperately ill and in need of organs.[73]

However, others express considerable concern about such a move, noting that the goal of satisfying the unexpressed wishes of the population may not in fact be met by removing the active consent model. Garwood-Gowers, for example, suggests that:

---

[72] BMA (2000), at pp. 15–16.

[73] Chadwick, R. (1994), 'Corpses, Recycling and Therapeutic Purposes', in Lee, R. and Morgan, D. (eds), *Death Rites: Law and Ethics at the End of Life*, Routledge: London, pp. 54 and 57.

> ... given that surveys typically show that around half of the public oppose presumed consent, there is a danger that it would alienate a significant section of the public to introduce it and have counterproductive consequences for procurement.[74]

He does concede that there is as yet no evidence to support this contention from those countries which have moved to a presumed consent position, but he also notes that there is no evidence to 'support the view that the effect of presumed consent on procurement will be dramatic'.[75]

Nonetheless, the possibility that organ removal will not *in fact* be consensual under such a scheme must be taken seriously. Price, for example, suggests that silence may also be equivalent to dissent, especially amongst those – such as the young – who have in fact given little or no thought to their own death. They may, therefore, be indifferent or overtly hostile to donation, but under a presumed consent regime their silence would be taken as assent.[76] Equally, as the American Medical Association pointed out:

> The claim that presumed consent enhances individual autonomy is dubious. In many cases it is incorrect to assume that an individual who does not clearly express a preference would in fact be willing to serve as an organ donor. If 69% of the population would be willing to donate their own organs, then the presumption of consent would be incorrect up to 31% of the time.[77]

The second strand running through the BMA's most recent position is that moving towards presumed consent will be likely to facilitate family discussion as to the wishes of their relatives. In a number of ways this is a peculiar reason. First, it is based on untested and untestable assumptions about what families will talk about and what will stimulate such conversation. Second, and perhaps more importantly, it also seems to renege on the very rationale for the move; namely that people by and large do want to donate. If that is true, there seems no clear justification for the relatives' views (or knowledge of the deceased's views) to be considered of any importance whatsoever. But this is essential to the BMA's strategy, as they also indicate that their scheme should ensure that 'close relatives' views are also taken into account ...'.[78]

Finally, the BMA's proposals rest on practical reasons of efficiency and cost-effectiveness. While these are real issues for an already stretched healthcare system, they can also arguably be seen as significant only if they are consequential on an ethically sound structure; yet as we have seen, there is in reality little consensus about the ethics of presumed consent. Indeed, some commentators doubt that

---

74 Garwood-Gowers, A. (1999), *Living Donor Organ Transplantation:: Key Legal and Ethical Issues*, Ashgate: Aldershot, at p. 25.

75 Garwood-Gowers (1999), at pp. 25–26.

76 Price, D. (2000), *Legal and Ethical Aspects of Organ Transplantation*, Cambridge University Press: Cambridge, at pp. 113 *et seq.*

77 Council on Ethical and Judicial Affairs of the American Medical Association (1994), 'Strategies for Cadaveric Organ Procurement: Mandated Choice and Presumed Consent', *Journal of the American Medical Association*, **272**, at pp. 809, 811.

78 BMA (2000), at p. 16.

presumed consent has any basis either in law or in ethics, and therefore that 'consent' cannot be taken to be the equivalent of absence of refusal.[79]

To continue for the moment on the practical, it might be that the objections to presumed consent would be significantly reduced in authority were it to be empirically clear that this model does in fact result in major improvements in the availability of life-saving organs for donation. However, the evidence for this remains equivocal. The BMA itself notes the difficulty of obtaining evidence which directly links changes in availability patterns to the system of presumed consent itself, and notes that other factors may also be relevant, such as:

- the predominant cause of death (such as the number of road traffic accidents);
- the availability of ICU beds and staff;
- the number, responsibility and organization of transplant co-ordinators;
- the number of transplant surgeons;
- the number of specialized units in the region;
- the number and characteristics of the patients on the waiting list (such as which organs they need); and
- the availability of training programmes for ICU staff such as the European Donor Hospital Educational Programme (EDHEP) and Donor Action.[80]

For this reason, the BMA's endorsement of presumed consent is linked to the need for the development of a variety of strategies, and its success would not be dependent solely on a change to the current, consent-based system.

Despite these caveats, for many, the fundamental solution to the problems of organ procurement is to be found in a radical move away from the consent-based model. Most, however, are agreed that evidence from those countries, like Belgium and Spain, which already have such systems, requires more detailed analysis before the conclusion can be drawn that the system *itself* has the capacity to improve the supply of organs for transplantation. Even if this is done, and the conclusion is reached that the system does have a positive effect, it will still be wise to heed the warning that follows:

> Wherever transplantation is considered the gold standard for treatment of organ disease, utility drives the impulse to procure sufficient organs to meet demand. Yet rights should be considered inviolable, including the living person's right to determine treatment of their body upon death as well as in life. The right not to be used for the purposes of others is a basic tenet of civilised society and any contravention of it represents a step away from pluralism toward totalitarianism.[81]

One final objection remains. It is unusual that people's views should be judged on the basis of their silence, as has already been noted. However, it is also the case that for some adherents to specific religions, such as Judaism, the sanctity of the whole body after death is of critical importance. Thus, for the person who wishes to adhere to his or her faith, it will be necessary effectively to register that faith in a public

---

79 Garwood-Gowers (1999), at p. 26.

80 BMA (2000), at p. 13.

81 Garwood-Gowers (1999), at p. 195.

way. For many, this is at best undesirable, and at worst discriminatory. However, UKTransplant's review of Judaism's approach to organ transplantation presents a much less clear-cut perspective, considerably reducing fears of discrimination, saying '[i]n principle Judaism sanctions and encourages organ donation in order to save lives ...',[82] and notes that this principle can sometimes override the otherwise imperative prohibition on interfering with the body after death, and the requirement for immediate burial of the whole body.

Despite the possible shortcomings of the presumed consent model, a Bill was introduced to the Scottish Parliament in January 2004, and was widely reported as having considerable support among MSPs.[83] The Human Organ Transplantation (Register) Bill was introduced as a Private Member's Bill on 21 January 2004. Although some 20 MSPs had immediately declared their support for the Bill, the First Minister was reported as having said, '[w]e are not yet convinced an opt-out system is the right way forward, but we will also look at the [bill] and consider that in due course'.[84] As we have already seen, this reluctance to consider presumed consent as a viable alternative has now been given legislative support by the terms of the Human Tissue Act 2004, and the Human Tissue (Scotland) Bill. For the moment, then, it appears that this option will have to be placed firmly on the back burner.

Non-Heart Beating Donors

Generally speaking, the largest number of cadaveric organs comes from those who have been declared brain stem dead, but – because of continued ventilation – their hearts remain beating and the body continues to be oxygenated, thereby maintaining the quality and usefulness of the organs. However, one further source of organs for donation might be those who have stopped breathing. Such individuals are likely to die from causes which differ from those of brain stem dead patients, who will almost certainly have been hospitalized following – for example – trauma, and will therefore either be in, or near to, an intensive care unit where facilities will be available for ventilation. The non-heart beating donor (NHBD), on the other hand, may well be someone presenting at Accident and Emergency, and suffering some fatal incident, such as a coronary or cerebral event leading to sudden death.

The classic case is described as follows:

> A patient is brought into an accident and emergency room and is declared dead. A small catheter is introduced into the main artery in the groin and this is used to perfuse the kidneys and keep them cold until such time as a discussion can be carried out with the relatives. If the relatives refuse to agree to organ donation the procedure goes no further, and the small cannula is removed and the groin is sutured. If, however, the relatives agree to organ donation the kidneys are removed by an operative procedure in a surgical theatre. Transplantation is then carried out in the usual fashion.[85]

---

82 http://www.uktranspant.org.uk, accessed on 10/02/04.

83 http://www.news.bbc.co.uk, accessed on 23/01/04.

84 http://www.news.bbc.co.uk, accessed on 23/01/04.

85 Scottish Transplant Group (2002), *An Organ Donation Strategy for Scotland*, HMSO: Edinburgh, June.

Historically, the NHBD was the primary source of organs for transplantation, despite the clinical imperatives that demand their use virtually instantly,[86] but developments in intensive care, the early lack of success of such transplants and the increased legal acceptance of brain stem death largely overtook the popularity of NHBDs as a source of organs. Price, however, notes a recent resurgence of interest in the NHBD as a source of viable tissue, and that '[i]n the US, twenty-nine out of the sixty-three Organ Procurement Organisations have NHBD protocols ...',[87] and 'nine British centres now have such protocols covering fifty donor hospitals'.[88] In addition, it has been estimated that the use of NHBDs could increase the 'number of potential organ donors by at least 50 per cent'.[89] Indeed, a recent report from the Scottish Transplant Group recommended that '[a] non-heartbeating programme should be established in Scotland as soon as possible ...'.[90] The terms of the Human Tissue (Scotland) Bill allow preservation for transplantation, giving authority to the NHBD programme.[91] Such preservation is also explicitly authorized by the Human Tissue Act 2004.[92]

Rothblatt notes that, '[t]he use of non-heart-beating donors has been called "back to the future" because it is with these kinds of organs that transplantation began ...',[93] and further that 'a reexamination of the utility of non-heart-beating donors' has been prompted by the worsening shortage of organs.[94] However, this system is not without its problems – both practical and ethical/legal. Practically, the short period of time within which organs will deteriorate, and thereby become unsuited for use, makes it imperative that medical staff are alert to the possibility of organ donation in cases of sudden death. The BMA recognized that NHBDs might represent hope for the future, but also that if this is to be the case, staff must be aware of the potential use of kidneys from such donors, and proactive in notifying the transplant co-ordinator in the event of a sudden death of a patient in their care.[95]

Even should medical staff be sufficiently alert to the possible uses of asystolic donation, further problems of a more ethical or legal nature must be circumvented. Given that respiration and circulation will have ceased, it will be necessary that some way be found to maximize the viability of the organs. This, as we have seen, is done by means of catheterizing the cadaver, in order that cooling and perfusion of the organs can take place. Younger and Arnold noted that this practice is by no means uncontroversial. As they say:

---

86 Price (2000), at p. 25.

87 Price (2000), at p. 26.

88 Price (2000), at p. 160.

89 Younger, S. and Arnold, R. (1997), 'Non-Heart-Beating Cadavers: The Beat Goes On', in Spielman, B. (ed.), *Organ and Tissue Donation: Ethical, Legal and Policy Issues*, Southern Illinois University Press: Southern Illinois, at pp. 69, 70 (quoted in Price (2000), at p. 26).

90 Scottish Transplant Group (2002), note 59, at p. 17.

91 S. 13.

92 S. 43.

93 Rothblatt, M. (2004), *Your Life or Mine*, Ashgate: Aldershot, at p. 12.

94 Rothblatt (2004), at p. 13.

95 BMA (2000), at pp. 12–13.

> The moral questions raised by the postmortem infusion without family consent are more substantial than its advocates contend. For instance, if the controversy about practising intubation on dead patients is any indication, there is little consensus about the moral acceptably of performing invasive procedures on dead patients to benefit others. Critics believe that these procedures are unethical because they are disrespectful of the dead, disregard families' wishes, and foster undesirable attitudes in health care professionals. The practice is also legally ambiguous.[96]

This objection must be addressed, and it can be countered – at least partially. It will, for example, not always be the case that families have not agreed to the catheterizing of their deceased relative (and their legal standing to do so is moot). Nonetheless, the exigencies of the situation may often mean that no prior consent was or could be obtained, leading to ethical and legal doubts about the capacity to harvest organs in this situation.[97] Of course, if the use of NHBDs were to be combined with a system of presumed consent, then arguably there would be no need for the views of the relatives to be considered at all (unless the BMA's caveat remained in place). Thus, the real potential of NHBDs to make major inroads into the organ shortfall would be enhanced under this system. In fact, even within the opting in system, UKTransplant reports that recent figures as to the number of transplants performed include 'a record number of kidney transplants from non-heartbeating donors – 143, 20% up on the previous year'.[98]

Equally, it would be possible (although perhaps not common) for an individual to declare in advance their consent to being used as an NHBD. The British Transplantation Society contends that, '[i]t is felt ethically acceptable to cannulate a potential NHBD if it can be established beyond reasonable doubt that that individual has indicated their wish to donate in life and the view of the next of kin is unknown ...'[99] although it concedes that '[t]here is room for further debate on what constitutes "beyond reasonable doubt".'[100] The Society also considers that the wishes of the deceased should not predominate, thus doubtless reducing the number of available organs. In its view, '[t]he distress caused to living persons and the negative overall effects of the publicity on organ transplantation should take precedence over the wishes of the deceased'.[101] Given the continued support for advance declarations or statements, it might be thought counter-intuitive to hold to this view. Arguably, any advance statement which is followed has the potential to cause distress to those remaining, yet nonetheless doctors are generally exhorted to follow them.[102] Additionally, there is considerable case law which would suggest

---

96 Younger, S. and Arnold, R. (1993), 'Ethical, Psychosocial, and Public Policy Implications of Procuring Organs from Non-Heart-Beating Cadaver Donors', *Journal of the American Medical Association*, **269**, at pp. 2769, 2770.

97 Orr, R. et al. (1997), 'Reanimation: Overcoming Objections and Obstacles to Organ Retrieval from Non-Heart-Beating Cadaver Donors', *Journal of Medical Ethics*, **23** (7).

98 UKTransplant website, accessed on 28/06/2005.

99 'Approved Position Statements', September 2003, available at http://www.bts.otg.uk/approvedstatements.htm, accessed on 20/01/04.

100 Ibid.

101 Ibid.

102 BMA (1994), *Statement on Advance Directives*, London.

that – where the directive applies to the circumstances in which the person now finds him or herself – it has a great deal of force in law. Initially, the law's approach was somewhat tentative. In 1994, for example, it was said that:

> The views of the patient may have been previously expressed, either in writing or otherwise. The High Court exercising its inherent jurisdiction may determine the effect of a purported advance directive as to future medical treatment ... In summary, the patient's expressed views, if any, will always be a very important component in the decisions of the doctors and the court.[103]

In the case of *Airedale NHS Trust* v *Bland*, two of the Law Lords seemed to indicate that advance directives would have legal standing, and in the case of *Re C*,[104] a mentally ill man was permitted to make an advance refusal of potentially life-saving treatment, with the full backing of the court. More recently, in the cases of *AK (adult patient)(medical treatment)*[105] and *Ms B* v *An NHS Trust*[106] the courts made it clear that an advance statement, which continues to represent the wishes of the individual, and is applicable to the presenting circumstances, has the force of law. By analogy, therefore, it must surely be the case that an equivalent advance statement regarding agreement to becoming a non-heart beating donor would have equal legal standing, *irrespective of the wishes of surviving relatives or others*. This hypothesis seems to be borne out by the judgement of the case of *R(Burke)* v *General Medical Council*,[107] in which Mr Justice Munby held that a validly executed and applicable advance requirement that treatment (in this case assisted nutrition and hydration) be continued was as valid as one which rejected treatment in the future. Indeed, refusal to follow the advance statement could amount, in his view, to breach of Articles 3 and 6 of the patient's Convention rights.[108]

Equally, the second objection – namely that it is possibly illegal to interfere with a corpse in this way – will, as has been noted, fall once the Bill becomes law in those parts of the UK to which it applies. However, and notwithstanding the pleas from the Scottish Transplant Group, arguably the use of NHBDs in Scotland – which is essentially unaffected by the terms of the Bill – remains potentially controversial. Moreover, clarifying the legal position will not affect the emotional response which the use of NHBDs may provoke. DuBois, for example, suggests that:

> If patients are already struggling with the source of their donated organs, knowing that the cause of death for some donors is the procurement process itself could only exacerbate feelings of guilt.[109]

---

103 *Practice Note* [1994] 2 All ER 413.

104 *Re C (adult: refusal of treatment)* 15 BMLR 77 [1994].

105 [2001] 58 BMLR 151.

106 [2002] All ER 449.

107 [2004] EWHC 1879 (Admin).

108 It should be noted that his judgement is likely to be appealed.

109 DuBois, J.M. (1999), 'Non-Heart-Beating Organ Donations: A Defense of the Required Determination of Death', *Journal of Law, Medicine and Ethics*, **27**, 2, pp. 126–136, at p. 132.

Interestingly, the objections to the retrieval of organs from non-heart beating donors are remarkably similar to those which surround the practice known as elective ventilation.

Elective Ventilation

One alternative to the current practice in human organ transplantation, shown to have some considerable success in terms of recruiting higher numbers of donors,[110] is the procedure called 'elective ventilation'. To a very large extent, of course, this description is a misnomer. There is, in fact, nothing elective about it, since the decision whether or not to maintain a dying patient in these circumstances is taken by others rather than the patient him or herself. As the Nuffield Council puts it, '[e]lective ventilation involves placing a patient for whom death is inevitable on a ventilator in order to maintain their organs in a suitable state for transplantation'.[111] Although the procedure was attempted in a small number of patients in Exeter between 1988 and 1990, it provoked considerable controversy and the Department of Health ultimately issued guidance which indicated that this practice would be unlawful.[112] Not least, this purported unlawfulness stems from the fact that the treatment of those who are otherwise incapable of providing consent should only be undertaken where it is in the best interests of the individual so to do. Indeed, in Scotland, the terms of the Adults with Incapacity (Scotland) Act 2000 would almost certainly preclude elective ventilation since the legislation is specifically designed to facilitate the authorization of treatment which will be of benefit to the individual incapable adult. The conclusion that elective ventilation would currently be unlawful is also endorsed by the Report of the Advisory Group on the Ethics of Xenotransplantation (Kennedy Report)[113] which says '... any intervention carried out on a patient without consent must be in the patient's best interests. If an intervention is not in the patient's best interests (and elective ventilation is not) then it is unlawful.'[114] Mason, McCall Smith and Laurie, noting that the practice of elective ventilation has been discontinued, comment:

> We believe this to be correct – one cannot exorcise a feeling that death is being pre-empted and it is certain that this form of organ husbandry must be very carefully controlled if a backlash of public reaction – and a return to a public fear of pre-empted death – is to be avoided.[115]

---

110 Feest, T.G., et al. (1990), 'Protocol for Increasing Organ Donation after Cerebrovascular Deaths in a District General Hospital', *The Lancet*, **335** (1133).

111 Nuffield Report (Report of the Nuffield Council on Bioethics) (1996), *Animal-to-Human Transplantation: The Ethics of Xenotransplantation*, Nuffield Council on Bioethics: London, p. 16, para. 2.9.

112 Acute Services Policy Unit (1994), *Identification of Potential Donors of Organs for Transplantation*, Department of Health: London, (HSG(94)1).

113 Kennedy Report (Report of the Advisory Group on the Ethics of Xenotransplantation) (1997), *Animal Tissue into Humans*, HMSO: London, p. 94, para. 5.18.

114 Ibid.

115 Mason et al. (2002), at p. 444.

Their objections, however, are contextual rather than principled. Recognition of the status of a relevant advance directive – that is, clarity that such decisions are made only with the authority of the individual donor him or herself – seems unlikely to generate or support the kinds of fears to which they refer.

Additionally, the Kennedy Report noted the possibility that there were ethical difficulties associated with the practice of elective ventilation, for example that there was a small risk 'of inducing a persistent vegetative state in the patient'.[116] At present, therefore, there seems to be a consensus that the practice of elective ventilation is not a practical, lawful or ethical way forward. The 'reanimation' of comatose and dying patients for the purpose of removing organs clearly does raise a number of potential problems. As Salih et al. have said:

> Organ donation has generally been justified in terms of better and longer lives for the recipients. A policy of elective ventilation may call into public question the necessary means to this end, and it is not yet clear that a public debate on this issue would endorse this move.[117]

Although neither the Kennedy Report nor the Report of the Nuffield Council on Bioethics (Nuffield Report)[118] addressed in any great depth the ethical objections to elective ventilation, they can perhaps best be encapsulated in the Kantian philosophy that people should never be used solely as a means to the ends of another.[119] In addition, it seems that elective ventilation could fly in the face of the established principles of medical ethics. These are described by Beauchamp and Childress[120] as being: beneficence, non-maleficence, respect for autonomy and justice. These, it has been argued, are in many senses individuated concepts.[121] Although justice might be taken to require the doctor to address the needs of all of his or her patients, by and large the tradition of medical ethics is to consider the relationship between the individual doctor and the individual patient, essentially to the exclusion of others. Thus, the doctor is exhorted to act in the best interests of a *particular* patient, arguably irrespective of the clinical condition of other patients. In other words, in this situation the doctor's primary obligation is to the comatose, terminally ill patient and not to any other patients who may benefit from that particular patient's death. It is, for example, with this in mind that transplantation teams are generally divorced from the teams who are caring for a dying patient. However, it is possible to interpret the Kantian ethic, which, after all, dictates only that people should not be used *solely* as a means to an end for other people, in a manner which renders it not inimical to elective ventilation, providing other

---

116 Kennedy Report (1997).

117 Salih, M.A.M. et al. (1991), at p. 1065.

118 Nuffield Report (1996).

119 Kant, I. (1990), 'Duties Towards the Body in Regard to Life', *Lectures in Ethics*, reprinted in Donnelly, J. (ed.), *Suicide: Right or Wrong?*, Prometheus: New York.

120 Beauchamp, T.L. and Childress, J.F. (2001), *Principles of Biomedical Ethics* (5th Ed.), Oxford University Press: Oxford.

121 See McLean, S.A.M. (1996a), 'The New Genetics: A Challenge to Clinical Values?', *Proceedings of the Royal College of Physicians of Edinburgh*, **26**, pp. 41–50.

safeguards are in place. The Kantian ethic need not be seen as precluding people from being free to agree to offer themselves as a means to an end, although other people could not do this on their behalf. Thus, it can be concluded that, although as practised in the Exeter experiment elective ventilation would undoubtedly be unlawful, there need be no general ethical objection to the use of elective ventilation which had been agreed to in advance by the individual who is to become the organ donor. Indeed, it would be entirely coherent with Kantian principles that individuals should be able to make just such a donation. As McLean has said:

> ... there is no fundamental ethical objection to the use of body parts, particularly when directed by the donor; ... people are entitled to make decisions about what treatment should be given or not in the event of their lapsing into incompetence.[122]

Indeed, this conclusion has been taken seriously by the Scottish Transplant Group Report referred to above, which recommends that '[t]he forthcoming review of the [Human Tissue] legislation should include consideration of the power of advance directives in relation to elective ventilation'.[123] Sadly, it appears that this has not in fact been done. The terms of the (England and Wales) Mental Capacity Act 2005 give legal authority to advance directives, but do not specifically address this question.[124]

It is, of course, the case that advance decisions, or directives as they are sometimes called, generally relate to the *refusal* of treatment rather than to its *imposition*. In other words, it is more common that people leave behind them information about treatment which they would refuse, for example continued ventilation, rather than leaving behind them directions for treatment which they would accept. The Law Commission recognizes that there may be a difference between these two, stating that there is a 'further important distinction ... to be drawn between the legal effect of a decision *in favour* of a particular (or all) treatment and a decision *against* such treatment'.[125] It has traditionally been assumed that individuals cannot oblige a doctor to treat against the doctor's clinical judgement[126] (although that position may now have changed following the *Burke* judgement mentioned above).[127] Equally, no advance directive can render lawful something which would otherwise be unlawful. Thus, if the treatment to which they were attempting to agree was not in itself lawful then obviously the directive would have no force whatsoever. However, ventilation is not unlawful *in se*, and with consent and a valid advance directive there is arguably no reason why elective

---

122 McLean, S.A.M. (1996b), 'Transplantation and the "Nearly Dead": The Case of Elective Ventilation', in McLean, S.A.M. (ed.), *Contemporary Issues in Law, Medicine and Ethics*, Dartmouth: Aldershot, pp. 143–162, at p. 151.

123 Scottish Transplant Group (2002), p. 54, recommendation 25.

124 S. 26.

125 The Law Commission (LAW COM No 231) (1995), *Mental Incapacity, Item 9 of the Fourth Programme of Law Reform: Mentally Incapacitated Adults*, HMSO: London, at p. 65.

126 See *R* v *Cambridge Health Authority ex p B (a minor)* (QBD) (1995) 25 BMLR 5; (1995) 25 BMLR 1 (CA).

127 For further information in respect of England and Wales, see the Mental Capacity Act 2005, ss. 24 *et seq*.

ventilation should not in fact be lawful. Not everything, however, is capable of being consented to.

In the United Kingdom, the law is clearly expounded in the case of *R* v *Brown*.[128] In this case, which was subsequently upheld by the European Court of Human Rights,[129] it was made clear that there were certain limitations to what even a competent adult could consent to. In this case, the behaviour in question related to sado-masochistic sexual practices performed in private by consenting male adults. In *Attorney General's reference (No. 6 of 1980)*, Lord Lane indicated that '[i]t is not in the public interests that people should try to cause, or should cause, each other actual bodily harm for no good reason'.[130] Or as Lord Jauncey put it in the original case of *R* v *Brown*, '[t]he infliction of bodily harm without good reason is unlawful and ... the consent of the victim is irrelevant'.[131] These statements taken together would seem to suggest that, if it were possible to agree to elective ventilation, then it would be necessary to establish that there was a good reason for the bodily harm being inflicted. It might be argued that the 'good reason' in these circumstances would be the facilitation of a programme of organ transplantation which by and large people seem to believe to be a good thing. Alternatively, the 'good' could be the vindication of the individual's autonomous prior decision.

In addition, Lord Mustill in the same case indicated that there were other considerations beyond consent which might be relevant in providing a defence to any allegation that an individual has been assaulted. As he said:

> ... in reality the reason why the perpetrator of the harm is not liable is not because of the recipient's consent, but because the perpetrator has acted in the situation where the consent of the recipient forms one, but only one of the elements which make the act legitimate.[132]

This might be interpreted as meaning that the good that can flow from a programme of organ transplantation could be one of the elements which make the act legitimate. Indeed, Lord Mustill made some considerable play of the fact that medical treatment by and large would be exempt from the general rules, saying that behaviour can be 'legitimate if performed in accordance with good medical practice and with the consent of the patient'.[133] As McLean has said, '... there may be arguments which would suggest that, in the right climate and with the requisite will, reanalysis would render it [elective ventilation] acceptable in certain circumstances'.[134] Thus, elective ventilation might become a possibility in these limited circumstances. As Lord Mustill also said, echoing the words of John Stuart Mill:

> ... the state should interfere with the rights of an individual to live his or her life as he or she may choose no more than is necessary to ensure a proper balance between the special

128 [1994] 1 AC 212.

129 *Laskey, Jaggard and Brown* v *UK* (1997) 24 EHRR 39.

130 [1981] 1 QB 715, at p. 718.

131 At p. 243.

132 *R* v *Brown*, at p. 259.

133 *R* v *Brown*, at pp. 258–259.

134 McLean (1996b), at p. 159.

> interests of the individual and the general interests of the individuals who together comprise the population at large.[135]

A Market in Human Tissue

Although often discounted, the creation of a market in human tissue has been actively called for by one leading British clinician,[136] despite the fact that the Council of Europe's Biomedicine Convention declares that, '[t]he human body and its parts shall not give rise to financial gain'.[137]

Mason, McCall Smith and Laurie note that there are two distinct situations here, each of which might raise different issues. In the case of a living donor, they argue that 'this is essentially a matter of valid consent by the donor'.[138] They suggest that:

> It is at least arguable that, in closing the door on the use of an inessential part of one's body for gain, Parliament is striking at the individual publican's autonomy in favour of the corporate pharisee's inner virtue.[139]

Although public opinion on this matter may not be as clear-cut as might be imagined,[140] the establishment view on a trade of organs from living people is pretty uniform. The British Transplantation Society 'considers that payment for organs or tissue where a donor accrues financial or material gain is unethical'.[141] The General Medical Council agrees:

> In no circumstances may doctors participate in or encourage in any way the trade in human organs from live donors. They must not advertise for donors nor make financial or medical arrangements for people who wish to sell or buy organs ... Doctors must also satisfy themselves that consent to a donation has been given without undue influence of any kind, including the offer of financial or material benefit.[142]

Recent professional disciplinary actions against doctors ignoring this advice have shown the tenacity of the objections to the sale of live organs. Yet, it could reasonably be argued that it is undue paternalism to interfere with the free choice of individuals to sell parts of their body, after appropriate consideration of the risks of

---

135 *R* v *Brown*, *supra cit*, at p. 273.

136 May 2003, 'Senior UK Doctor Calls for a Regulated Trade in Organs', http://www.news.bbc.co.uk, accessed on 20/05/03.

137 Convention for the Protection of Human Rights and Dignity of the Human Being with Regard to the Application of Biological Medicine: Convention on Human Rights and Biomedicine, European Treaty Series – No. 164, Oviedo, 4.iv.1997 Article 21.

138 Mason et al. (2002), at p. 445.

139 Ibid., at p. 434.

140 Davies, I. (1991), 'Live Donation of Human Body Parts: A Case for Negotiability?', *Medico-Legal Journal*, **59** (100).

141 'Approved Policy Statements', September 2003, available at http://www.bts.org.uk/approvedstatements.htm, accessed on 20/01/04.

142 General Medical Council (1992), 'Guidance for Doctors on Transplantation of Organs from Live Donors', *News Review*, December, Supplement.

live donation, which the WHO describe as 'low but not negligible'.[143] Of course, this would require an assessment of what is in fact a 'free' decision; presumably one would only sell an organ if one were in desperate need of the money. The question of whether this form of 'coercion' or 'persuasion' is sufficient to override an otherwise apparently autonomous act is moot; many people engage in perfectly lawful, yet hazardous, activity for reward.

Mason, McCall Smith and Laurie, amongst others, raise yet another potential problem – at least within the context of the UK healthcare system. As they say:

> It is difficult to see the sale of organs as other than a way for the rich to obtain priority essential care, the iniquity being compounded by the corollary that the poor, who would form the pool of such donors, would be positively disadvantaged in the role of supplier.[144]

However, as they also point out, such concerns could perhaps be alleviated by controlling the market, perhaps using the Unrelated Live Transplant Regulatory Authority, and 'legalising paid donations'.[145]

Indeed, not only is the public apparently divided on this issue, but reputable commentators in the UK have also lent their weight to this possibility. Radcliffe Richards, for example, has said that:

> The prohibition of organ sales is derived not from the principles usually invoked in its support, but from a powerful feeling of repugnance that apparently numbs ordinary moral sensitivities and anaesthetises the intellect, making invisible the obvious harms of prohibition, giving plausibility to arguments whose inadequacy would in less fraught contexts proclaim itself from the rooftops, and, in doing both these things, hiding the extraordinary force of its own influence.[146]

Harris and Erin maintain that an 'ethical market in organs' could be created, but that:

> To meet legitimate ethical and regulatory concerns any such scheme must have built into it safeguards against wrongful exploitation and show concern for vulnerable people, as well as taking into account considerations of justice and equity. If all this can be done then a market in human body products will be shown to be, at the very least, not prima facie unethical.[147]

Although some of the issues in respect of what might loosely be called commodification are relevant also to any sale of cadaveric organs, still others are unique to that area. While it could be argued that a voluntary donation (even for financial gain) lies within the competence of the competent individual, in the case of cadaveric organ sales there is clearly no direct benefit to the deceased donor.

---

143 WHO (2003).

144 Mason et al. (2002), at p. 434.

145 Ibid., at p. 435.

146 Radcliffe Richards, J.R. (1996), 'Nephrarious Goings On: Kidney Sales and Moral Arguments', *Journal of Medical Philosophy*, **21** (375), at p. 406; see also Radcliffe Richards, J. et al. (1998), 'The Case for Allowing Kidney Sales', *The Lancet*, **351** (1950).

147 Harris, J. and Erin, C. (2002), 'An Ethically Defensible Market in Organs', *British Medical Journal*, **325**, at pp. 114–115. This article provoked considerable response in the *British Medical Journal*

Rather, 'the selling of cadaver organs is, at root, directed to the enticement of the next of kin'.[148] Interestingly, in the face of this controversy, it was announced in 2002 that the American Medical Association had 'voted to encourage studies that would determine whether financial incentives could increase the pool of cadaveric organ donors'.[149] The US position is not dissimilar to that which currently exists in the UK; namely, organ sales are outlawed by the National Organ Transplant Act 1984. At the same time, it is reported that around '80000 people are on transplant waiting lists, and an estimated 15000 people die on these lists while waiting for an organ'.[150] Exploring the possibility of a market in human organs has the potential to reduce this terrible toll.

Finally, 'payment' for organs need not, it must be remembered, simply relate to financial inducement. In much the same way as egg-sharing schemes operate in some countries, incentives could also include guaranteeing a living donor priority treatment should any of the possible adverse consequences of providing the organ actually occur, or offering preferential treatment to the families of cadaveric 'donors'. However, whichever route is proposed, it would realistically seem that the UK is a long way from seriously considering a market in organs, and the Human Tissue Act[151] and the Scottish Bill[152] expressly outlaw trafficking in human organs as we have already noted. This option, therefore, clearly will have no impact on the number of available organs in the UK[153] for the foreseeable future. The debate, however, remains real and – given the reality of the need for organs – the last word may not yet have been said. Gill and Sade, for example, argue that:

> Undoubtedly, many people will continue to oppose kidney sales….Many people will continue to find the sale of a kidney repugnant, a feeling that rational argumentation alone may be incapable of dislodging. But we should not let this feeling of repugnance hold hostage our moral thinking. For a great many things we now hold in the highest esteem – including organ transplantation itself – occasioned strong repugnance in times past.[154]

On the other hand, Cohen suggests that:

– see, for example, in 2002, 'Letters, Ethical Market in Organs', *British Medical Journal*, **325** (835). See also Erin, C. and Harris, J. (2003), 'An Ethical Market in Human Organs', *Journal of Medical Ethics*, **29** (137); Harris, J. (2003), 'In Praise of Unprincipled Ethics', *Journal of Medical Ethics*, **29** (303).

148 Mason, McCall Smith and Laurie (2002), at p. 445.

149 Josefson, D. (2002), 'AMA Considers Whether to Pay for Donation of Organs', *British Medical Journal*, **1541**.

150 Ibid.

151 S. 32.

152 S. 17.

153 In Scotland, at least this will be true of donations from living donors as the 1989 Act will continue to apply, unless specific reference is made to this in the anticipated new legislation. As there is generally said to be 'no property' in the human body, presumably common law would also not be able to accommodate the sale of an organ from a deceased person; whether or not a criminal offence would be committed is moot.

154 Gill, M.B. and Sade, R.M. (2002), 'Paying for Kidneys: The Case against Prohibition', *Kennedy Institute of Ethics Journal*, **12** (1), at p. 19.

> If organ donation from living persons, in particular, can be justified in terms of its risks to donors and benefits to recipients, we ought to promote the altruistic donation of organs from living donors in a more communitarian fashion, rather than promote their sale.[155]

Artificial Organs and Tissue

A further option worth contemplating briefly is the possible development of artificial organs and tissue for transplantation purposes. As the Nuffield Report notes, '[a]rtificial implants currently under development range from totally mechanical devices to organs consisting of a combination of artificial materials and human cells'.[156] Considerable work has been done on the possibility of replacing living human parts with those which have been artificially created. Opinion is divided on the potential of these technologies. For example, two prominent exponents of xenotransplantation claim of artificial heart devices:

> Even though these devices are steadily being improved and will likely provide an option for some patients, it seems that it will be many years before a power source for such a device can be made small enough to be inserted into the patient ... When this can be achieved, then these devices may well prove strong competition to heart transplants. Unfortunately, it seems unlikely that we shall see this within our lifetimes.[157]

However, in his 2002 Ravdin Lecture to the American College of Surgeons, artificial organs expert Robert Bartlett said:

> The use of artificial devices to replace the function of vital organs is only about 50 years old. This transition from basic science research to routine clinical application has proceeded so quickly that it is now commonplace, even to the lay public. It is considered routine to have an artificial heart valve, pacemaker, hip joint, or artery; to be on an artificial kidney or mechanical ventilator ... Organ replacement makes it possible to bridge organ recovery or organ transplantation. Millions of people have had their lives extended and improved by artificial organs.[158]

This positive assessment of the contribution made by artificial organs to human well-being is, arguably, somewhat misleading because the technological advances to which Bartlett refers often fall short of being artificial organs *per se*. Furthermore, the devices to which he refers which do replicate organ functions (haemodialysis and ventilation) are employed *ex vivo*. Thus, while such artificial devices have, as Bartlett suggests, extended the lives of many people, in their current form they do not address the need to supply more organs that can be transplanted into patients as a destination therapy.

---

155 Cohen, C.B. (2002), 'Public Policy and the Sale of Human Organs', *Kennedy Institute of Ethics Journal*, **12** (1), at p. 62.

156 Nuffield Report (1996), p. 17, para. 2.11.

157 Cooper, D. and Lanza, R. (2000), *Xeno: The Promise of Transplanting Animal Organs into Humans*, Oxford University Press: Oxford, at p. 20.

158 Bartlett, R.H. (1993), 'Artificial Organs: Basic Science Meets Critical Care,' *Journal of the American College of Surgeons*, **196** (2), pp. 171–179, at p. 171.

Bartlett also suggests that artificial 'organ replacement' can be used to bridge patients to transplantation or organ recovery, while another researcher in the field claims that such devices also represent an option for permanent organ replacement.[159] If true, suggestions that clinical work with implanted artificial organs is sufficiently advanced to provide bridge and destination therapy to patients would indicate that this technology is much closer to being able to fulfil the shortage of organs than other alternatives. Hence, we must briefly consider what clinical work is being undertaken with artificial organs.

Currently there are two types of cardiac device employed as a treatment option; namely, cardiac assist devices and total artificial hearts. Left Ventricular Assist Devices (LVADs) are used either as a bridge,[160] or a destination treatment option to support circulation.[161] Thus, while some patients still require an organ transplant, LVADs also provide temporary support to allow patients to recover normal organ functioning after operations and act as permanent support to others, so reducing the need for transplantation. There are a number of difficulties with such devices including infection risks,[162] and the devices are not totally implanted; patients wear some parts externally.

The other form of cardiac device, that which perhaps more correctly can be named an 'artificial organ', is the Total Artificial Heart (TAH). Currently, the most well-known TAH is Abiomed's AbioCor.[163] The company explains:

> The AbioCor is intended for use in end-stage heart failure patients whose hearts have irreversible left and right ventricular failure and for whom surgery or medical therapy is inadequate. Currently, heart transplantation is the only proven method of cardiac replacement for extending the lives of such patients; however, there remains a consistent shortage of available donor hearts for transplantation.[164]

The Food and Drug Administration provided Abiomed with an exemption to allow it to start trials of its TAH in January 2001.[165] To participate in AbioCor clinical

---

159 Nose, Y. (2004), 'Artificial Organs for Bridge to Therapy', *Artificial Organs*, **28** (2), pp. 127–128, at p. 127; Nose, Y. and Okubo, H. (2003), 'Artificial Organs Versus Regenerative Medicine: Is it True?', *Artificial Organs*, **27** (9), pp. 765–771, at p. 767f.

160 Frazer, O.H. et al. (1995), 'Improved Morality and Rehabilitation of Transplant Candidates Treated with a Long Term Implantable Left Ventricular Assist System', *Annals of Thoracic Surgery*, **222**, pp. 327–28; Kumpati, G.S. et al. (2001), 'Left Ventricular Assist Device Bridge to Recovery: A Review of the Current Status', *Annals of Thoracic Surgery*, **71**, ss. 103–108.

161 Letsou, G.V. et al. (2001), 'Continuous Axial-Flow Left Ventricular Assist Device (Jarvik 2000) Maintains Kidney and Liver Perfusion for up to 6 Months', *Annals of Thoracic Surgery*, **76**, pp. 1167–1170; Beyersdorf, F. (2001), 'Economics of Ventricular Assist Devices: European View', *Annals of Thoracic Surgery*, **71**, ss. 192–194.

162 Malani, P.N. et al. (2002), 'Nosocomial Infections Associated with Left Ventricular Assist Devices', *Clinical Infectious Diseases*, **34** (10), pp. 1295–1300; McCarthy, P. et al. (1996), ' Implantable LVAD Infections: Implications for Permanent use of the Device', *Annals Thoracic Surgery*, **61** (1), pp. 359–365.

163 Information at http://www.abiomed.com/abiocor/prodback.html, accessed on 13/03/04.

164 Ibid.

165 Ibid.

trials patients must have a life expectancy of under 30 days, be over 18 years old, have bi-ventricular failure, be ineligible for allotransplantation and have failed to respond to other therapies.[166] The first AbioCor patient, 59-year-old Robert Tools, received the device in July 2001.[167] After a period he was able to take exercise, including walking to the local park.[168] However, after anti-coagulation problems and a stroke, Mr Tools died in November 2001, 151 days after receiving the TAH.[169] Dowling reports that, of the six other patients who took part in the initial clinical trials of the device, two patients were discharged from hospital, one of these eventually went home, another died 142 days after transplantation, another after 56 days and two died shortly after surgery.[170] Of the two patients who were discharged from hospital, one – a 51-year-old man – was later readmitted with pneumonia and respiratory failure and died 294 days after transplant.[171] The other, Tom Christerson – who received TAH in September 2001 – was discharged from hospital 209 days after transplantation and died in February 2003.[172] Dowling suggests that in many cases the multiple deaths experienced following the trial could be explained by the fact that:

> These patients have all been ill, with 30-day mortality of more than 75%. A significant number of postoperative complications have been related to the preoperative comorbidities, including the presence of end-organ dysfunction and severe malnutrition.[173]

Other shortcomings of the AbioCor include the fact that its internal battery life only permits free movement for a short time; Christerson, for example, survived so long (17 months) that he had to have an additional operation to replace the internal battery.[174] In addition, TAHs, like LVADs, have external parts which make the devices less ideal than an allotransplant. However, it has been claimed that:

> ... the AbioCor system has demonstrated a high degree of reliability. No pump failures have been experienced and only minor technical problems have been encountered. The system has functioned as intended, and hemodynamic stability is easily achieved.[175]

Despite the potential of artificial heart devices, there is relatively little progress in replicating the functions of other organs in ways that would address the shortage of

---

166 Information at http://www.abiomed.com/abiocor/clinfact.html, accessed on 13/03/04.

167 http://www.heartpioneers.com/releases/070301.html, accessed on 13/03/04.

168 http://www.news.bbc.co.uk/1/hi/health/1564244.stm, accessed on 13/03/04.

169 http://www.heartpioneers.com/releases/113001-2.html, accessed on 13/03/04; Dowling, R.D. (2003), 'The AbioCor Implantable Replacement Heart', *Annals of Thoracic Surgery*, **75**, ss. 93–99, at s. 96.

170 Ibid., at s. 96f.

171 Ibid., at s. 97.

172 http://www.heartpioneers.com/releases/020703.html, accessed on 13/03/04.

173 Dowling (2003), at s. 98.

174 Ibid.

175 Myers, T.J. (2003), 'Continuous Flow Pumps and Total Artificial Hearts: Management Issues', *Annals of Thoracic Surgery*, **75**, ss. 79–85.

organs. For example, although there have been both research and clinical trials of an *ex vivo* bioartificial liver to bridge patients to transplantation,[176] it is acknowledged that far more work is required to make this a viable alternative to liver transplantation.[177] Research is also being conducted on a wearable bioartificial kidney,[178] although at present it is far from providing a reliable alternative to kidney transplantation. Furthermore, the artificial kidney and the bioartificial liver are artificial organs in a wider sense than the mechanical cardiac devices we have already examined. That is, they belong under the broader classification of regenerative medicine.[179] Thus, while these bioartificial devices may develop to provide some respite to organ shortage, potential benefits for transplantation itself are likely to come from devices which are not solely mechanical. For the foreseeable future, then, their main value may lie in maintaining patients awaiting transplant; even in this role, much remains to be done before their actual impact can be evaluated.

Stem Cell Research

In 2001, the United Kingdom Parliament agreed to expand the categories of research which were permissible on the human embryo to include the possible development of stem cell research.[180] The joint report from the Human Genetics Commission and the Human Fertilisation and Embryology Authority,[181] published in 1998, concluded that, although reproductive cloning should be outlawed, therapeutic cloning should be permissible. A report from both the Nuffield Council[182] and the Government's Chief Medical Officer[183] also agreed that developments in stem cell research would be of potential future benefit.[184] As far as

---

176 Chen, S. et al. (1997), 'Treatment of Severe Liver Failure with a Bioartificial Liver', in Prokop, A. et al. (eds), *Bioartificial Organs: Science, Medicine and Technology*, New York Academy of Sciences: New York, pp. 350–360.

177 Thalheimer, U. and Capra, F. (2002), 'Liver Transplantation: Making the Best out of what we have', *Digestive Diseases and Sciences*, **47** (5), pp. 945–953, at p. 951; Court F.G. (2003), 'Bioartificial Liver Support Devices: Historical Perspectives', *Australian and New Zealand Journal of Surgery*, **73**, pp. 739–748; Hayes, P.C. and Lee, A. (2001), 'What Progress with Artificial Livers?', *The Lancet*, **358**, pp. 1286–1287.

178 Saito, A. (2004), 'Research into the Development of a Wearable Bioartificial Kidney with a Continuous Hemofilter and a Bioartificial Tubule Device Using Tubular Epithelial Cells', *Artificial Organs*, **28** (1), pp. 58–63; Humes, H.D. (1999), 'Replacement of Renal Function in Uremic Animals with Tissue-Engineered Kidney', *Nature Biotechnology*, **17** (May), pp. 451–455.

179 Saito (2004), at p. 58.

180 Human Fertilisation and Embryology (Research Purposes) Regulations 2001.

181 Human Genetics Commission and Human Fertilisation and Embryology Authority (1998), *Cloning Issues in Reproduction, Science and Medicine*, London, December.

182 Nuffield Council (2000), *Stem Cell Therapy: The Ethical Issues*, Nuffield Council of Bioethics: London, April.

183 Chief Medical Officer (2000), *Stem Cell Research: Medical Progress with Responsibility*, Department of Health: London, June. Also available at http://www.doh.gov.uk/cege/stemcellreport.pdf.

184 For discussion of these reports, see McLean, S.A.M. (2000), 'Aspects ethiques, juridiques et reglementaires de l'utilisation de cellules souches embryonnaires humaines en Grande-Bretagne', in Dodet, B. and Vicari, M. (eds), *Cellules souches pluripotentes: perspectives therapeutiques et aspects ethiques*, John Libbey Eurotext: London, pp. 35–44.

therapeutic research is concerned, this would entail the possible development of nerves, skin and possibly solid organs derivative from stem cells preferably from the individual patient him or herself which would allow the development of replacement organs.

Brownsword describes the possibilities of stem cell research in this way:

> If cell-based therapies were to be delivered in future health care regimes, the current thinking is that this might be sourced in one of two ways. One way would be to draw on cell lines held in a national cell bank; it is unlikely that the bank would hold cell lines that would be perfect matches for patients but they would aim to hold at least some lines that would be close enough to serve. The other way would be to use the patient's own tissue, and then generate a custom-made embryo and embryonic stem (ES) cells using cell nuclear replacement (CNR) technology. Such bespoke cells should be perfectly compatible with the patient and, in many popularised and schematic accounts, this is seen as the answer to degenerative diseases.[185]

It is, however, the case that this is also something which is very much in the future and certainly will not make an immediate impact on the shortage of organs for transplantation purposes. As the House of Lords Select Committee on Stem Cells[186] said:

> From the evidence we have received we are clear that over the next few years most studies on stem cells, whether adult, foetal or embryonic in origin, will be basic research. This research will not in itself be therapeutic, but will be undertaken with the aim of gaining the understanding necessary if stem cells are to be used widely for therapeutic benefit.[187]

Moreover, there may be some international constraints on the development of embryonic stem cell research, for example the prohibition on the creation of embryos for research contained in the Council of Europe's Bioethics Convention,[188] although it should be noted that this is not prohibited in the UK which has not ratified the Convention. Despite potential disagreement on the use of embryos in research on a European or international basis, interest in stem cell research continues to thrive and develop. As has been said, '[i]f such cells can be cultivated in the laboratory, then it may be possible to prompt them to differentiate into types of tissue found in particular organs which can be used to repair organ damage'.[189] In 2002, the House of Lords report on stem cell research[190] concluded as follows:

---

185 Brownsword, R. (2002), 'Stem Cells, Superman, and the Report of the Select Committee', *Modern Law Review*, **65** (4), pp. 568, 569.

186 House of Lords Select Committee on Stem Cells, 13 February 2002. Available at http://www.publications.parliament.uk/pa/ld200102/dselect/ldstem/83/8302.htm.

187 Para 2.12.

188 Convention for the Protection of Human Rights and Dignity of the Human Being with Regard to the Application of Biology and Medicine: Convention on Human Rights and Biomedicine (Oviedo, 4 April 1997), Article 18(2).

189 Mason, McCall Smith and Laurie (2002), p. 611.

190 House of Lords Select Committee on Stem Cells, 13 February 2002. Available at http://www.publications.parliament.uk/pa/ld200102/dselect/ldstem/83/8302.htm.

(i) Stem cells appear to have great therapeutic potential for the treatment of many disorders that are both common and serious and for the repair of damaged tissue.
(ii) Until recently most research on stem cells has focussed on ES cells from animals and the derivation of ES cell lines from them; cell lines from human ES cells have the potential to provide a basis for a wide range of therapies.
(iii) Recent research on adult stem cells, including stem cells from the placenta and umbilical cord, also holds promise of therapies; and research on them should be strongly encouraged by funding bodies and the Government.
(iv) To ensure maximum medical benefit it is necessary to keep both routes to therapy open at present since neither alone is likely to meet all therapeutic needs.
(v) For the full therapeutic potential of stem cells, both adult and ES, to be realised, fundamental research on ES cells is necessary, particularly to understand the processes of cell differentiation and dedifferentiation.
(vi) Future developments might eventually make further research on ES cells unnecessary. This is unlikely in the foreseeable future; in the meantime there is a strong scientific and medical case for continued research on human ES cells.[191]

In July 2002, the Government published its response to the House of Lords Report,[192] which 'agrees completely with the Select Committee over the exciting prospects that stem cell research may deliver'.[193]

However, it must be said that stem cell research is by no means entirely uncontroversial, particularly where the research is conducted on human embryos. Such research is outlawed in a number of European countries, and is permitted only within clear limits in the USA. In 2001, President Bush declared that funding for research would only be considered using human ES (embryonic) cells from 'cell lines that had been derived and cultured by August 9, 2001'.[194] However, the American Society for Reproductive Medicine's Ethics Committee 'regards embryo research as ethically acceptable if it is likely to provide significant new knowledge that will benefit human health and if it is conducted in ways that accord the embryo respect'.[195] In 2003, the European Union proposed guidelines which would allow financial support for projects using human embryonic stem cells using so-called 'spare' embryos.[196] Some, however, argue that there is no such thing as a surplus or spare embryo, and recommend rather that all such embryos should where possible be used for implantation.[197] However, it is also noted that:

> Most in vitro fertilisation programmes discard hundreds of healthy human eggs each year because they are immature or do not fertilise with the partner's sperm. If these eggs were

191 Ibid., para 3.22.

192 *Government Response to the House of Lords Select Committee Report on Stem Cells*, Cm 5561/2002.

193 Ibid., at p. 7.

194 American Society for Reproductive Medicine Ethics Committee (2002), 'Donating Spare Embryos for Embryonic Stem-cell Research', *Fertility and Sterility*, **78** (5), November, p. 957.

195 Ibid., at p. 958.

196 British Medical Council (2003), 'EU Will Fund Research on Stem Cells Only from Embryos Created before June 2002', *British Medical Journal*, **327**, p. 124.

197 Brison, D.R. and Lieberman, B.A. (2003), 'Use Eggs, not Embryos, to Derive Stem Cells', (Letter to the Editor), *British Medical Journal*, **327**, p. 872.

> fertilised with sperm from a fertile donor, many would form viable embryos that could be used for stem cell derivation.[198]

It is not immediately clear, however, that this avoids any real ethical problems. Irrespective of source, once an embryo is created, its use will be subject to the same debate which has been alluded to above. Whatever the extent of the debate, proponents of stem cell research will doubtless derive some consolation from the findings of a poll commissioned by, amongst others, the Medical Research Council, which found that '[s]even out of ten of those surveyed said the use of human embryos was acceptable in research to find treatments for serious diseases and in fertility research'.[199]

It seems likely that there will be considerably less debate about the use of adult stem cells, although evidence as to efficacy is currently ambivalent.[200] In any event, as the House of Lords Select Committee noted:

> Although adult stem cells may ultimately fulfil many therapeutic needs, the strong weight of evidence is that the full potential of adult stem cell research and its therapeutic application is unlikely to be realised without research on ES cells.[201]

In a report published in October 2003, the European Commission Joint Research Centre was reasonably confident about the future of adult stem cell research, although they also note that embryonic stem cell research will continue to be necessary, at least initially. The report says:

> It is probable that adult stem cells will be one of the main cell sources for tissue engineering in the medium-term future, with the advantage of avoiding immune rejection. Embryonic stem cells would mainly be used for basic research on cell differentiation and the necessary molecular signals, the results of which could be applied to tissue engineering.[202]

One fascinating potential, however, derives from the possibility of taking stem cells from umbilical cord blood. Already this practice is increasing in the UK (and elsewhere), and – given consent from the parent, and its lack of harm to the born child – this may pave the way for considerable, non-ethically ambivalent research and the development of therapies. For one thing, there are few who oppose the taking of stem cells from living people (with valid consent, of course) or the umbilical cord.[203] For another, again given appropriate regulation, the very real need for financial investment

---

[198] Ibid.

[199] http://www.news.bbc.co.uk, accessed on 08/04/03.

[200] See House of Lords Select Committee on Stem Cells, *supra cit*; 'Stem Cell Research Doubts', http://ww.news.bbc.co.uk, accessed on 14/03/02.

[201] House of Lords Select Committee on Stem Cells, *supra cit*, para. 3.17.

[202] European Commission Joint Research Centre, European Science and Technology Observatory (2003), *Human Tissue-engineered Products: Today's Markets and Future Prospects*, Report EUR 21000 EN, October.

[203] See McCartney, J.J. (2004), 'Recent Ethical Controversies about Stem Cell Research', in Humber, J.M. and Almeder, R.F. (eds), *Stem Cell Research*, Humana Press: New Jersey, at p. 99 *et seq.*

in stem cell research would be less open to criticism, were the rights of property and use related, as in this case, to tissue which would otherwise be discarded. Although very much in the future, stem cell research, it can be concluded, may offer real hope in the treatment of a number of medical conditions, including organ failure.

Required Request

One final option which is worthy of brief consideration is the use of the system of 'required request'. This system was essentially developed to meet the apparent problem that families were not approached for their agreement to organ donation, thus sacrificing many potentially viable organs. It would, therefore, be most valuable in situations where the default position is consent-based, and the deceased or dying individual has left no instructions behind. Although this approach has not been tried in the United Kingdom, and it expressly does not have the backing of the BMA,[204] it was first introduced at Federal level in the United States under the terms of the Uniform Anatomical Gift Act 1987,[205] although Oregon had passed required request legislation in 1985.

Price identifies two strands to 'required request', one of which is more commonly referred to as 'routine enquiry'.[206] 'Required request' laws 'require documentation on the death certificate of a request and its outcome',[207] whereas 'routine enquiry' laws 'require simply that hospitals develop policies or protocols to ensure that families are asked to donate'.[208] Presumably because of the potential that such laws had to increase the availability of organs, they became relatively popular in the United States, with a majority of states passing laws incorporating one or other of the forms identified above. However, Siminoff et al. report that:

> Required Request legislation has not ... resulted in the expected increase in the number of procured organs, tissues or corneas. Studies in several states have shown that although there was a small immediate increase in procurement after the passage of required request laws, these increases were modest and levelled off after the first 2 years.[209]

Given their relatively minimal effect on organ procurement, it is not necessary to consider such laws in much greater detail. However, it should also be noted that they are difficult – even emotionally painful – to implement. For many, confronting recently bereaved relatives at such a time as part of a routine policy dehumanizes the relationship between doctors and the bereaved, and inappropriately prioritizes the needs of others over the interests of the families. Of course, such an intrusion is also present when relatives are asked under any system for their views on transplantation, but arguably there is an increased lack of sensitivity where the conversation becomes

204 BMA (2000), at p. 24.

205 Section 5.

206 Price (2000), at pp. 102–105.

207 Price (2000), at p. 102.

208 Ibid.

209 Siminoff, L.A. et al. (1995), 'Public Policy Governing Organ and Tissue Procurement in the United States', *Annals of Internal Medicine*, **10**, at p. 11.

merely part of clinical routine. In addition, it has been suggested that required request 'compromises the clinical autonomy of the medical staff concerned',[210] and can be extremely costly in terms of scarce or limited resources.

Conclusion

This overview of the legal situation in the United Kingdom has demonstrated that the system did undoubtedly require to be re-addressed, in light both of the scandals which came to light and the need to increase the number of organs available to a transplantation programme which has both wide support and increasing success. Equally, however, the brief review of alternative systems has not demonstrated with any confidence that any one of them would be preferable to a consent – or authorization – based model. Nonetheless, as has been noted:

> Generally, the 1990s has seen some improvements in the numbers of organs procured but these have generally been outstripped by increases in demand for transplantation. Waiting lists in most countries are growing year upon year.[211]

We have seen that concern over the use of organs following death was particularly acute following inquiries into practice in Bristol,[212] Liverpool[213] and Scotland[214] in the removal and retention of organs without consent for diagnostic, research or educational purposes. Although these inquiries were not directly about organ transplantation, the fact that the relevant law for both situations could be found in the same piece of legislation meant that the law needed to cover both situations. Moreover, there was concern that, at least in respect of cadaveric donation, the public might – in light of the revelations from these inquiries – be less rather than more willing to trust the motivation of those carrying out the necessary medical procedures. As Neuberger has said:

> There is little doubt that, at present, public faith in the organ donor system has been dented very badly. That loss of faith is extremely damaging for staff. But it is also an opportunity to rebuild public confidence by rebuilding the system for obtaining meaningful consent for organ donation.[215]

DuBois reinforces this point, noting that '... some evidence supports claims that the public will not donate organs unless it trusts the medical community ...'.[216]

If organ donation is indeed the 'good' that most people seem to believe it is, arguably there must be fewer legislative impediments to its practice. If the toll of human tragedy exacerbated by the shortage of organs is to be minimized it is necessary that the legal framework within which organ transplantation is carried out

---

210 Mason, McCall Smith and Laurie (2002), at p. 441.

211 Garwood-Gowers (1999), at p. xviii.

212 HMSO (2001a).

213 HMSO (2001b).

214 Independent Review Group on Retention of Organs at Post-Mortem (2001).

215 Neuberger, J. (2001), 'Restoring Faith in the Organ Donor System', *The Guardian*, 16 February.

216 DuBois, J.M. (1999), at p. 132.

in the United Kingdom is clear and unambiguous. This, it can be postulated, may now be the case given the law reforms described briefly above. Whether or not the dismissal of presumed consent will prove to be a barrier to enhancing the programme remains to be seen.

In the UK between 1 April 2004 and 31 March 2005:

- A total of 1,783 people received a kidney transplant of whom 475 (27 per cent) were given their kidney by a friend or relative – the highest number of living kidney transplants ever recorded in the UK.
- The figures also include a record number of kidney transplants from non-heart beating donors – 143, 20 per cent up on the previous year.
- Organs from 752 people who died were used to save or dramatically improve many people's lives through 2,242 transplants.
- A further 2,375 people had their sight restored through a cornea transplant – the highest number for eight years.
- 86 people received a pancreas or combined kidney/pancreas transplant – the highest number on record.
- A million more people pledged to help others after their death by registering their wishes on the NHS Organ Donor Register.[217]

Nonetheless, there remain insufficient organs for transplantation; a 'serious problem requiring serious action…'.[218] The BMA's vision of developing 'a modern, efficient and effective service for the twenty-first century'[219] is entirely laudable, but the desire to enhance services neither comes without cost, nor does it mandate the use of anything and everything that might be technically feasible.

Paradoxically, as Price points out:

> ... transplantation has become a victim of its own success. In the US in 1998 patients had an average survival rate after five years of 80+ per cent for kidneys, 73 per cent for livers and 69 per cent for hearts. These results in turn stimulated demand to the point where there are typically now (often woefully) insufficient numbers of donor organs for transplantation, compounded by an even wider class of individuals becoming eligible recipients, for example elderly patients, a phenomenon which could be unremittingly repeated in the future.[220]

Even should all cadavers become the property of the state, as seems to be the case in some countries,[221] and assuming ethical objections to this could be overcome, it is clear that there are practical reasons why not every salvageable organ will be removed and successfully transplanted. Although some commentators wish to ask an even more fundamental question – namely whether we should always strive to

217 UKTransplant website, accessed 28/06/05.

218 BMA (2000), at p. 28.

219 Ibid.

220 Price (2000), at pp. 4–5.

221 For discussion see Blasszauer, B. (1998), 'Autopsy', in Ten Have, H., Welie, J. and Spicker, S. (eds), *Ownership of the Human Body*, Kluwer: Dordrecht, at p. 19.

push back the frontiers of death[222] – it seems plausible that the cause of organ transplantation will remain both popular and powerful in the years to come. However, it has been said that:

> ... even if all human cadaveric organs were somehow made available for transplant, the supply would still not meet the potential demand. The hidden pool of potential transplant recipients would quickly become visible were these organs and tissue to become available. The search for alternatives to the use of human cadaveric organs rests on the recognition that scarcity is an insurmountable obstacle.[223]

Given the apparent intractability of the problems of organ procurement, attention has in recent years been focused on alternatives to donation as it is currently understood. In particular, as the following chapters will show, considerable interest has been aroused by the possibility of animal to human transplants (xenotransplantation). As the BMA says:

> In the future the use of animal organs and tissue for transplantation (xenotransplantation) and the use of cell nuclear replacement technology to develop compatible tissue for transplantation (sometimes referred to as 'therapeutic cloning') may, at least partially, resolve the problem. Both of these developments are, however, still at the research stage and will then need to progress through a series of clinical trials; even if these trials are successful, it will be many years, if ever, before they are available routinely in clinical practice. In the meantime, serious consideration needs to be given to how to improve the present situation.[224]

Equally, neither of these potential developments is without its legal and ethical concerns. In passing, it may be of interest to note that the scientific inquiry into both options has raised widespread concerns. In particular, the use of embryonic (ES) stem cells (which has already been discussed) and the use of animals as sources of organs for human survival have formed the basis of considerable debate. However, arguably any and all of the alternatives to the consent-based model may merit a response to the question:

> Are the boundaries of health, or indeed life itself, destined for inevitable extension or have we reached a point at which it is time to say that enough really is enough, and that for ethical reasons, including resource allocation, our energies would be better devoted to other health care issues?[225]

Putting this question slightly differently, Brazier says:

---

[222] See, for example, Fox, M. and McHale, J. (1998), 'Xenotransplantation: The Legal and Ethical Ramifications', *Medical Law Review*, **6** (1), pp. 42–61.

[223] Caplan, A.L. (1992), 'Is Xenografting Morally Wrong?', *Transplantation Proceedings*, **24** (2), April, pp. 722–727, at p. 723.

[224] BMA (2000), at p. 5.

[225] Fox and McHale (1998), at p. 61.

> The most important single issue in the context of organ and tissue transplantation is to find means of ensuring an adequate supply of organs ... In the end society will have to decide what price can be paid to improve supply.[226]

One of the potential ways of improving supply is, of course, xenotransplantation; the price – if any – that we might need to pay if we were to utilize this option will be the subject of the remainder of this book.

226 Brazier, M. (2003), *Medicine, Patients and the Law*, (3rd Ed.), Penguin Books: London, at p. 436.

Chapter 2

An Introduction to Xenotransplantation

Definitions

By definition, xenotransplantation is the transplantation of body tissue between 'foreign' or different species. Much of the biomedical research that takes place in this area is conducted by transplanting tissue and organs between different non-human animal species. But the primary objective of such research is to transplant animal organs and tissue into humans for therapeutic benefit. The Council of Europe highlights that it is also widely agreed that xenotransplantation does not include the use of non-living parts such as heart valves or vaccines that are made from animal sources.[1] This agreement over the general features of xenotransplantation is disrupted somewhat by debates over precisely which biomedical techniques should be included within this broad definition for reasons of public policy. Some of the issues raised by the efforts of nation states to identify what their public policy will include under the title 'xenotransplantation' can be illustrated by briefly examining how the definition has developed within the United States and the United Kingdom.

In 1996 the United States Public Health Service published its 'Draft Public Health Service Guidelines on Infectious Disease Issues in Xenotransplantation'. This document defines xenotransplantation as:

> ... any procedure that involves the use of live cells, tissues, and organs from a non-human animal source, transplanted or implanted into a human or used for *ex vivo* perfusion.[2]

While this definition appeared to include the fundamental features of animal to human transplantation, in June 1999 a meeting of the Food and Drug Administration (FDA) Xenotransplantation Subcommittee expanded it to cover:

> ... the use of live cells, tissues, or organs from a non-human animal source transplanted or implanted into a human, or used for *ex vivo* contact with human body fluids, cells, tissues, or organs that are subsequently given to a human recipient.[3]

The difference between these two definitions is that the second includes not just *ex vivo* perfusion but other forms of *ex vivo* contact, such as culturing skin for grafts to

[1] Council of Europe (2003), *Report on the State of the Art in the Field of Xenotransplantation*, Council of Europe: Strasbourg, p. 16.

[2] Public Health Service (1996), 'Draft Public Health Service Guidelines on Infectious Disease Issues in Xenotransplantation', *Federal Register*, **61** (185), pp. 49919–49932.

[3] *Draft Report of the Biological Response Modifiers Advisory Subcommittee on Xenotransplantation*, Meeting of 3 and 4 June 1999. Available at: http://www.fda.gov/ohrms/dockets/ac/99/other/6_3-4mtg.doc, accessed 8/3/04.

treat burns patients and other plastic surgery procedures. The subcommittee raised a number of concerns in relation to this broader understanding of what constitutes a xenotransplant. For example, it was thought that the new definition could generate 'a potentially enormous range of products that might require FDA regulation'.[4] In addition, it was also noted that under this definition it still:

> ... might be possible for humans to be exposed to some of the infectious risks associated with xenotransplantation in ways that fall outside of this definition. For example, Porcine Factor 8, used for the treatment of hemophilia, could expose, and may conceivably already have exposed, human patients to PERV. These products are currently regulated appropriately through other branches of the FDA and would not fall under the proposed definition of xenotransplantation.[5]

At a Xenotransplantation Subcommittee meeting in January 2000, concern was expressed about the fact that – under the new definition – xenotransplantation had been taking place in various forms for a number of years. Furthermore, it had not been subject to the stringent regulations that now had to be adhered to by those wishing to conduct xenotransplantation procedures.[6] Thus, the problems raised by the new definition ranged from concerns over the potential omission of certain practices from the definition, to the possibility that a large number of unregulated xenotransplantation procedures had already been conducted.

In response to these concerns it was suggested that not all forms of xenotransplantation included within the new definition required the same degree of monitoring. In some cases it was thought that the risk of animal diseases passing to humans was so low that they could be regulated less stringently. For example, it was claimed that:

> ... the use of cell lines, as opposed to whole organs from living animals, would not require the extensive documentation of parental breeding sources that has been required by the FDA thus far. In addition, the co-culture of human cells with cell lines derived from invertebrate animals was felt by the subcommittee to represent an exceptionally low risk ...[7]

Finally, the concerns that xenotransplantation had already been conducted for many years were partially addressed by the conclusion that not many patients had received animal tissue. This suggested that any potential risk to public health was minimized by the relatively small number of potential disease vectors existing within the human community. In addition, it was thought that patients who had had *ex vivo* contact with animal tissue had received it from well-established, relatively safe cell lines.[8]

---

[4] Ibid.

[5] Ibid.

[6] Food and Drug Administration (2000), *Xenotransplantation Subcommittee of the Biological Response Modifiers Advisory Committee*, 13 January, available at http://www.fda.gov/cber/xap/trans.htm, accessed on 19/9/04.

[7] Ibid.

[8] Food and Drug Administration (2000), 13 January, available at http://www.fda.gov/cber/xap/trans.htm, accessed on 19/9/04.

Despite the problems that surrounded the decision to alter the definition of xenotransplantation in the United States, the United Kingdom also decided to expand its definition. In the UK xenotransplantation had originally been defined as:

> Any procedure that involves the use of live cells, tissue and organs from a non-human animal source, transplanted or implanted into a human or used for ex vivo perfusion.[9]

However, the revised US definition found favour with the United Kingdom Xenotransplantation Interim Regulatory Authority (UKXIRA).[10] Before recommending to the Secretary of State for Health that the definition should be changed, the UKXIRA stated that it:

> ... had to consider the extent of the risk of infectious agent transmission from these processes. In skin replacement therapies, well-established murine cell lines are usually used and they have been used for a variety of scientific and medical purposes for more than 20 years. However, there is considered to be a theoretical risk of infectious disease transmission, albeit small.[11]

Given this small risk, in its *Fourth Annual Report* UKXIRA stated that it had recommended to the Secretary of State for Health that the UK definition should be changed to correspond with the new US definition. The alteration must now be approved by the devolved Parliaments in the UK.[12] However, by 2004 UKXIRA's *Fifth Annual Report* still referred to the UK definition as including 'ex-vivo perfusion but not other forms of ex-vivo contact'.[13]

The more inclusive definition of xenotransplantation incorporates surgical procedures that are thought to pose only a small risk of transmitting animal diseases to humans, although in the future they would be regulated as rigorously as whole organ xenografting. Although it is thought that some techniques involving *ex vivo* contact may well pose less of a risk than, for example, the transplantation of whole organs, this cautious approach is intended to function as a holding position until more information is available on the risk of relative factors. Given the incubation periods of diseases that are thought to have spread from animals to humans, such as HIV/AIDS and CJD, this circumspect position may be required for years to come. However, as the Organization for Economic Co-operation and Development (OECD) and the World Health Organization (WHO) point out, the decision to adopt a cautious, inclusive definition of xenotransplantation is not a move that has been taken by all nation states.[14] These divergent positions raise questions over the relationship between the international and

9 UKXIRA (1998), *First Annual Report May 1997–August 1998*, Department of Health: London.

10 UKXIRA (2001), *Third Annual Report September 1999–November 2000*, Department of Health: London.

11 UKXIRA (2002), *Fourth Annual Report December 2000–December* 2001, Department of Health: London, p. 4.

12 Ibid.

13 UKXIRA (2004), *The UKXIRA Fifth Annual Report January 2002–September 2003*, Department of Health: London, p. 4.

14 See OECD/WHO (2001), *Consultation on Xenotransplantation Surveillance: Summary Report*, OECD/WHO: Paris, p. 9.

national regulation of animal to human transplantation. This is because the potential infection risk posed by xenotransplantation is not one that can be restricted within national boundaries. Hence, the question of how best to define xenotransplantation also highlights the need to forge consensus over issues that could have global ramifications. These are issues to which we will return throughout this book.

The History of Xenotransplantation

Attempts to transplant tissue between human and non-human animals have been under way for hundreds of years. Cooper and Lanza report a number of very early attempts at animal to human transplantation. For example, they relate that efforts were made to transfuse humans with sheep blood as early as 1628 in Padua and London,[15] and that a Russian soldier's skull was repaired with bone from a dog's skull in 1682.[16] They also report the use of frog skin for grafting in the late 1800s,[17] while Williams notes that in 1894 the first known instance of islet xenotransplantation took place as sections of a sheep's pancreas were transplanted into a 15-year-old child. The treatment failed and resulted in the death of the patient.[18] This was followed by a number of attempts at kidney xenotransplantation using a variety of species as source animals, including rabbit, pig, goat, primate and sheep.[19] Of these transplants, two grafts failed and the other recipients died after 32 hours (primate donor), 16 days (rabbit donor) and 9 days (sheep donor).[20]

Although such stories reveal the interest that has long surrounded efforts to sustain human lives by using parts taken from animals, they form the pre-history of what we can now regard as xenotransplantation research. Our interest is more appropriately directed at the transplants which began in the 1960s and have continued intermittently until the present time. In this section we will consider how xenotransplantation, or 'heterotransplantation' as it was originally known during the modern period,[21] has developed. One reason why attempts to conduct xenotransplantation redoubled during this period was due to the development of new immunosuppressive medication.[22] All of the previous attempts were conducted

---

15 Cooper, D.K.C. and Lanza, R.P. (2000), *Xeno: The Promise of Transplanting Animal Organs into Humans*, Oxford University Press: Oxford, at p. 27f.

16 Ibid., p. 28f.

17 Ibid., p. 30.

18 Williams, P.W. (1894), 'Notes on Diabetes Treated with Extract and by Graft of Sheep's Pancreas', *British Medical Journal*, **2**, pp. 1303–1304.

19 White, S.A. and Nicholson, M.L. (1999), 'Xenotransplantation', *British Journal of Surgery*, **86**, pp. 1499–1514 at p. 1500; Princeteau, M. (1905), 'Greffe Renale', *Journal Medicine de Bordeaux*, **26**, p. 549; Jaboulay, M. (1906), 'Greffe de reins aupli du coude par soudres arterielles et veineuses', *Lyon Medicale*, **39**, pp. 575–577; Unger, E. (1910), 'Nierentransplantation' [Kidney Transplantation], *Berlin Klin Wochenschr*, **47**, p. 573; Neuhof, H. (1923), *The Transplantation of Tissues*, Appleton: New York.

20 White and Nicholson (1999), at p. 1499f.

21 Reemtsma, K. (1969), 'Renal Heterotransplantation from Nonhuman Primates to Man', *Annals of the New York Academy of Sciences*, July, **162**, pp. 412–418, at p. 412.

22 Hancock, W. (2000), 'Xenotransplantation: Is this the Future?', *Seminars in Nephrology*, **20** (2), pp. 217–229, at p. 218.

without immunosuppression. Porter notes that although various immunosuppressants existed in the late 1950s, cyclosporine, the most sophisticated immunosuppressant of its time, was not available until the late 1970s.[23]

Kidney

In the modern period, xenotransplantation (heterotransplantation) can be considered to have commenced in 1963 with Keith Reemtsma's efforts to transplant chimpanzee and monkey kidneys into humans.[24] Reemtsma et al. explain:

> In our renal homografting program we had increasing difficulty obtaining donor organs. Attempts to use cadaveric kidneys met with no prolonged success, and the supply of expended kidneys was inadequate. We were reluctant to press the use of volunteer humans for ethical, scientific and legal reasons.[25]

Elsewhere Reemtsma explains that the decision:

> ... to explore heterotransplantation was prompted in part by clinical urgency and in part by the belief that the pessimism surrounding heterotransplantation, derived largely from studies between widely disparate species, might not be applicable among higher primates, including man. Furthermore, it was impossible to test this basic conjecture in the laboratory, as there was no nonhuman animal system that would be a valid parallel to chimpanzee-to-man grafting.[26]

Clinical urgency gave such impetus to the desire to transplant animal organs into humans that the surgery took place despite the apparent lack of success. As Reemtsma says:

> The fact that no significant, sustained success had accompanied any previous attempt at renal heterotransplantation into man was disquieting but hardly conclusive that failure was inevitable.[27]

This suggests that the surgery took place without much (if any) available evidence that there was a reasonable to fair chance of it being successful. In addition, the commitment to continuing also points to the optimism of the surgical teams attempting to develop allogenic and xenogeneic transplantation. Reemtsma explains

---

[23] Porter, R. (1997), *The Greatest Benefit to Mankind: A Medical History of Humanity from Antiquity to the Present*, Fontana Press: London, p. 619; Borel, J-F. (2003), 'Xenotransplantation in the Cyclosporine Era', *Xenotransplantation*, **10**, pp. 383–386.

[24] Reemtsma, K. et al. (1964a), 'Heterotransplantation of the Kidneys: Two Clinical Experiences', *Science*, **143**, pp. 700–702; Reemtsma, K. et al. (1964b), 'Renal Heterotransplantation in Man', *Annals of Surgery*, **160** (3), pp. 384–410; Reemtsma K. et al. (1964c), 'Reversal of Early Graft Rejection After Renal Heterotransplantation in Man', *Journal of the American Medical Association*, **187**, pp. 691–696.

[25] Reemtsma, K. et al. (1964b), at p. 386.

[26] Reemtsma, K. (1969), at p. 414.

[27] Reemtsma, K. (1989), 'Xenotransplantation: A Personal History', in Hardy, M.A. (ed.) *Xenograft 25: Proceedings of the International Congress, Xenograft 25, held at Arden House, Harriman, New York, 11–13 November 1988*, Excerpta Medica: Oxford, pp. 7–16, at p. 9.

that a number of criteria were thought to make clinical trials acceptable. All the patients were 'terminal uremics, maintained on dialysis'.[28] In addition, other options were investigated before resorting to xenografting. Thus, Reemtsma et al. state that, for the first two xenotransplants they performed, searches were made for a human kidney but none could be found.[29] In fact the patients were alerted that they had various options including:

> (1) supporting treatment only; (2) homograft from a human volunteer, with the word 'volunteer' defined in the strictest sense; (3) cadaveric homograft, if and when available; or (4) cross-species graft ...[30]

Reemtsma suggests that clinical trials were considered to be acceptable because the patients had no other ways in which to sustain their lives. In addition, those involved had been appraised of the risks and still wanted to proceed with the novel surgery. In his account of the surgeries Reemtsma explains:

> The risks, the uncertainties, the experimental nature of the work were discussed with the patients and their families. If they chose to proceed with transplantation and had no volunteer donor, a search was made for a cadaveric kidney. If no suitable cadaver kidney became available in a stated period of time, a heterograft was used, with the patient's understanding and consent.[31]

Reemtsma's first xenograft was conducted on 8 October 1963 and saw a kidney from a rhesus monkey transplanted into a 32-year-old female patient.[32] The graft only functioned for ten days and was then removed. The patient was placed on dialysis but died two days later, on 20 October.[33] Reemtsma performed a second kidney xenograft into a 43-year-old man, this time using a chimpanzee as a source animal on 5 November 1963.[34] After rejection problems were overcome the patient was discharged from hospital on 18 December, but was readmitted on 20 December with pneumonia and died on 6 January 1964.[35] It is interesting to note that Reemtsma reports the second of the above procedures in a number of papers.[36] But the first xenograft that he conducted in 1963 (using a rhesus monkey kidney) is only recorded in one paper.[37] The reasons why the first, less successful, xenograft is not given more attention in Reemtsma's work remain unclear.

Reemtsma performed a number of other kidney xenografts sourced from chimpanzees after these initial transplants.[38] On 23 December 1963, a 12-year-old

28 Ibid., at p. 9.
29 Reemtsma, K. et al. (1964a).
30 Reemtsma, K. (1989), at p. 9.
31 Ibid., at p. 9.
32 Reemtsma, K. et al. (1964a), at p. 700f.
33 Ibid., at p. 701.
34 Reemtsma, K. et al. (1964a), at p. 701f; Reemtsma, K. et al. (1964b), at pp. 387–390.
35 Reemtsma, K. et al. (1964a), at p. 701f; Reemtsma, K. et al. (1964b), at pp. 387–390.
36 Reemtsma, K. et al. (1964a), at p. 701f; Reemtsma, K. et al. (1964b), at pp. 387–390.
37 Reemtsma, K. et al. (1964a).
38 Reemtsma, K. et al. (1964b), at pp. 387–390.

male child received a kidney xenograft and survived for seven weeks.[39] On 13 January 1964, a 23-year-old female teacher received a renal xenotransplant.[40] This patient was discharged from hospital and 'although unexplained fever persisted for 3 months', she 'was asymptomatic and had normal renal function 6.5 months after transplantation'.[41] In fact the patient's condition improved sufficiently to allow her to return to work. However, nine months after transplantation the patient died after a short illness of 'undetermined etiology'.[42] This 1964 xenotransplant remains the most successful solid organ xenotransplant to date. That is, none of the other xenografts conducted by Reemtsma and his team at this time, or by others since, have extended the length, or apparently the quality, of the patient's life for so long as did this particular transplant.

Of the other kidney transplants performed by Reemtsma it should be noted that on the 16 January 1964 a chimpanzee kidney was transplanted into a 35-year-old man. However, the source animal had a different blood type (type A) from the patient (type O).[43] The transplanted organ failed to function and two days later the patient received another transplant from a source animal which shared his blood type. During this surgery it was discovered that using an organ with a blood type that did not match that of the patient had led to the wound becoming 'grossly infected'.[44] Despite the re-transplantation the patient died 11 days after the second operation.[45] Finally, two other transplants were performed by Reemtsma in February 1964, but neither patient lived for a month after transplantation.[46]

The dismissal of Reemtsma's most successful surgery as 'only' attaining nine months' survival does not afford sufficient attention to the positive aspects and considerable influence of this procedure, or indeed of Reemtsma's ground-breaking transplant programme.[47] In addition to allowing one patient to return to work for a period of time, Reemtsma's work inspired other surgical teams. Thus, James Hardy has explained that his decision to go ahead with the first clinical cardiac xenograft was influenced '... by the surprising degree of at least early clinical success ...' [48] achieved by Reemtsma's kidney transplants. Similarly, Thomas Starzl writing in 1989 describes how the relative success of the xenotransplants conducted by Reemtsma gave encouragement to his own surgical team,[49] and suggested to him that xenotransplantation would soon be clinically viable. He states:

---

39 Ibid., at p. 392.

40 Ibid., at p. 392f.

41 Reemtsma, K. (1989), at p. 13.

42 Ibid., at p. 15.

43 Reemtsma, K. et al. (1964b), at p. 395f.

44 Ibid., at p. 396.

45 Ibid.

46 Ibid., at p. 397ff.

47 White and Nicholson (1999), at p. 1500.

48 Hardy, J.D. et al. (1964), 'Heart Transplantation in Man: Developmental Studies and Report of a Case', *Journal of the American Medical Association*, **188** (13), pp. 1132–1140, at p. 1137.

49 Starzl, T.E. (1989), 'Baboon Renal and Chimpanzee Liver Heterotransplantation', in Hardy, M.A. (ed.) *Xenograft 25: Proceedings of the International Congress, Xenograft 25, held at Arden House, Harriman, New York, 11–13 November 1988*, Excerpta Medica: Oxford, pp. 17–28, at p. 17.

> ... I am convinced that animal to human transplantation is close to the horizon. The main reason to believe this is how close efforts at both chimpanzee-to-human and baboon-to-human transplantation came to succeeding in that now distant time. However, failure to complete the task over a span of 25 years introduces a note of very real caution because the inability to exploit this kind of breakthrough generally means that the problem is deeper and more unfathomable than was actually appreciated.[50]

This need for caution was also suggested by other attempts at kidney xenotransplantation in the 1960s (1964–1969), all of which achieved shorter survival times than those conducted by Reemtsma.[51] Like Reemtsma's xenotransplants, Starzl's attempts at xenografting baboon kidneys into six humans in 1964 were only carried out if the patients were in a terminal condition and efforts to obtain familial or cadaveric kidneys had failed.[52] Starzl et al. report that while all patients showed initial improvement the longest survival with the transplanted organ in place was 60 days; the shortest 19 days.[53] Most of the transplants failed due to the inability of the surgical team to deal with the rejection problems that arose.[54]

In 1969 Reemtsma assessed the clinical evidence that had been provided by the kidney xenografts performed by his team and that of Starzl. He claimed:

> On the basis of existing studies, it is difficult to define with precision clinical or biochemical features that would distinguish heterografts from homografts. With the exception of one instance, in which major blood group incompatibility occurred in a chimpanzee-to-man heterograft, prompt function occurred in all instances.[55]

However, Reemtsma concedes that most of the xenografts had failed within two months. The xenograft that lasted nine months was an exception.[56] Despite this he presents the clinical trials of xenotransplantation as taking small steps forward in overcoming the shortage of organs.[57] In addition, he claims that another benefit of animal to human transplantation is that it 'removes the ethical concern' that surrounds the use of human organs.[58] Thus, he deemed xenografting to be an issue that 'deserves close scrutiny and continued effort'.[59]

---

[50] Ibid.

[51] Cortesini, R. et al. (1970), 'Heterotransplantation in Primates: Current State of Affairs', in Balner, H. and Beveridge, W. (eds), *Infection and Immunosuppression in Subhuman Primates*, pp. 239–248, Munksgaard: Copenhagen; Hardy, J.D. et al. (1964), pp. 1132–1140; Traeger, J. et al. (1965), 'Heterotransplantation chez l'homme. Premiers Resultats', *Proceedings of the European Dialysis and Transplant Association*, **2**, pp. 214–217; Hitchock, C.R. et al. (1964), 'Baboon Renal Graft', *Journal of the American Medical Association*, **189** (12), pp. 934–937.

[52] Starzl, T.E. et al. (1964), 'Renal Heterotransplantation from Baboon to Man: Experiences with Six Cases', *Transplantation*, **2**, pp. 752–776, at p. 753.

[53] Ibid., at p. 754.

[54] Ibid., at p. 772.

[55] Reemtsma, K. (1969), at p. 414.

[56] Ibid., at p. 415.

[57] Ibid., at p. 416.

[58] Ibid., at p. 417.

[59] Ibid.

Heart

In the spring of 1963 the surgical team led by Hardy at the University of Mississippi Medical Center considered that their research 'justified a planned approach directed toward eventual heart transplantation in man'.[60] The development was approved by the Medical Center's management board.[61] Like others before him, Hardy had planned to carry out an allograft, not a xenotransplant. However, the experience of the team led them to realize that it was unlikely that the potential human donor and recipient would die at the same time so allowing a human organ to be transplanted without delay.[62] Hence, they decided the only way to overcome this difficulty was to try to save the life of a terminally ill patient by using the heart of a lower primate that could provide the organ when needed.[63] On 27 January 1964 Hardy's team performed the first cardiac xenotransplant into a human on a 68-year-old male patient. Thus, although this is not often realized, the first heart transplant into a human was in fact a xenotransplant.[64] However, the first choice of source for this transplant was:

> ... a young man near death from irreversible brain damage who might serve as a suitable donor, and the responsible relatives of the heart patient were appraised of the situation. They were well aware that death was imminent and were willing to have heart transplantation performed in the event of terminal collapse.[65]

The next of kin of the prospective recipient of the transplant had signed a consent form saying that they understood that the novelty of the treatment weighed against it being successful. The document stated:

> I hereby give full permission for leg amputation and heart surgery on Boyd Rush. I understand that any clots present will be removed from the heart to stop them from going to still more arteries of his body. I further understand that his heart is in extremely poor condition. If for any unanticipated reason the heart should fail completely during either operation and it should be impossible to start it, I agree to the insertion of a suitable heart transplant if such should be available at the time. I further understand that hundreds of heart transplants have been performed in laboratories throughout the world but that any heart transplant would represent the initial transplant in man.[66]

Although it did not feature on the consent form, the patient's relatives were also informed as follows:

---

60 Hardy, J.D. et al. (1964), at p. 1132.

61 Ibid.

62 Ibid., at pp. 1134 and 1136.

63 Ibid.

64 Ibid., at p. 1136.

65 Ibid., at p. 1136.

66 The consent document or 'operative permit' reproduced in Hardy, J. and Chavez, C. (1969), 'The First Heart Transplant in Man: Historical Reexamination of the 1964 Case in Light of Current Clinical Experience', *Transplantation Proceedings*, **1** (2), pp. 717–725, at p. 721.

> The possibility of using a lower primate heart was acknowledged in discussion with the recipient's relatives, should the anticipated death of the patient with massive brain injury not occur.[67]

As the surgical team had forecast, when Mr Rush went into terminal shock, '... the condition of the prospective donor was not such that death appeared to be immediately imminent'.[68] Thus, as a last resort the larger of two chimpanzees was tranquillized and a xenograft conducted.[69] Unfortunately, the graft only survived for two hours because the smaller animal heart could not accommodate the larger volume of blood required by the human. The patient died.[70]

Annas makes the point that Rush did not consent to the procedure himself and that Hardy had a reputation for performing experimental surgeries on poor, uneducated patients.[71] In this respect, Annas explains that Boyd Rush:

> ... was particularly vulnerable because he was a deaf-mute. He was brought to the hospital unconscious and never regained consciousness. A search for relatives turned up only a stepsister who was persuaded to sign a consent form authorizing 'the insertion of a suitable heart transplant' if this should prove necessary. The form made no mention of a primate heart; in later written reports Dr. Hardy contended that he had discussed the procedure in detail with *relatives*, although there was only one. Mr. Rush survived two hours with the chimpanzee heart.[72]

Annas is correct to suggest that the omission of details about the animal organ from the consent form is troubling and suggests that the surgical team were not completely open. However, one reason why it may not have seemed necessary to mention on the consent form that an animal organ may be used is that it was not thought necessary to alert the relatives to the particular problems that we now associate with xenotransplantation, because at this time allotransplantation and xenotransplantation were developing in tandem. Transplantation itself was a risky operation regardless of the origin of the organ to be transplanted. Thus, it could be the case that there was insufficient knowledge about the risks particular to either form of transplantation to warrant specific attention on a consent form. Yet Hardy et al. state that there was awareness that the announcement that a heart transplant had been performed may in itself have been controversial; but the fact that a primate heart had been used 'was even more likely to arouse controversy'.[73] This suggests that the consent form omission may, as Annas suggests, have been an attempt to conceal the fact that an animal organ might be used. However:

> ... it was felt that to perform this transplant, under the specific set of circumstances which existed at that instant, was well within ethical and moral boundaries. Thus, the five

---

67 Ibid., at p. 720.

68 Hardy, J.D. et al. (1964), at p. 1136.

69 Ibid.

70 Hardy, J.D. et al. (1964), pp. 1132–1140; Hardy, J. and Chavez, C.M. (1969), pp. 717–725.

71 Annas, G. (1985), 'Baby Fae: The "Anything Goes" School of Human Experimentation', *Hastings Center Report*, **15** (1), February, pp. 15–17 at p. 15.

72 Ibid., at p. 15.

73 Hardy, J.D. et al (1964), at p.1137.

> primary team members were individually polled and their votes made a matter of record. Four voted to proceed and the fifth abstained. The first author [Hardy] believed that the circumstances justified the heterotransplant, and from this point on the transplantation proceeded smoothly.[74]

In addition, Hardy et al. report that the hospital management realized that the basic facts surrounding the case 'could not be suppressed'.[75] However, they also acknowledge that the 'initial announcement did not specify that a chimpanzee heart had been used'.[76] This was to be announced at an international conference a few days later, but false media reports necessitated that the hospital produced a fuller account of the operation.

Despite the outcome of Hardy's surgery, Cooley made a second attempt at xenogeneic heart transplantation in 1968, when a sheep's heart was implanted into a 48-year-old man. The graft failed within ten minutes.[77] Ross (1968) and Marion (1969) made two further attempts at cardiac xenotransplantation using porcine and sheep organs respectively; neither achieved graft function.[78] The results of these transplants for some time led to a decrease in the number of cardiac xenotransplantations conducted. However, in 1977, ten years after his relatively successful attempts at allografting,[79] Barnard carried out two cardiac xenografts using a baboon and a chimpanzee as sources.[80] Both were attempts to save the lives of patients who could not be weaned off by-pass following valve replacement. The first graft into a 25-year-old woman failed due to the inadequate capacity of the donor heart. However, in the second patient (a 60-year-old man) the heart functioned for a short time before gradually being rejected over a period of four days.[81]

In 1984 Leonard Bailey performed what is perhaps the most well-known xenotransplant to have been conducted to date, at Loma Linda University Medical Center. Bailey and his team transplanted a baboon heart into a neonate with hypoplastic left heart syndrome (HLHS).[82] Bailey et al. explain that, following the diagnosis of HLHS, the parents discharged the child from hospital, but after being

---

74 Ibid., at p. 1137.

75 Ibid., at p. 1139.

76 Ibid.

77 Cooley, D.A. et al (1968), 'Human Heart Transplantation. Experience with Twelve Cases', *American Journal of Cardiology*, **22**, pp. 804–810.

78 Ross, D.N. (1969), 'Experience with Human Heart Transplantation', in Shapiro, H.A. (ed.), *Proceedings of the Cape Town Symposium 13–16 July 1968*, Butterworths: Durban, pp. 111–146; Marion, P. (1969), 'Les Transplantations Cardiaques et les Transplantations Hepatiques', *Lyon Medical*, **222**, pp. 545–607.

79 Porter, R. (1999), *The Greatest Benefit to Mankind: A Medical History of Humanity from Antiquity to the Present*, Fontana Press: London, at p. 621.

80 Barnard, C.N. et al. (1977), 'Heterotopic Cardiac Transplantation with a Xenograft for Assistance of the Left Heart in Cardiogenic Shock after Cardiopulmonary Bypass', *South African Medical Journal*, **52**, pp. 1035–1038.

81 Ibid.

82 Bailey, L.L. et al. (1985), 'Baboon-to-human Cardiac Xenotransplantation in a Neonate', *Journal of the American Medical Association*, **254**, pp. 3321–3329.

contacted by the hospital and told that there may have been various surgical options with which to improve the child's life span, including xenotransplantation, she was readmitted.[83] The family then 'chose to pursue plans for xenotransplantation' and rejected palliative surgery.[84] Both parents signed the consent form to allow the xenotransplant to proceed on 24 October and for a second time on 25 October.[85] The surgery was performed on 26 October.[86] Unlike previous xenotransplants, this surgery was performed following the development of the immunosuppressant cyclosporine and attempts were made to match the infant's tissue with that of the chosen baboon.[87] Initially, the graft functioned but then failed after 20 days and the infant died.[88] Despite this outcome Bailey commented:

> ... it has been demonstrated that cardiac replacement by orthotopic xenotransplantation is technically feasible in the small neonate with HLHS. A gratifying early recovery and survival to 20 days were documented.[89]

The 'Baby Fae' case, as it became known, generated considerable debate because of the manner in which the transplant was conducted. Firstly, it seems that one of the reasons why the transplant failed was that it was not possible for Bailey to match the blood type of the patient with that of the baboon donor – a factor that led Bailey et al. to suggest that this:

> ... placed the graft and host in a highly vulnerable situation. Crossing this barrier does not necessarily preclude graft survival, but is generally avoided in human allotransplantation.[90]

However, Bailey failed to acknowledge the lesson highlighted by Reemstma's 1964 transplant; namely, that it is important to match the blood types of the source animal and recipient. Cooper and Lanza have recently stated:

> It is interesting to speculate whether the baboon heart might have survived longer had Baby Fae had a different blood type. The rules of organ transplantation are fundamentally identical to those governing blood transfusions: there must be blood group compatibility between donor and recipient ... Baboon blood groups are confined to A, B, and AB, however, and so a baboon of blood type B had to be chosen as the donor for Baby Fae. This increased the chance of rejection of the heart and may well have played a role in the child's death. However, subsequent experimental research suggests that the immunosuppressive drugs available at the time may not have been powerful enough to prevent graft rejection even if the blood groups of the donor and recipient had matched.[91]

83 Ibid., at p. 3321.
84 Ibid.
85 Ibid., at p. 3322.
86 Ibid., at p. 3323.
87 Ibid., at p. 3324.
88 Ibid., at p. 3324.
89 Ibid., at p. 3327.
90 Ibid., at p. 3327.
91 Cooper, D.K.C. and Lanza, R.P. (2000), p. 39.

Secondly, it appears that insufficient effort (or perhaps no effort at all) was made to find an allograft for the infant before turning to xenografting. Bailey et al. record that efforts to find an allograft for the infant were only made after the xenotransplant had taken place. They state:

> The Regional Organ Procurement Agency was notified during the first post transplant week to begin searching for a satisfactory replacement allograft. No allograft was found during the patient's lifetime.[92]

Thus, unlike the early xenotransplants conducted by Reemtsma and Hardy – when an animal organ was only used as a last resort and after a search had been made for cadaveric organs – Bailey performed this surgery without apparently investigating the other options that were available. Furthermore, the surgeons who conducted xenografts in the 1960s could legitimately have argued that they did not know which, if either, type of transplant would be most beneficial or most risky to the patient. However, by the time Bailey conducted his cardiac xenograft it was clear that cardiac allografts had greater success rates than xenografts. A review of the surgery by the National Institutes of Health made a number of recommendations including that any future protocol should '... clearly state whether a search will be made for an appropriate human donor heart and the risks and benefits associated with that decision'.[93]

Thirdly, the age of the transplant recipient was also a cause for concern. However, it will be noted below that 'Baby Fae' was not the first infant to have received a xenotransplant – although it is the case that attracted most attention. Despite all of these difficulties, the criticism attracted by the case appears to have been a surprise to at least one surgeon involved in xenotransplantation. Starzl comments:

> We realized what a firestorm of publicity and of condemnation further heterografts trials were apt to bring down on us. I was stunned when I saw the reaction to the Baby Fae case. In the earlier trials (mine and all of Reemtsma's) ... there was no particular sense of outrage. These earlier trials were not secret. Perhaps, the climate was different.[94]

In 1992 Czaplicki performed the first heart transplantation following the 'Baby Fae' case, using a porcine heart, but the graft failed after 24 hours.[95] Most recently, Indian surgeon Dhani Ram Baruah claimed to have performed a cardiac xenograft on New Year's Day 1997. The patient reputedly survived for a week. However, as a result of his (illegal) action his laboratory in Assam was burned down and he was sent to prison.[96]

---

92 Bailey, L.L. et al. (1985), at p. 3323.

93 Dommel, W.F. et al. (1986), 'The NIH Report of Its Review of the Baby Fae Case', *IRB: A Review of Human Subjects Research*, **8** (2), pp. 1–4, at p. 4.

94 Starzl, T.E. (1989), at p. 27.

95 Czaplicki, J. et al. (1992), 'The Lack of Hyperacute Xenogeneic Heart Transplant Rejection in a Human', *Journal of Heart and Lung Transplantation*, **11**, pp. 393–397.

96 The case is unreported but see www.bbc.co.uk/1/hi/world/south_asia/122680.stm and *British Medical Journal* (1999), 'Indian Surgeon Challenges Ban on Xenotransplantation', **318**, p. 79.

Liver

In 1989 Starzl drew attention to a number of liver xenografts he had performed in the 'dark ages when we had primitive immunosuppression by today's standards'.[97] The transplants to which he referred were performed in 1966, 1969 and 1973.[98] Of these, Starzl has said:

> Although I reported them, I may have tried subconsciously to hide the experiences by stashing the reports in obscure corners and funny places. Hugh Auchincloss smoked me out by some marvellous detective work in his review of heterotransplantation ...[99]

The first of these transplants took place in July 1966 when Starzl transplanted a chimpanzee liver into a 28-month-old male infant with biliary atresia.[100] The child's condition had deteriorated and no suitable cadaveric organs could be found, so in 'desperation' a xenograft was performed.[101] Starzl explains that:

> The procedure was finally decided upon because of the encouraging results already obtained after renal homotransplantations with the triple drug immunosuppressive regimen ...[102]

After a number of rejection problems, three days post-transplant the patient improved sufficiently to eat.[103] However, nine days after the transplant, he died.[104] Starzl suggests that the patient's immunosuppression was 'badly managed', including medication being given in doses that were too small. As a result 'rejection was uncontrolled'.[105] However, he claims:

> Even if the immunosuppressive drugs had been administered more efficiently, it is doubtful that prolonged survival could have been obtained; there have been difficulties enough in achieving this objective in subsequent cases using homografts. Consequently, no plans have been made for additional heterotransplantations unless there is a fundamental improvement in the treatment protocol which can be offered.[106]

---

97 Starzl, T.E. (1989), at p. 24.

98 Starzl, T.E. et al. (1966), 'Avenues of Future Research in Homotransplantation of the Liver', *American Journal of Surgery*, **112** (3), pp. 391–400; Starzl, T.E. (1969a), 'Orthotopic Heterotransplantation', *Experience in Hepatic Transplantation*, Saunders: Philadelphia, pp. 408–421; Giles, G.R. et al. (1970), 'Clinical Heterotransplantation of the Liver', *Transplantation Proceedings*, **2** (4), pp. 506–12; Starzl, T.E. et al. (1974), 'Progress in and Deterrents to Orthotopic Liver Transplantation, with Special Reference to Survival Resistance to Hyperacute Rejection, and Biliary Duct Reconstruction', *Transplantation Proceedings*, **6**, pp. 129–139.

99 Starzl, T.E. (1989), at p. 25; also see Auchincloss, H.J. (1988), 'Xenogeneic Transplantation: A Review', *Transplantation*, **46**, pp. 1–20.

100 Starzl, T.E. (1969b), 'Orthotopic Heterotransplantation', in *Experience in Hepatic Transplantation*, with the Assistance of Putnam, C.W., W.B. Saunders Company: London, pp. 408–421, at p. 415f.

101 Ibid.

102 Ibid., at p. 415.

103 Ibid., at p. 418.

104 Ibid., at p. 418.

105 Ibid., at p. 419.

106 Ibid., at p. 419.

This suggests that even Starzl saw xenotransplantation as being too experimental to make it a clinically viable procedure. Nonetheless, in December 1969 Starzl deemed it appropriate to perform another liver xenotransplant. The recipient again was an infant of seven-months old.[107] The heterograft was only conducted when a search for a cadaveric organ had failed and the child's condition was thought to necessitate such a 'desperate therapeutic effort'.[108] However, the '... child died 26 hours after the heterotransplantation without having awakened'.[109]

Finally, Starzl performed the third of his 'hidden' liver xenografts in June 1973. Little information is presented on the circumstances surrounding the operation, but Starzl et al. note that in case number:

> ... OT 71, the homograft seemed to have been severely damaged by ischemia, as well as cellular rejection, although its poor initial function could have been a manifestation of acute antibody-mediated injury. After 10 days the organ was removed and replaced by a chimpanzee heterograft, against which the recipient cytotoxins also reacted. The chimpanzee liver functioned for most of the 14 subsequent days of the patient's life ... This was our third trial of chimpanzee-to-man heterotransplantation, the other two having been previously reported.[110]

A table informs the reader that the age of the patient in case OT 71 was 1 year 11 months and that the reason for the initial homograft was biliary atresia, the cause of death pulmonary edema and bronchial haemorrhage.[111] The xenograft only functioned for 14 days.[112] During this period (1969–1971) other transplant teams were also conducting liver xenografts, but none achieved graft survival beyond three days.[113]

In June 1992 Starzl transplanted a baboon liver into a 35-year-old male patient who was positive for Hepatitis B and HIV.[114] The patient had been rejected for an allograft because it was thought the organ would be destroyed by Hepatitis. It was hypothesized that a baboon liver would be resistant to Hepatitis and the transplant would stand a better chance of surviving.[115]

The surgery took place even though the patient's HIV positive status was deemed 'undesirable' given its potential impact on his immune system.[116] The surgery

107 Giles, G.R. et al. (1970), at p. 506.

108 Ibid., at p. 510.

109 Ibid., at p. 508.

110 Starzl, T.E. et al. (1974), at p. 137.

111 Ibid., at p. 136.

112 Ibid., at p. 136f.

113 Bertoye, A. (1969), 'Essais de traitement de certaines insuffisances hepatiques graves par geffe heatique heterologue', *Lyon Medical*, **222**, p. 345; Leger, L. et al. (1970), 'Greffe heterotopique d'un foie de babouin sur une malade atteinte d'hepatite fulminante', *Chirurgie*, **96**, p. 249; Marion, P. (1969), at p. 585; Marion, P. et al. (1970), 'Traitement du coma hepatique par Transplantation Auxiliaire Heterologue du Foie', *Chirurgie*, **96**, p. 152; Pouyet, M. and Berard, P.H. (1971), 'Deux cas de Transplantation Heterologues du foie de babouin au cours d'hepatites aigues malignes', *Lyon Chirurgical*, **67**, p. 287.

114 Starzl, T.E. et al. (1993), 'Baboon-to-human Liver Transplantation', *The Lancet*, **341** (8837), January, pp. 65–71.

115 Ibid., at p. 66.

116 Ibid.

proceeded in these less than ideal conditions because of its clinical urgency – the patient had fallen into a coma and had no other treatment options available.[117] After surgery the transplanted liver functioned well and after a month the patient was moved from intensive care.[118] However, a number of difficulties then arose, including a series of infections and renal failure.[119] Seventy days after transplantation the patient had a massive stroke and was declared dead.[120] Starzl held that the surgery failed due to 'technical' problems including the oversuppression of the patient's immune system.[121]

Extra-Corporeal Perfusion of the Liver[122]

The motivation behind efforts to temporally filter (perfuse) the blood of a patient through a non-native liver is that although the prognosis for patients with liver failure is poor, the liver has the ability to regenerate. Hence, if the native organ can be allowed time to recover by means of perfusion, the patient's condition may improve.[123] Eiseman et al. explain that, although perfusion through a human organ would be ideal, this:

> ... requires the simultaneous availability of a patient with reversible yet severe liver failure and a fresh, undiseased liver from a patient with the proper blood type whose family is available and willing to authorise quick post-mortem harvest of the cadaver liver. Such a fortuitous set of circumstances is obviously unlikely. In an effort to resolve this clinical dilemma, it was decided to investigate the feasibility of utilizing a heterologous liver washed free of its own blood for such temporary hepatic support.[124]

Hence, in 1964 Eisman's team endeavoured to perfuse the blood of a number of patients through porcine livers.[125] After a number of animal trials, eight patients were perfused with a porcine liver for periods of 1 to 6.6 hours.[126] While some patients improved, the treatment had little impact on the health of others. Moreover, none of the patients achieved long-term survival as a result of the perfusion.[127]

117 Ibid., at p. 67.

118 Ibid.

119 Ibid., at p. 67f.

120 Ibid., at p. 68.

121 Ibid., at p. 70.

122 It should be noted that work on renal extracorporeal perfusion has also been conducted but is less advanced than trials with livers. Thus, we will concentrate on hepatic perfusion here. For a discussion of clinical work with kidneys see Dobson, J.M. and Dark, J.H. (2002), *The Physiology of Xenotransplantation*, Department of Health: London, at p. 66.

123 Eiseman, B. et al. (1965), 'Heterologous Liver Perfusion Treatment of Hepatic Failure', *Annals of Surgery*, **162** (3), pp. 329–345; Chalstery, L.J. and Parbhoo, S.P. (1971), 'Circuitry and Technique of Extracorporeal Porcine Liver Perfusion for the Treatment of Hepatic Coma', *British Journal of Surgery*, **58** (7), pp. 522–524.

124 Eiseman, B. et al. (1965), at p. 329.

125 Ibid.

126 Ibid., at p. 343.

127 Ibid.

Similarly poor results were achieved by other studies.[128] Yet some surgical teams have reported the development of techniques that led to patients surviving for up to eight months after transplant,[129] while other teams found that baboon livers produced better results that porcine livers. Abouna et al. state:

> Pig liver perfusions generally were disappointing, since only 30% of episodes of coma were reversed by the porcine perfusions, and it usually required two to four consecutive livers to effect reversal of coma. In contrast, each of the seven baboon livers and the two human livers used in this series resulted in recovery of normal consciousness. Only one single perfusion was required.[130]

However, the relatively poor results achieved by extra-corporeal perfusion and the increasing success of liver transplantation meant that the procedure was neglected for a period.[131] Yet Chari et al. have recommended that although extra-corporeal perfusion was abandoned due to its difficulties and its failure to produce convincing results:

> On the basis of our limited experience, we believe that hepatic xenoperfusion should be reconsidered in the management of otherwise untreatable acute liver failure in selected patients.[132]

Despite this suggestion, the results achieved by this team were poor.[133] However, recent efforts to bridge patients with liver failure to a time when an allograft can be provided have proved more successful.[134]

Makowka et al. have reported that they were the first to use a pig liver xenograft in an attempt to bridge a patient until an allograft could be found – without removing the native liver.[135] However, a day after surgery, at a time when a human liver had become available, it was decided:

---

128 Ranek, L. et al. (1971), 'Pig Liver Perfusion in the Treatment of Acute Hepatic Failure', *Scandinavian Journal of Gastroenterology*, **6** (Suppl 9), pp. 161–169.

129 Chalstery, L.J. and Parbhoo, S.P. (1971), at p. 524.

130 Abouna, G.M. (1973), 'Experience in the Treatment of Hepatic Failure by Intermittent Liver Hemoperfusions', *Surgery, Gynecology and Obstetrics*, **137** (5), pp. 741–752, at p. 750.

131 Prentice, E.D. et al. (1994), 'History, Donor Considerations and Ethics of Xenotransplantation and Xenoperfusion', *Research Animal Anesthesia, Analgesia and Surgery*, pp. 25–36; Smith, A. and Swindle, M. (eds) (1994), SCAW, Greenbelt: Maryland, at p. 27; Dobson, J.M. and Dark, J.H. (2002), at p. 53.

132 Chari, R.S. et al. (1994), 'Brief Report: Treatment of Hepatic Failure with Ex vivo Pig-Liver Perfusion Followed by Liver Transplantation', *The New England Journal of Medicine*, **331** (4), pp. 234–237.

133 Ibid., at pp. 235–237.

134 Levy, M. et al. (2000), 'Liver Allotransplantation After Extracorporeal Hepatic Support with Transgenic (hC555/hCD59) Porcine Livers: Clinical Results and Lack of Pig-to-Human Transmission of the Porcine Endogenous Retrovirus', *Transplantation*, **69** (2), pp. 272–280; Horslen, S.P. et al. (2000), 'Extracorporeal Liver Perfusion using Human and Pig Livers for Acute Liver Failure', *Transplantation*, **70** (10), pp. 1472–1478.

135 Makowka, L. et al. (1995), 'The Use of a Pig Liver Xenograft for Temporary Support of a Patient with Fulminant Hepatic Failure', *Transplantation*, **59** (12), pp. 1654–1659, at p. 1654.

> Due to the deteriorating condition of the patient, the allotransplantation procedure was not attempted and the patient was sent to the intensive care ward where brain death was declared.[136]

Despite this poor outcome, Makowka et al. are keen to stress that the surgery provided 'new information relevant to the use of porcine organs and tissues for xenotransplantation'.[137] They continue:

> While this attempt to rescue a desperately ill patient was of limited effectiveness, it has had the effect of stimulating a renewed interest in the use of pig liver xenografts as ex vivo support for patients with acute hepatic failure and the use of bioartificial liver devices using pig hepatocytes as additional methods to provide temporary support for patients awaiting liver allotransplantation.[138]

In 2000 Horslen et al. announced that extra-corporeal liver perfusion is a 'safe and effective' way to bridge patients to transplantation. They also claim of the 14 patients treated with eight human and eight pig livers that 'the pig livers appeared to work as well as the human livers'.[139] Of the eight patients who were perfused using porcine liver, half survived to receive an allograft and three of these survived to the post-transplantation period.[140]

Cellular Transplantation

Xenotransplantation is perhaps most often associated with the transplantation of whole animal organs into humans. However, xenogeneic cellular therapies have emerged to treat a number of conditions and are seen by many as the form of animal to human transplantation to hold the most promise, although in 2005 the National Health and Medical Research Council of Australia indicated that it did not find it acceptable to proceed with clinical trials of cellular therapies at this time.[141] In its 2003 review of xenotransplantation the Council of Europe reported:

> Cell transplantation is leading clinical developments in xenotransplantation. Several 100 [sic] patients have been exposed to cellular xenotransplants using pigs as well as other non-primate species as source animals.[142]

As with the xenotransplantation of solid organs, xenogeneic cellular therapies have arisen to meet the shortfall in the human tissue that is available for transplantation.[143] The allografting techniques which xenografting may be able to

---

136 Ibid., at p. 1656.

137 Ibid., p. 1659.

138 Ibid.

139 Horslen, S.P. et al. (2000), at p. 1475f.

140 Ibid., at p. 1474, Table 1.

141 Available at http://www7.health.gov.au/nmhrc/news/media/rel04/xenocom.htm, accessed 04/02/05. For further information on the Nhmrc's position, see Chapter 5.

142 Council of Europe (2003), at p. 19.

143 Fink, J.S. et al. (2000), 'Porcine Xenografts in Parkinson's Disease and Huntington's Disease Patients: Preliminary Results', *Cell Transplantation*, **9** (2), pp. 273–278; Koulmanda, M. et al. (2003),

aid include the use of human fetal tissue to treat Parkinson's Disease,[144] the transplantation of the pancreatic gland or injection of cells from the pancreas to treat diabetes,[145] and neural transplantation with fetal cells for the treatment of Huntington's Disease.[146]

In addition to offering a way to alleviate the shortage of tissue it has also been suggested that cellular xenografting offers a number of other benefits. For example, the use of human fetal material for the treatment of neurological conditions raises ethical concerns,[147] which some of those working in xenotransplantation hope to overcome.[148] It has also been claimed:

> Cell transplantation as opposed to whole organ transplantation carries a number of significant advantages: the immune barrier is more easily overcome, the infusion of cells is far less invasive than the surgery involved in organ removal and replacement, and cells are easily manipulated genetically.[149]

Shumakov et al. reported that between April 1981 and December 1985 they conducted a series of transplants of pancreatic cells. The transplants included 53 fetal porcine xenotransplants and 18 fetal bovine xenotransplants.[150] They also conducted 97 allografts.[151] The Russian team stated that a large number of the allografts functioned and produced clinical improvement, but the performance of

---

'Pig Islet Xenografts are Resistant to Autoimmune Destruction by Non-obese Diabetic Recipients after Anti-CD4 Treatment', *Xenotransplantation*, **10**, pp. 178–184; Ehrnfelt, C. (2004), 'Adult Porcine Islets Produce MCP-1 and Recruit Human Monocytes in Vitro', *Xenotransplantation*, **11**, pp. 184–194.

144 For example, see Lindvall, O. et al. (1994), 'Evidence for Long-term Survival and Function of Dopaminergic Grafts in Progressive Parkinson's Disease', *Annals of Neurology*, **35**, pp. 172–180; Freed, C. et al. (1992), 'Survival of Implanted Fetal Dopamine Cells and Neurologic Improvement 12 to 24 Months after Transplantation for Parkinson's Disease', *New England Journal of Medicine*, **327**, pp. 1549–1555; Borlongan, C.V. and Sanberg, P.R. (2002), 'Neural Transplantation for Treatment of Parkinson's Disease', *Drug Discovery Today*, **7** (12), pp. 674–682.

145 For example, see Scharp, D.W. et al. (1990), 'Insulin Independence after Islet Transplantation into Type I Diabetic Patient', *Diabetes*, **39**, p. 515; Tzakkis, A.G. et al. (1990), 'Pancreatic Islet Transplantation after Upper Abdominal Exenteration and Liver Replacement', *The Lancet*, **336**, p. 402.

146 Rosser, A.E. and Dunnett, S.B. (2003), 'Neural Transplantation in Patients with Huntington's Disease', *CNS Drugs*, **17** (12), pp. 853–867.

147 Boer, G.J. (1994), 'Ethical Guidelines for the Use of Human Embryonic or Fetal Tissue for Experimental and Clinical Neurotransplantation and Research', *Journal of Neurology*, **242**, pp. 1–13.

148 Brevig, T. et al. (2001), 'Xenotransplantation for Brain Repair', *Transplantation*, **72** (2), pp. 190–196, at p. 190; Xiao, Y. (2004), 'Immunosuppression and Xenotransplantation of Cells for Cardiac Repair', *Annals of Thoracic Surgery*, **77**, pp. 737-44; Borlangan, C.V. and Sanberg, P.R. (2002), at p.675; Larsson, L.C. and Widner, H. (2000), 'Neural Tissue Xenografting', *Scandinavian Journal of Immunology*, **52**, pp. 249–256; Harrower, T.P. (2004), 'Complement Regulation Protein are Expressed at Low Levels in Embryonic Human, Wild Type and Transgenic Porcine Neural Tissue', *Xenotransplantation*, **11** (1), pp. 60–71, at p. 61.

149 Edge, A.S.B. (2000), 'Current Applications of Cellular Xenografts', *Transplantation Proceedings*, **32** (5), pp. 1169–1171.

150 Shumakov, V.I. et al. (1987), 'The Principal Results of Pancreatic Islet Cell Culture Transplantation in Diabetes Mellitus Patients', *Transplantation Proceedings*, **19** (1), p. 2372.

151 Ibid.

the xenografts was relatively poor. However, they provided no specific data to support their claims that the xenografts had a 'positive' impact on the patients' condition.[152]

In 1993, Groth et al. reported that they had conducted eight clinical trials transplanting porcine islets into diabetic patients. The first transplant took place in June 1990 and the last in March 1992.[153] They record that although three of the eight grafts may have taken, 'no clinical benefit was achieved'.[154] The surgical team felt that the move to clinical trials was justified on a number of grounds, including: the ability of porcine fetal cells to correct diabetes in animal models; the failure to identify harm in such animal models; that 'contaminated porcine material could be identified by the use of a stringent microbiologic screening program'[155] and, finally, because porcine tissue survives in culture containing human material.

In 1994 Groth et al. reported that ten patients had now received porcine fetal transplants.[156] Although it was found that the porcine cells could survive in the human body and were not hyperacutely rejected, there was no improvement in the condition of the patients.[157] However, there was no evidence that porcine endogenous retroviruses (PERVs) were transmitted to the patients.[158] Elsewhere the team comments:

> The porcine cells survived and functioned for almost 1 year while protected with conventional immunosuppression alone. No clinical benefit was, however, achieved. To achieve a larger and more consistent insulin production, additional measures are obviously required. Probably, a larger amount of ICC [islet-like cluster cells] should be transplanted.[159]

In 1997, Deacon et al. claimed to provide the first evidence of long term (seven months) survival of porcine neural grafts in patients with Parkinson's Disease.[160] Although the study, which was based on the post-mortem evaluation of one patient with Parkinson's Disease,[161] found that pig fetal cells can survive in the human brain, this should not be equated to improvement in the patient's condition.[162] However, as part of the same study, Schumacher et al. have published details on the clinical benefits

---

152 Ibid.

153 Groth, C.G. et al. (1993), 'Transplantation of Porcine Fetal Islet-Like Cell Clusters into Eight Diabetic Patients', *Transplantation Proceedings*, **25** (1), p. 970.

154 Ibid.

155 Andersson, A. and Groth, C.G. (1992), 'Transplantation of Porcine Fetal Islet-Like Cell Clusters to Three Diabetic Patients', *Transplantation Proceedings*, **24** (2), pp. 677–678, at p. 678.

156 Groth, C.G. et al. (1994), 'Transplantation of Porcine Fetal Pancreas to Diabetes Patients', *The Lancet*, **344**, November 19, pp. 1402–1404.

157 Ibid.

158 Heneine, W. et al. (1998), 'No Evidence of Infection with Porcine Endogenous Retrovirus in Recipients of Porcine Islet-Cell Xenografts', *The Lancet*, **352**, August 29, pp. 695–699.

159 Anderson, A. and Groth, C.G. et al. (1992), at p. 678.

160 Deacon, T. et al. (1997), 'Histological Evidence of Fetal Pig Neural Cells Survival after Transplantation into a Patient with Parkinson's Disease', *Nature Medicine*, **3** (3), pp. 350–353.

161 Ibid., at p. 350.

162 Ibid.

and safety of porcine fetal transplants in 12 patients with Parkinson's disease.[163] The transplants took place between April 1995 and October 1996 and the patients were observed for one year post-operatively.[164] The impact of the transplant was measured on the Unified Parkinson's Disease Rating Scale. In this respect:

> ... the changes in standardized PD clinical rating instruments after unilateral transplantation of 12 million embryonic porcine VM cells were variable. Three patients have experienced substantial improvement in clinical rating scores ... in others, improvement has been less marked, or there has been no clinically meaningful improvement.[165]

More specifically, three patients made a 30 per cent improvement, two patients a 'mild improvement' (25 per cent and 19 per cent) and five patients a less than 11 per cent improvement.[166] The other main finding of the study was that cellular xenotransplantation of this type presented 'no serious adverse events', including a failure to find evidence of PERVs.[167] The Council of Europe reports that the company behind this Parkinson's trial, Diacrine, also conducted similar trials with Huntington's disease patients and found no clinical benefits.[168] However, they say:

> ... 3–4 patients who were transplanted reasonably early in their disease seemed to have stabilised after the transplantations. The significance of the observation is uncertain as this was a phase I trial. A phase II trial is being discussed.[169]

Such clinical examples suggest that cellular xenografting is more advanced than whole organ xenotransplantation. It also implies that cellular xenotransplantation raises fewer difficulties than whole organ transplantation. O'Connell states of the transplantation of pancreatic islet cells that:

> It is not as technically demanding as vascularised organ Xtx, it may be possible to protect the islets from the strong innate immune response that is directed against other forms of xenotransplants, and there are many patients who could potentially benefit from the procedure. Most importantly, we already know that there are no physiological incompatibilities between pig islets and humans, as porcine insulin has been clinically used for years. Despite this optimism the level of investment and development in pancreatic Xtx has lagged behind that of its solid organ counterparts.[170]

The Council of Europe concludes:

---

163 Schumacher, J.M. et al. (2000), 'Transplantation of Embryonic Porcine Mesencephalic Tissue in Patients with PD', *Neurology*, **54**, pp. 1042–1050.

164 Ibid., at p. 1043f.

165 Ibid., at p. 1047.

166 Ibid., at p. 1045.

167 Ibid.

168 Council of Europe (2003), p. 21.

169 Ibid., p. 21.

170 O'Connell, P. (2003), 'Pancreatic Islet Xenotransplantation', *Xenotransplantation*, **9**, pp. 367–375, at p. 367.

Cell transplantation often only requires a minor intervention. This may partly explain why several clinical trials have been initiated without significant experience first being obtained in primate models. From a physiological perspective, present data indicate that some xenotransplants including dopaminergic neurons, pancreatic islets and cells from the adrenal medulla can have a therapeutic effect in humans but more studies on the physiological aspects of xenotransplantation are obviously needed.[171]

Obstacles to the Clinical Success of Xenotransplantation

Immunology

It has recently been suggested that the immunological obstacles to the successful clinical conduct of xenotransplantation are amongst the 'most difficult of hurdles' to overcome.[172] These immunological difficulties exist because the human immune system rejects what it identifies as alien tissue. Such rejection takes place in a number of stages; namely, hyperacute rejection (which occurs in seconds or minutes), acute vascular rejection (AVR) (which takes place within days) and cellular rejection (which occurs weeks after a graft).

Hyperactive rejection was long regarded as the 'first hurdle' that needed to be overcome to make xenotransplantation clinically viable.[173] A number of developments in the field mean that it is now regarded as preventable.[174] The announcement that two different research teams had successfully produced 'knockout' pigs without the α –1, 3, galactosyl transferase gene was widely viewed as an important step in overcoming hyperacute rejection.[175] The tissue from these pigs lacks a molecule that leads to hyperacute rejection. In addition, as Vanderpool points out, hyperacute rejection is also addressed by transgenic porcine tissue that actually expresses a human protein.[176] While various researchers agree on the

---

171 Council of Europe (2003), p. 23.

172 Ogata, K. and Platt, J.L. (2004), 'Cardiac Xenotransplantation: Future Limitations', *Cardiology*, **101**, pp. 144–155, at p. 147.

173 Cooper, D.K.C. and Lanza, R.P. (2000), p. 62ff.

174 Sachs, D.H. et al. (1995), 'Tolerance and Xenograft Survival', *Nature Medicine*, **1** (9), p. 969; Vanderpool, H.Y. (1999a), 'Xenotransplantation: Progress and Promise', *British Medical Journal*, **319**, 13 November, pp. 1–3 [at http://www.bmj.com]; Ogata, K. and Platt, J.L. (2004), at p. 149; Cozzi, E. et al. (2000), 'Long-term Survival of Non-human Primates Receiving Life-supporting Transgenic Porcine Kidney', *Transplantation*, **70** (1), pp. 15–21; Cowan, P.J. et al. (2000), 'Renal Xenografts from Triple-transgenic Pigs are Not Hyperacutely Rejected but Cause Coagulopathy in Non-immunosuppressed Baboons', *Transplantation*, **69** (12), pp. 2504–2515; Platt, J. (1997), 'Hyperacute Xenograft Rejection', in Cooper, D.K.C. et al. (eds), *Xenotransplantation* (2nd Ed.), Springer-Verlag: London and Heidelberg, p. 13.

175 Lai, L. (2002), 'Production of α-1, 3-Galactosyltransferase Knockout Pigs by Nuclear Transfer Cloning', *Science*, **295**, February, pp. 1089–1092; Dai, Y. (2002), 'Targeted Disruption of the α1, 3-galactosyltransferase Gene in Cloned Pigs', *Nature Biotechnology*, 20 March, **5**, pp. 251–255; Frankish, H. (2002), 'Pig Organ Transplantation Brought One Step Closer', *The Lancet*, 12 January, **359**, p. 137.

176 Vanderpool (1999a), at p. 1 [at http://www.bmj.com].

importance of transgenic pigs in overcoming hyperacute rejection,[177] Platt has pointed out that:

> Unfortunately, solving the problem of hyperacute rejection does not make xenotransplantation feasible, but rather reveals a more vexing problem called acute vascular rejection ... I believe that acute vascular rejection is the greatest hurdle to the transplantation of animal organs into humans and that the solution to this problem will be advanced, but not solved, by knocking out α1, 3GT.[178]

In 2002 a report for the Department of Health stated that 'AVR remains a significant obstacle to the use of porcine xenografts in human recipients'.[179] However, considerable effort is now being focused on trying to understand the immune mechanisms that lead to AVR, so that ways to overcome it can be developed.[180] In fact, some research in animal models has been successful in delaying or preventing AVR.[181] Recently, Ogata and Platt have summarized the primary ways in which scientists are attempting to address AVR.[182] Although knowledge about the nature of AVR is clearly increasing, all of the primary methods being used to address it have their limitations.[183] In addition, Ogata and Platt state that even when 'acute vascular rejection is prevented, xenografts are susceptible to cellular rejection ...'.[184]

Efforts to address cellular rejection are even less well developed than those to tackle AVR. In addition, it is also thought likely that xenografts will be chronically rejected.[185] As a response to chronic rejection, Ogata and Platt have recently suggested that, given that xenotransplantation would supply an unlimited number of organs, chronic rejection could be overcome by replacing the organ.[186]

---

177 Niemann, H. and Kues, W.A. (2003), 'Application of Transgenesis in Livestock for Agriculture and Biomedicine', **79**, pp. 291–317, at p. 298; Vanderpool (1999a).

178 Platt, J.L. (2002), 'Knocking out Xenograft Rejection', *Nature Biotechnology*, 20 March, **5**, pp. 231–232, at p.231f.

179 Dobson, J.M. and Dark, J.H. (2002), at p. 20.

180 Saadi, S. et al. (2004), 'Pathways to Acute Humoral Rejection', *American Journal of Pathology*, **164** (3), pp. 1073–1080; Chen, G. et al. (2004), 'Improved Suppression of Circulating Complement Does Not Block Acute Vascular Rejection of Pig-to-Rhesus Monkey Cardiac Transplants', *Xenotransplantation*, **11** (2), pp. 123–132.

181 Kuwaki, K. et al. (2004), 'Suppression of Natural and Elicited Antibodies in Pig-to-Baboon Heart Transplantation using a Human Anti-Human CD154mAb based Regimen', *American Journal of Transplant*, **4** (3), pp. 363–372; Gollackner, B. (2003), 'Pig Kidney Transplantation in Baboons Treated Intravenously with a Bovine Serum Albumin-Galα 1-3Gal Conjugate', *Xenotransplantation*, **10** (6), pp. 606–614.

182 Ogata, K. and Platt, J.L. (2004), at p. 149ff.

183 Ibid.

184 Ibid., at p. 151.

185 Ogata, K. and Platt, J.L. (2004), at p. 151; Cooper, D.K.C. (2003), 'Clinical Xenotransplantation – How Close are We?', *The Lancet*, **362**, pp. 557–559.

186 Ogata and Platt (2004), at p. 151.

Physiology

Given the immunological difficulties that exist with xenotransplantation, there is currently limited information on whether animal organs and tissues will function physiologically in humans.[187] That is, assessments of how successfully xenotransplants will function cannot be made until longer graft survival is achieved to allow more evidence to be gained. However, this lack of information means that:

> ... questions remain as to whether a pig's heart can continue to pump the volumes needed by a human which walks upright, and whether or not the organ will age at the rate of a pig or of a human organ. Concerns also exist as to whether the organ will produce the appropriate biochemicals that humans require, or respond to the hormones that other human organs produce.[188]

In 2002, a number of reviews that considered the physiological aspects of xenotransplantation pointed both to specific problems that may arise when transplanting animal organs into humans and to the uncertainty which surrounds this topic.[189] For example, in the United States the National Heart, Lung and Blood Institute Heart and Lung Xenotransplantation Working Group reported that:

> Physiological Barriers stem mainly from incompatibilities of the biochemical systems of disparate animals ... Although these 'molecular incongruities' are generally acknowledged to be detectable, investigators differ in their views on the significance of these. There may be tens to hundreds of proteins and processes that may be affected by imperfect compatibilities between species, and there is uncertainty about which of these might limit the function or survival of a xenograft.[190]

In their more detailed review of *The Physiology of Xenotransplantation* for the Department of Health in the United Kingdom, Dobson and Dark outline some of the specific difficulties that may befall clinical xenotransplantation.[191] Thus, they suggest that:

> ... cardiac xenotransplantation appears to be the least susceptible to major physiological incompatibility problems compared to the transplantation of xenogeneic kidney, liver and lung. The good survival rates achieved in concordant cardiac xenotransplantation suggest that the main barrier to overcome may be immunological and not physiological. However, the available data highlight several key areas that will present major problems for possible future clinical xenotransplantation. For example, pig-to-non-human-primate cardiac

---

187 Council of Europe (2003), p. 29; Dobson and Dark (2002), at p. 12; Hammer, C. (1997), 'Evolution: Its Complexity and Impact on Xenotransplantation', in Cooper, D.K.C. et al. (eds), at p. 721; Soin, B. et al. (2001), 'Physiological Aspects of Pig-to-Primate Renal Xenotransplantation', *Kidney International*, **60** (4), pp. 1592–1597, at p. 1592.

188 Council of Europe (2003), p. 29.

189 Dobson, J.M. and Dark, J.H. (2002); Platt, J. et al. (2002), 'Recommendations of the National Heart, Lung, and Blood Institute Heart and Lung Xenotransplantation Working Group', *Circulation*, **106**, pp. 1043–1047.

190 Platt, J. et al. (2002), at p. 1044.

191 Dobson, J.M. and Dark, J.H. (2002).

> xenotransplantation has achieved survival rates of one month but the onset of lethal disrhythmias in some experimental animals suggests that anatomical differences ... may be a major factor in morbidity ...[192]

In respect of kidney transplantation, Dobson and Dark note that although some of the longest survival times have been attained in this area, 'extended survival times' are required to help determine whether porcine kidneys will function physiologically in a human.[193] The authors suggest that liver xenotransplantation presents the greatest physiological difficulties:

> ... since many enzymes and hormones and regulatory pathways depend on species-specific interactions which may be non-functional in the xenogeneic setting. Erythropoietin incompatibility between pigs and man will potentially cause severe anaemia but can be managed in a clinical situation using recombination human EPO therapy. However, major differences are apparent in the structure and serum concentration of important transport proteins such as serum albumin between pigs and man.[194]

In respect of cellular xenotransplantation it is noted that, although this is now a clinical reality in the treatment of conditions like Parkinson's disease, few cellular grafts have survived to enable them to produce long-term clinical benefits. Dobson and Dark suggest that:

> A good knowledge of the native biochemical environment of neural tissue and the processes of proliferation, migration and differentiation are therefore essential to the survival and function of xenogeneic tissue in the host brain.[195]

At the very least, more research is required in animal models to ensure that xenotransplantation moves to clinical trials only when there is a high probability that they are likely to function in their human recipients, or at least that prolonged and reliable graft survival has been attained in animal models. Dobson and Dark conclude:

> ... in the medium term, it appears that the physiological incompatibilities encountered to date, and those still to be discovered, constitute a significant stumbling block to the progress of xenotransplantation towards clinical trials.[196]

Infectious Disease Risk

It has long been acknowledged that allotransplantation can spread diseases between the donor and recipient of transplanted organs and tissue.[197] As Meslin notes:

---

192 Ibid., at p. 99.

193 Ibid.

194 Ibid.

195 Ibid. at p. 101.

196 Ibid.

197 Ho, M. and Drummer, J.S. (1990), 'Risk Factors and Approaches to Infections in Transplant Recipients', in Mandell, G.C. et al. (eds), *Principles and Practice of Infectious Diseases*, (2nd Ed.),

> A risk of disease transmission is present in any transplantation system. In allotransplantation, disease transmission is a major cause of illness and death in recipients. This is largely due to the required level of recipient immunosuppression but is also attributable to infected, but usually asymptomatic, human donors.[198]

In addition, it is also acknowledged that animal diseases (zoonoses) can cause diseases in humans. Thus, Chapman emphasizes that:

> Zoonotic viruses have been responsible for at least two major pandemics: the 1918 Spanish influenza pandemic, attributed to infection of humans with a swine influenza virus, and the current HIV/AIDS pandemic, believed to have originated with the infection of humans by a simian immunodeficiency virus endemic to chimpanzees.[199]

Interestingly, it was a zoonosis (HIV infection) that led to calls for 'even more careful screening' of transplant donors.[200] This is required not least because the spread of zoonoses via transplantation is likely to be even more efficient than it is by natural means.[201] However, the knowledge that transplantation can transmit disease and that animal diseases can pass to humans did not immediately lead to attention being given to the public health implications of xenotransplantation. In his 1998 review of the risks associated with xenotransplantation, Butler noted:

> The emphasis on the risk of xenozoonosis – the transmission of animal diseases to humans via organ transplants or blood – is relatively recent. Louisa Chapman, an expert on xenotransplantation at CDC, recalls that when the issue was first raised at CDC in 1993 her first thought was 'why would we spend taxpayers' money on that, as it's only once in a blue moon that someone puts a baboon liver [or] heart into someone, they die within 72 hours and that is the end of the story?'[202]

Indeed, there is agreement that the immunological problems associated with the development of xenotransplantation initially attracted more attention than those related to infection.[203] There are a number of reasons for what now may appear from

---

Churchill Livingstone: Edinburgh; Gottesdiener, K.M. (1989), 'Transplanted Infections: Donor-to-Host Transmission with the Allograft', *Annals of Internal Medicine*, **110**, pp. 1001–1016; Eastlund, T. (1995), 'Infectious Disease Transmission through Cell, Tissue, and Organ Transplantation: Reducing the Risk Through Donor Selection', *Cell Transplantation*, **4** (5), pp. 455–477.

198 Meslin, F.X. (1997), 'Global Aspects of Emerging and Potential Zoonoses: A WHO Perspective', *Emerging Infectious Diseases*, **3** (2), pp. 223–228, at p. 227.

199 Chapman, L.E. (1999), 'Xenogeneic Infections and Public Health', *Clinical and Experimental Pharmacology and Physiology*, **26**, pp. 1005–1008, at p. 1005.

200 Gottesdiener, K.M. (1989), at p. 1001.

201 Chapman, L.E. and Fishman, J.A. (1997), 'Xenotransplantation and Infectious Disease', in Cooper, D.K.C. et al. (eds) (1997).

202 Butler, D. (1998), 'Last Chance to Stop and Think on Risks of Xenotransplants', *Nature*, **391**, pp. 320–324, at p. 320.

203 Finch, J.D. (1996), *A Review of the History of Animal to Human Transplantation (Xenotransplantation) and the Risk of Infectious Disease Transmission*, The University of Wales: Aberystwyth, Prepared for the Department of Health, p. 22; Michaels, M.G. and Simmons, R.L. (1994), 'Xenotransplant-Associated Zoonoses', *Transplantation*, **57** (1), pp. 1–7, at p. 1.

an ethical and regulatory perspective to be a dubious allocation of research attention. Firstly, as Chapman notes, the early xenografts of solid organs did not survive long enough for public health to be threatened. Secondly, Finch points out that:

> Poor documentation of the perceived risk of the transmission of infectious agents from the animal donor to the human recipient following xenotransplantation before the mid-1980s partly reflects the limited technology which was available to detect the infectious agents or to provide serological evidence of previous infection.[204]

Thus, there was not seen to be a need to focus on public health and the tools for facilitating this focus were in any case still developing. However, in the late 1980s and early 1990s the impetus to focus on the public health issues raised by xenotransplantation began to emerge, for a number of reasons. Advances in overcoming rejection and attempts at cellular xenografting both meant that patients with xenografts survived longer and made the infectious disease issue more acute.[205] Also at this time other zoonoses such as HIV/AIDS and CJD led to more awareness of the attention being afforded to public health. Allen, for example, highlights the 'explosion of interest surrounding emerging viral diseases'.[206]

As infectious disease began to be discussed in the context of xenotransplantation, different aspects of the issue were highlighted. Thus, it was noted in 1992 that infectious disease experts:

> ... fear that insufficient precautions were taken to prevent the liver of the baboon from transmitting to the patient simian viruses, which could in turn be spread to other humans, potentially unleashing a new epidemic as devastating as AIDS.[207]

Many other articles around this time only present parts of the infectious disease issues raised by xenotransplantation. That is, attention is variously given to the risk posed to xenograft recipients,[208] or to transplant recipients and their close contacts.[209] Others note in passing the potential risk to public health; for example, Nelson comments on the '... possibility that xenografting will serve as a vector by which new and possibly virulent viruses become established in humans ...'.[210] However, it was not until the 1995 papers of Allen and Chapman et al. that extensive

---

204 Finch, J.D. (1996), p. 22.

205 Chapman, L.E. et al. (1999), 'Xenotransplantation: The Potential for Xenogeneic Infections', *Transplantation Proceedings*, **31** (1–2), pp. 909–910, at p. 909.

206 Allen J.S. (1995), 'Xenograft Transplantation and the Infectious Disease Conundrum', *ILAR Journal*, **37** (1), pp. 37–48.

207 Nowak, R. (1992), 'Hope or Horror? Primate-to-Human Organ Transplants', *The Journal of NIH Research*, **4**, September, pp. 37–38, at p. 37.

208 Van der Riet, J.F. de ST et al. (1987), 'Virological Implications of the Use of Primates in Xenotransplantation', *Transplantation Proceedings*, **19** (5), pp. 4068–4069, at p. 4068; Chiche, L. et al. (1993), 'Xenotransplantation: Baboons as Potential Liver Donors?', *Transplantation*, **55** (6), pp. 1418–1421, at p. 1420.

209 Douglas, M. (1993), 'Endogenous Retroviruses in Xenografts', *The New England Journal of Medicine*, **328** (2), pp. 142–143, at p. 143.

210 Nelson, J.L. (1993), 'Moral Sensibilities and Moral Standing: Caplan on Xenograft "Donors"', *Bioethics*, **7** (4), pp. 315–322, at p. 316.

attention began to be consistently afforded to the public health risk dimension of the infection risks associated with xenotransplantation.[211] Chapman et al. drew attention to the fact that:

> If the risk of xenotransplant-associated infections is restricted to the recipient, it simply constitutes one more factor affecting the risks and benefits of transplantation. However, there may be wider implications for the human community.[212]

Arguably, the topic to have received most attention in the scientific literature that considers the infection risks associated with animal to human transplantation is the potential of Porcine Endogenous Retroviruses (PERVs) to pass to humans. PERVs have been thought to pose a particular risk because they cannot be removed from porcine tissue. Thus, although other viruses can be managed by the introduction of biosecurity procedures, this is not the case with PERVs. In addition, it was unknown how these retroviruses would react when grafted into a human. Such concern was heightened by the fact that PERVs did infect human cells in culture.[213] However, evidence also exists to support the suggestion that PERVs do not transmit to humans or animals.[214] Thus, seven patients with acute liver failure who were bridged to transplantation extra-corporeally with porcine liver therapy did not show any signs of being infected with PERVs after two years.[215] Similarly, no PERVs were discovered in ten diabetic patients who received transplants of porcine foetal islet cells between 1990–1993.[216] On the other hand, a number of studies have found PERVs to be transmitted in immunodeficient mice.[217] Despite such results a number of researchers in this area now think the risks posed by PERVs are overstated.[218] Ogata and Platt recently claimed that:

---

211 Allen, J.S. (1995), pp. 37–48; Chapman, L.E. et al. (1995), 'Xenotransplantation and Xenogeneic Infections', *The New England Journal of Medicine*, **333** (22), pp. 1498–1501.

212 Chapman, L.E. et al. (1995), at p. 1499.

213 Patience, C. et al. (1997), 'Infection of Human Cells by an Endogenous Retrovirus of Pigs', *Nature Medicine*, **2**, pp. 282–286; Martin, U.V. et al. (1998), 'Expression of Pig Endogenous Retrovirus by Primary Porcine Endothelial Cells and Infection of Human Cells', *The Lancet*, **352**, pp. 692–964.

214 Paradis. K.G. (1999), 'Search for Cross-species Transmission of Porcine Endogenous Retrovirus in Patients with Living Pig Tissue', *Science*, **285**, pp. 1236–1241; Patience, C.G.S. (1998), 'No Evidence of Pig DNA or Retroviral Infection in Patients with Short-Term Extracorporeal Connection to Pig Kidneys', *The Lancet*, **352**, pp. 699–701; Pitkin, Z. and Mullon, C. (1999), 'Evidence of Absence of Porcine Endogenous Retrovirus (PERV) Infection in Patients Treated with a Bioartificial Liver Support System', *Artificial Organs*, **23** (9), pp. 829–833; Martin, U. et al. (2002), 'Absence of PERV Specific Humoral Response in Baboons after Transplantation of Porcine Cells of Organs', *Transplant International*, **15**, pp. 361–368.

215 Irgang, M. (2003), 'Porcine Endogenous Retroviruses: No Infection in Patients Treated with a Bioreactor Based on Porcine Liver Cells', *Journal of Clinical Virology*, **28**, pp. 141–154, at p. 146.

216 Heneine, W. et al. (1998), pp. 695–699.

217 Van der Laan, L.J.W. et al. (2000), 'Infection by Porcine Endogenous Retrovirus after Islet Xenotransplantation in SCID Mice', *Nature*, **407**, September, pp. 90–94; Deng, Y. et al. (2000), 'Transmission of Porcine Endogenous Retroviruses in Severe Combined Immunodeficient Mice Xenotransplanted with Fetal Porcine Pancreatic Cells', *Transplantation*, **70** (7), pp. 1010–1016.

218 Platt, J.L. (2002), at p. 232; Niemann, H. and Kues, W.A. (2003), at p. 297; Suling, K. et al. (2003), 'Packaging of Human Endogenous Retrovirus Sequence is Undetectable in Porcine Endogenous Retrovirus Particles Produced from Human Cells', *Virology*, **312**, pp. 330–336.

> While the question of the relevance of PERV to public health cannot be entirely dismissed, the question may now be viewed as one that might be resolved by careful attention to the recipients of xenografts, rather than as a reason for abandoning xenotransplantation.[219]

However, it should be noted that in 2001 a Department of Health report stated that, although there is no sign that humans have been infected in trials, 'there are precedents for the adaptation of and spread of animal retroviruses within the human population'.[220] This is a possibility that has still not been discounted.

Conclusion

One issue that comes through strongly in this chapter is that the development of xenotransplantation has been led by clinical urgency. That is, in the vast majority of cases surgical teams or their lead surgeons stressed that the experimental use of xenografting only occurred when no other potential therapies were available. For example, we have seen that Reemtsma, Hardy and Starzl all report turning to xenografting as a last resort. However, ethico-legal questions are raised by the operating assumption of surgeons like Reemtsma; namely, that an experimental treatment is likely to be acceptable if there are no alternatives. The early efforts at xenotransplantation may not have been subjected to critical appraisal. However, examining these historical cases can help to highlight why assessments of contemporary initiatives to develop xenotransplantation are necessary.

Another noticeable feature of the early xenotransplantation case reports is that the surgeons were able to classify as advances events which – to the non-clinical eye – were in fact failures. For example, despite the death of his patient, Starzl asserted that that it was 'encouraging' that the xenograft of a baboon liver to a patient positive for Hepatitis and HIV failed for identifiable technical reasons which could be remedied. Similarly, in his report of the 'Baby Fae' case, Bailey was able to claim that, despite its failure, the transplant showed that the surgery was 'technically feasible'. Such statements inadvertently portray the lost lives at the centre of such surgery as the collateral damage of medical progress. However, progress is rarely desirable at all costs. Thus, it is important that biomedical advances are assessed and outcomes presented in a transparent manner.

We have discovered, for example, that on one occasion the lead surgeon decided to report cases in a manner that would protect them from wider scrutiny in case they were regarded as problematic. Similarly, we have discovered that the way in which consent has been gained for xenotransplantation procedures has at times been dubious. For example, the consent form used for Hardy's first cardiac xenograft neglected to acknowledge that an animal organ might be used. This was despite the fact that the surgical team realized that such a procedure would be controversial. On a number of occasions we found decisions over whether to proceed with a xenograft highly questionable. For example, in the 'Baby Fae' case it appears that no efforts

---

219 Ogata, K. and Platt, J.L. (2004), at p. 152.

220 Muir, D.A. and Griffin, G.E. (2001), *Infection Risks in Xenotransplantation*, Department of Health: London, p. 38.

were made to find a suitable human organ before deciding to use a heart harvested from an animal, or to match the blood type of the patient and the source animal. It seems likely that the success of the surgery may well have been compromised by these decisions. It will be also be recalled that Starzl acknowledged that technical limitations led to the failure of the first of his 'hidden' transplants in 1966, but went on to suggest that even if this had not been the case it is unlikely that the surgery would have succeeded. Such a statement from the lead surgeon suggests that his decision to proceed with the xenograft was questionable. These examples again highlight some of the reasons why it is important to ensure that efforts to develop clinical xenotransplantation are transparent and subject to ethico-legal assessment. This is required to prevent the potential of xenotransplantation being tarnished and undermined by questionable decision-making.

It is perhaps easier for those who stand at a distance from surgical disciplines to see any progress that has been made in the field in more abstract terms. Our thematic outline of the immunological, physiological and infectious obstacles to xenotransplantation allows us to see that progress has been made in, for example, overcoming hyperacute rejection. However, this assessment has also suggested that considerable work still needs to be done. The ease with which a thematic treatment of the issues can advance a broad account of progress (and work that is still required) is enhanced by the fact that it is partially detached from the specifics of particular cases. However, such a thematic account of biomedical progress can hide the costs of making such progress. The often single-minded perspective of medical researchers and clinicians seeking to make animal to human transplantation clinically viable needs to be balanced by the perspectives of other disciplines to determine whether or when the costs of progress are reasonable or too great.

Chapter 3

The Regulation of Xenotransplantation in the United Kingdom: The Background Reports

Introduction

In the United Kingdom efforts to investigate the ethical and regulatory issues presented by the development of animal to human transplantation commenced in earnest with reports by the Nuffield Council on Bioethics (Nuffield Report)[1] and the Advisory Group on the Ethics of Xenotransplantation (Kennedy Report).[2] In this chapter the contribution of these reports will be elucidated and critically appraised.

Nuffield Council on Bioethics

The Nuffield Council began its consideration of xenotransplantation by clarifying the assumptions on which its work was predicated. The first assumption was: 'a recognition that it is unrealistic to expect consensus across society on the issues addressed in this report'.[3] The Nuffield Report charged itself with the task of trying to identify as much common ethical ground as was possible, given these circumstances. Their second assumption was that 'no single ethical framework can capture all of the reasonable perspectives that may be taken on the issues raised by xenotransplantation'.[4] Thus, it was accepted from the outset that the conclusions of their deliberations were unlikely to satisfy all perspectives within the community. Nonetheless, the Nuffield Council believed that a major consequence of its Report would be to inform any debate that took place in the future, and – perhaps more importantly – to ensure that whatever decision society reached on the ethics of xenotransplantation would be based on identifiable principles that were capable of justification. In this way, they hoped to reconcile, or at least accommodate, the views of those who, as they put it, 'dissent from the majority decision'.[5]

---

1 Nuffield Report (Report of the Nuffield Council on Bioethics) (1996), *Animal-to-Human Transplants: The Ethics of Xenotransplantation*, Nuffield Council on Bioethics: London.

2 Kennedy Report (Report of the Advisory Group on the Ethics of Xenotransplantation) (1997), *Animal Tissue into Humans*, HMSO: London.

3 Nuffield Report (1996), p. 10, para. 1.29.

4 Ibid., p. 10, para. 1.30.

5 Ibid., p. 10, para. 1.29.

As a preliminary to consideration of specific issues, the Nuffield Council listed a number of benefits and concerns which might flow from the use of animals as sources of organs for transplantation. As they noted, '[e]ven if one accepts in principle the use of animals in medicine and in medical research, their use in xenotransplantation may raise particular difficulties'.[6] However, they also conceded that there were some relatively obvious advantages to the use of animals as source organs for humans desperately in need of life-saving measures. According to the Nuffield Council, the benefits would be as follows:

> Enough animals could be reared to avoid the organ shortfall which has been described ...; animal organs would then be available to a wider group of people; xenotransplantation has the potential to eliminate the careful tissue matching which is currently needed in human-to-human organ donation; the availability of animal organs might also reduce the problems posed by the shortage of organs available for certain ethnic groups in the community; the use of animals would avoid the need to consult the relatives of dead people, a problem which has already been discussed ...; the ready availability of animal organs would give both patients and their clinicians the opportunity of preparing for the operation, rather than needing to act with the urgency required when cadaveric organs become available; xenotransplantation, it was also believed, would eliminate any possibility of future commercial dealings in human organs; and finally, the capacity to use animal organs would avoid the development of potentially more controversial measures such as elective ventilation.[7]

However, the Nuffield Council also identified a number of ethical matters which could be the subject of concern. For example, they highlighted the clear potential public health implications of xenotransplantation, not least resulting from the possibility of the spread of infectious organisms both to individual recipients and to the wider community.[8] In addition, they noted that the use of animal organs, at least in the early stages, would be of an experimental nature, and were concerned that the usual ethical concerns about the use of human subjects as experimental 'fodder' would apply also in xenotransplantation.[9] It was also clear that there may be cost implications for the healthcare system, in that the more organs that were available, the more transplantation would be likely to be carried out, with obvious resource implications.[10] These issues will be considered below.[11] It was also clear that there were potentially considerable social implications for recipients of animal organs or tissue, and concern was expressed about the possible personal effect on those who had received them.[12] Finally, the Nuffield Council posed the question whether or not the ready availability of animal organs would impact on people's willingness to donate organs.[13] Clearly, even were a regime of xenotransplantation successful,

6 P. 8, para. 1.19.
7 P. 7.
8 P. 8.
9 Ibid.
10 Ibid.
11 See chapters 7 and 8, below.
12 Nuffield Report (1996), p. 8.
13 Ibid.

there would – at least in the first years of the programme – still be a need for human organ donation to continue.

Much of the Nuffield Council Report concentrates on issues concerning animals. This it does by addressing a number of questions. First, the Report considers the kinds of animals whose use in xenotransplantation might be most appropriate. So far, they concede, a major ethical concern has been the possibility of the use of non-human primates in xenotransplantation.[14] Primates are often regarded as being sufficiently close to humans to render their use as sources of body parts ethically unacceptable.[15] Thus, as the Nuffield Council notes, attention has turned to the possibility of breeding other animals for use as organ donors.[16] The animal that has been the subject of particular focus has been the pig. This, according to the Nuffield Report is because:

> Pig organs are comparable in size and, to a lesser degree, physiology to those of human beings, and they reproduce quickly and produce large numbers of offspring. The use of pigs as a domestic animal that is farmed and eaten is long established and many would have fewer concerns about their use in xenotransplantation as compared with the use of primates.[17]

However, even if one is prepared to accept the use of pigs as being less ethically problematic than the use of primates, the Nuffield Council identifies practical considerations which might militate against their use. Noting that the heart is a relatively simple organism,[18] they feel that in principle animal hearts might be able to perform the same function in a human.[19] However, they state that there would be issues concerning the size of the animal organ to be transplanted, and the possibility that in the case of some organs – perhaps particularly the liver – there may be what they describe as 'complicated biochemical functions' that differ between the animal and the human.[20] As they say, '[i]t is simply not known whether an animal liver will support human life'.[21]

The Nuffield Council also raises the question, which was also incidentally of scientific interest in the cloning of Dolly the sheep, as to whether or not the lifespan of animals would have any impact on the length of time for which a transplanted organ could survive in a human.[22] If the animal organ does in fact age more rapidly than the human into whom it is transplanted, the Nuffield Council notes that this might mean that a recipient would require multiple transplants in order to survive to a normal life expectancy.[23]

---

14 P. 25, para. 3.4.
15 P. 46, para. 4.29.
16 P. 25, para. 3.4.
17 Ibid.
18 P. 26, para. 3.6.
19 Ibid.
20 Ibid.
21 Ibid.
22 Ibid.
23 Ibid.

Despite recent announcements from two of the companies most closely associated with the development of xenotransplantation in the United Kingdom that they were either abandoning or reducing their investment in xenotransplantation,[24] the Nuffield Council notes that the development of transgenic pigs has produced some successes, albeit with limited life expectancy in animal research.[25]

Of course, for many people the major ethical issue in xenotransplantation is the question of whether or not it is appropriate for human beings to use animals in this way. There are arguably three main ethical considerations that flow from this concern. The first relates to the transgenic nature of source animals. In order that pigs, or any other animals, may be successfully used as organ donors for human subjects, it is necessary that they are modified – that is become transgenic – in order to lower the likelihood of the human immune system rejecting them immediately.[26] As the Nuffield Report says:

> The essence of transgenesis is that a gene from one species is incorporated into another. The transferred gene enables the transgenic animal to produce a particular protein. The transgenic pigs bred for xenotransplantation contain a human gene which produces a complement regulating protein. This reduces the immune response to transplanted organs.[27]

Just as allotransplantation requires the use of immunosuppressive drugs to prevent rejection, the use of organs from another species would probably require an even more major immunosuppressive regime to be applied, unless the organs have already been sufficiently and successfully modified so as to minimize the possibility of rejection; that is, unless they have been genetically modified. Although it is not clear whether or not genetically modifying animals directly causes them suffering, some concern is undoubtedly raised by the possibility of so doing.

The second major concern relates to the fact that, if xenotransplantation did become feasible, then it is likely that it would be widely used. This would require the breeding and killing of animals on a potentially massive scale in order to provide the relevant tissue and organs for transplantation.[28] This dominance of human interests over animal interests (actual or potential) questions the nature of the relationship between human beings and the animal world. Finally, as the Nuffield Council notes, there are many who believe that animals *do* have interests; indeed some who believe that animals have specific rights. Thus the infliction of any suffering on animals, even if we believe them only to have interests rather than rights, needs to be justified. The Nuffield Council's conclusion on this matter is:

> Many would endorse the view that animals have interests, particularly in the avoidance of suffering, that should be respected, but that in certain limited circumstances those interests may be outweighed by the interests of human beings provided that everything possible is

---

24 As reported on 14 August 2000; see http://bbc.co.uk/news, accessed on 14/8/04.

25 Nuffield Report (1996), p. 33, para. 3.29.

26 P. 26, para. 3.5, 'There is evidence from experiments with animal recipients that the immune response is reduced when transgenic pig organ or tissue is transplanted.'

27 P. 52, para. 4.45.

28 P. 37, para. 4.1.

> done to minimise distress to the animals ... others hold the opinion that all use of animals for medical purposes is wrong, no matter how great the benefits. The view that there should be an absolute prohibition on the use of animals for medical purposes is a minority position within UK society.[29]

The Nuffield Council Report then seeks some justification for the use of animals in this way, by addressing the question of how, if at all, it is possible to draw a distinction between animals and human beings. In their view, 'if animals are to be used for medical purposes in ways that would not be considered ethically acceptable if applied to human beings, then there must be some basis for drawing the distinction between animals and human beings'.[30] This, the report concedes, is not by any means an easy task. To an extent, their consideration of this difficult question is premised on the concept of personhood. Seemingly accepting that persons have a higher status than non-persons, the Report nonetheless comes up against the obvious problem that 'the boundaries of personhood and of the human species do not exactly coincide, but rather overlap. Some non-human animals might be considered persons and some human beings might not be considered persons.'[31] Thus, for those who would argue that non-persons may legitimately be used as a source of life-saving treatment for those who do possess personhood, the thorny question of speciesism arises, since it is not suggested by the Report that humans who lack the characteristics of personhood should be used as a source of organs. Speciesism is, however, according to the Nuffield Report, a notion which should be treated 'with some caution'.[32] In their view, it is not self-evident that we should treat non-human animals in the same way as we should treat human beings. Rather, in their view, we should treat non-human animals in their own terms and not in terms which would apply to humans.[33]

However, they do concede that any pain and suffering caused to animals cannot be disregarded.[34] For example, they note that some animals may form social relationships with one another, and that their deliberate killing would clearly cause distress to other animals. This, they say, is an issue which cannot be ignored. Although not claiming to answer the problems of alleged speciesism, the Nuffield Council takes seriously the concerns that our uses, or abuses, of animals may reflect in a negative way on the relationship which humans have with the rest of the animal kingdom.[35] As they say, 'if there is continual unjustifiable exploitation of other species for human use, then it would be wrong to allow the development of a new technology that increased that exploitation'.[36] However, they also note the relative impossibility of actually identifying the rationale underpinning the development of new technologies and innovations. They conclude that there is 'undoubted force in

29 P. 37, para. 4.3.
30 P. 38, para. 4.4.
31 P. 40, para. 4.12.
32 P. 40, para. 4.15.
33 Ibid.
34 P. 42, para. 4.18.
35 P. 44, para. 4.22.
36 Ibid.

the moral argument that rests upon the question: what sort of people do our social and technical practices reveal us to be?',[37] and that 'if we do not like what we see when we look honestly in the mirror, then there is cause for thought at least'.[38]

Turning then to the animals deemed most appropriate for use in xenotransplantation, should it proceed, the Nuffield Council notes that at first sight the most obvious group to use would be non-human primates. However, as we have already seen, the fact that primates are close to humans in evolutionary terms, although it might lead one to assume that this would render them the most appropriate animals for use, is often the primary reason for people to object to their use.[39] Additionally, the Nuffield Council notes that it might be thought that any reservation about the use of primates could and should be extended to other animals. As its report says:

> Many non-primate species, possibly including pigs, display comparable capacities of intelligence and sociality, albeit in forms that less clearly resemble the human and thus appeal less strongly to human moral sensibility. To limit reservations to those species closest to human beings, in this view, is to be swayed by sentimental anthropomorphism.[40]

Nonetheless, the Nuffield Council also believes that there are additional arguments against using primates, which would tip the balance away from their use and towards the use of other less well-developed animals. In part, this argument rests on the basis of the nature of primates themselves. For example, it is known that chimpanzees are an endangered species, and it could therefore be argued that there are powerful arguments from a conservationist perspective which would rule out their use.[41] This argument, however, does not apply in the case of other primates, such as baboons. They are apparently able to survive reasonably well in captivity and it is relatively easy to establish colonies of baboons for possible xenotransplantation in captivity.[42] The Nuffield Report, however, argues nonetheless that:

> ... establishing breeding colonies of baboons to provide organs for transplantation would require the capture of large numbers of animals. Hence, although baboons are abundant at present, their use to provide organs for xenotransplantation might have a significant effect on their numbers.[43]

Moreover, the Nuffield Report poses the question as to whether or not the very similarity – in evolutionary terms – between humans and primates might make it more, rather than less, likely that any infectious organisms would transfer between the species, thus risking the health of the individual recipient of organs or tissue and potentially exacerbating any other public health problems associated with xenotransplantation.[44]

---

37 Ibid.
38 Ibid.
39 P. 46, para. 4.29.
40 P. 47, para. 4.29.
41 P. 49, para. 4.33.
42 P. 49, para. 4.35.
43 Ibid.
44 P. 50, para. 4.36.

Turning to the question of transgenesis, the Nuffield Report notes that there may be objections inherent in this process, which, as we have seen, seems to be essential for the production of organs which have a reasonable chance of successful transplantation. For example, there may be specific religious objections to inserting human genes into animals, particularly from the Judeo-Christian tradition, which holds that human beings are created in the image of God.[45] However, the Report also suggests that:

> ... species boundaries are not, in fact, inviolate, but change as evolution occurs. Some regard transgenic techniques as no more than an extension of traditional breeding techniques that artificially produce new animal breeds. There is also evidence that, at a low level, the transfer of genetic material from one species to another occurs naturally.[46]

Leaving aside the question of whether or not the introduction of human genes into animals causes the animal any suffering, the Nuffield Council's conclusion on the issue of transgenesis is that the actual modification to the source animal would be so minor as not to render the animal unidentifiable as an animal, nor would it mean that the modified animal would be more like a human being.[47]

A further matter of concern, which has been briefly referred to above, is the possibility of the transmission of organisms between species. Although there are some organisms which may be common between humans and animals, it is also clear that there will be organisms which are present in animals, whether or not they actually cause the animal any suffering, which are not usually present in humans.[48] Thus, if xenotransplantation is to proceed, it would be necessary to ensure as far as possible that such organisms were not transferred to the recipient human being who may thereby develop diseases which were previously unknown in humans and for which there is no apparent therapy. Until the science is clear on the extent to which the transmission of such organisms is a risk, the Nuffield Report concludes that it would not be ethical to begin clinical trials of xenotransplantation using human beings as recipients.[49]

As the Nuffield Report notes, it is also possible that these organisms may affect the organ that is being transplanted, thereby reducing its effectiveness as well as possibly putting the recipient at risk.[50] Thus, the Report turns its attention to the question of the circumstances in which animals must be bred and reared in order, if possible, to avoid the transmission of such organisms. This too may be a source of concern. It is known, for example, that certain animals are highly sociable, not least the pig, but breeding techniques to ensure minimization of infection risks would almost certainly involve delivery by caesarean and the maintenance of the animal in completely sterile, and by definition isolated, circumstances.[51]

---

45 P. 53, para. 4.45.

46 P. 53, para. 4.46.

47 Pp. 53–54, para. 4.48.

48 P. 67, para. 6.3.

49 P. 116, para. 10.28.

50 Ibid.

51 P. 125, para. 10.21.

Of course, it seems plausible that it may never be entirely possible to rule out the possible spread of organisms into human beings, but rather that a risk-benefits calculation may require to be made once the science is in place. This being the case, were animal to human transplants ever to be seriously attempted, the Report concludes that it would be necessary to ensure that the recipients of xenografts were carefully monitored.[52] They also recommend that no clinical trials of xenotransplantation should take place unless there is sufficient evidence as to the risk(s) associated with them.[53] However, and perhaps more controversially, given the residual risk either of the transmission of previously unknown organisms into humans, and in order to monitor the success of early clinical trials in xenotransplantation, it will be necessary for the recipient of an organ to agree to life-long surveillance.[54]

The Kennedy Report[55]

Following the publication of the Nuffield Council Report, the Government invited Professor Ian Kennedy to chair a review of the ethics of xenotransplantation. The intention was that this Report would produce a definitive statement on the ethics associated with xenotransplantation, and indicate the way forward.

The Report begins by making it clear that it bases its enquiry on certain assumptions. These, it says, are that:

1. Ethical judgements are inescapable. They are not simply for rarefied people in rarefied circumstances but are unavoidable in medicine, science and ordinary life.
2. Ethical judgements are all pervasive. Dramatic issues which happen to be topical tend to be highlighted, but ethical decisions are made many times in the course of a normal working day.
3. Ethical considerations are indivisible in the sense that there are not separate public and private areas of ethics. Ethical judgements made by the professions should be open to attitudinal changes in society. Moreover, we should take note of science, public health and economics.
4. Ethical decisions must be made in the every day world of 'give' and 'take' and of constantly changing information. In other words, 'absolutes' may need to be tempered by realities.
5. Ethical decisions can change as new knowledge becomes available which shifts the balance of arguments.[56]

Interestingly, and this will be returned to later, the Kennedy Report's position was that when formulating public policy, a critical aim would be the balancing of risks and benefits.[57] Although they say that they do not ignore other theories of ethics,

---

52 P. 117, para. 10.28.

53 P. 116, para. 10.25.

54 P. 117, para. 10.28.

55 Kennedy Report (1997), *Animal Tissue into Humans*, HMSO: London.

56 Pp. 4–5, para. 1.9.

57 P. 5, para. 1.11.

they clearly position themselves in this camp from the beginning of their consideration.[58]

Perhaps this ethical perspective, then, predicts the questions that the Kennedy Report regards as being critical, namely:

1. In the light of current scientific knowledge, does xenotransplantation offer an ethically acceptable solution to the problems associated with the shortage of tissue for transplantation and to the problems caused by other medical conditions?
2. Are there ways to improve the current programme for obtaining human tissue so as to meet all or a greater part of the demand for transplantation of tissue?
3. Are there currently other procedures for responding to the needs of those whose conditions call for transplantation and are such procedures likely to be developed in a relevant timescale?[59]

Of course, these questions underpin virtually any ethical approach to xenotransplantation, with the possible exception of those that concentrate exclusively on the welfare of animals. In line with its assertion that other ethical perspectives would not be ignored, the Kennedy Report then proceeds to discuss briefly a number of possible objections to xenotransplantation.

It first addresses religious arguments. As they note, certain of these arguments would hold all living things to be sacred and therefore would apparently preclude the destruction of animals for human use.[60] This, presumably, would remain true even if there were considerable benefit to be obtained by human subjects. A second kind of religious argument that they refer to is that animals are 'unclean' and therefore should not be used for transplantation into human beings.[61] Having very briefly outlined these arguments, the Kennedy Report concludes that 'these arguments depend on beliefs which not everyone shares and which cannot be established beyond doubt'.[62]

This cursory consideration is followed by consideration of whether xenotransplantation is unacceptable because it is unnatural.[63] Of course, it could be countered that much of medicine – if not all of medicine – is 'unnatural' in that its primary aim is to defeat the diseases which nature inflicts on human beings. The Kennedy Report adds to this argument that '... any conclusion as to whether a transplantation is or is not "natural" will not prevent the need to examine the various arguments which suggest that xenotransplantation may bring more harm than good'.[64]

Having dispensed with these two arguments, the Report then turns its attention to what is arguably one of the major concerns in ethical terms; namely the issue of animal welfare or animal rights. The Report is careful not to preclude the possibility that animals are worthy of consideration, but even though it is conceded that animals

58 Ibid.

59 P. 6, para. 1.15.

60 P. 60, para. 4.7.

61 Ibid.

62 Ibid.

63 Pp. 60–61, paras 4.8–4.11.

64 P. 61, para. 4.11.

may have rights, these rights are not held to be absolute, nor indeed are they necessarily more significant than those which human beings may have. As the Report says:

> ... if animals are to be said to have rights it can only be in the sense of claims (as distinct from powers, liberties or immunities). The essential claim will be to have their interests considered. If this position is accepted we are granting or recognising in animals moral rights (although of course these moral rights may become legal rights if they are recognised by a system of law). Presumably, the animal interests which rights would principally protect would be that (sic) of protecting and preserving animal life and having animal suffering minimised.[65]

Therefore, from the perspective of the Report, the claim of animals to be:

> ... free from suffering must weigh in any assessment of the benefits and harms of any proposed course of action. They have a right to consideration. The extent of this right will vary according to the capacity which the animal has for suffering, and clearly higher primates have greater capacity than lower animals, and human beings have greatest of all ... we consider that animals have rights in this minimal sense.[66]

However, the claim that animals have minimal rights does not clarify exactly what these rights would encapsulate. The Report concludes that they certainly do not encapsulate the right not to be used for xenotransplantation, but cautions that they may not be 'so used in circumstances which violate unjustifiably the minimum rights they may have'.[67]

Like the Nuffield Report, the Kennedy Report then turns its attention to the question of whether or not it would be appropriate to use non-human primates for xenotransplantation. In what must be said to be a somewhat inconsistent argument, the Report concludes of non-human primates:

> We consider that these animals can be distinguished from other animals not least by virtue of their greater self-awareness and mental capacity. We consider that these features increase their capacity for suffering, particularly given the conditions under which source animals would be kept in order to ensure proper controls (e.g. biosecure and isolated accommodation). To use them for xenotransplantation would therefore, in our view, constitute too great an infringement of their right to be free from suffering.
>
> **We therefore conclude that it would be ethically unacceptable to use primates as source animals for xenotransplantation, not least because they would be exposed to too much suffering.**[68]

In making this statement the Advisory Group appears to prioritize the suffering which would be endured by primates if they were to be used as source animals for xenotransplantation. However, the Report continues to state that:

---

65 P. 63, para. 4.17.

66 P. 64, para. 4.22.

67 P. 64, para. 4.26.

68 P. 64, para. 4.28, emphasis in the original.

> A primate used for research purposes may (indirectly) provide benefit for a large number of humans, due to the information generated from the research. Thus, the ratio of benefit to humans against harm to the primate may provide an ethical basis for the use of primates in research. By contrast, a primate used as a source animal could only benefit one or at best a very small number of humans ...
>
> **We conclude that it would be ethically acceptable to use primates in research into xenotransplantation, but only where no alternative method of obtaining information exists and this use should be limited so far as is possible.**[69]

The prohibition on the use of primates as source animals recommended by the Advisory Group was expressed in a manner that suggested its primary, if not sole, concern was the capacity of primates to suffer. However, its judgement that primates can be used in xenotransplantation research seems to owe more to the extent to which they may be valuable for human beings, rather than *in fact* being about suffering.

The Kennedy Report is much more sanguine about the use of pigs as source animals for xenotransplantation. In line with the conclusions of the Nuffield Report, the Report concludes that – although pigs may be exposed to harm as a result of their involvement in xenotransplantation – this harm is not 'so unjustifiable as to make the use of the pig unacceptable in principle'.[70] Instead, they say:

> ... as regards the pig, the issue is one of balancing the rights of the pig to be free from harm, as we understand them, against the rights of the human who, as we have seen, could benefit from xenotransplantation. The ethical acceptability of the use of the pig then becomes a matter of balancing the potential benefits, which we have already outlined, against the human harm involved ... and reaching a view.[71]

In passing, this does raise the question as to whether or not this balancing act would need to take account of whether or not human beings have inflicted the condition, as a result of which they need xenotransplantation, upon themselves. For example, would it become impermissible to use pig organs for someone who has ruined their liver by excessive alcohol consumption? If the entire issue hinges on the balancing of risks and benefits, then it does seem to leave the door open to a calculation of whether or not either the pig or the individual should either suffer the harm or receive the benefits.

The Report then turns its attention to the question of transgenesis. Noting that not all xenotransplantation requires genetic modification,[72] they nonetheless agree that genetically modified animals are more likely to be used in the future, in an attempt to prevent the human immune system from rejecting any transplanted organs.[73] As we have already seen, the question of genetic modification of animals is one which has caused some concern. The Kennedy Report's response to this concern is as follows:

---

69 P. 65, para. 4.29, emphasis in the original.

70 P. 65, para. 4.30.

71 Ibid.

72 P. 67, para. 4.33.

73 Ibid.

> The current procedure for genetically modifying pigs by the addition of genes has not seemed to cause the pigs any physical harm. The pigs do not appear to recognise themselves as anything but pigs. Furthermore, the pigs do not look like anything but a pig. The current transgenic pigs, modified and bred for xenotransplantation would, therefore, seem to have all the actions, reactions and habits of a 'normal pig'. We take the view that some degree of genetic modification is ethically acceptable providing that there is a concomitant benefit to humans and that the pig neither suffers unduly nor ceases recognisably to be a pig.[74]

After what might appear to be a somewhat cursory consideration of the potential harm to animals, and in particular pigs, the Report turns its attention to the potential of harm for human recipients. One concern that is discussed briefly is the question of whether or not the distinction between humans and animals might 'break down'[75] given the genetic modification of the source animals. As they say, '[a]n anxiety about the human/animal divide has been a constant theme in the history of human culture ...'.[76] However, the Committee does not believe that the extent of the genetic modification which is contemplated at present would go beyond any limits which might be regarded as acceptable. In particular, its view is that the ethical acceptability of xenotransplants depends more on the function which the transplanted tissue would perform than on the extent to which it is genetically modified by human genes.[77] However, it does not rule out the possibility that future developments might raise concerns of this sort and recommends that any future developments should be carefully monitored to evaluate whether or not they exceed acceptable limits.[78]

There are three major types of risk that the Report identifies for human subjects. These are:

> (i) The risk that the tissue will not function physiologically once transplanted and the consequence of possible harm caused to the tissue recipient should the tissue not function normally. This is of particular, but not exclusive, relevance to the transplant of solid organs.
> (ii) The risk of the organ or tissue being rejected and the risk to the tissue recipient of an excessive immunosuppressive regimen which may be needed to prevent rejection but which also increases the risk of infection and possibly cancers.
> (iii) The risk of infection transmitted from the source animal to a) human tissue recipients and b) their contacts in the wider population.[79]

While concluding that research into these possible risks should continue, and that further analysis of the results of this research should be undertaken, the Kennedy Committee concluded that at present there is insufficient evidence about any of these three possible risks to justify the move to clinical trials.[80] In addition, in

---

74 P. 67, para. 4.36.
75 P. 68, para. 4.42.
76 Ibid.
77 Pp. 68–69, para. 4.43.
78 P. 69, para. 4.44.
79 P. 69, para. 4.46.
80 Pp. 69–70, para. 4.47.

specific relation to the second and third concerns mentioned above, it again feels that the evidence about the possibility of rejection is insufficiently robust at the moment to justify moving to clinical trials. However, the Committee does feel that there is a justification for further research being carried out.[81]

One of the major concerns about xenotransplantation is, of course, the possibility that infection may spread from animal to recipient, and thence to the population as a whole. The Committee concludes that the risks of certain kinds of infection associated with xenotransplantation would be ethically acceptable, citing 'fungi, parasites, bacteria and prions, provided that source animals are maintained in conditions which aim to minimise the risk of infection and provided that the infections which arise are monitored'.[82] However, the Report also takes account of the fact that it would only be possible at present positively to identify and diagnose the presence of prions after death.[83] It was, therefore, further recommended that in respect of 'prion-related disease there should be a programme of culling of sentinel pigs over a wide age range to test for neuropathological changes'.[84] The Report concludes that, because of the lack of available information about the viruses which might be spread between animals and humans, it is inappropriate to proceed to clinical trials at this stage.[85] Given the potential known and unknown risk of the spread of infectious agents, the Committee was forced to ask whether it would ever be appropriate to use xenotransplantation. The Committee consideres that:

> ... there will be a stage at which researchers will have done as much as possible to learn about infectious risks associated with xenotransplantation but that, even at this point, unknowns will still remain.[86]

Notwithstanding this, however, the Report concludes that:

> ... at the stage where it is considered that a full investigation of potential infection risks has been carried out, and the risks have been shown to be within tolerable margins, it would be ethical to proceed. This is subject to there being a system in place to monitor the emergence of any unusual disease or any unknown pathogens and to require, as a consequence, that appropriate additional research be completed in a proper fashion.[87]

Interestingly, the Committee also believes that the issues surrounding animal welfare will not simply disappear if and when it appears that the scientific merit of xenotransplantation has been established. For example, the Committee recommends that the sequential removal of solid organs is ethically unacceptable,[88] as is the sequential removal of any tissue.[89]

---

81 P. 70, para. 4.50.
82 Pp. 71–72, para. 4.55.
83 P. 72, para. 4.56.
84 Ibid.
85 P. 72, para. 4.58.
86 P. 74, para. 4.63.
87 Ibid.
88 P. 80, para. 4.93.
89 P. 80, para. 4.94.

The Report then turns to the interests of patients or potential recipients of xenografts. As it seems likely that the first recipients of xenotransplants will be those potentially most at risk, and therefore most vulnerable, the Report concludes that a number of vitally important considerations must be taken into consideration. It therefore concentrates on a number of issues. These comprise the selection of appropriate patients, issues surrounding consent and information provision, matters concerning confidentiality and privacy, and the position of patients who refuse xenotransplantation.

Agreeing with the Nuffield Committee that children should not be included in trials, at least initially,[90] they also hold that neither should those adults who are incapable of providing a legally valid consent.[91] Equally, those who are so ill that they are unlikely to benefit from the clinical trials of xenotransplantation should also be excluded.[92]

The central platform of the Kennedy Report's attitude to clinical trials in this area is based on the concept of these trials as being therapeutic rather than non-therapeutic.[93] In other words, trials should not take place unless there is some reason to believe that the patients involved might benefit. For that reason, the selection criteria for suitable patients become doubly important. For the moment, the Report concludes that it is not possible to provide any real guidance as to how judgements about which patients should benefit from xenotransplantation in the early stages should be made.[94] However, if it were possible to deduce that xenotransplantation trials were indeed beneficial, then it may be that questions concerning patient selection would become substantially clinical rather than ethical.[95]

The second consideration in this part of the Kennedy Report relates to the provision of consent to involvement in a clinical trial. Once the patient has been selected for inclusion, then in the view of the Kennedy Report the general legal and ethical rules which apply to all human experimentation or research would be equally applicable in xenotransplantation trials.[96] The question of consent is described in the report as 'an exceptionally complex concept from both an ethical and legal standpoint'.[97] However, the Report identifies a number of issues which it regards as being of particular significance in any consent arrangements in respect of xenotransplantation trials. First, they recommend that consent should always be sought.[98] Interestingly, given their earlier comments about using those who are otherwise incompetent, they also include in the requirement for the obtaining of consent a recognition of the importance of the views of those closest to an adult who is otherwise incapable of consenting.[99] This at first sight would appear to contradict

90 P. 112, para. 7.7.

91 Ibid.

92 P. 112, para. 7.6.

93 P. 112, para. 7.5.

94 P. 113, para. 7.9.

95 Ibid.

96 P. 113, para. 7.10.

97 P. 113, para. 7.11.

98 Ibid.

99 Ibid.

their earlier position that such persons should not be used in xenotransplantation trials.

In the search for a truly informed consent, it would also be necessary that intended recipients were informed about the current status of xenotransplantation, including information about the research that has been undertaken, any procedures which have previously been carried out and their success.[100] The problems of immunology and physiology and the potential risks of infection must also be made known.[101] Moreover, patients should also be informed of the alternatives to xenotransplantation, including the likelihood of the patient concerned actually receiving benefit from any alternative programmes, such as human-to-human transplantation.[102] The Report is also concerned that, for a consent to be valid, information must be provided that would allow people to make decisions which take account of their own personal preferences. Therefore, information about the source of the tissue, the way in which the tissue has been preserved and modified and any suffering which it is thought might have been caused to the animals should also form part of the disclosure process. In particular, disclosure should include any information which might be specific to certain types of tissue, for example brain tissue, where people might be concerned that personality could be affected.[103] Finally, the potential recipient should be informed of any psychological and social effects that xenotransplantation might have.[104]

As the Report concedes, the obtaining of consent in routine medical circumstances is not unproblematic. It is, almost by definition, much more difficult to obtain a meaningful and valid consent in circumstances where much of the information being disclosed is information about uncertainty.[105] Thus, the Report concludes that it will be necessary to institute a system of counselling, so that potential recipients of xenotransplants can be counselled in advance of involvement in any clinical trial or established xenotransplantation programme. This counselling should be independent of the transplant team.[106] In conclusion of this section, the Report emphasizes the need for those who refuse or do not opt for xenotransplantation to be dealt with without any penalty being imposed in respect of their medical care.[107]

In respect of matters of confidentiality and privacy, the Committee notes that there is likely to be considerable media and other interest in any person who has undergone a xenograft.[108] Additionally, it is clear that if the monitoring of xenotransplantation is to be carried out effectively, there will be a requirement for certain information about the progress of the patient to be stored and checked.[109] As

100 Ibid.
101 Ibid.
102 Ibid.
103 Ibid.
104 Ibid.
105 P. 114, para. 7.13.
106 Ibid.
107 P. 115, para. 7.15.
108 P. 115, para. 7.17.
109 Ibid.

the Kennedy Report suggests, this is part of the information which must be provided to a potential recipient in advance of seeking their agreement. Of particular relevance to xenotransplantation is, of course, that, unlike many other medical treatments, relatives and others may also be affected by the fact that someone has had a xenograft. For example, if any infection does transfer between the source animal and the recipient, then relatives and close contacts may run the risk of also being infected. And, as the Kennedy Report points out, at least in the early stages when the success of xenotransplantation is unknown, 'they have the emotional burden of having a loved one undergoing major surgery with uncertain outcomes'.[110] Therefore, relatives will have an ongoing interest in the information gathered from xenotransplantation, even should the recipient subsequently die. The needs of relatives, as well as the individual recipient, must, in the view of the Kennedy Report, therefore be addressed.[111]

The Report then turns its attention to the interests of the professionals involved in xenotransplantation trials or programmes. A wide range of individual professionals may be involved in this process; both those who are involved with the rearing of the animal and those who are involved with the care of the human patients. The Report suggests that '[x]enotransplantation demands that those who work with the source animals have regard to the needs of health care professionals and that health care professionals understand certain aspects of the source animals breeding and raising'.[112] In the view of the Committee, this requires consideration of the relationships between the various professionals involved, including training and identification of the appropriate roles of the professions involved.[113] Equally, the Committee recognizes the probability of a diversity of views amongst those who are involved in this procedure as professionals.[114] Not only, therefore, should patients or prospective patients be permitted to opt out of xenotransplantation, but in the view of the Committee so too should professionals.[115]

Finally, like the Report of the Nuffield Council, the Kennedy Report recommends the establishment of a national body to regulate the development of xenotransplantation.[116] The Kennedy Report suggests that the fact that there are no legislative provisions that delimit or constrain the use of human subjects in experiments makes the formation of such a body particularly important.[117] Thus, while it acknowledges that an informal network of local and multi-centre ethics committees exists, it concludes that:

> ... in view of the complexity of the issues presented by xenotransplantation, we are persuaded that trials should not be left only to local consideration and that proposals for clinical trials of xenotransplantation should be considered by a national body.[118]

---

110 P. 116, para. 7.19.
111 P. 116, para. 7.20.
112 P. 116, para. 7.22.
113 P. 117, para. 7.25.
114 P. 116, para. 7.22.
115 P. 117, para. 7.26.
116 See pp. 141–146.
117 P. 135, para. 8.68.
118 Pp. 136–137, para. 8.74.

The Kennedy Report also views the formation of a National Standing Committee as the best way to ensure that its other recommendations are implemented.[119] In the following chapter we will examine the remit and work of the body which was formed at the behest of the Kennedy Report – The United Kingdom Xenotransplantation Interim Regulatory Authority (UKXIRA) – in more detail. However, here it will be useful to consider the responsibilities that the Kennedy Report recommends the Standing Committee should discharge, when created.

The Report recommends that the Standing Committee should have responsibility for the 'setting of standards for continued research into and, if appropriate, the introduction of xenotransplantation'.[120] The Report also suggests that the Committee should have responsibility for ensuring that the standards it sets are implemented.[121] More specifically, in terms of standard setting, the Kennedy Report recommends that the Standing Committee should advise on research that needs to be conducted on infection risks, immunology and physiology.[122] On the basis of the data it receives the Standing Committee would decide:

> ... whether conditions had been met so as to permit clinical trials in xenotransplantation and, if appropriate, the introduction of a therapeutic programme.[123]

Other tasks that the Kennedy Report recommends the Standing Committee should conduct as part of its responsibility to set standards centre on the need to minimize the risk of animal diseases being transmitted to human transplant recipients. Hence, the Report states that the Standing Committee should be responsible for formulating measures to minimize the transmission of disease from a transplant recipient to the wider population.[124] This task requires the creation of biosecurity conditions for the rearing of animals and methods for removing tissue from source animals.[125] It is also recommended that long-term surveillance measures are put in place to monitor individuals who receive animal tissue and the creation of a 'mechanism to discontinue any therapeutic programme if necessary'.[126] Finally, as part of its responsibility to set standards the Kennedy Report suggests that the Standing Committee should liaise with 'appropriate professional groups'.[127]

In respect of its responsibility to ensure the standards it sets are implemented, the Kennedy Report recommends that the Standing Committee: liaise with the Home Office over research on animals;[128] monitor and (under legislation) license clinical sites and animal facilities.[129] Finally, it is recommended that the Standing Committee, under a statutory licensing system, develop 'methods of approving

119 P. 141, para. 9.3.
120 Ibid.
121 Ibid.
122 P. 141f, para. 9.3, 1.
123 Ibid.
124 P. 142, para. 9.3, 2.
125 P. 142, para. 9.3, 2–3.
126 P. 142, para. 9.3, 4.
127 P. 142, para. 9.3, 5.
128 P. 142, para. 9.3, 6.
129 P. 142, para. 9.3, 7–8.

those who propose to undertake xenotransplantation procedures involving humans'.[130]

The Kennedy Report also requires a number of 'additional functions' and 'executive functions' of the Standing Committee:[131] namely, that it provides 'advice to Health Ministers on the safety and efficacy' of xenotransplantation;[132] keeps under review national and international developments in xenotransplantation and offers advice on developments that may cause concern.[133] The Standing Committee's final 'additional function' as recommended by the Kennedy Report is:

> ... advising on such issues as arrangements for consent, confidentiality, appropriate groups of patients to be offered xenotransplantation and monitoring of the psychological effects of xenotransplantation.[134]

The 'executive functions', which the Kennedy Report recommends should be performed by the Standing Committee, include maintaining a database of information on individuals who receive transplants of animal tissue and of source animals,[135] and inspecting clinical sites and animal facilities.[136]

It is important to note that the Kennedy Report recommends that the National Standing Committee should perform all of these tasks within a statutory framework.[137] However, it appreciates that a packed Parliamentary timetable will make it difficult to quickly make the Standing Committee a statutory body.[138] Hence, the Kennedy Report proposes:

> ... as an interim measure only, that our recommendations, particularly with regard to the National Standing Committee, are taken forward on a non-statutory basis until such a time as legislation can be brought forward. Such an interim body should not be regarded as a substitute for legislation not least because many of our recommendations are dependent on the existence of the National Standing Committee as well as the fact that, more obviously, such a body will only operate by consent.[139]

By implication, it would be insufficient for a Committee with responsibility for overseeing the safe development of xenotransplantation to rely on the decisions of companies and individuals voluntarily to comply with or consent to the standards it produces. Despite this, no legislation to place UKXIRA on a statutory footing has yet seriously been made.

In light of the wide range of tasks that the Kennedy Report attributes to the Standing Committee, it will prove useful to summarize the fundamental

---

130 P. 143, para. 9.3, 9–10.

131 P. 144, para. 9.3, 11–14 and p. 144, para. 9.4.

132 P. 144, para. 9.3, 11.

133 P. 144, para. 9.3, 12–13.

134 P. 144, para. 9.3, 14.

135 P. 144, para. 9.4, a.

136 P. 144, para. 9.4, b.

137 P. 141, para. 9.1, 9.2.

138 P. 141, para. 9.2.

139 Ibid.

preconditions which the Committee would have to oversee. The Kennedy Report recommends:

> **... that only if the conditions which we have outlined are met could xenotransplantation be considered to be ethically acceptable.**
>
> The conditions include:
>
> - primates must not be used as a source animal for xenotransplantation. They may be used only in the limited circumstances of tissue recipients in research to develop xenotransplantation, and then only where no alternative method of obtaining the necessary information exists.
> - the limits to which xenotransplantation can be developed, both in terms of the genetic modification of the animal and in terms of the tissue which may be transplanted, must be monitored to assess possible effects and harm caused. Those charged with these developments should bear in mind the concerns we have outlined.
> - further evidence should be obtained on certain elements of risk to the potential tissue recipient and to the wider population. This would include further research on the risk relating to physiology, immunology, and infection. *In the current state of knowledge it is not acceptable to move to clinical trials involving humans.*
> - measures to minimise the risk of infection to the human recipient and to the wider population should be designed and put in place. These relate to the methods in which the source animals would be kept, the monitoring source animals would undergo and the methods which would be used to remove the tissue (that is, the production methods of the tissue). Measures should also be put in place to monitor observance of these measures.
> - systems designed to collect data on the source animals used and the human patients involved in xenotransplantation should be designed and put into operation. The data and, where relevant, tissue samples to be collected should be agreed, after appropriate consultation, to ensure consistency.
> - the welfare of animals, compromised by the infection control measures which we consider to be necessary, should be protected so far as is possible.
> - the sequential removal of tissue from source animals should be forbidden.
> - given that any therapeutic programme of xenotransplantation would make demands on the resources available to the NHS, the National Specialist Commissioning Advisory Group should consider the purchase of the various xenotransplantation services.
> - given the recognition that the effects of xenotransplantation could extend to other therapies which exist or are being developed, attention must continue to be given to allotransplantation and any other new or existing therapy which could meet the needs of patients.[140]

The Standing Committee is charged with ensuring that all of these conditions have been met before xenotransplantation can be considered acceptable. In the following chapter we will consider how UKXIRA has gone about attempting to address these issues and meet these responsibilities. However, we will first critically assess the contribution of the Nuffield and Kennedy Reports to the development of animal to human transplantation in the United Kingdom.

---

140 P. 105f, para. 6.2–6.3.

A Critique of the Nuffield and Kennedy Reports

Perhaps unsurprisingly, some aspects of the approach taken by the two Reports have been subject to a certain amount of criticism. However, there has been wide agreement on the need for the provision of an adequate consent and support for the recommendations relating to counselling and the quality of information disclosure. Equally, it appears that there has been unanimous support for a national standing body, which now exists in the United Kingdom in the shape of the United Kingdom Xenotransplantation Interim Regulatory Authority (UKXIRA).[141] However, it has been suggested by some commentators that both Reports have underplayed some of the negative aspects of xenotransplantation, while at the same time emphasizing the positive.[142] Fox and McHale, for example, would take issue with the very premise that underpins both the Nuffield and the Kennedy Reports. As they say:

> We have followed the Kennedy and Nuffield reports in using the chronic shortage of human organs as a starting point for discussion, but are conscious that a major problem with structuring discussion in this way is that it inevitably skews the terms of the debate. In consequence, human needs are rendered paramount and both reports are essentially premised on satisfying what are represented as pressing human needs. The upshot is that the debate as played out in the Kennedy and Nuffield reports is bounded and some of the most troubling moral issues are obscured.[143]

Additionally, they note that – as conceded by both Committees – it is unlikely that a consensus will be reached on the ethical issues raised by the development of xenotransplantation.[144] Whether or not this ought to be fatal to the development of animal to human transplantation is, however, a different question. In addition, for Fox and McHale, there is significance in the fact that trials of xenotransplantation to date have been unsuccessful. As they say:

> ... since the early 1960s over 30 organs have been transplanted from nonhuman animals to humans, without a single organ recipient being able to return to a normal life, or even survive the operation for more than a month or two.[145]

Whether or not this continues to be of significance will of course depend on scientific progress being made. In a general sense, the acceptability of xenotransplantation may still hinge on the success or failure of alternative schemes for obtaining organs for transplantation. As Clark says:

> High profile national campaigns to increase the supply of available donor organs have not had much success. The interesting dynamic is that families give consent in only half the cases where a dying or dead patient has previously given permission to have organs

---

[141] For a discussion of the work of UKXIRA, see chapter 4, below.

[142] Fox, M. and McHale, J. (1998), 'Xenotransplantation: The Legal and Ethical Ramifications', *Medical Law Review*, **6** (1), pp. 42–61, at p. 42.

[143] Fox and McHale (1998), at p. 44.

[144] Ibid., at p. 60.

[145] Ibid.

donated. And yet, more people claim they would allow an organ donation from a dying relative. Over 50 per cent of Americans say they are designated organ donors.[146]

On the other hand, Vanderpool would argue that:

> ... a moratorium on xenotransplantation research for the sake of public debate over easily exaggerated medical and infectious disease risks is unwarranted. This does not mean that extensive public discussion and debate is not warranted ... This can and should be done without a moratorium that cripples its progress.[147]

As has been said, much of the content of the Kennedy and Nuffield Reports rests on the question of animal welfare and animal rights. Fox and McHale are highly critical of the Kennedy Report's approach to animal suffering saying that 'the failure to explore the moral implications of pain is significant, given the report's endorsement of suffering as the relevant moral criterion'.[148] In particular they highlight the Kennedy Report's arguably intuitive conclusion in respect of the use of primates for xenotransplants. As they say:

> ... adopting the criterion of ability to suffer as the relevant moral consideration renders it unconvincing to then *presume*, without adducing any evidence, that primates have a higher capacity for pain than other animals, when so much depends upon this assumption.[149]

Other commentators are equally concerned about the justifications provided for the use of pigs as source animals for xenotransplantation. Taking account of the criticism made by Fox and McHale of the use of unknowable pain thresholds in animals as the basis for excluding primates and including other animals, Hughes also notes that one of the arguments sometimes tendered to support the use of pigs as source animals is that these are animals already reared and killed for food.[150] However, as Hughes points out:

> ... since the animal harms as well as the human benefits of xenotransplantation may be greater than those of meat eating, a simple inference from the permissibility of the latter to the permissibility of the former will be invalid.[151]

Additionally, although both Reports pay considerable attention to the question of whether or not animals have rights, or perhaps simply strong interests, they conclude that any such rights will not, except in the case of primates because of pain, be sufficient to justify their non-use in xenotransplantation. Some

---

146 Clark, M.A. (1999), 'This Little Piggy Went to Market: The Xenotransplantation and Xenozoonosis Debate', *Journal of Law, Medicine and Ethics*, **27**, pp. 137–152, at p. 137.

147 Vanderpool, H.Y. (1999b), 'Commentary: A Critique of Clark's Frightening Xenotransplantation Scenario', *Journal of Law, Medicine and Ethics*, **27**, pp. 153–157, at p. 156.

148 Fox and McHale (1998), at p. 46.

149 Ibid., at p. 47.

150 Hughes, J. (1998), 'Xenografting: Ethical Issues', *Journal of Medical Ethics*, **24**, pp. 18–24.

151 Ibid., at p. 23.

commentators are unhappy about that conclusion. Garwood-Gowers, for example, argues that there is a reasonable critique to be made of both Reports' consideration of animal welfare and animal suffering issues.[152]

For Fox and McHale '[o]ther ethical concerns, not directly linked to the status of animals, are canvassed even less adequately'.[153] They note, for example, that in the Kennedy Report objections which stem from religious beliefs are dealt with very briefly;[154] thus, a consideration which for many might be felt to be particularly important is effectively dismissed because of its lack of universality. Also, they are critical of the extent to which consideration is given in either Report to the blurring of boundaries between humans and other animals, and in particular whether or not it is legitimate to alter, perhaps irrevocably, the nature of the animals used as sources for xenotransplantation.[155]

Fox and McHale are also critical of the extent to which the Reports consider in sufficient depth a number of other issues, most notably legal issues, which would flow from xenotransplantation.[156] Additionally, although the Kennedy Report indicates that xenotransplantation should only proceed where it can be described as therapeutic research, and would therefore fall within the type of intervention to which people could legitimately consent, Fox and McHale question whether or not this is indeed likely to be the case. As they point out, there are restrictions on the types of harms to which people may lawfully consent, even in respect of private behaviour, never mind in respect of behaviour such as becoming a recipient of a xenotransplantation trial which would have considerable public as well as private implications.[157] For Fox and McHale:

> At least in the early years, xenotransplantation will be experimental in nature, and the nature of the risks are such that the legal validity of any purported consent may be questionable.[158]

Of course, the validity of consent may indeed hinge on the categorization of the trials as therapeutic or not. Arguably, if trials are therapeutic, then the limitations placed on the decision of private individuals to participate in them would be significantly reduced, if not totally obviated. However, it may be that it is not appropriate simply to accept that any such early trials would be purely or even primarily therapeutic, particularly given the range of uncertainties which would surround them. If, then, it is conceded that such trials – especially in their early stages – might more appropriately be seen as non-therapeutic, the question of whether or not people could indeed validly consent to the harm of involvement in them (irrespective of any potential benefits) is a question worth posing.

---

152 Garwood-Gowers, A. (1999), *Living Donor Organ Transplantation: Key Legal and Ethical Issues*, Ashgate: Aldershot.

153 Fox and McHale (1998), at p. 51.

154 Ibid.

155 Ibid.

156 Fox and McHale (1998), at pp. 57–58; for further discussion, see chapters 7 and 8, below.

157 Ibid., at p. 56.

158 Ibid.

Additionally, Fox and McHale raise the question of patenting. As they note, the law tends to regard animals as property, and therefore it may well be that attempts are made to patent genetically modified animals.[159] This question in some sense is slightly different from that as to the uses which may appropriately be made of animals, but it arguably reinforces the perception that animals are significantly less worthy of respect than humans, by legitimizing their commodification through commerce. Finally, Fox and McHale point to the fact that even were legal systems individually to regulate the development of xenotransplantation, and even were these jurisdictions to produce legal regimens which were thought by the majority of the population to be sufficiently stringent, there are transnational problems which might also arise.[160] Of course, this is a criticism which could be levelled at very many areas. For example, the regulations which describe and define the development of new pharmaceutical products are manifestly more strict in some countries than in others. Nonetheless, the fact that this is not a problem unique to xenotransplantation does not in any sense deny the validity of the critique, particularly as it seems probable that 'achieving global consensus on such issues is unlikely'.[161]

One of the most formidable tasks confronting those who must evaluate the possibilities and potential of xenotransplantation, as is true with the introduction of virtually any new medical technology, is calculating the risks and benefits likely to be associated with it. Arguably, however, in the case of xenotransplantation there is a need for an increased and enhanced observation and analysis of such potential risks and benefits. As Clark says:

> The medical risks to individual patients from xenotransplantation are formidable, as are the public health risks to society. These risks raise unprecedented and unanticipated ethical, legal, and psychological issues that will challenge even the most sophisticated professionals in these fields.[162]

Indeed, it may not be overstating the case to suggest that xenotransplantation is unique in the history of medical innovation. It is especially the potential problems associated with solid organ animal to human transplants – on which both Reports tend to focus – which point to the need for particularly sensitive and careful evaluation of xenotransplantation. Not only will the risks of xenotransplantation relate to the inherent potential limitations of animal organs, or to the possibility of the transmission of hitherto unknown diseases into the human population, but there may be psychological and emotional consequences of xenotransplantation which transcend even those which are known to arise in the case of allotransplants. As has been said:

> The emotional risks associated with xenotransplants are less well understood than the immunity or other clinical issues. Besides the stress of acute illness, radical treatments, and social issues, transplantation may tap deeper emotions that no one really understands

159 Fox and McHale (1998), at pp. 57–58.

160 Ibid., at p. 59.

161 Ibid.

162 Clark (1999), at p. 138.

... Recipients of allografts sometimes report emotional difficulty accepting a grafted organ ... How might these emotions surface when animal organs are transplanted?[163]

It is questions such as these that both Reports seek to address in their evaluation of the potential benefits and the potential harms of xenotransplantation. This risk-benefits calculation will be considered in more detail below, but as Vanderpool says:

> Risk/benefit determinations are a dominant feature in contemporary medico-ethical decision-making, and relate to both donors and recipients. Even where there are few or no harms attaching to the donor, there are generally perceived to be limits in terms of the extent to which it is legitimate to carry out highly experimental transplantation procedures, even with the full consent of the patient. Assuming such consent is freely given (problematic some would allege where the recipient might inevitably succumb without such an intervention) and with full knowledge of the known and unknown risks and consequences, there is an anticipated 'threshold of benefit' which must accompany the procedure.[164]

However, he also perceives some benefits which may derive from xenotransplantation should it become 'a customary feature of the transplant landscape'.[165] Not least, and assuming that the other fears surrounding xenotransplantation are proved to be groundless, he rightly points to the fact that xenotransplantation opens up the possibility that those who are currently not even considered for transplants – even though they might need one – because of the current shortage of human organs could become recipients of animal organs, thereby reducing the incredible toll on humanity of avoidable deaths.[166]

Conclusion

The Nuffield and Kennedy Reports on xenotransplantation stress the extent to which it is unlikely that a consensus on the ethics of xenotransplantation can easily be reached. There are many powerful emotional and other arguments against xenotransplantation that it would be difficult to refute. Equally, perhaps most importantly for those not opposed to xenotransplantation and in urgent need of life-saving treatment, there are strong interests in the development of a safe xenotransplantation programme. What seems lacking, however, is the mechanism which would permit the kind of full and informed public debate which each of the Reports believes to be of importance. As Clark says:

> All those involved in developing this technology agree that more public debate on moral and ethical issues needs to occur, but no one seems to know exactly how to make that happen.[167]

---

[163] Ibid., at p. 140.

[164] Vanderpool (1999b), at p. 11.

[165] Ibid., at p. 5.

[166] Ibid.

[167] Clark (1999), at p. 137.

To an extent, and this will be explored in the next chapter, the Government's acceptance of the need to establish a regulatory authority provides some kind of forum for the debate to be held. However, in addition to the need for public debate on the ethical issues presented by animal to human transplantation, there is a range of scientific, psychological, practical and public health concerns on which more information is needed.

Chapter 4

The Regulation of Xenotransplantation in the United Kingdom: The Work of UKXIRA

Introduction

This chapter will assess the regulatory initiatives that have taken place in the United Kingdom since the publication of the reports by the Nuffield Council and the Advisory Group on the Ethics of Xenotransplantation. The focus here is on the work of the United Kingdom Xenotransplantation Interim Regulatory Authority (UKXIRA) which was founded in 1997 following the recommendation of the Kennedy Report.[1] The assessment of UKXIRA's work will address the question as to how it has endeavoured to fulfil both the recommendations made by the Kennedy Report and those contained in its own terms of reference.

The Role of UKXIRA, Its Terms of Reference and Methods of Working

UKXIRA's terms of reference, as they appear in its *First Annual Report*, state that its role is:[2]

> To advise the Secretaries of State of the UK Health Departments on the action necessary to regulate xenotransplantation, taking into account the principles outlined in *Animal Tissue into Humans*, and world-wide developments in xenotransplantation. In particular to advise:
>
> a. on safety, efficacy and considerations of animal welfare and any other preconditions for xenotransplantation for human use, and whether these have been met;[3]
> b. on research required to assess safety and efficacy factors in xenotransplantation procedures;
> c. on the acceptability of specific applications to proceed with xenotransplantation in humans; and
> d. to provide a focal point on xenotransplantation issues within the government.[4]

---

[1] The Kennedy Report (Report of the Advisory Group on the Ethics of Xenotransplantation) (1997), *Animal Tissue into Humans*, HMSO: London.

[2] United Kingdom Xenotransplantation Interim Regulatory Authority (UKXIRA) (1998a), *First Annual Report May 1997 – August 1998*, Department of Health; London.

[3] This is a revised version of UKXIRA's original terms of reference in which the first sub-point did not include any explicit reference to animal welfare.

[4] UKXIRA (1998a), at p. 24.

Although UKXIRA's terms of reference provide it with a fairly broad mandate, many of its responsibilities concern the need to ensure that animal to human transplantation is developed safely in the United Kingdom. The Kennedy Report called for a variety of measures that impacted on the safety of the procedure and UKXIRA's terms of reference seek to respond to these recommendations.[5] Thus, amongst UKXIRA's most important responsibilities is the requirement to put in place mechanisms to minimize and monitor the risk of animal infections spreading to individuals and the general population. This requires it to develop ways to monitor the safety of the animal tissue that is to be transplanted, individuals who receive transplants and the wider community in which these individuals live. As its terms of reference show, it is also responsible for assessing the suitability of applications to conduct clinical trials. It is important to note that efforts to produce regulatory frameworks to perform these tasks not only have to be pragmatically beneficial, but ethically and legally acceptable. This is a requirement to which the chapter will return later.

One pressing task for the newly created Authority has been to provide information on the physiological, immunological and infection risks posed by xenotransplantation. The significance of this responsibility rests on the fact that the failure to provide data to show that the risks in these spheres are at acceptable levels would mean, according to the Kennedy Report upon which UKXIRA's work is based, that xenotransplantation is unethical and should not proceed to clinical trials.[6] Of course, it could be argued that a preliminary review of the ethical and legal questions should have been amongst UKXIRA's first tasks. However, it seems that the view taken was that these had been adequately covered by the Kennedy report. We will examine UKXIRA's position on the ethical assessment of xenotransplantation later in this chapter.

This chapter will consider the ways in which UKXIRA has sought to fulfil its regulatory role. This will be accomplished by focusing on two areas of the Authority's work. Initially the chapter will consider the ways in which UKXIRA has addressed the need to generate greater knowledge and certainty on the risks presented by animal to human transplantation. The regulatory procedures that UKXIRA has established will then be examined. This approach is not intended to record all of the activities in which UKXIRA has been involved since its creation, but rather to outline some of its central initiatives. The final section of the chapter will critically assess UKXIRA's work.

Information Gathering

Porcine Endogenous Retrovirus Workshop

One of UKXIRA's earliest endeavours to generate a sound information base on the infection risks associated with xenotransplantation took the form of a workshop

---

5 Kennedy Report (1997), at p. 105f.

6 Ibid.

held in August 1998 on Porcine Endogenous Retroviruses (PERVs).[7] The workshop had two objectives:

- To assess whether the available information on PERVs answers key questions.
- To identify whether there is further pre-clinical research that could usefully be carried out – and if so, where priorities for research lie.[8]

More specifically, the questions that the workshop set out to address included whether: there is any breed of pig that does not have PERVs; it would ever be possible to breed PERVs out of pigs; there are any analogies that help us to know, if PERVs were transmitted to humans, whether they would cause infection and how severe the infection would be; any pre-clinical research could be devised to help answer these questions.[9]

It was concluded that all breeds of pigs appear to have PERVs and that, if it were possible to remove these retroviruses from porcine material, it would take at least ten years to accomplish this.[10] In respect of the potential impact of PERVs on humans, the workshop concluded only that it 'might be feasible to model the effects' of the retrovirus on humans.[11] In his treatment of this issue at the workshop, Robin Weiss reported that the limited information available at this time failed to show that these retroviruses were transmitted to humans.[12] Weiss also stressed that, should PERVs be transmitted to humans, this would not necessarily mean that the virus would become pathogenic. However, if the retrovirus became pathogenic, the most likely diseases to emerge would include: leukaemia, lymphoma, sarcoma, immunodeficiency, anaemia, motor neurone disease and osteopetrosis.[13] Weiss went on to acknowledge that the need of some individuals for a transplant may be so great that they would find it acceptable to risk the possibility of an animal retrovirus being transmitted to them if the transplant promised to improve their quality or length of life. However, he concluded that:

> It is the onward spread that matters. I suspect that if this type of C-type retrovirus took hold in an immuno-suppressed patient that the transmission route would be parenteral and possibly sexual transmission.[14]

Based on its inconclusive findings, participants at the workshop agreed that there were a number of areas on which more research should be conducted before moving to clinical trials.[15] These included the possibility of developing vaccines,

---

7 United Kingdom Xenotransplantation Interim Regulatory Authority (UKXIRA) (1998b), *Report of the Workshop on Porcine Endogenous Retroviruses*, 6 August, Department of Health: London.

8 Ibid., at p. 7.

9 Ibid.

10 Ibid., at p. 38.

11 Ibid., at p. 39.

12 Ibid., at p. 32.

13 Ibid.

14 Ibid., at p. 34.

15 Ibid., at p. 37.

epidemiological studies of abattoir workers, computer modelling of viruses and further work in cell culture to help understand the potential expression of PERVs.[16] The workshop's conclusions were understandably tentative. However, its effort to consider pragmatic issues such as the direction of future research, and the relationship between research and when it would be appropriate to move to clinical trials, was undoubtedly beneficial.

UKXIRA also endeavoured to provide more information about the potential impact of PERVs on humans by seeking advice on the infectious disease risks that could be associated with xenotransplantation procedures from a sub-group of the Advisory Committee on Dangerous Pathogens (ACDP). The report of the group, received in August 1998, also suggested that at that time there was insufficient knowledge of PERVs to determine which xenotransplantation procedures posed the greatest risk of transmitting infections. More specifically, it was not thought possible at this stage to 'differentiate between the infection risks posed by different procedures'.[17]

Literature Reviews

In its first year of work, UKXIRA also began to investigate the possibility of conducting a more detailed systematic literature review on various aspects of xenotransplantation.[18] The Authority explained:

> Another example of UKXIRA's desire to have access to the best available evidence was the decision to establish a Systematic Literature Review on certain aspects of xenotransplantation. This will concentrate initially on physiology, immunology and infectious disease. It is likely to be some months before there are any results from this Review ...[19]

After discussions with the Research and Development Directorate of the Department of Health, it was agreed that a review of this type would be commissioned but would include two different pieces of work. The first would address infection risks and immunology and the second, the ethical and legal issues raised by animal to human transplantation.[20] In fact, by 2001 UKXIRA had commissioned three separate literature reviews: one on infection risks, another on physiology and a review on ethics and law.[21]

The first review published by UKXIRA was *Infection Risks in Xenotransplantation*.[22] In his Foreword to the review, UKXIRA's then Chairman, Lord Habgood, noted that:

---

[16] Ibid.

[17] UKXIRA (1999a), *Second Annual Report September 1998 – August 1999*, Department of Health: London, p. 21.

[18] UKXIRA (1998a), p. 5, para. 1.5.

[19] Ibid.

[20] UKXIRA (1999a), p. 21.

[21] UKXIRA (2001), *Third Annual Report September 1999 – November 2000*, Department of Health: London, p. 10.

[22] Griffin, G. and Muir, D. (2001), *Infection Risks in Xenotransplantation*, Department of Health: London.

> The advice that the UK Xenotransplantation Interim Regulatory Authority (UKXIRA) is able to offer government on xenotransplantation is dependent on keeping abreast of developments in the field ... This document is the first review and has been produced primarily to assist the UKXIRA in its role as the regulatory body responsible for xenotransplantation matters in the UK.[23]

As Lord Habgood suggested, the use of accurate, up to date information is crucial to the regulatory actions of a body like UKXIRA.[24] However, it should also be recalled that the Kennedy Report regarded the need to obtain more evidence on 'the risk relating to physiology, immunology and infection' to be a precondition for the ethical acceptability of xenotransplantation in its own right.[25] A failure to provide such data would mean that it remains unacceptable to proceed to clinical trials.[26] Thus, UKXIRA should also be actively assessing whether such preconditions are fulfilled and whether xenotransplantation can proceed at all.

Infection Risk Review

Infection Risks in Xenotransplantation surveys a vast amount of literature on known viruses, prions, endogenous retroviruses, bacteria, parasites and fungi that are associated with transferring animal tissue into humans.[27] It also considers the potential impact of infections that are currently unknown.[28] The work only considers the risks associated with porcine tissue because it notes that the use of non-human primates is 'now recognised as being unacceptable for a number of reasons, including technical, ethical and safety issues'.[29] The review notes that while viruses are widely thought to pose the greatest risk:

> ... there is currently a lack of information about the infectious potential of a number of porcine organisms, particularly viruses. In view of this lack of knowledge, it is impossible to make accurate predictions concerning the relative risks of infection associated with the different organisms. In addition, although relatively few porcine pathogens are currently considered to be of high zoonotic potential, a long-term xenograft would represent an extremely sheltered environment, within an immunosuppressed host, providing an optimal opportunity for the survival and replication of organisms and their subsequent spread and adaptation to the human recipient. [30]

Thus, the first stage of UKXIRA's literature review highlights the uncertainty that still exists on the infectious disease risks that may be associated with

---

23 Ibid., at p. 3.

24 A point that is made more explicitly in his Foreword to the second literature review; see Dobson, J.M. and Dark, J.H. (2002), *The Physiology of Xenotransplantation*, Department of Health: London, p. 7.

25 Kennedy Report (1997), at p. 106.

26 Ibid.

27 Griffin and Muir (2001), chapters 1–3.

28 Ibid., chapter 4.

29 At p. 4.

30 At p. 118, para. 5.1.

xenotransplantation. This inability to provide assurances on the safety of animal to human transplantation suggests that more work is required before it is possible to adequately evaluate the risks associated with the procedure. In this respect, it seems that little advance had been made on the Kennedy Report's claim that there was insufficient knowledge on infection risks to allow clinical trials to commence.[31] The review itself concludes by saying:

> Xenotransplantation's potential for tangible benefits to the individual has to be balanced against the less certain but nevertheless substantial risks it presents to the human population.[32]

Physiology Review

UKXIRA's second literature review, *The Physiology of Xenotransplantation*, examines whether the physiological incompatibility of animal and human tissue will result in xenotransplants being dysfunctional.[33] The review notes that considerable advances have been made in preventing the hyper acute rejection of animal organs by the human immune system, but suggests that more work is required to overcome acute vascular rejection (AVR) which remains a 'significant obstacle' to successful xenotransplantation.[34] Dobson and Dark also express concern over the potentially more 'violent' impact of cellular rejection even if AVR itself is overcome.[35]

The review then provides a detailed assessment of the risks and benefits that are associated with different forms of solid organ transplantation.[36] In respect of xenografts, it is noted that hearts 'may be the only organ which can potentially be considered for clinical xenotransplantation at the present time'.[37] Despite this, the authors highlight that a number of problems exist even in cardiac xenotransplantation. They state:

> The intrinsic neural properties of the porcine heart may ... create problems for the control of the heart rate and contractility in a human recipient, and may lead to fatal ventricular arrhythmias.[38]

However, Dobson and Dark also suggest that advances in cardiac assist devices may remove the need for cardiac xenotransplantation altogether.[39] In relation to the transplantation of other solid organs, the review notes that due to its complex functions the liver is likely to prove the most difficult organ to transplant successfully between species.[40] Furthermore, the poor survival times associated with

---

31 Kennedy Report (1997), at p. 106.
32 Griffin and Muir (2001), at p. 122.
33 Dobson, J.M. and Dark, J.H. (2002).
34 At p. 19f.
35 Ibid.
36 Chapters 4–7.
37 At p. 9.
38 At p. 37.
39 At p. 40ff.
40 At p. 49.

xenotransplanted livers mean that there is too little information at present to allow for an accurate assessment of its physiological performance.[41] The review also reports failures to advance significantly in the areas of renal and pulmonary xenotransplantation.[42]

The Report suggests that techniques which transplant animal cells rather than whole organs may be closer on the clinical horizon. Thus, while Dobson and Dark report that there remains a lack of information on the transplantation of porcine pancreatic islet cells into humans as a treatment of diabetes, the lack of rejection problems experienced to date is encouraging.[43] However, the use of neural cells to treat Parkinson's and Huntington's disease is the form of xenotransplantation – although still at an experimental stage[44] – which is deemed to be closest to clinical practice.[45] Despite advances in these areas, the rejection of cells is reported to remain a major obstacle and more work is needed to maximize the survival of transplants.[46] Similarly, in respect of the use of xenogeneic stem cells, the authors state that:

> Despite the excitement in the field at the present time, there remain many fundamental questions, which need to be addressed before stem cells can be used in future therapeutic applications.[47]

Dobson and Dark conclude:

> If the physiological limitations to xenotransplantation can be fully identified, it is possible that new technologies and suitable therapies can be employed to overcome some of these additional problems. However, in the medium term, it appears that the physiological incompatibilities encountered to date, and those still to be discovered, constitute a significant stumbling block to the progress of xenotransplantation towards clinical trials.[48]

This conclusion again raises concerns that insufficient information is available on animal to human transplants to fulfil the preconditions of the Kennedy Report and – at least in Kennedy's terms – make it ethically justifiable to proceed to clinical trials.

Other Sources of Information

It should be noted that UKXIRA also gains information on developments in xenotransplantation by liaising with representatives of the industries it regulates and various international organizations. In respect of industry, exchanges allowed those attempting to develop xenotransplantation procedures to gain insight into the

41 At p. 57.
42 Chapters 6 and 7.
43 At p. 75f.
44 At p. 84.
45 At p. 80.
46 At p. 83.
47 At p. 91.
48 At p. 101.

regulatory procedures under which they must work and afforded UKXIRA insights into issues which will emerge as xenotransplantation procedures are developed. For example, UKXIRA reports that some of its members had meetings with University Hospital Birmingham and Genzyme during its first working year to discuss the development of a bioartifical liver and a cellular treatment for Parkinson's and Huntington's diseases.[49] In 2000, meetings were held with Circe Biomedical and Reneuron, again to discuss the development of a HepatAssist bioartifical liver system and the development of murine treatment for Parkinson's disease.[50]

As specified in UKXIRA's terms of reference, the Authority's regulatory work is also informed by international developments in the area of xenotransplantation. Particularly in its first year, UKXIRA had to monitor a period of increased activity on xenotransplantation issues at an international and European level. The World Health Organization (WHO), the Organization for European Co-operation and Development (OECD) and the Council of Europe all published reports on aspects of xenotransplantation.[51] In addition, the Council of Europe Working Group on Organ Transplantation produced a Recommendation on Xenotransplantation that was adopted in March 1998. This required xenotransplantation to be treated as distinct from allotransplantation procedures; suggested that public debate should take place over xenotransplantation; and recommended that a Working Party on xenotransplantation should be established within the Council of Europe. A number of international conferences were held, and attended by some UKXIRA members, which focused on concerns similar to those that were being prioritized by UKXIRA.[52]

Regulatory Procedures[53]

Guidance on Making Applications

The first and arguably most significant piece of regulatory work published by UKXIRA to date is its *Guidance on Making Proposals to Conduct*

[49] UKXIRA (1998a), p. 22.

[50] UKXIRA (2001), p. 5.

[51] OECD (1996), *Advances in Transplantation Biotechnology and Animal to Human Transplants (Xenotransplantation)*, OECD: Paris; WHO (1996), *Draft WHO Recommendations on Xenotransplantation and Infectious Disease*, WHO: Geneva; Council of Europe (1997), *Xenotransplantation State of the Art*, Council of Europe: Strasbourg; WHO (1997), *The Report of the WHO Consultation on Xenotransplantation, Geneva, Switzerland 28–30 October 1997*, WHO: Geneva; WHO (1998), *Xenotransplantation: Guidance on Infectious Disease Prevention and Management*, WHO: Geneva.

[52] See, for example, UKXIRA (1998a), p. 21f; UKXIRA (1999a), p.8f; UKXIRA (2001), p. 7f; UKXIRA (2002), *Fourth Annual Report December 2000 – December 2001*, Department of Health: London, p. 9f.

[53] It should be pointed out that UKXIRA's regulatory remit does not extend to the use of animals in transplantation procedures. This is the responsibility of the Animals Procedures Committee. See, for example, UKXIRA (2002), at p. 2.

Xenotransplantation on Human Subjects.[54] The work is important because its publication allows applications to conduct xenotransplantation clinical trials to be submitted in the United Kingdom. Most generally, the document explicates the standards and procedures that should be adopted by those submitting applications to carry out xenotransplantation procedures. In this respect, the Guidance seeks to meet part of the Kennedy Report's recommendation – and one of UKXIRA's own terms of reference – that the Standing Committee should formulate ways to approve applications under legislation by developing a licensing system.[55] However, the document states that 'UKXIRA is developing a non-statutory system'.[56] This non-statutory approach meets with another recommendation of the Kennedy Report; namely, that as an 'interim measure only' the Standing Committee could proceed on a non-statutory basis.[57] However, UKXIRA's Guidance document gives no indication of when or how the proposed framework will take on a statutory form. The advisory (non-statutory) nature of UKXIRA is an issue to which we will return later in this chapter.

The framework under which applications to conduct different forms of xenotransplantation (solid organs, cell therapies, medical devices and gene therapies) will be considered has six stages. Basically, the application is submitted to UKXIRA, scrutinized by external referees and then reviewed by UKXIRA. If the application has been successful in these stages it is then forwarded to the Secretaries of State for consideration and the decision is communicated to the applicant. If the application is still successful it then goes through the usual Local Research Ethics Committee (LREC) decision-making process.[58] Exceptions to this procedure are applications that involve gene therapy, which are submitted initially to the Gene Therapy Advisory Committee rather than UKXIRA.[59]

This procedure was tested for the first time in September 1998 when UKXIRA received its first application to conduct a xenotransplantation clinical trial. On this occasion the external assessors believed the applicants had provided insufficient information regarding the proposal. UKXIRA advised the applicants of this and the application was withdrawn.[60] A second application was received in October 1998. This was reviewed by assessors and then submitted to UKXIRA for formal consideration. In this case also, the Authority decided there was insufficient information for the application to proceed. A response was provided to the applicant in April 1999. Given advances in other areas of their research, the applicant decided not to continue with this application, but was expected to submit a new application in 2000.[61] However, in the event UKXIRA did not receive any applications to conduct clinical trials in this year. A third application was received by the Authority

---

54 UKXIRA (1998c), *Guidance on Making Proposals to Conduct Xenotransplantation on Human Subjects*, Department of Health: London.

55 Kennedy Report (1997), p. 143, paras 9.3, 10.

56 UKXIRA (1998c), at p. 4, para. 2.4.

57 Kennedy Report (1997), p. 141, para. 9.2.

58 UKXIRA (1998c), at p. 6f.

59 At p. 6, para. 4.5.

60 UKXIRA (1999a), at p. 13.

61 At p. 13f.

in October 1999. This was also returned to the applicant because it failed to provide sufficient information.[62] UKXIRA's *Fourth Annual Report*, covering the period 2000–2001, states that no further applications had been received and that the next application was thought most likely to come from a company that would conduct its trials outside the UK.[63] The *Fifth Annual Report* records that an application to perform a trial using a bioartificial liver assist device was received in January 2003.[64] The application was withdrawn two months later.[65]

The Guidance document acknowledges that it forms only part of the regulatory procedures being formulated by UKXIRA. It states that it has also initiated work:

> ... to develop standards of tissue quality (to include consideration of the biosecurity standards that animal facilities should maintain) and to develop a surveillance system, for any xenotransplant recipients. Once these systems are fully established, compliance with standards and approval of sites by inspectors will be a pre-condition for making an application to UKXIRA.[66]

UKXIRA commissioned Steering Groups to consider the biosecurity and infection surveillance issues raised by xenotransplantation in June 1998.[67] The reports by the Biosecurity and Infection Surveillance Steering Groups were published in draft form for consultation in August and September 1999, respectively;[68] in April 2005 both reports remained in draft form.[69] This highlights that UKXIRA initially considered submissions from applicants who were unaware of the necessary biosecurity and surveillance standards, as the first applications to conduct trials were received in September and October 1998. Thus, crucial aspects of the regulatory framework (based on the Kennedy Report's preconditions[70]) were not in place while applications to conduct clinical xenotransplantation procedures were nonetheless being made to UKXIRA. Of course, the fact that applications can be submitted does not mean they will be approved. Indeed, UKXIRA still has not approved any clinical trials. But it is questionable whether applications to commence trials in the UK should be reviewed at all until all of the relevant regulatory mechanisms (preconditions) have been completed.

The Biosecurity Guidance

The introduction to the Biosecurity Guidance provides a number of caveats regarding its scope. These endeavour to take account of the dynamic nature of the field and the manifold ethical issues presented by animal to human transplantation.

---

62 UKXIRA (2001), at p. 12.

63 UKXIRA (2002), at p. 2.

64 United Kingdom Xenotransplantation Interim Regulatory Authority (UKXIRA) (2004), *Fifth Annual Report December 2002 – December 2003*, Department of Health: London, at p. 3.

65 Ibid.

66 UKXIRA (1998c), at p. 4, para. 2.4.

67 UKXIRA (1998a), p. 19f.

68 UKXIRA (2001), at pp. 16, 21.

69 See http://www.advisorybodies.doh.gov.uk/ukxira/publications.htm, accessed on 19/9/04.

70 Kennedy Report (1997), at p. 106.

In this respect, the Guidance states that, because xenotransplantation science is constantly developing, 'these guidance notes cannot be definitive and Regulatory Authorities will expect applicants to take account of all relevant advances'.[71] In addition:

> It is outwith the scope of these notes to discuss the ethical issues involved but they try to address some of the important areas of concern and outline systems for managing the infectious disease risks associated with this technology.[72]

The areas that are of concern to the Biosecurity Steering Group are given in an Annex to the document that provides its terms of reference:

> 1. To specify the biosecurity conditions for each stage in the xenotransplantation procedure which minimise the risks to human health from infections and other disorders resulting from the handling of source animals or as a consequence of the transplantation process.
> 2. To give priority to the consequences of the use of pigs as source animals but to address issues which might arise from the use of other species.
> 3. To liaise with the Home Office to ensure, as far as possible, that the biosecurity requirements which minimise the risk to humans are compatible with the Home Office Code of Practice relating to the housing, husbandry, and care of source animals for use in xenotransplantation.
> 4. To ensure familiarity with all appropriate and relevant legislation, codes of practice and guidance notes relating to xenotransplantation.[73]

The Guidance document begins by considering which species should be chosen for xenotransplantation.[74] Primates are considered unsuitable because it would be difficult to provide sufficient numbers of primate organs that are safe from a biosecurity perspective. The Guidance suggests, however, that in certain circumstances primate cells could be used.[75] Porcine organs are deemed acceptable, based on their size and because genetic alteration of pigs may prevent the human immune system from rejecting the organ.[76] The use of other animals should be determined by risk assessment criteria.[77] The decisions taken by the Steering Group are, as the introduction to the report suggests, based purely on pragmatic considerations. Indeed, the report reiterates that:

> There are important ethical considerations regarding the choice of species for xenotransplantation but these fall outwith the scope of these guidance notes.[78]

---

71 UKXIRA (1999b), *Guidance Notes on Biosecurity Considerations in Relation to Xenotransplantation*, Department of Health: London, at p. 4.

72 Ibid.

73 UKXIRA (1999b), Annex One, p. 30–31.

74 Ibid., at p. 7f.

75 Ibid., at p. 7.

76 Ibid.

77 Ibid., at p. 7.

78 Ibid.

In its work on the 'Health Status' of animals, the Steering Group notes that the animal welfare implications of Gnotobiotic (germ-free) conditions are too serious to allow this method, but states that Qualified Pathogen Free (QPF) conditions are 'acceptable from the point of view of animal welfare'.[79] This is the first indication given in the Guidance that the Steering Group is uncertain whether it should be discussing ethical issues, or perhaps that there was internal disagreement on this point. Alternatively the Steering Group might have been confused over what constitutes an ethical issue. Determining the acceptability of a practice on the basis of whether it will have negative consequences on the welfare of other humans or animals is an ethical decision as to how things 'should' be treated. Although the Steering Group categorically states that ethical issues are not within its remit, it seems to find it impossible to ignore the ethical questions that emerge when giving serious consideration to biosecurity issues.

This issue occurs again, when the Guidance recommends in respect of animal husbandry the use of a barriered system which aims to:

> ... reduce the risks of contamination from the environment by ensuring that all materials entering the barrier are sterilised, if possible, or decontaminated. ... All potential sources of contamination should be controlled including air, water, materials and personnel.[80]

The report further states that within this barrier:

> It is essential that adequate environmental enrichment be provided. Pigs are intelligent animals and require an environment with provision for exercise, play and interaction. In the wild they exhibit rooting behaviour and interact with their peers. Within the scope of a microbiologically controlled environment attempts should be made to provide good welfare standards for animals.[81]

Thus, the Steering Group again takes serious account of welfare (ethical) considerations. These glimpses of a more nuanced, sophisticated and integrated approach to science and ethics are to be welcomed. However, under the circumstances such statements reveal an approach that is not entirely consistent with the Steering Group's self-professed aims.

The Guidance explains that under QPF conditions the dams (production animals) of source animals are delivered by hysterotomy and by establishing QPF breeding colonies by using barrier conditions,[82] although the organisms that should be excluded from QPF conditions are still to be 'determined'.[83] That is, while the Steering Group provides general advice for applicants on the organisms that should be excluded, 'the onus is on the applicant to provide a list of excluded pathogens and justification for the strategy adopted'.[84] This parallels its earlier insistence that

---

79 Ibid., at p. 9, para. 1.4, a.

80 Ibid., at p. 12.

81 Ibid., at p. 13.

82 Ibid., at p. 10.

83 Ibid.

84 Ibid., at p. 10. The guidance is provided in an Appendix, p. 28ff.

applicants should be responsible for keeping abreast of developments in the field. The Appendix to the report explains:

> Responsibility for the detailed content of the programme rests with the applicant who will be expected to have developed animal surveillance programmes which specify organisms that must be eliminated from production and source animals, methods of testing and actions to be taken should breakdown occur in the biosecurity system. The Regulatory Authorities will pay particular attention to the sensitivity and robustness of test methods.[85]

The Guidance also identifies the standards that should be maintained in respect of the staff of the facilities in which animals are raised.[86] The Steering Group states that it is important that staff are sufficiently experienced and work under a project manager.[87] It emphasizes that because the animals used in xenotransplantation are likely to be transgenic, the procedures and staff who conduct them will come under the control of the Animals (Scientific Procedures) Act 1986.[88] This requires that all staff are adequately qualified and that:

> Establishments which carry out work under Animals (Scientific Procedures) Act 1986 must have an approved system of ethical review for such work carried out [i]n the establishment. This should address aspects of ethics of particular experiments using animals, animal care and welfare, staff training and implementation of the principles of refinement, reduction and replacement.[89]

Again, the efforts of the Biosecurity Steering Group to avoid ethical questions fail and the difficulties of formulating policies in the area without discussing ethics is apparent. Interestingly, the Guidance does not suggest that a similar system of ethical review should be part of UKXIRA's regulation of the use of xenotransplantation source animals. Presumably, the Steering Group's claim that ethical issues do not fall within its remit precludes it from having to consider such questions.

The Guidance document further identifies standards that should be maintained when animal tissue is harvested.[90] These include the need to maintain QPF conditions, to ensure that the surgical specifications meet those for human surgery and to keep a record of all those who enter the facility.[91] Particular attention is given to the need to prevent the tissue that is harvested from coming into contact with the skin of the source animal because this presents the greatest risk of the tissue becoming infected.[92] Recommendations are made about the storage of tissue, post-mortem examination of source animals and disposal of carcasses.[93] The final chapter

85 Ibid., at p. 28.
86 Ibid., at p. 15ff.
87 Ibid., at p. 15.
88 Ibid., at p. 15.
89 Ibid., at p. 16.
90 Ibid., at p. 18ff.
91 Ibid., at p. 18.
92 Ibid., at p. 19.
93 Ibid., at p. 19f.

of the Guidance identifies the need for accurate records to be maintained on production and source animals and the need to archive samples.[94]

Infection Surveillance Guidance

In its draft consultation document, the Infection Surveillance Steering Group states that, most generally, its aim is to address the safety concerns that appear in UKXIRA's terms of reference.[95] More specifically:

> The document outlines a way forward for the monitoring and surveillance of potential infections associated with xenotransplantation. It describes the overall approach and principles, and provides a draft model framework to implement infection surveillance, initially for clinical trials.[96]

The draft Guidance states that among the objectives of a surveillance framework must be the ability to care for the sick, control and contain the spread of infection, monitor the effectiveness of control measures and prevent a recurrence.[97] Importantly, infections must be recognized and dealt with quickly.[98] The Steering Group recommends that, to enable this type of rapid response, samples must be collected and stored from animals, animal workers, xenotransplant recipients, the household/close contacts of recipients and recipients' healthcare workers.[99] In addition, it recommends that all of those affected by the risks associated with the procedure should be provided with adequate information.[100] It is suggested that xenotransplant recipients should 'undergo pre- and post-xenotransplantation clinical and laboratory screening'.[101] Others, such as close contacts and healthcare staff, should also provide samples to be archived.[102]

The work of the Infection Surveillance Steering Group, like that of the Biosecurity Group, encountered a number of ethical issues. That is, efforts to address the safety issues that lay within the Group's remit had to consider not only the ways in which it is possible to prevent the spread of infection, but which surveillance strategies are ethically acceptable. The ethico-legal content of the report of the Surveillance Steering Group appears as an Annex entitled 'Consent Issues Arising from Requirements for Infection Surveillance'.[103]

The discussion of consent issues begins with an outline of the post-operative surveillance requirements which patients and their close contacts will be required to follow. These measures include the need for patients to: remain within a surveillance

---

94 Ibid., at p. 21ff.

95 UKXIRA (1999c), *Draft Report of the Infection Surveillance Steering Group of the UKXIRA*, Department of Health: London, at p. 5.

96 Ibid.

97 Ibid., at p. 17.

98 Ibid., at p. 8.

99 Ibid., at p. 10.

100 Ibid., at p. 10.

101 Ibid., at p. 11.

102 Ibid., at p. 12.

103 UKXIRA (1999c). This report will be analyzed in more depth in chapter 7, below.

programme for life; use barrier contraception for life; refrain from having children; keep their name and address on a register; identify their contacts in case of a xenotransplant event; agree to storage of samples; agree that any future GP will be told of their status as a xenotransplant recipient; and agree that anonymized data can be divulged for research purposes.[104] Patients must not donate their organs and they must also agree to post-mortem examination.[105] In addition, transplant recipients:

> ... must agree to their contacts being informed about the patient's condition, the xeno-procedure, subsequent treatment, possible side effects in the patient and symptoms in themselves. By contacts UKXIRA means:
>
> 'household members and sexual partners and others with whom the xenotransplant patient may engage in activities in which bodily fluids may be exchanged'.[106]

The Guidance suggests that the close contacts of the patients 'may need' to comply with check-up and testing requirements, be contactable and agree to the storage of data and samples and to the divulging of anonymized data.[107]

The Steering Group acknowledges that there is currently no legislation able to force patients or their contacts to comply with surveillance measures. However, it is anticipated that patients will understand the need to participate in surveillance, and are likely to be compliant.[108] If an infectious disease did result from a xenograft, the Committee noted that it may be possible to amend the Public Health (Infectious Disease) Regulations 1988 and so make that person subject to the Public Health (Control of Disease) Act 1984 which would allow for the examination of patients.[109] Of course, before such legislation could be invoked, the diseases would have to be identified.

Before any xenotransplantation procedures take place, UKXIRA will insist that properly 'informed' consent has been obtained and that participants agree to post-operative surveillance measures.[110] For patients to give valid consent it would be necessary for them to have adequate information on the procedure and its possible consequences. It is acknowledged that even if consent to surveillance measures is given explicitly in advance, the patient could still withdraw from surveillance programmes.[111] However, the Steering Group suggests that as a minimum requirement it may be possible to insist that xenotransplant recipients cannot withdraw from patient registers, thus enabling them to be traced in an emergency.[112] To pre-empt any problems that could arise if patients refused to take part in surveillance programmes, the Guidance insists that applicants should make every effort to ensure that their choice of patients, and the information patients are given, minimize the chances that surveillance procedures will be breached.[113]

---

104 Ibid., at p. 31ff.
105 Ibid., at p. 32.
106 Ibid., at p. 32.
107 Ibid., at p. 32f.
108 Ibid., at p. 34.
109 Ibid., at p. 34.
110 Ibid., at p. 35.
111 Ibid.
112 Ibid.
113 Ibid., at p. 36.

The ethical and legal issues raised by the surveillance and biosecurity reports, such as consent and animal welfare, will be discussed in greater detail in later chapters. However, here it is sufficient to point out that neither of the UKXIRA Steering Groups considered it their responsibility to investigate the ethical and legal issues raised by their remits in detail. This, therefore, leaves open the question as to the extent to which the recommendations of these groups are either ethically acceptable or legally viable. Arguably, the basic desire to avoid the ethical and legal issues which are inherent in the subjects of UKXIRA's work to date leaves some cause for concern about the robustness or sophistication of the ensuing recommendations.

A Critique of the Work of UKXIRA

In this section it will be argued that UKXIRA's work is characterized by a number of methodological features that are proving detrimental to the ethical and legal standing of its regulatory initiatives. These features include the ongoing failure to make UKXIRA into a statutory body and, secondly, the failure to identify how the ethical issues raised by xenotransplantation will be considered by UKXIRA in a strategic, thoroughgoing manner.

The Kennedy Report stated that the implementation of the measures it had recommended would be 'best guaranteed by the establishment of a National Standing Committee that was backed by legislation'.[114] Despite this recommendation the Kennedy Report also acknowledged:

> ... that there is always pressure on Parliamentary timetables. We therefore recommend, as an interim measure only, that our recommendations, particularly with regard to the National Standing Committee, are taken forward on a non-statutory basis until such time as legislation can be brought forward. Such an interim body should not be regarded as a substitute for legislation ...[115]

However, seven years after UKXIRA was established as a non-departmental public body (NDPB) there has been no concerted effort to give it statutory backing. The fact that UKXIRA has remained an NDPB has undoubtedly influenced the Authority's regulatory role. For example, UKXIRA is unable to work to the primary legislation that the Advisory Group on the Ethics of Xenotransplantation regarded as necessary. Thus, the force of UKXIRA's regulatory recommendations is dependent upon its ability to secure the agreement of those being asked to comply with them. As it stands, the Authority would be unable to impose penalties on those who ignored the guidance it offered should an application be accepted. This means that in its efforts to regulate xenotransplantation, UKXIRA must work in co-operation with industry, and its impact and success as an advisory body are dependent upon good relations with industry. However, biomedical companies involved in the development of xenotransplantation procedures may be reluctant to

114 Kennedy Report (1997), at p. 141.

115 Ibid.

release all of the relevant information concerning their research into the public domain for commercial reasons.

This suggests that there may be a tension in the working relationship between UKXIRA and commercial companies. As an NDPB, UKXIRA is bound by principles of openness and transparency. The Model Code of Practice issued by the Cabinet Office in 1998 for NDPBs lists openness, accountability, objectivity and integrity as being among the principles that should shape the conduct of UKXIRA and its members.[116] These requirements have led UKXIRA to publish annual reports,[117] establish a website which contains its annual reports, guidance documents, summaries of its most recent meetings and a list of members' interests.[118] To date the Authority has held four public meetings at which its annual reports are launched and UKXIRA's work is summarized.[119] However, such requirements for openness do not sit easily with the confidentiality that is demanded by the commercial companies developing various forms of xenotransplantation. Given that UKXIRA is reliant on the compliance of such companies, this risks compromising the force of the Authority's regulatory work.

UKXIRA's efforts to monitor the development of xenotransplantation are also challenged by its failure to afford the fundamental ethical and legal issues anything other than relatively cursory attention. The problem is rooted in a number of sources. UKXIRA's own terms of reference, the legacy of the Kennedy Report and apparent confusion over the relationship between ethics, law and science all impact on the ethico-legal quality of UKXIRA's work.

UKXIRA's terms of reference do not explicitly commit the Authority to conducting an ethical assessment of animal to human transplantation. The terms of reference do state that UKXIRA has a responsibility to consider the 'acceptability of specific applications'.[120] However, it is not entirely clear whether this is a mandate only to determine the scientific feasibility and potential of specific acts, or whether it does in fact charge the Authority to consider whether certain procedures are 'right' or 'wrong'. For example, a biomedical procedure can be unacceptable (not accepted) because it fails to respect the known laws of science, but this is not necessarily an ethical issue. Similarly, applications to UKXIRA could be unacceptable, as they have been to date, because they fail to supply sufficient information, but this too is not itself an ethical issue. Alternatively, an application to UKXIRA could be deemed (ethically) unacceptable because the risk it poses to the prospective transplant recipient is too great, or because it inflicts too much suffering on the animals used.

There are a number of other references in UKXIRA's documents to its relationship with the ethical assessment of xenotransplantation that may help us to

---

116 For further discussion of the requirements see the following publications: Cabinet Office (1997), *Model Code of Practice for Board Members of Advisory Non-Departmental Public Bodies; Opening up Quangos*, HMSO: London; Cabinet Office (1998), *QUANGOS Opening the Doors*, HMSO: London; Cabinet Office (1981), *Non Departmental Public Bodies: A Guide for Departments*, HMSO: London.

117 UKXIRA (1998a); UKXIRA (1999a); UKXIRA (2001); UKXIRA (2002); UKXIRA (2004).

118 www.advisorybodies.doh.gov.uk/UKXIRA.

119 The meetings took place on 7 December 1998, 6 December 1999, 7 February 2001, 1 December 2003.

120 UKXIRA (1998a), at p. 24.

shed light on the confusion over the ethical content of UKXIRA's remit. In his Foreword to UKXIRA's First Annual Report the Authority's Chairman at the time, Lord Habgood, stated that UKXIRA's role includes examining the ethical issues that underlie the scientific ones raised by xenotransplantation.[121] However, later in the same report the Authority states that the Kennedy Report is 'the ethical underpinning for the regulatory work it [UKXIRA] would put in hand'.[122] Thus, the Authority's first Chairman understood UKXIRA to have a responsibility to consider the ethical issues raised by xenotransplantation, but the *First Annual Report* suggests that UKXIRA is responsible for regulating xenotransplantation on the basis of the ethical work already conducted by the Kennedy Report. We must investigate whether, as Lord Habgood suggested, UKXIRA's work reveals a commitment to ethics and also assess the implications of UKXIRA's reliance on the 1997 Kennedy Report for its ethical convictions.

In this chapter we have seen that, arguably, the most significant piece of ethical work published by UKXIRA to date is the Annex on consent in the draft Guidance of the Surveillance Steering Group.[123] However, we have also noted that the focus of this work is on whether it is feasible to enforce the surveillance mechanisms.[124] It does not examine in any detail whether such measures *should* be initiated, or whether different aspects of the framework are right or wrong. Thus, even this document fails to provide a detailed ethical assessment of the issues involved. Indeed as the report says:

> It is not intended to set out in detail the legal and ethical guidelines that operate in the UK: it provides an overview to the consent issues arising from the requirements for infections surveillance post xenotransplantation.[125]

This begs the question as to where such discussion is to take place and certainly confirms that this UKXIRA Steering Group does not regard it as its responsibility to investigate the ethical issues. Similarly, we have seen that the Authority's Steering Group on Biosecurity stressed that its work does not examine the ethical aspects of xenotransplantation. The Biosecurity document states that it is 'outwith the scope of these notes to discuss the ethical issues involved',[126] although, as we have seen, this Steering Group does not always successfully avoid ethical issues. UKXIRA did commission a third literature review on ethics and law – on which this book is based – but took the decision not to publish it. This decision, along with UKXIRA's failure to give any indication of whether it intends to fill the gap by commissioning other work on ethics and law, does little to promote confidence in its commitment to self-critical ethico-legal work. Thus, in the very least, it seems prudent to suggest that UKXIRA should have a more overtly ethical aspect to its remit and that its Steering Groups should have the expertise to address the ethical issues with which they are

[121] Ibid., p. 3.
[122] Ibid., at p. 9, para. 3.4.
[123] UKXIRA (1999c).
[124] UKXIRA (1999c), at p. 31.
[125] Ibid.
[126] UKXIRA (1999b), at p. 4

confronted. Alternatively, if the legal and ethical issues raised by xenotransplantation are not addressed in the United Kingdom by UKXIRA, an alternative agency for conducting such examinations should be identified.

The suggestion made in UKXIRA's *First Annual Report* is that the ethical assessment of xenotransplantation had already been conducted in the Kennedy Report. Thus, its own regulatory work would take account of this. However, this presents a number of difficulties. Firstly, as the Kennedy Report itself stressed, biomedical work is dynamic. This means that 'ethical decisions can change as new knowledge becomes available'.[127] This infers that ethical work on xenotransplantation must also be ongoing if it is to stand any chance of addressing the new challenges that arise. That is, ethical work should be iterative and not reliant on outdated empirical data. An ethical analysis of xenotransplantation that is not based on the most up to date scientific data could overlook the promise of new developments, or fail to consider data which reveal new risks.

Related to this need for ongoing ethical work is the possibility that previous ethical assessments could be flawed. In the previous chapter a number of difficulties were identified with the report of the Advisory Group (and with that of the Nuffield Council). Thus, by basing its regulatory and ethical responsibilities on the work of the Kennedy Report, UKXIRA's work could replicate the same limitations and not move assessments of animal to human transplantation forward. The Kennedy Report, for example, considered it unnecessary to investigate those established ethical principles of therapeutic research, such as consent and confidentiality, in the context of xenotransplantation procedures, although it held that these principles provided standards that should be maintained for the practice to be considered ethically acceptable.[128]

Furthermore, it is possible to argue that UKXIRA's claim to rely on the recommendations and analyses of the Kennedy Report is itself unreliable. For example, the Kennedy Report's recommendation that UKXIRA should have statutory powers has failed to materialize. Indeed, when commissioning the report which forms the basis of this book, the Department of Health made it clear that the need for regulation should not form part of our consideration. Secondly, the Kennedy Report argued that xenotransplantation 'could' be ethically acceptable and clinical trials permissible once certain preconditions were fulfilled.[129] However, UKXIRA's programme of work has sought to deliver these preconditions in a manner that appears somewhat muddled. The first major document published by UKXIRA implemented a framework that allowed applications to be submitted. This led to a situation in which applications to conduct clinical trials were submitted before additional research had been conducted on the immunological, physiological and infection risks and before biosecurity and surveillance measures were in place. It could be argued that instituting a procedure to consider applications at the beginning of its working life, before these other fundamental tasks had been accomplished, has allowed UKXIRA to have firm control over whether and when clinical trials should be performed. Indeed, this argument is supported by the fact

127 Kennedy Report (1997), at p. 5, para. 1.9, 5.

128 Ibid., at p. 113, para. 7.10f; 7.17.

129 Ibid., at p. 105.

that UKXIRA is yet to approve a clinical trial. However, permitting applications at such an early stage also suggests that UKXIRA assumed that clinical trials *would* take place, despite the fact that many preconditions have not been fulfilled. It seems that this predicament has been a factor in so many of UKXIRA's initiatives overlooking crucial ethico-legal issues. That is, because applications can be submitted it is easy to assume that the debate has advanced beyond the consideration of fundamental ethical and legal questions, when in fact many issues remain unresolved, but are frequently placed outside the remit of UKXIRA's reports and internal investigating bodies.

The implications of UKXIRA's decision to receive applications for clinical trials so early in its existence for the other preconditions made by the Kennedy Report is evidenced by a recent description of the Authority's responsibilities in the House of Commons. In response to a written question concerning the Government's policy on xenotransplantation, Rosie Winterton, Minister of State for Health, replied that UKXIRA had been established to:

> ... advise the Government on the acceptability of specific applications to undertake xenotransplantation procedures (the transplantation of live cells, tissues and organs from a non-human source into a human), it also acts as a focal point for xenotransplantation issues.[130]

Indeed, because UKXIRA remains a non-statutory body, one of its tasks is to provide advice to Ministers on the 'acceptability of specific applications'; while another of its terms of reference requires it to 'provide a focal point on xenotransplantation issues within Government'.[131] However, the Minister fails to mention two of UKXIRA's other responsibilities. Namely, to advise:

> a. on safety, efficacy and considerations of animal welfare and any other preconditions for xenotransplantation for human use, and when these have been met;
> b. on research required to assess safety and efficacy factors in xenotransplantation procedures.[132]

The omission of these responsibilities from her statement of UKXIRA's role has the effect of drawing a veil over the substantial work that is still required before clinical trials should be contemplated. In this respect, it replicates the impact of UKXIRA's decision to publish its Guidance document on applications before real headway had been made to address the other preconditions. That is, it suggests that the United Kingdom is closer to conducting clinical trials than it ought to be, given the remit and standing of the Authority that regulates the procedure.

Conclusion

To date UKXIRA has conducted a considerable amount of work needed to evaluate and regulate xenotransplantation in the United Kingdom. However, its efforts to

130 HC Deb (2002–2003) 408, Column 354W.

131 UKXIRA (2004), at p. 20.

132 Ibid., at p. 20.

gather data on xenotransplantation have not provided sufficient clarity on when it might be ethically acceptable to conduct animal to human transplantation in the United Kingdom, or indeed whether such a development will ever be ethically or legally acceptable. As we have seen, this is in part because there remains a lack of information on the main risk factors in xenotransplantation. In terms of regulatory initiatives, UKXIRA has done substantial work on all of the tasks that are clearly identified by its terms of reference. However, in this chapter concerns have been raised over the ordering and ethico-legal content of this work. It has been suggested that the premature decision to allow applications to be submitted may, inadvertently, obscure the work that remains to be done before clinical trials could be approved.

In respect of the ethico-legal features of UKXIRA's work, the Authority's non-statutory standing and its close relationship to industry may well compromise its regulatory role. Given that UKXIRA is charged with regulating a biotechnological development that may pose a substantial risk for public health, its lack of regulatory teeth is a cause for concern. In addition, it has been suggested that even UKXIRA's terms of reference do not clearly identify the Authority's responsibility to assess the ethical standing of xenotransplantation procedures. This problem is exacerbated by documents published by the Authority, which frequently state that ethical issues do not fall within their remit. Such statements appear to be based on the mistaken assumption that it is both desirable and possible to separate the technico-scientific issues on which such reports usually focus from ethico-legal questions. This chapter has endeavoured to show that efforts to regulate biotechnology procedures like animal to human transplantation must test not only what is possible, but also what is ethically acceptable and legally permissible.

Chapter 5

A Review of National and International Responses to Xenotransplantation

Introduction

A review of international and national responses to the issues raised by xenotransplantation has an important role to play in the ethico-legal assessment of the procedure, particularly because efforts to address the issues – particularly surrounding infectious disease – associated with xenotransplantation require some form of international co-operation. To be efficient, such liaison requires knowledge of national and international policies that impact on xenotransplantation. This chapter will begin by reviewing the work of a number of international and European agencies on xenotransplantation. This examination will assess the contributions of the World Health Organization (WHO), the Organization for Economic Co-operation and Development (OECD), the European Parliament and the Council of Europe to debates on animal to human transplants. This will be followed by a survey of how various nation states are choosing to regulate the actual or potential development of xenotransplantation.

International and European Initiatives

World Health Organization

In October 1997 the World Health Organization held a Consultation on Xenotransplantation.[1] The issue that dominated the proceedings was the identification and prevention of xenozoonoses. It was suggested that a number of measures would be necessary to make xenotransplantation safe: first, the recipients of animal organs should be screened for infection and, second, samples from patients and source animals should be archived in national and international registries.[2] It was also thought likely that the recipients of animal organs would have to be monitored for life and be expected to adapt their behaviour to protect public health.[3] Furthermore, surveillance measures would have to extend to the recipient's close contacts.[4]

---

[1] World Health Organization (1997), *The Report of the WHO Consultation on Xenotransplantation, Geneva, Switzerland 28–30 October 1997*, WHO: Geneva.

[2] Ibid., at p. 2ff.

[3] Ibid., at p. 3f.

[4] Ibid., at p. 4.

Despite this focus on the scientific and practical issues that surround endeavours to address the infectious disease risks associated with animal to human transplants, the Report also acknowledges that:

> The implications of this technology are not solely biomedical. It also raises philosophical issues, including questions of ethical, social, cultural and religious acceptability. Public acceptance should not be assumed. Psychological, cultural and societal concerns call for accurate information and frank public discussion.[5]

A number of socio-ethical issues were identified during the consultation. It was, for example, noted that because xenotransplantation is unlikely to overcome the shortage of organs in the 'near future' it is important to continue to promote human organ donation.[6] Thus, the consultation report represents xenotransplantation as 'one alternative to human organ and tissue donation'.[7] Social and personal attitudes towards animal to human transplants were identified as another area that requires consideration.[8] As the Report states:

> The appropriateness or acceptability of xenotransplantation will differ between cultures and societies and may change over time ... Cultural norms, attitudes, and belief systems shape the perceptions of societies and individuals. A major influence on people's attitudes towards xenotransplantation will be their perception of the scientific validity and medical justification for the procedure.[9]

The consultation document suggests that the ethical legitimacy of xenotransplantation should be determined by applying traditional ethical concepts such as beneficence, non-maleficence, autonomy and justice to both the individual recipients of organs and the community as a whole.[10] On this basis patients and the community should expect the principle of precaution to be exercised and the rights of individuals, if necessary, could be restricted to protect public health.[11] Despite this desire to limit risk, the Report continues to stress that 'a balance of risks, not a total absence of risk is expected'.[12]

Recommendations are made to Member States regarding features which they should consider in their xenotransplantation policies.[13] These include: the development of mechanisms to protect individual and public health; additional research on the potential infectious disease risks posed by animal to human transplants; and quality assurance measures concerning the health of the source animals.[14] It was also thought necessary for nation states to provide mechanisms to

---

5 Ibid., at p. 10.
6 Ibid., at p. 5.
7 Ibid.
8 Ibid.
9 Ibid.
10 At p. 6.
11 Ibid.
12 Ibid.
13 At p. 11.
14 At p. 11ff.

allow participants to receive adequate counselling on the technique, and to encourage informed public discussion on the ethical issues raised by the procedure.[15] Another recommendation concerns the need for international co-operation on the issues raised by xenotransplantation. It is claimed:

> International co-operation and co-ordination are needed to help promote the safety and efficacy of xenotransplantation as well as equity of access to the technology. International co-operation is also needed to ensure that xenotransplantation is developed in conformity with accepted ethical and legal standards based on the need to respect human dignity and individual rights together with community interests.[16]

The next document published by the WHO on animal to human transplantation, *Xenotransplantation: Guidance on Infectious Disease Prevention and Management* focuses on the practical aspects of preventing disease transmission.[17] The document states that it 'does not examine the important ethical issues surrounding this technology' but is concerned with practical questions of how to prevent the spread of animal diseases within the human population.[18] The working assumption of the document is that xenotransplantation 'might be implemented'.[19] The report considers the nature of the risk xenotransplantation presents to individuals and the general population. A list of infectious agents that should be excluded from source animals is provided and the potential risk from unknown agents is noted.[20] The report then outlines measures that will minimize the risk to public health. The issues discussed include the careful selection of source animals, the conditions in which source animals should be kept, the surveillance of source animals and the need for reliable diagnostic tests.[21]

The WHO's *Guidance on Xenogeneic Infection/Disease Surveillance and Response: A Strategy for International Cooperation and Coordination*[22] is based on the presupposition that 'international systems for disease surveillance and response do not completely meet the unique challenges posed by xenogeneic infection disease events.[23] The document aims to '... facilitate consideration [of] the development and implementation of an international xenogenic infection/disease event surveillance network ...'.[24] In this document, the WHO does consider the ethical issues that will arise when performing this task. It is suggested that there are two main issues which should be taken into account; namely, the need to protect patients and the need to protect public health. The protection of patients is accounted for by traditional

---

15 At p. 12f.

16 At p. 14.

17 World Health Organization (1998), *Xenotransplantation: Guidance on Infectious Disease Prevention and Management*, WHO: Geneva.

18 Ibid., at p. 1.

19 Ibid.

20 At p. 3f.

21 At pp. 7–13.

22 World Health Organization (2001), *WHO Guidance on Xenogeneic Infection/Disease Surveillance and Response: A Strategy for International Cooperation and Coordination*, WHO: Geneva.

23 Ibid., at p. 1.

24 Ibid.

bioethical standards and guidelines, which are summarized in Annex 6 of the document[25] as follows:

> Individual recipients of xenotransplantation products must be informed of all the possible benefits and risks, and must be guaranteed protection of privacy and confidentiality. They must be at liberty to withdraw from the 'experiment' at any stage, including xenogenic infection/disease even surveillance.[26]

Despite this reliance on traditional bioethical principles, it is acknowledged that the risk to public health means that xenotransplant recipients and their contacts may have to consent to life-long monitoring, which will 'possibly be in the absence of true informed consent'.[27] This leads the WHO to suggest that '[t]he exact meaning of informed consent with respect to xenotransplantation requires much further discussion'.[28] Thus, the WHO sees a need to develop the principles that have traditionally been used to assess biomedical issues if they are to meet the challenges of animal to human transplantation.

In 2003 the WHO Executive Board established an expert group to prepare a report to advise the WHO on how to advance their transplantation policies.[29] This Report was published in November 2003 and considered by the Executive Board in January 2004.[30] The Report summarizes the major obstacles to allotransplantation and xenotransplantation. In respect of xenotransplantation, it emphasizes that before successful animal to human transplantation can take place, immunological and infection risks need to be addressed.[31] In addition, it is noted:

> Ethical questions in xenotransplantation include whether potential recipients (and possibly their family and other close contacts) have given voluntary, informed consent, and whether monitoring of recipients may be mandated along with containment measures when transmission of an animal pathogen is suspected. Other considerations relate to the ethics of the use of animals as sources of material.[32]

The Report raises concern that xenotransplantation research and clinical trials sometimes take place in countries that have no regulatory procedures in place.[33] In response to this, the Report recommends that Member States should 'give urgent attention' to ensuring that they have procedures in place to regulate all forms of

---

25 At p. 42f.

26 At p. 11.

27 Ibid.

28 Ibid.

29 It should be noted that before the publication of this document, the WHO published the results of a consultation it had held with the OECD in 2001. OECD/WHO (2001), *OECD/WHO Consultation on Xenotransplantation Surveillance: Summary Report*, OECD/WHO: Paris, October. This document will be considered when we assess the contribution of the OECD to the regulation of xenotransplantation.

30 *Human Organ and Tissue Transplantation*, Report by the Secretariat, 27 November 2003, EB113/14.

31 P. 3, para. 12.

32 P. 3, para. 13.

33 P. 3. para. 14.

organ and tissue transplantation.[34] The Report concludes by producing a draft resolution to be considered by the Executive Board. It recommends that Member States should only permit xenotransplantation when regulatory procedures are in place containing measures to prevent secondary infection and to support international collaboration on the safety measures that are required. In addition, it calls on the Director-General of the WHO to promote international collaboration and to create a global evidence base.[35] The recommendations were adopted by the World Health Assembly in May 2004.[36]

World Health Organization: Summary The WHO's work on xenotransplantation is influenced by its responsibility to public health, or in the words of Article 1 of the WHO Constitution, to support the 'attainment by all peoples of the highest possible level of health'.[37] This interest in protecting the health of 'all peoples' means that the WHO is concerned with the health of individuals who may be helped by a form of xenotransplantation, as well as with the health of those who could experience the negative consequences of xenozoonoses. The WHO endeavours to discern the characteristics of a surveillance system that would be able to perform this dual task. As we have seen, the WHO suggests that the protection of individual recipients can be based on traditional bioethical principles. It holds that these principles will support the life-long monitoring of transplant recipients and require them to adapt their behaviour to protect public health. The reliance on traditional ethical principles also means that the WHO maintains that participants in clinical trials must be able to withdraw from them at any time. This may seem to suggest that the WHO underestimates the novel challenges presented by xenotransplantation. Yet it also suggests that the requirement of life-long monitoring may have to take place without what can be regarded as truly free and informed consent. This leads the WHO to suggest that it may be necessary to re-evaluate this traditional ethical (and legal) concept. Finally, the WHO affords considerable importance to the need to establish and maintain international surveillance measures. In this, it concurs with other European and international agencies.

Organization for Economic Co-operation and Development

In March 1998 the OECD and the New York Academy of Sciences held a joint workshop on the 'International Issues in Transplantation Biotechnology, Including the Use of Non-human Cells, Tissues and Organs'.[38] The aim of the workshop was to review scientific progress on xenotransplantation and to 'facilitate productive international co-operation and co-ordination',[39] with a view to formulating 'an OECD opinion on current developments on xenotransplantation'.[40] Despite this aim,

---

34 P. 4, para. 15.

35 At p. 6.

36 World Health Assembly, *Human Organ and Tissue Transplantation*, WHA57.18, 22 May 2004. Available at http://www.who.int/transplantation/en/A57_R18-en.pdf.

37 World Health Organization, *The Constitution of the World Health Organization*, was signed on 22 July 1946 by the representatives of 61 states and came into force 7 April 1948. Available at http://policy.who.int/cgi-bin/om_isapi.dll?infobase=Basicdoc&softpage=Browse_Frame_Pg42.

38 OECD (1999), *Xenotransplantation: International Policy Issues*, OECD: Paris.

39 Ibid., at p. 3.

40 Ibid., at p. 73.

the workshop 'revealed a substantial divergence of opinion among OECD countries'.[41] However, there was consensus among participants at the workshop on the need for international co-operation and that efforts to initiate this type of approach should be started 'immediately'.[42] The report notes that:

> Although many of the direct challenges raised by xenotransplantation will be met by domestic health policies, the understanding, monitoring and treatment of possible adverse events will demand global co-operation.[43]

In this respect, it suggests that although xenotransplantation will be subject to national legislation, such regulation can lack clarity. It is therefore important to acknowledge that international agreement on 'appropriate standards can influence national legislation'.[44] The issues addressed within this internationalist strategy include the need for databases, principles for risk assessment and an international research agenda. It was decided that international co-operation should be interdisciplinary and incorporate industry, doctors, veterinary surgeons, policy makers, patient representatives and ethics experts.[45]

The report highlights that an obstacle to efforts to address the socio-legal issues raised by the development of animal to human transplantation is that the procedures and issues involved cross a number of 'regulatory boundaries'.[46] In this regard, it is explained that:

> Regulatory frameworks which cover medical devices, medicinal products, gene therapies, as well as sanitary, phytosanitary and animal welfare measures, might all be relevant to xenotransplantation. In addition, animals subjected to biotechnology procedures would be covered not only by the relevant sections of animal, health and welfare legislation, but also by the laws on genetically modified organisms.[47]

It is also contended that there are 'few subjects in biomedicine that have raised as many challenging socio-legal and ethical questions as xenotransplantation'.[48] The report concentrates on three topics: namely, the use and welfare of animals, the public perceptions of xenotransplantation and the necessary consent and monitoring procedures.[49]

In respect of the use of animals in xenotransplantation, it is noted that although the 'highest microbiological standards' must be maintained, animal welfare also needs to be safeguarded.[50] The report emphasizes that:

> ... it should be recognised that countries differ with respect to specific standards for the housing and transport of animals, personnel qualifications, and record-keeping

41 Ibid., p. 9.
42 Ibid., p. 10.
43 Ibid., p. 46.
44 Ibid., p. 78.
45 Ibid., p. 10.
46 Ibid., p. 64.
47 Ibid.
48 At p. 66.
49 Ibid.
50 At p. 78f.

> requirements. Until now, these differences have not hindered the exchange of research animals across borders, but they might become problematic in the case of the import/export of animals for research on xenotransplantation.[51]

In respect of the public perception of xenotransplantation, it is highlighted that this will be influenced by the different socio-cultural systems that exist internationally.[52] Thus, the workshop found that while there are universal ethical principles, diverse contexts mean they are interpreted in different ways.[53] Among the issues that influence public perceptions of xenotransplantation the report names the shortage of human organ donors, the concept of brain death and the need for informed decision making.[54]

On the issue of patient monitoring and consent the report concurs with the suggestion of the WHO that the surveillance requirements will require the development of traditional bioethics concepts.[55] The OECD suggests that this is because xenotransplantation will 'involve not only the subject but also close contacts and ultimately the community'.[56] Thus, while consent is only usually required from the participant in a trial or medical procedure, the risks to third parties who are associated with xenotransplantation will make consent from those close to the participant necessary.

The workshop also heard concerns surrounding the ambiguous impact xenotransplantation may have on resource-poor countries. While it may help to stem the black market in human tissue that can instrumentalize the poor in such countries, the hope offered by the procedure is likely to remain beyond the reach of the majority in these nations due to its expense.[57] In order to address the diverse ethical issues raised by animal to human transplants, the OECD report insists:

> Universal guidelines and legal protection of human dignity and autonomy are needed to address these concerns. The visible presence of such protection will facilitate the development of appropriate research. Therefore, to ensure universal observance of the principles and rules, international agreements and standards should be formulated by committees with representatives from both the developed and developing world.[58]

The report concludes that to date the economic ramifications of developing animal to human transplantation have not been examined. The costs and benefits associated with xenotransplantation must be assessed by viewing the procedure in the context of the burden associated with the diseases for which xenotransplantation may prove a remedy and the potential of other technologies to address these conditions.[59] The report ends by highlighting the remaining scientific obstacles and gaps in research

---

51 At p. 79.
52 Ibid.
53 Ibid.
54 Ibid.
55 At p. 80.
56 Ibid.
57 Ibid.
58 Ibid.
59 At p. 73f.

that must be overcome for xenotransplantation to become a clinical reality. These include issues surrounding the potential infection risk associated with the procedure and the uncertainty of whether animal organs will function successfully in humans.[60]

In 2000 the OECD held a joint consultation exercise with the WHO on the surveillance issues raised by xenotransplantation.[61] The executive summary of the consultation encourages member countries to: establish national registries; designate surveillance facilities linked to international facilities; adopt internationally agreed criteria; facilitate the free exchange of information while protecting confidentiality; provide means by which non-confidential information could be easily updated; and develop education programmes.[62]

In its consideration of the ethical issues raised by xenotransplantation surveillance the Report acknowledges:

> ... it has become clear that a broad range of ethical implications, including the feasibility of xenotransplantation and of the surveillance schemes, will have to be addressed.[63]

The consultation holds that animal to human transplantation 'raises issues that are not adequately covered in current literature'.[64] Among the areas which require more attention are: privacy and confidentiality; conflicts between public and private interests; potential infringements of the human rights of the first recipients; and the relationship between international and domestic law.[65] It is regarded as particularly important to consider how the public can be engaged in xenotransplantation debates, the kind of consent process that is most appropriate and whether there are types of clinical study that can answer important scientific questions while minimizing public risk.

In terms of the consent question, and particularly the duration of compliance needed, the Report claims that there are precedents for patients binding themselves in advance to medical treatment. Thus, it says:

> One potentially applicable approach is referred to as 'The Ulysses Contract'. In this situation, a person binds him-/herself in advance to a future therapeutic course of action. Such contracts have been advocated, for example, for patients with severe bipolar disease who fluctuate between ability and inability to consent.[66]

It is highlighted that 'in the case of xenotransplantation, such binding consent would be enforced also to protect others, not only actual contractors'.[67] The thorny problem of consent will be considered below.[68]

---

60 Ibid.
61 OECD/WHO (2001).
62 Ibid., p. 5.
63 Ibid., p. 20.
64 Ibid.
65 Ibid.
66 At p. 21.
67 At p. 21.
68 See chapter 7 for discussion.

The document proposes to formulate a network of national and international exchange on the public health response necessitated by xenotransplantation.[69] The different participants in the proposed network are the local community, larger regional bodies, countrywide decision-making executives and the international community.[70] The consultation found that a framework that encourages co-operation at these different administrative levels is well placed to address the three features it holds to be necessary for successful xenotransplantation surveillance: the ability to harmonize norms and standards, flexibility and the timely detection of adverse disease events.[71]

It should be noted that, although the consultation is based on the need to establish an international surveillance system, it was thought that formulating one from scratch would be most likely to fail.[72] With this concern in mind it was deemed preferable to:

> ... strengthen communication between the scientific and policy making communities, and among public health officials, the private sector and the public.[73]

To this end:

> The WHO in co-operation with the OECD and other relevant international bodies (e.g. Council of Europe) was invited to take a leadership role in facilitating the development of internationally agreed norms for testing and reporting, and of an effective xenogenic infectious disease surveillance network.[74]

OECD: summary The OECD workshop presents xenotransplantation as an issue that raises difficult socio-ethical and ethico-legal issues. It emphasizes that these require the same level of international co-operation as the technical issues. The OECD's interest in the socio-ethical issues raised by xenotransplantation leads it to consider the possible impact of the procedure on resource-poor countries. The joint OECD/WHO consultation moves away from the WHO suggestion that the recipients of animal organs would have to be free to leave trials at anytime. Instead the consultation notes ways in which it may be possible to bind individuals to treatment regimes. In addition, its joint consultation with the WHO notes that the traditional understanding of consent may need to develop in order to incorporate third parties. The involvement of the OECD in discussions on xenotransplantation has helped to broaden the scope of international debates, because its remit means that it places socio-economic and ethico-legal issues at the centre of its analysis.

---

69 At p. 28f.

70 At p. 28ff.

71 At p. 28.

72 At p. 36.

73 Ibid.

74 Ibid.

The European Commission

The European Commission published the final version of its *Opinion on the State of the Art Concerning Xenotransplantation* in October 2001.[75] The document was intended to inform the European Commission of issues that are important in the area of xenotransplantation and 'to identify issues that may require community-wide action'.[76] The report gives considerable importance to the infection risks posed by xenotransplantation.[77] It identifies the pig as the animal most likely to be used as source for tissue and organs because it is easier to breed than non-human primates and presents less chance of transmitting infections to humans.[78] However, it is acknowledged that even raising pigs under barriered conditions will not completely eliminate the risk that they will transmit animal viruses to the human population.[79] Furthermore, transplanting animal tissue into individual patients who have suppressed immune systems may prove particularly risky.[80]

In respect of surveillance measures, the report highlights that although various supranational organizations, including the Council of Europe, have examined the issues raised by xenotransplantation, no mechanism has been created to collate and share information between Member States and no Europe-wide legislation or regulations have been formulated.[81] This is despite the fact that the infection risk posed by xenotransplantation could be more successfully treated by a Europe-wide approach that unites the efforts of individual Member States.[82] Given this shortcoming the European Commission suggests:

> ... it is important that there should be some form of registration of the clinical trials, and collation and exchange of information. An agency like the WHO seems a likely candidate to function as office for the distribution of information to local governments.[83]

The report acknowledges that there are ethical questions concerning humans and animals that must be addressed.[84] In respect of humans, the report states:

> Xenotransplantation raises ethical as well as scientific considerations for all those involved. Whilst these will not be discussed in detail they include practical consideration such as obtaining informed consent from the early clinical trial patients, the gaining of consent from non-transplanted persons in contact with the patient for surveillance purposes ... archiving of samples, data protection of personal details, dissemination of results, confidentiality conditions by contributing commercial

[75] European Commission (2001), *Opinion on the State of the Art Concerning Xenotransplantation*, European Commission: Brussels.

[76] Ibid., p. 2.

[77] Ibid., p. 6ff.

[78] Ibid., p. 6.

[79] Ibid., p. 8.

[80] Ibid., p. 9.

[81] Ibid., p. 4.

[82] Ibid., p. 10.

[83] Ibid., p. 11.

[84] Ibid., p. 11ff.

companies, and even, perhaps, how to handle breaches of agreed contracts when others may be put at risk.[85]

On the ethical issues that concern the treatment of animals, the Commission suggests that because animals are eaten by humans, using animals will not be regarded as ethically problematic by many – although some will object to this particular use of animals.[86] However, animals that are used in xenotransplantation would not be caused 'avoidable suffering' and should be 'killed painlessly'.[87]

In its conclusion and recommendations, the report suggests that the European Parliament's Directive 2001/20/EC, which outlines standards for maintaining good clinical practice in clinical trials, might provide a suitable legal framework for regulating xenotransplantation trials.[88] In addition, its recommendations include:

- The establishment of a centralized regulatory body.
- An iterative risk analysis by the European Commission.
- That specific measures for clinical trials dealing with authorization, informed consent, registration, surveillance of patients and those at risk should be defined on the basis of Directive 2001/20/EC.
- The maintenance of appropriate standards in animal welfare and the procurement of organs.
- Additional research by the European Commission to determine the risks of viral infection and the risks associated with severe immunosuppression.
- The need to implement surveillance measures for source animals.[89]

The European Commission: summary The document published by the European Commission is not intended to analyze or advance the debate on animal to human transplantation, but rather to inform the Commission of the current standing of research in the area. Thus, while the document notes the ethical issues that exist, it does not examine them in any detail. However, in terms of regulation the Commission does emphasize that, despite much discussion about the value of having some form of Europe-wide or international regulation of xenotransplantation, nothing of this nature exists. The Commission adds its voice to the calls for such a framework to be established.

The Council of Europe

On 30 September 1997 the Council of Europe's Committee of Ministers adopted Recommendation No R (97) 15. This asks Member States to establish a mechanism for the regulation of the following aspects of xenotransplantation: research and clinical trials; the selection and care of animals; xenotransplantation programmes; and the long-term follow up of recipients and source animals. This recommendation

85 Ibid., p. 11f.

86 Ibid., p. 12.

87 Ibid.

88 At p. 14.

89 At p. 14f.

appears to sanction the development of xenotransplantation providing that certain standards are upheld, and proposes that:

> Governments of member States should establish a mechanism for the registration and regulation of the following aspects of xenotransplantation with a view to minimising the risk of transmission of known or unknown diseases and infections to either the human or animal population:
>
> i. basic research and clinical trials;
> ii. the source and care of animals for their use in xenotransplantation;
> iii. xenotransplantation programmes;
> iv. long-term follow-up and review of xenograft recipients and the xenograft source animals.[90]

However, on 29 January 1999 the Parliamentary Assembly of the Council of Europe adopted Recommendation 1399. This statement recommends to the Council of Ministers that they should:

> i. work for the rapid introduction in all member states of a legally-binding moratorium on all clinical xenotransplantations;
> ii. take steps to make this moratorium a worldwide legal agreement;
> iii. ask its European Health Committee and Steering Committee on Bioethics to work out, in co-operation with the World Health Organization, a strategy for balancing the ethical, medical, scientific, legal, social and public health aspects of xenotransplantation, before the scientific and medical establishment is permitted to proceed with clinical trials on humans.[91]

The Council of Ministers did not adopt this cautious recommendation. Instead it established a Working Party, directed by the Steering Committee on Bioethics and the European Health Committee, to examine the issues raised by animal to human transplants. The Working Party's remit ran from 1999 to 2001. Its terms of reference state that, among other things, it had a responsibility:

> a. to monitor developments in the field of xenotransplantation in member States and in other States, in particular in co-operation with other international organisations, currently addressing the issue (including the WHO, OECD and EU).
>
> - to collect and make available information concerning regulations and research, clinical trials and current practice in this field,
> - to make, at appropriate intervals, a report on the state of the art ...
>
> b. to consider ... the implications of xenotransplantation for the member States of the Council of Europe, concerning:
>
> i. respect of ethical and legal principles
> ii. protection of safety and quality regarding xenotransplantation

---

[90] Recommendation No R (97) 15, www.coe.int/T/E/Social_Cohesion/Health/Recommendations/Rec(1997)15.asp.

[91] Recommendation 1399 (1999) 1 http://assembly.coe.int/documents/adoptedtext/ta99/erec1399.htm.

iii. efficiency and cost-effectiveness, taking into account alternative solutions
iv. protection of animals.

c. to make recommendations on informing the public and media about xenotransplantation.

d. to prepare draft guidelines on xenotransplantation, taking into account the activities carried out by other bodies, in particular international organisations, and the necessity of world-wide co-operation.[92]

The Working Party published the final version of its *Report on the State of the Art in the Field of Xenotransplantation* in February 2003.[93] The group explains that the aim of the report is to put:

> ... xenotransplantation into context while providing interested parties and those responsible for drafting the Recommendation of xenotransplantation with the most recent information concerning advances in this new therapeutic field.[94]

The Recommendation informed by the *State of the Art Report*, Recommendation Rec (2003) 10 of the Council of Ministers to Member States on Xenotransplantation, was published in June 2003.[95] The content of the Recommendation will be assessed after we have noted some of the points raised by the *State of the Art Report*.

As required by the Working Party's terms of reference, its *State of the Art Report* provides a broad survey of the development of xenotransplantation. More specifically, it reports on the state of research on whole organs, cellular treatments, extra-corporeal treatments and the immunological and physiological features of xenotransplantation.[96] It then considers the various pre-clinical procedures that are underway using both pigs and primates,[97] before advancing to explore the cultural, ethical, religious and legal aspects of animal to human transplantation.[98]

The Working Party records that there has been very little success in the field of whole organ xenotransplantation.[99] In respect of cellular transplants, the Working Party concludes that, although such techniques are less complicated than clinical work with whole organs, more research is required to ascertain the physiological complexities associated with cellular treatment. Furthermore, on the issue of cellular transplants, concern is raised that because they only necessitate a 'minor intervention':

---

92 Terms of reference available at http://www.xenotransplant.ineu.org/xenotrans/news/19990302a.htm.

93 Council of Europe (2003), *Report on the State of the Art in the Field of Xenotransplantation*, Council of Europe: Strasbourg. The full report is available at http://www.coe.int/T/E/Legal_Affairs/Legal_co-operation/Bioethics/ Activities/Xenotransplantation/XENO(2003)1_SAR.pdf.

94 Ibid., p. 7.

95 http://www.coe.int/T/E/Social_Cohesion/Health/Recommendations/Rec(2003)10.asp.

96 Council of Europe (2003), pp. 17–30.

97 At pp. 31–52.

98 At pp. 53–76.

99 At p. 17ff.

> This may partly explain why several clinical trials have been initiated without significant experience first being obtained in primate models.[100]

In respect of the clinical extra-corporeal use of animal tissue, the Working Group notes that mouse cells have been used to grow skin to treat burns victims, without any signs of adverse effects, for many years.[101] But the group reports that generally there is 'little evidence' on the clinical effectiveness of other extra-corporal treatments, or cellular treatments such as those used to treat Parkinson's disease and in liver assist devices.[102]

In relation to the immunological difficulties that exist for xenotransplantation, the Working Group notes that while advances have been made in overcoming hyperacute rejection, problems remain with other responses such as acute vascular rejection.[103] In fact acute vascular rejection, which occurs within days of the transplant, is considered to present such an obstacle to successful xenotransplantation that the Working Group states that strategies to prevent it 'are not yet effective enough to enter clinical xenotransplantation of solid porcine organs, tissues or cells within the near future'.[104] The group reports that there is also insufficient information on the physiological risks associated with xenotransplantation,[105] but states that it may not be possible to gain such information without advances in the area of immunology that will allow transplant recipients to live longer.[106]

The *State of the Art Report* then considers in some detail the arguments for and against the use of non-human primates.[107] It concludes that xenotransplantation using non-human primates 'should not be performed at present or in the near future'.[108] The Working Party suggests that risk management strategies for the use of porcine tissue have been identified,[109] but concludes that despite such work 'there is still a need for additional risk assessment and refinement of the risk management procedures'.[110] This is not least because there are particular concerns surrounding the problems that may be created by 'transplanting pig tissue into an immuno-suppressed human'.[111]

The Working Group then addresses the 'Cultural, Ethical and Religious Aspects of Xenotransplantation'.[112] The general socio-cultural attitudes that exist towards 'science, technology, medicine and death' are noted to be significant because the public acceptance of xenotransplantation 'will be crucial if the technology is to

100 At p. 23.
101 At p. 24.
102 At p. 25.
103 At p. 27.
104 Ibid.
105 At p. 30.
106 Ibid.
107 At pp. 32–48.
108 At p. 48.
109 At p. 48f.
110 At p. 52.
111 At p. 49.
112 Section 7.

become accepted as a medical practice'.[113] More specifically, the Report highlights the concern that exists about the development of new biomedical techniques, given the unknown risks they pose;[114] a situation that has led to suggestions that techniques like xenotransplantation should not be used 'unless we can be sure of the consequences'.[115] The Report also states that there is concern that xenotransplantation is being developed primarily for the huge financial benefits it offers and not for health reasons.[116] In light of such issues the Report insists that:

> If the technology is to be accepted and used, there are various questions that must be answered. These include demonstrating that:
> - there are no appropriate alternative options which are available;
> - there is a genuine medical need for xenotransplantation;
> - the technology is efficacious;
> - the highest possible levels of safety for patients and the wider human population can be guaranteed;
> - all issues of animal husbandry, care, welfare and use can be properly dealt with; and
> - there are real benefits for patients, families and society and not just for the commercial companies who stand to make a profit from this procedure.[117]

The Working Party focuses on a number of ethical issues raised by xenotransplantation. For example, in response to suggestions that biomedical procedures like xenotransplantation are in some way against nature, the Working Party explains:

> The line between what is natural and unnatural is often very difficult to draw. Medicine seems to intervene in order to prevent the 'natural' breakdown caused by diseases, while at the same time medicine is trying to restore 'natural' functions and well being. In other words, it is extremely difficult to be categorical about what is natural in our modern technological world.[118]

On the issue of consent, the Working Party notes that all of the requirements usually expected in experimental medical procedures should apply to xenotransplantation. Thus, patients should be fully informed regarding risks, benefits and the likely outcome.[119] However, the Working Party goes on to suggest:

> In xenotransplantation, there are particular problems since the first recipients are likely to be those in fairly extreme situations, whose medical condition, lack of alternative treatments, and level of desperation may make consent a difficult issue.[120]

The Working Party further outlines a number of factors that complicate the issue of consent. For example, the potential public health risks associated with

113 At p. 53.
114 Ibid.
115 Ibid.
116 At p. 54.
117 Ibid.
118 At p. 66.
119 At p. 67.
120 Ibid.

xenotransplantation make it 'difficult to see how the normal right to withdraw from a procedure can be allowed in the case of xenotransplantation',[121] and concedes that the legal enforcement of surveillance measures is unlikely to be either 'possible or acceptable'.[122] Yet it also claims that the concerns that surround the implementation of surveillance requirements may not be insuperable because:

> Those engaged in transplant work stress that the recipients' choice should be well known and therefore it will be easy to assess how willing patients will be to conform (transplant patients are known to be conformists).[123]

In relation to the restrictions and high degree of risk that early participants in clinical trials are likely to have to accept in order to receive a transplant, the Working Party stresses that it is permissible for patients to infringe their rights to participate in such trials.[124] It states:

> The ability to give consent means that patients may accept risky procedures fully understanding those risks and may set limits to others rights or freedoms to which they are entitled. It is ethically permissible for patients to choose to set aside such human rights such as the right to begin a family or the freedom to donate blood, if there is some overwhelming public good to be attained or public harm avoided.[125]

Like the OECD, the Council of Europe Working Party suggests that the risks associated with xenotransplantation mean 'informed consent should usually be obtained from close contacts such as relatives and family',[126] while acknowledging that obtaining freely given consent from close contacts will prove difficult. Thus, it suggests close contacts should, as a minimum requirement, be informed about the procedure and the risks associated with it.[127] However, the Working Party states:

> Ideally, the informed consent of close relatives and family should be obtained even if this might set aside other moral principles like autonomy, privacy and confidentiality. These principles are never absolute obstacles and communities are entitled to limit them where there is serious harm to the individual concerned or to other people. A high level of risk to public health would be considered an adequate basis for limiting these principles.[128]

The report pays considerable attention to the use and welfare of animals in xenotransplantation.[129] In this respect, two issues are deemed particularly important; namely, whether it is acceptable to use animals as a source of organs and tissue and, if so, what limits should be imposed to protect their welfare.[130] The report provides

---

121 Ibid.
122 Ibid.
123 Ibid.
124 Ibid.
125 Ibid.
126 Ibid.
127 Ibid.
128 Ibid.
129 At p. 68ff.
130 At p. 69.

a review of the different features that impact on the acceptability of the use of animals in xenotransplantation. The main welfare issues are identified as:

> The manner in which animals are produced and subsequently bred – techniques in transgenesis with associated wastage rates, surgical interventions, hysterotomy derivation, segregated and/or medicated early weaning.
>
> The husbandry, care and transport of animals; the use of isolators and biocontainment systems.
>
> Routine procedures carried out on animals, e.g. blood and tissue sampling.
>
> Harvesting of tissues and organs, and the humane killing of animals.[131]

The report indicates that there is wide variation in the attitude towards xenotransplantation both within and between different religious traditions.[132] These diverse perspectives are often influenced by the value a particular tradition affords to animal life.[133] It is noted that only Buddhists, Hindus and Native Americans – Hindus and Native Americans are also noted to oppose allotransplantation – are entirely opposed to animal to human transplants.[134]

Finally, between 1999 and 2000, as part of its remit, the Working Party of the Council of Europe surveyed 27 countries on the state of research and regulations on xenotransplantation in their jurisdiction. The results of these surveys form the final section of the *State of the Art Report*.[135] The surveys will be employed later in this chapter as the framework for the responses different nation states have made to animal to human transplants. Thus, the surveys will not be given extensive treatment here. However, it is interesting to note the main findings of the survey. The Working Party states that the survey reveals that a minority of the states which responded to the survey have a legal framework specifically to address xenotransplantation.[136] It concludes:

> ... this survey shows that the legal and regulatory framework for xenotransplantation is incomplete in many States and pleads in favour of the development of European guidelines with a twofold aim of (a) harmonising regulations in Europe and (b) contributing to the preparation of such a framework in States where no such guidelines exist.[137]

In light of these concerns, the Council of Europe Recommendation, published after the *State of the Art Report*, emphasizes that efforts to harness the promise of xenotransplantation for human health must be conducted within properly regulated, authorized systems.[138] Furthermore, the Recommendation states that

131 At p. 71.

132 At p. 74f.

133 At p. 74.

134 Ibid.

135 At pp. 75–86.

136 At p. 85.

137 At p. 86.

138 Recommendation Rec (2003) of the Committee of Ministers to Member States on Xenotransplantation, Articles 4 and 5.

xenotransplantation should only be authorized within a Member State if it is 'highly probable that there is no risk in particular of infection, for public health'.[139] Thus, although the Recommendation falls short of adopting the moratorium recommended by the Parliamentary Assembly in 1999, it does require considerable advances to be made before it will consider it acceptable to move to clinical trials.

The Committee of Ministers also calls for Member States to have procedures in place to deal with any disease events that may arise from xenotransplantation,[140] and to trace and monitor recipients, their close contacts and professional staff.[141] These groups must also be provided with sufficient information on the procedure and its risks.[142] Furthermore,

> The patient should also ensure that such information is provided to any future close personal contacts.[143]

The provision of adequate information is a key feature of transplant recipients being able to consent to a xenotransplant.[144] The Recommendation states that patients should be able to withdraw consent to monitoring procedures 'prior to xenotransplantation'.[145] However,

> If, after the xenotransplantation has been carried out, the recipient or his or her close personal contacts refuse to comply with the constraints associated with xenotransplantation, public authorities should intervene and take appropriate measures, where public health protection so requires, in conformity with principles of necessity and proportionality.[146]

Thus, although patients can withdraw their consent before the transplant takes place, this is not the case once it has taken place. This recommendation is based on the suggestion of the Working Group in its *State of the Art Report* that 'it is difficult to see how the normal right to withdraw from a procedure can be allowed in the case of xenotransplantation'.[147]

The Recommendation also requires Member States to co-operate in their efforts to develop and manage animal to human transplantation.[148] States should:

> ... co-operate through international surveillance procedures and agreements. They should also take appropriate steps to facilitate the co-ordination of research in xenotransplantation in order to improve its efficacy and safety, to avoid unnecessary duplication and to minimise animal use and suffering.[149]

---

139 Article 5, point 1a.
140 Article 7.
141 Article 9.
142 Articles 13 and 14.
143 Article 14.
144 Article 16.
145 Article 16, point 2.
146 Article 21.
147 Council of Europe (2003), p. 67.
148 Recommendation Rec (2003), articles 31 and 32.
149 Article 32.

The Council of Europe: summary Since 1999, when the Parliamentary Assembly called for a legally binding moratorium on clinical xenotransplantation to be adopted, the attitude of the Council of Europe towards the development of animal to human transplantation has become more permissive. The Working Party on Xenotransplantation that was formed as a response to the call for a moratorium has recommended that animal to human transplantation can proceed providing certain preconditions are fulfilled. These preconditions include the need for nation states to have a regulatory framework in place and a greater amount of certainty on the risks posed by the procedure. To provide such confidence in the procedure, the Working Group suggests that more research is required on all forms of xenotransplantation. The *State of the Art Report* gives considerable attention to the ethical and legal issues raised by xenotransplantation. Like the WHO and the OECD, the Council of Europe affords special attention to consent, because it is an ethico-legal principle that has the potential to be an important element in an effective and appropriate xenotransplantation surveillance system. However, in its *State of the Art Report* the Working Party suggests that the consent of transplant recipients and their close contacts to life-long surveillance is highly desirable, but concedes that no mechanisms exist to deal with a subsequent failure to abide by the terms of that consent. However, should participants and their contacts not comply with surveillance measures, the Committee of Ministers suggests that constraints could be used.

Nation States

In this section the perspectives of different countries on animal to human transplantation will be examined. This task will be informed by the results of the Council of Europe questionnaire on xenotransplantation issued to 27 countries in September 1999. The responses of the countries surveyed reveal various levels of interest in xenotransplantation and equally diverse efforts to provide a regulatory framework to monitor the procedure.[150] Provided that countries have reported their positions accurately, it is possible to ascertain from these surveys which countries are developing xenotransplantation and their regulatory response to the issues it presents. We will also draw on documentation and reports that have been issued by individual countries as part of their regulatory response to xenotransplantation. Our examination will be conducted under three headings: countries not developing xenotransplantation; those that are conducting research in animal models; and, finally, countries that report they are conducting xenotransplantation clinical trials.

Countries Not Developing Xenotransplantation

Some of the 27 countries surveyed by the Council of Europe, including Albania, Bulgaria, Croatia, Cyprus, Finland, Hungary, Turkey, Latvia, Malta, the Slovak

150 In reporting these responses we draw directly on the surveys returned to the Council of Europe, as well as from the summary the Council of Europe provides of these results in its *State of the Art Report on Xenotransplantation* (2003).

Republic, Georgia and Andorra, report they are not developing xenotransplantation. Furthermore, these countries have no, or few, regulations that apply to xenotransplantation procedures.[151] Regardless of their own decision not to develop animal to human transplantation, the failure of such countries to regulate xenotransplantation techniques is a matter of concern since it could undermine international and European-wide efforts to regulate the procedure. Certainly, those wishing to develop xenotransplantation in an environment free of legislative restrictions could choose to conduct their research in a nation state without prohibitive policies. A case in point is Albania, which reported that it does not require any authorization to carry out xenotransplantation procedures in animal or human models.[152] Efforts to manage the international public health risks associated with xenotransplantation will prove difficult while such regulatory gaps remain. Thus, it is of concern that the Council of Europe found that 20 per cent of the countries responding to its survey reported that xenotransplantation could be conducted in their jurisdiction without any specific authorization being required.[153]

Countries Developing Xenotransplantation in Animal Models

The Council of Europe reports that 48 per cent of the countries it surveyed were conducting xenotransplantation research involving animals.[154] These countries were Belgium, Canada, the Czech Republic, France, Germany, Italy, the Netherlands, Spain, Sweden, Switzerland, the United Kingdom and the United States.[155] Seventeen countries, including all of those carrying out xenotransplantation research using animals, reported that their general animal protection laws are applicable to xenotransplantation research.[156] In this section we will examine the regulatory work being undertaken by some of these countries – Sweden, France and Canada. In addition, we will consider the regulatory response of Australia to the development of xenotransplantation. Although this country was not part of the Council of Europe survey, xenotransplantation has been the object of considerable interest and activity in Australia, and its cultural and legal similarities to many European countries make it a useful paradigm.

Sweden Although Sweden is not currently conducting clinical trials, two xenotransplantation trials did take place in Sweden in 1995, when it had no legislation on animal to human transplants in place. To fill this void the Swedish Committee on Xenotransplantation was established in 1997, and began its work in January 1998. The Committee's terms of reference include the 'medical, ethical,

[151] *Responses Given to the Working Party on Xenotransplantation: Questionnaire on Xenotransplantation.* However, the Slovak Republic and the Republic of Georgia both claim that animal protection laws are applicable to xenotransplantation.

[152] Recorded in Albania's response to *Working Party on Xenotransplantation: Questionnaire on Xenotransplantation.*

[153] Council of Europe (2003), p. 79, Table 25.

[154] Council of Europe (2003), p. 82, Table 27.

[155] Ibid.

[156] At p. 77, Table 24.

legal and animal protection aspects' of xenotransplantation.[157] Under its terms of reference it has a responsibility to: establish the conditions under which clinical trials could take place; identify the authority that should be responsible for implementing these standards; propose safety guidelines for animal to human transplants; ensure the quality control of organs and tissue from source animals; and report on any necessary statutory changes. Furthermore, the Committee must make decisions on the allocation of organs and determine which patients receive allografts and which xenotransplants.[158] The Committee has sought to determine public opinion on xenotransplantation by commissioning a survey of attitudes. The survey found a generally positive attitude towards xenotransplantation, providing the risks involved are minimal.[159]

The main topic addressed in *From One Species to Another*, the report of the Swedish Committee on Xenotransplantation, is how clinical trials should be monitored.[160] More generally, the report provides a summary of the issues examined by the Swedish Committee on Xenotransplantation and the statutory proposals it makes for regulating animal to human transplants. A number of ethical principles underpin the Committee's evaluations:

> One principle is the principle of beneficence (you ought to do good), interpreted as a requirement for knowledge ... The other is the principle of non-maleficence (you should not do harm), applied as the principle of precaution. The principle of precaution aims at minimising risks for harm by influencing the design of the system of rules and other elements in the infrastructure concerning xenotransplantation.[161]

This places an ethical framework at the heart of the Committee's work, and integrates ethico-social concerns with the practical interests of the report. Despite its commitment to these principles, the Committee acknowledges that difficulty arises when they conflict.[162] Having identified the relevant principles, the report then highlights the issues that must be addressed in order for policy decisions on xenotransplantation to make a positive contribution to human well-being and avoid causing harm. For example, the need to obviate the possibility of zoonoses being transmitted to humans is considered. So too are the attitudes of recipients towards the animal organs they receive; the well-being of animals; and the gaps in scientific knowledge that make an accurate risk assessment and appropriate action difficult to determine.[163] Given its philosophical foundations, to be internally consistent the Committee deems it necessary to recommend that:

> ... only carefully controlled clinical trials of a limited extent and where the risks are assessed to be manageable should be allowed. The current system of rules is, in our

157 The Swedish Committee on Xenotransplantation (1999), *From One Species to Another*, Swedish Committee on Xenotransplantation: Stockholm, at p. 7.

158 At p. 4.

159 At p. 7f.

160 At p. 7.

161 At p. 8.

162 At p. 8f.

163 At p. 11ff.

> opinion, insufficient to deal with these issues. We therefore propose that these rules are supplemented with a special system of rules for xenotransplantation.[164]

The recommended system involves a procedure to evaluate applications to carry out clinical trials, a register of recipients and a tissue bank. In addition, among the proposals in the report are those for a special Act, the Xeno Licensing and Control Ordinance, to regulate clinical trials.[165] It also recommends that a special authority, the Xenotransplantation Board, be established to regulate xenotransplantation.[166] Further consideration should be given to the issue of informed consent and the status of the patient. Regardless of the outcome of these investigations, a psychologist should be part of the transplant team and the Xenotransplantation Board should have a role in choosing those who are suitable to take part in early trials.[167] Finally, until the proposals in the document have been evaluated by Parliament, no clinical trials should take place.[168] The report ends with recommendations for new legislation and an amendment to current law. These statutory proposals concern the regulation of clinical trials, proposals for a biobank, an amendment to the Secrecy Act and instructions to the Xenotransplantation Board.[169] These legislative recommendations highlight the conviction of the Committee that there is a need for the statutory regulation of xenotransplantation. As Stefan Reimer, a member of the Xenotransplantation Committee, stresses:

> ... the decisions of the committee should be binding and not just advisory. This means that there should be appeal to administrative courts.[170]

France France established an expert committee on xenotransplantation in 1995. This group published a document, *Good Practice Guidelines for the Production of Pigs* in 1996,[171] and the ethical issues raised by xenotransplantation were examined subsequently by the French Advisory Ethics Committee. In *Opinion on Ethics and Xenotransplantation*, the Advisory Ethics Committee identifies the scientific issues raised by xenotransplantation before considering its ethical dimensions.[172] The report identifies the scientific issues that must be addressed as being rejection, physiology, immunology and the risk that animal infections will pass to humans. It also concludes that even if these scientific problems are overcome it remains necessary to consider a number of ethical questions. These ethical issues include the need to decide at what point in scientific progress on xenotransplantation it will be ethical to undertake clinical trials; who the first transplant recipients will be; what

164 At p. 14.

165 At p. 14.

166 At p. 15.

167 At p. 16.

168 At p. 17.

169 At pp. 19–40.

170 Reimer, S. (2000), 'Xenotransplantation in Sweden', *Pathologie Biologie*, **48** (4), pp. 440–442, at p. 442.

171 As referenced in Council of Europe (2003) at p. 63.

172 National Consultative Bioethics Committee for Health and Life Sciences (1999), *Opinion on Ethics and Xenotransplantation*, Paris, **61**, 11 June (pages unnumbered).

safety precautions should be taken, and the type of information that should be given to patients. A 'major' ethical issue is identified as that encountered by patients who may have to decide whether it is better to wait an unknown length of time for an allograft, that will stand a better chance of success, or to accept an immediate xenotransplant with unknown results.

Despite such concerns, at a number of points the report downplays the ethical dilemmas that are raised by xenotransplantation. For example, the Advisory Committee suggests that the use of pigs in xenotransplantation will not present substantial ethical obstacles because of their other social uses. Furthermore, although consent is often viewed as a particularly problematic aspect of xenotransplantation, this report suggests:

> Patient's consent to xenografting, even initially, does not appear to be very different from what is generally practised now for human organs. Patients must be completely informed about the experimental nature of the procedure, the successive phases, the risks, and the alternatives. Such information must definitely be given by qualified personnel capable of coping with psychological, scientific, and ethical issues. Consent should be requested in the same manner as for allografts.[173]

However, it is acknowledged that one problem which could arise in relation to consent is that:

> ... patients will have to consent and even commit themselves in writing for this procedure to take place for some considerable period of time during which they would be obliged to accept the possible constraints of quarantine measures.[174]

The report concludes that it is acceptable to use animals as a source of organs for humans. However, it also notes that, on the basis of current knowledge, it is uncertain whether the disease risk posed by xenotransplantation is sufficient to permit clinical trials.

Canada In November 1997 a National Forum on Xenotransplantation was held in Canada.[175] The proceedings of the Forum report that its purpose was to:

> ... present information and initiate discussion on the risks, benefits and ethics of xenotransplantation; to identify key regulatory issues; and define areas where research and new information is required.[176]

Among the ethical issues addressed were those surrounding the legitimate use of animals, issues of patient ethics and questions raised by efforts to review xenotransplantation proposals. These issues were considered within the wider

---

173 Ibid.

174 Ibid.

175 Therapeutic Products Program, Health Canada (1997), *Excerpts from the Report of the National Forum on Xenotransplantation: Clinical, Ethical and Regulatory Issues November 6–8*, Health Canada: Ottawa, Canada, www.islet.org/25.htm (pages unnumbered).

176 Ibid.

context of the ethical issues raised at the 'human/-animal/-gene/-machine interface'.[177] Discussion considered fundamental questions such as whether xenotransplantation was 'intrinsically acceptable', or 'inherently right or wrong'.[178] Efforts to address this question involved an examination of whether the use of animals as a source of organs is fundamentally different from using them as a source of food and an examination of the genetic modification of animals. A second facet of this discussion was whether the risks associated with xenotransplantation were too great to permit the procedure to be developed. More generally, it was suggested that there was a:

> ... need to consider the impact that the advent of xenotransplantation technology will have on our societal paradigm, that collection of attitudes, values, myths, beliefs, symbols – the 'shared story' – that we buy into in order to form society and which we use to give meaning to our individual and collective lives.[179]

Other issues discussed, and deemed to need further treatment, in the area of animal welfare included: whether international standards or a national committee should regulate the use of animals; whether the genetic modification of animals is legitimate; and whether the seclusion of animals to protect public health was acceptable.[180]

The issue of informed consent dominated exchanges on patient ethics. This discussion included considerations of what constitutes truly informed consent, the minimum of information that should be given to patients to make consent possible, whether informed consent should be required from close contacts of the transplant recipient and whether stringent surveillance measures are feasible. It was also asked whether some groups of patients should be excluded from early clinical trials because of their inability to consent to or comply with surveillance. Of primary concern was the 'highly desirable' suggestion that patients would have to consent to life-long surveillance – although the issue was thought to need additional discussion.[181] It was recommended that a number of changes should be made to the traditional informed consent framework. That is, consent should be gained from third parties; restrictions on patient autonomy should be put in place to protect the health of individuals and the community; there should be efforts made to evaluate whether patients would comply with surveillance measures; and transplant recipients should be required to consent to undergo an autopsy on death. On the topic of Ethical Review Boards, participants considered whether such groups had sufficient knowledge to review proposals to conduct xenotransplantation trials and how these Review Boards might balance the benefits to individuals against the risks to the wider community. It was decided that a National Advisory Board should be founded to supplement the work of local research review boards. However:

---

177 Somerville, M. (1997a), Plenary Session I: Overview, 'Xenotransplantation: Ethics at the Human/ -Animal/ -Gene/ -Machine Interface', in Therapeutic Products Program, Health Canada (1997).

178 Ibid.

179 Ibid.

180 Therapeutic Products Program, Health Canada (1997), www.hc-sc.gc.ca.

181 Summary of Key Issues and Recommendations, Section 10 Surveillance (Registeries and Sample Banks).

> The major ethical issue articulated at the forum, on which the participants were seriously divided in their views, was whether clinical trials of xenotransplantation in the human context should be allowed to commence.[182]

In seeking to address this question, participants were primarily concerned with the risk the procedure posed to public health. On this issue the forum decided:

> ... that the ethics of xenotransplantation must be embedded in the science – bad ethics is bad science and, in this area in particular, ethics cannot just be an add-on after the science had been carried out. Second, it was agreed that it is essential to proceeding with any human trials of xenotransplantation that there first be an informed public debate and that, ultimately, it is Canadian society which must decide whether xenotransplantation will proceed.[183]

In response to this requirement for public involvement in the decision as to whether Canada should proceed with xenotransplantation, in March 1999 public opinion was surveyed.[184] Canada's Therapeutic Products Programme (TPP) questioned 2,526 Canadians on their attitudes to organ transplantation and xenotransplantation.[185] The survey found that educational levels influenced whether participants had heard of xenotransplantation and their attitude towards it. Thus, 85 per cent of graduates, 61 per cent of unskilled workers and 62 per cent of school and university students were familiar with xenotransplantation,[186] although only 45 per cent indicated that they were aware that the procedure carried any risk to the patient. Only 18 per cent of those surveyed were aware that xenotransplant recipients have the potential to transmit diseases to others.[187] Over half of the respondents (54 per cent) said they would consider a xenotransplant for themselves or their family if a human organ were not available. This positive assessment of xenotransplantation encouraged the TPP to initiate a further, more extensive, consultation exercise intended to help in the development of an appropriate regulatory framework.

Before this project commenced in 1999, the TPP produced a draft *Proposed Canadian Standard for Xenotransplantation*.[188] This document was intended to:

> ... provide performance requirements to prevent disease transmission and to assure optimum clinical performance of viable transplanted organs, tissues and cells from animal sources. This Standard includes all aspects of care and humane treatment of the potential and actual animals, and the safety of recipients, personnel and others who may be exposed to or affected by the transplant of animal tissue.[189]

---

182 Summary of Key Issues and Recommendations, Section 11 International Harmonization.

183 Somerville, M. (1997b), 'Closing Remarks: A Retrospective Overview of the Discussion of the Ethical Issues', in Therapeutic Products Program, Health Canada (1997), www.hc-sc.gc.ca.

184 Therapeutic Products Programme (1999a), *Survey on Human Organ Donation and Xenotransplantation*, TPP: Ottawa, Canada, 17 December, pp. 1–5.

185 At p. 1.

186 Ibid.

187 At p. 2.

188 Therapeutics Products Programme, Health Canada (1999b), *Proposed Canadian Standard for Xenotransplantation*, TPP: Ottawa, Canada.

189 At p. i.

The primary concerns expressed in the Standard are for the ethical, successful and safe conduct of xenotransplantation. Like the National Forum, it highlights the need to 'address the larger social, ethical and privacy issues of animal to human transplants'.[190] To this end, following an explanation of why xenotransplantation is thought necessary, the TPP considers the ethical principles associated with animal to human transplants. Initially the need for public consultation on the ethical dimensions of xenotransplantation is restated.[191] The issues which require attention in such a debate include the acceptability of using animals for their organs, the genetic modification of animals and the concerns that surround the use of baboons for their organs. In relation to the issues raised by clinical xenotransplantation, it was of concern that, to date, the outcomes for xenotransplant recipients had been very poor. This raises difficult ethical issues regarding when it will be acceptable to proceed with clinical trials, given the need for such research to be therapeutic. The public health issues raised by xenotransplantation require that principles and procedures to deal with the unknown level of risk associated with xenotransplantation are identified.[192] Furthermore, the economic impact of animal to human transplants on Canada's healthcare system, and its impact on the donation of human organs, must be addressed. It is suggested that all of these issues concerning animal and human ethics are sufficiently important to require national review and should not be solely the responsibility of local ethical review boards.[193]

Particular attention is given to the need to develop 'counselling, monitoring and informed consent requirements specific to xenotransplantation'.[194] It is suggested that consent should:

> ... indicate that the patient is obligated to follow all of the requirements of the program which include: blood and biopsy sampling, clinical follow-up, compliance with medication, possibility of quarantine due to zoonoses, safe sex practices, family notification and other measures necessary to ensure the safety of the recipient, the recipient's close contacts and the public at large.[195]

Furthermore, many consent requirements should be extended to third parties. The surveillance measures necessary for the safe conduct of xenotransplantation received additional consideration at a workshop sponsored by Health Canada in March 2000. The *Report of the Xenotransplantation Surveillance Workshop: Infection Control Database and Sample Archiving* shows that the aim of the workshop was to initiate discussions on the issues raised and to encourage public debate.[196] Amongst the issues discussed were the identification of adverse disease events, endemic and endogenous viruses, the need for tissue archives and measures that could reduce the

---

190 Ibid.

191 At p. 4.

192 Ibid.

193 At p. 5.

194 At p. 6.

195 Ibid.

196 Laderoute, M. (2001), *Report of the Xenotransplantation Surveillance Workshop: Infection Control Database and Sample Archiving, Canada Communicable Disease Report*, vol. 2751, Health Canada: Ottawa.

risks posed by source materials. Thus, of all the Canadian documents discussed, this one is primarily concerned with practical and not ethical issues.

In 2000 its was announced that the Canadian Public Health Association had received funding to conduct an extensive public consultation exercise on xenotransplantation. The results of this consultation were published in 2001 under the title *Animal-to-Human Transplantation: Should Canada Proceed?*[197] A number of methods were used to survey public opinion: citizens' forums, stakeholder groups, a consultation website and a telephone poll. The results gained from the citizens' forums, in which members of the public were questioned over their attitudes before and after an information weekend on xenotransplantation, are given particular importance in the report.

The consultation found that amongst those involved in the citizens' forums, the more information people were given on animal to human transplants, the less likely they were to be in favour of the procedure.[198] The conclusion, therefore, was that in order to reassure respondents about the risks involved, strict regulation would be required. However, of those who thought Canada should not develop xenotransplantation as a treatment option, one reason for their decision was that they 'doubted if adequate and enforceable regulations could ever be put in place'.[199] Of those who wanted xenotransplantation to proceed, most thought that: 'regulations covering all aspects of the clinical trials must be in place before xenotransplantation is undertaken in Canada'.[200]

In respect of the ethical dimensions of xenotransplantation, the respondents are reported to have been concerned primarily with general issues such as whether the procedure is unnatural and whether humans should interfere with nature. Among the more specific issues raised by respondents were 'the invasiveness of the procedure, the ethics of surveillance, and the potential stigmatization of the xenotransplantation recipient'.[201] Of those who participated in the citizens' forums, 56 per cent raised concerns about ethical issues at the end of the programme,[202] compared to 96 per cent who stated concerns over regulatory issues.[203]

On the basis of the information gained from the consultation, the main conclusion of the Public Advisory Group was that:

> ... the majority of informed Canadians do not support xenotransplantation involving humans at this time. The main reasons pertain to the potential health risks, the need to explore alternatives to xenotransplantation, and the inadequacy of current regulations and legislation governing xenotransplantation.[204]

---

197 Canadian Public Health Association (2001), *Animal-to-Human Transplantation: Should Canada Proceed? A Public Consultation on Xenotransplantation*, Canadian Public Health Association: Ottawa.

198 At p. 10. This finding conflicts with the work of Julvez et al. (1999), 'Survey in France of Response to Xenotransplantation', *The Lancet*, **353**, p. 726. This found that the more education people had, the more likely they were to approve of xenotransplantation.

199 At p. 41.

200 At p. 22.

201 At p. 27.

202 Ibid.

203 At p. 21.

204 At p. vi.

Australia In 2002 the Xenotransplantation Working Party established by Australia's National Health and Medical Research Council (NHMRC) published a substantial discussion paper and draft guidance on animal to human transplantation for public consultation.[205] One of the key tasks of the discussion document was to provide information to stimulate public debate.[206] The discussion paper considers the ethical, social, scientific, animal welfare and regulatory issues that must be considered to determine whether xenotransplantation clinical trials should take place in Australia.

The Working Party considered both the 'inherent' and 'practical' ethical issues that impact on humans and animals;[207] that is, the impact xenotransplantation is likely to have on the dignity of humans and animals, and pragmatic issues associated with allowing clinical trials. The Working Party recommended that certain principles must be adhered to before xenotransplantation involving humans is allowed to proceed. These are that the work must respect the common good, be scientifically sound and therapeutic, the benefits must justify the risks, it should not expose individuals to unreasonable risk, the dignity of participants must be respected and they must consent to procedures in which they take part.[208] Two requirements are identified as being 'unique' to xenotransplantation: transplant recipients 'may need' to be monitored for years to come; and the need to protect the rights and safety of close contacts.[209] In respect of these concerns the Working Party suggested that it would be unsatisfactory to assume that transplant recipients will choose to remain in surveillance programmes.[210] To support this claim it cited the example of female participants in clinical trials who often ignore requests not to become pregnant during the trial.[211] The Working Party held that requesting participants in xenotransplantation trials to remain in stringent surveillance programmes would not be deemed acceptable in terms of the principles espoused by international ethical codes.[212] It also claimed that it would not be feasible to require the close contacts of transplant recipients to remain in surveillance programmes.[213] Thus, it was concluded that the safety of xenotransplantation should be based on scientific evidence and risk assessment criteria so that restrictive monitoring is unnecessary.[214]

On the basis of its consideration of these and other issues, the Working Party presented a set of draft guidelines for public consultation.[215] The principles that form the foundation of the draft guidelines are: efficacy, safety, information giving, consent, monitoring and surveillance, data and tissue storage and the management

---

205 National Health and Medical Research Council, Xenotransplantation Working Party (2002), *Draft Guidelines and Discussion Paper on Xenotransplantation*, NHMRC: Canberra.

206 At p. 5.

207 At p. 25ff.

208 At p. 29.

209 Ibid.

210 At p. 82.

211 Ibid.

212 Ibid.

213 At p. 84.

214 At p. 83.

215 At p. xxiii.

of public health risks.[216] It recommended that clinical trials must be based on pre-clinical research that demonstrates that there is 'likely therapeutic benefit' to the participants in the trials.[217] The public health risks must be 'minimal' and 'acceptable to the community'.[218] The guidelines required that any applications to conduct clinical trials have procedures in place to provide the transplantation recipient and their close contacts with sufficient information on the procedure and any surveillance measures that will be required.[219] The consent of potential research participants must be based on sufficient information, and appropriate procedures, to explain what the individual is consenting to.[220] In addition, applications to conduct xenotransplantation should base their monitoring and surveillance measures on the most up to date methods, store the necessary tissue samples and have measures to protect public health.[221]

The NHMRC Working Party on xenotransplantation published a response to the 2002 public consultation and launched a second round of public consultation on revised draft guidelines in 2003.[222] The Working Party summarized that although many people have concerns over the development of xenotransplantation 'there are no significant *in-principle* ethical objections' that are sufficient to prevent more research being undertaken.[223] However, it stated that for such research to be approved there must be 'clear benefits' for individuals and the public.[224] Furthermore, animal to human proposals should only be sanctioned if they 'have shown a clearly documented therapeutic benefit for the participant'.[225] Proposals should also provide 'a detailed analysis of the risks of infectious disease transmission'.[226] Despite these preconditions the Working Party indicated that it did not agree with the view of some respondents to the 2002 consultation exercise that a ban should be imposed on xenotransplantation.[227] That is, although it understood the concerns surrounding disease risk which may encourage calls for a ban, the Working Party felt that any such ban would also prevent progress and would not stop other countries from developing the technique, or prevent Australians from travelling abroad to obtain a xenograft.[228]

These draft guidelines differed from the Working Party's initial list by including requirements on animal welfare (Guideline 1) and patient selection (Guideline

---

216 Ibid.

217 Guideline 1.

218 Guideline 2.

219 Guideline 3.

220 Guideline 4.

221 At p. xxiv, Guidelines 5–7.

222 NHMRC (2003a), *Animal-To-Human Transplantation Research: How Should Australia Proceed? Response to the 2002 Public Consultation on Draft Guidelines and Discussion Paper on Xenotransplantation*, NHMRC: Canberra; NHMRC (2003b), *Animal-To-Human Transplantation Research: A Guide for the Community*, NHMRC: Canberra.

223 NHMRC (2003a), p. 146.

224 At p. 147.

225 At p. 149.

226 At p. 150.

227 At p. 12.

228 Ibid.

4).[229] In respect of animal welfare the draft guidelines required that pre-clinical and clinical xenotransplantation 'must be conducted with due regard for high standards of animal welfare'.[230] The additional guideline on patient selection required that research protocols must contain clear information on the criteria that will be used to select patients.[231]

In September 2004 the Xenotransplantation Working Party submitted its final report and final draft guidelines to the NHMRC. The NHMRC debated these documents at its 154th session and announced it was to impose a five-year moratorium on solid organ animal to human transplantation.[232] In March 2005 the NHMRC, as a result of further discussions at its 155th session in December 2004, published in draft form the final report and guidelines of the Working Party which it had decided not to endorse.[233] At this time the NHMRC explained that it deemed a five-year moratorium on xenotransplantation clinical trials using whole organs necessary because:

> ... the risks of transmission of animal viruses to transplant recipients and the wider community have not as yet been adequately resolved. In addition, xenotransplantation research is at an early stage and clinical trials in the foreseeable future are unlikely to be of significant benefit to the research participants.[234]

Indeed, the Working Party's own position on whether a moratorium on solid organ xenotransplantation was needed had changed in its final (unendorsed) report to the NHMRC. The Working Party now held that:

> ... trials should not be considered for at least the next five years, on the basis that theoretical concerns suggest that this type of transplant carries the greatest risk of infection, current evidence indicates that this risk is not outweighed by likely prospects of success, and there is a high level of public concern about animal welfare for the animals involved in this type of research.[235]

The NHMRC decided not to endorse the report and guidelines produced by the Working Party because of a difference of opinion between the two bodies over

229 At p. 158.

230 Guideline 1.

231 Guideline 4.

232 Press release available at http://www7.health.gov.au/nhmrc/ethics/human/issues/xeno.htm, accessed on 4/07/05.

233 Press release available at http://www7.health.gov.au/nhmrc/ethics/human/issues/xeno.htm, accessed on 4/07/05; National Health and Medical Research Council, Xenotransplantation Working Party (2005a), *Animal-To-Human Transplantation (Xenotransplantation): Final Report and Advice to the National Health and Medical Research Council, September 2004*, NHMRC: Canberra; National Health and Medical Research Council, Xenotransplantation Working Party (2005b), *Guidelines for Clinical Animal-To-Human Transplantation (Xenotransplantation) Research, Draft for NHMRC Consideration (September 2004)*, NHMRC: Canberra.

234 National Health and Medical Research Council (2005), 'National Health and Medical Research Council Statement on Animal-to-Human Transplantation (Xenotransplantation) Research', 10 March, available at http://www7.health.gov.au/nhmrc/ethics/human/issues/xeno.htm, accessed on 4/07/05.

235 National Health and Medical Research Council, Xenotransplantation Working Party (2005a), at p. 27.

whether to permit clinical trials of cellular and external xenogeneic therapies. The Working Party recommended in its final report that cellular and external therapies should be given an 'extremely cautious "green light"' if such trials were strictly regulated in Australia.[236] The NHMRC felt unable to endorse the Working Party's position on such treatments,[237] and decided that its moratorium on xenotransplantation should apply to whole organ, cellular and external therapies.[238] In its March 2005 press release the NHMRC states that its Gene and Related Therapies Research Advisory Panel (GTRAP) has been asked to keep the use of cellular and external therapies under review. Should relevant information arise the moratorium on these therapies will be reconsidered.[239] However, until additional information is available the NHMRC has decided that the potential risks associated with *all* forms of animal to human transplantation are not outweighed by any benefits the procedures may offer in the short or long term.

Countries Conducting Clinical Trials

The Council of Europe reports that its surveys show that eight of the twelve countries conducting xenotransplantation research in animal models plan to, or currently do, carry out clinical trials.[240] These countries are named as Belgium, Germany, Italy, the Netherlands, Russia, Spain, Switzerland and the USA.[241] This section will consider the regulatory work that has been undertaken in the United States, the Netherlands and Spain. The Council of Europe also reported that (in 1999/2000) only five countries had legislation in place to cover clinical xenotransplantation.[242]

United States The OECD reports that a number of xenotransplantation clinical trials are under way in the United States, including those using extra-corporeal devices to assist patients with liver failure and foetal pig neuronal cells to treat Parkinson's and other neurological disease.[243] The OECD also reports that since 1996 animal to human transplantation has been regulated in the US by a Department of Health and Human Services Xenotransplantation Committee, which had members from various agencies including the Food and Drug Administration (FDA), Centers for Disease Control (CDC), National Institutes of Health (NIH) and Health Resources and Services Administration (HRSA).[244] In 1999 a committee – the Secretary's Advisory Committee on Xenotransplantation (SACX) – was established to advise the Secretary of Health and Human Services on 'the full range of complex scientific, medical, social, and ethical issues and public health concerns

236 Ibid.

237 http://www7.health.gov.au/nhmrc/ethics/human/issues/xeno.htm, accessed on 4/07/05.

238 Ibid.

239 Ibid.

240 Council of Europe (2003), at p. 82, Table 27.

241 Ibid.

242 Ibid., at p. 77.

243 http://www.oecd.org/document/14/0,2340,en_2649_201185_2347598_1_1_1_1,00.html.

244 See discussion at http://www.fda.gov/cber/xap/comp.htm.

raised by xenotransplantation'.[245] Governmental agencies in the United States have produced a number of draft Guidance documents that are primarily intended to address the technical measures needed to manage the public health concerns associated with xenotransplantation.

In 1996 the Public Health Service published its *Draft Public Health Service Guideline on Infectious Disease Issues in Xenotransplantation*.[246] The draft Guidance identifies measures to minimize 'the risk of transmission of infectious agents to recipient, health care workers, and the general public'.[247] The measures recommended to control infection are the screening of source animals, the post-xenotransplant surveillance of transplant recipients and healthcare workers, hospital infection control practices, the archiving of samples from source animals and participants, and the creation of a centralized data base.[248] Various criticisms were levelled against the Guidance during the consultation exercise, including that it placed too much emphasis on the role of local Institutional Review Boards and tended to overlook the need for national regulation.[249] A revised *PHS Guideline on Infectious Disease Issues in Xenotransplantation* was published in January 2001.[250]

The revised draft Guideline identified the need for the xenotransplantation team to have expertise in areas other than clinical transplantation.[251] The team should include specialists in infectious disease, zoonoses, animal husbandry, epidemiology and microbiology.[252] The importance of this requirement is influenced by the fact that the 'primary responsibility for designing and monitoring the conduct of xenotransplantation clinical trials rests with the sponsor',[253] although 'all clinical trials involving xenotransplantation are subject to regulation by the FDA'.[254]

The Introduction to the Guidance declares that it is beyond the scope of the document to consider 'the array of complex and important ethical issues raised by xenotransplantation'.[255] However, it does identify some of the issues that involve consent.[256] In this respect, the Guidance requires applicants to adhere to the ethical principles that are usually applied to protect humans in biomedical research.[257] More

---

245 Charter, Secretary's Advisory Committee on Xenotransplantation, at http://www4.od.nih.gov/oba/sacx/xenomtg.htm. SACX (1999), 'Notice of Establishment', *Federal Register*, **64** (165), p. 4667. SACX did not actually hold its first meeting until February 2001. For a complete programme of SACX meetings, see http://www4.od.nih.gov/oba/sacx/xenomtg.htm.

246 Public Health Service (1996), 'Draft Public Health Service Guidelines on Infectious Disease Issues in Xenotransplantation', *Federal Register*, **61** (185), September 23, pp. 49919–49932.

247 At para. 1.2.

248 At para. 1.3.3–1.3.7.

249 See, for example, Allan, J.S. (1996), 'Xenotransplantation at a Crossroads: Prevention Versus Progress', *Nature Medicine*, **2** (1), pp. 18–21.

250 Available at http://www.fda.gov/cber/gdlns/xenophs0101.pdf.

251 At p. 18, para. 2.1.

252 Ibid.

253 At p. 5, p. 18, para. 2.2, p. 19, para. 2.3.

254 At p. 18f para. 2.3.

255 At p. 16, para. 1.4.

256 At pp. 19–22, paras 2.5–2.5.13.

257 At p. 20, para. 2.5. Specific reference is made to the Belmont Report (1979), *Ethical Principles and Guidelines for the Protection of Human Subjects of Research*, available at http://ohsr.od.nih.gov/guidelines/belmont.html.

specifically, it suggests that, as a minimum, consent documentation given to potential xenotransplant recipients should explain the risks of a xenozoonosis being transmitted to them and to their close contacts.[258] The Guidance also requires that the consent process should inform transplant recipients of the need to educate their close contacts of the risks and behavioural changes that may be necessary.[259] Participants themselves must be informed of a number of other requirements including: the prospect of isolation procedures,[260] the importance of complying with life-long surveillance,[261] the need to register their contact details,[262] the need to undergo an autopsy on death,[263] and the need to defer from donating blood or blood products.[264] The Guidance also states:

> Xenotransplantation product recipients who may wish to consider reproduction in the future should be aware that a potential risk of transmission of xenogenec infectious agents not only to their partner but also to their offspring during conception, embryonic/fetal development and/or breast-feeding cannot be excluded.[265]

The conditions that are required for the production of source animals to minimize infection risks are then outlined.[266] As a minimum, the Guidance recommends that only animals bred in captivity within barriered conditions are suitable for xenotransplantation.[267] The animals should be housed in facilities that allow for the successful operation of barriered conditions.[268] The Guidance also provides details on the maintenance, screening and disposal of source animals.[269]

In its consideration of clinical issues the Guidance emphasizes the importance of post-xenotransplantation surveillance, as it provides 'the means of monitoring for any introduction and propagation of xenogeneic infectious agents'.[270] Such surveillance is built around the need to monitor xenotransplant recipients for life,[271] the archiving of biological specimens,[272] and the need to develop protocols for the surveillance of healthcare workers.[273] Despite the need to maintain medical records the Guidance acknowledges that all records should remain confidential.[274]

---

258 At p. 20, para. 2.5.2–2.5.3.
259 At p. 20, para. 2.5.4.
260 At p. 21, para. 2.5.5.
261 At p. 21, para. 2.5.7.
262 At p. 21, para. 2.5.8.
263 At p. 21, para. 2.5.9.
264 At p. 21f, para. 2.5.11.
265 At p. 22.
266 At pp. 22–35, para. 3.1–3.8.
267 At p. 24, para. 3.1.1–3.1.2.
268 At p. 25f, para. 3.2.
269 At pp. 29–35.
270 At p. 35, para. 4.1.1.
271 Ibid.
272 At p. 36, para. 4.1.2.
273 At p. 40, para. 4.2.3.2.
274 At p. 41, para. 4.3.

In addition to the development of a national database and archive for information and tissue storage,[275] the Guidance also reports on the Secretary's Advisory Committee on Xenotransplantation (SACX) that has now been formed by the DHHS.[276] The Committee's Charter explains:

> The Secretary's Advisory Committee on xenotransplantation considers the full range of complex scientific, medical, social and ethical issues and public health concerns raised by xenotransplantation ...
>
> The recommendations of the Committee will facilitate DHHS efforts to develop an integrated approach to addressing emerging public health issues in xenotransplantation.[277]

In April 1999 the *Guidance for Industry: Public Health Issues Posed by the Use of Non-human Primate Xenografts in Humans* was published.[278] This document recommends that, because of the public health risks associated with the use of tissue and organs from non-human primates:

> ... clinical protocols proposing the use of non-human primates xenografts should not be submitted to the FDA until sufficient scientific information exists addressing the risks posed by non-human primate xenotransplants.[279]

In December 1999 the *Guidance for Industry: Precautionary Measures to Reduce the Possible Risk of Transmission of Zoonoses by Blood and Blood Products from Xenotransplantation Product Recipients and their Contacts* was published.[280] The draft Guidance aimed to inform establishments which manage blood and blood products that xenotransplantation recipients and their contacts must defer from donating these products.[281]

Of a different status to the guidance documents is the 'Availability for Public Disclosure and Submission to FDA for Public Disclosure of Certain Data and Information Related to Human Gene Therapy or Xenotransplantation'.[282] In this proposed regulation, the FDA recommends 'changes to the biologics licensing regulations regarding confidentiality of information' to allow for the disclosure of certain data regarding clinical xenotransplantation procedures.[283] The change is

---

275 At p. 42 paras 5.1–5.2

276 At p. 42, para. 5.3; SACX (1999).

277 Charter at http://www4.od.nih.gov/oba/sacx/xenomtg.htm.

278 U.S. Department of Health and Human Services, Food and Drug Administration, Center for Biologics Evaluation and Research (1999a), *Guidance for Industry: Public Health Issues Posed by the Use of Non-human Primate Xenografts in Humans*, April, http://www.fda.gov/cber/guidelines.htm.

279 At p. 5.

280 U.S. Department of Health and Human Services, Food and Drug Administration, Center for Biologics Evaluation and Research (1999b), *Guidance for Industry: Precautionary Measures to Reduce the Possible Risk of Transmission of Zoonoses by Blood and Blood Products from Xenotransplantation Product Recipients and their Contacts*, December, http://www.fda.gov/cber/guidelines.htm.

281 At p. 1. A revised version of this draft document was issued for consultation in February 2002.

282 FDA (2001), 'Availability for Public Disclosure and Submission to FDA for Public Disclosure of Certain Data and Information Related to Human Gene Therapy or Xenotransplantation', *Federal Register*, **66** (12), p. 4688.

283 At p. 4688.

proposed on the grounds that it would facilitate public education and discussion of public health issues, as well as allowing the FDA to participate more easily in such public discussions. This would make it easier to address the unique public health risks associated with xenotransplantation. Under the changes, the FDA would be able to disclose information such as the names of sponsors, the protocols for the planned study, and sample informed consent forms.

Another draft Guidance, *Source Animal, Product, Preclinical and Clinical Issues Concerning the Use of Xenotransplantation Products in Humans*, was released in February 2001.[284] The focus of the document is again on '... scientific questions that should be addressed by sponsors during protocol development and during the preparation of submissions to the Food and Drug Administration'.[285] The final version of this Guidance was published in April 2003.[286] It 'provides guidance on the production, testing and evaluation of products intended for use in xenotransplantation',[287] and explains that:

> The document addresses issues such as the characterization of source animals, source animal husbandry practices, characterization of xenotransplantation products, considerations for the xenotransplantation product manufactory facility, appropriate preclinical models for xenotransplantation protocols, and monitoring of recipients of xenotransplantation protocols.[288]

The Guidance generally focuses on 'scientific questions'.[289] However, the advice it provides on the monitoring of xenotransplant recipients leads it to outline issues associated with informed consent.[290] In this respect, the document largely reiterates the requirements that are made in the *PHS Guidelines on Infectious Disease Surveillance*. That is, it requires recipients to inform their current and future contacts of the risks associated with their treatment,[291] transplant recipients and their contacts to defer from giving blood or blood products,[292] and reinforces the need for the transplant recipient to receive counselling on necessary behaviour changes.[293] Information should also be provided on the need for life-long surveillance,[294] the archiving of tissue samples,[295] the need to keep the contact details of transplant

284 U.S. Department of Health and Human Services, Food and Drug Administration, Center for Biologics Evaluation and Research (2001), *Guidance for Industry: Source Animal, Product, Preclinical and Clinical Issues Concerning the Use of Xenotransplantation Products in Humans*, February, http://www.fda.gov/cber/guidelines.htm.

285 At p. 1.

286 U.S. Department of Health and Human Services, Food and Drug Administration, Center for Biologics Evaluation and Research (2003), *Guidance for Industry: Source Animal, Product, Preclinical, and Clinical Issues Concerning the Use of Xenotransplantation Products for Humans*, Final Guidance, April, http://www.fda.gov/cber/gdlns/clinxeno.pdf.

287 At p. 1.

288 Ibid.

289 Ibid.

290 At pp. 52–56.

291 At p. 52f, para. 2i.

292 At p. 53, para. 2ii.

293 At p. 53, para. 2iii.

294 At p. 53, para. 2iv.

295 At p.54, para. 2v.

recipients on a register and provide access to their medical records as required,[296] and the need for transplant recipients to undergo an autopsy.[297]

Despite the need to adhere to these and other consent measures, there has been no extensive treatment of the ethical issues raised by xenotransplantation in official documentation from the United States. That is, although the consent and surveillance requirements for xenotransplantation are outlined, there is no systematic or conceptual consideration of whether they are ethically acceptable, or feasible. However, examinations of the ethical issues raised by xenotransplantation have taken place within other fora in the United States, for example, the Institute of Medicine workshop on public policy and xenotransplantation in 1995.[298] As part of the workshop, ethical and public policy issues were addressed.[299] However, even this document includes the caveat that it is not 'intended as an in-depth analysis and summary of the complex issues of ethics and public policy related to xenotransplantation'.[300] This led the Institute to recommend:

> ... further investigation into the special ethical issues that are raised by xenotransplantation, particularly those related to informed consent in light of the requirement for lifetime surveillance of patients and those related to fairness and justice in allocating organs.[301]

Despite this recommendation, and the acknowledgement by health authorities that the ethical issues presented by xenotransplantation require consideration, initiatives to address such issues in the United States have been relatively slow to commence.

The Netherlands In its 1998 report, *Xenotransplantation*, the Committee on Xenotransplantation of the Health Council of the Netherlands states that it would only find clinical trials ethically acceptable when the concerns surrounding infection risks and rejection problems had been addressed.[302] But the Committee felt that, even with more research, the obstacles to xenotransplantation would not be overcome quickly.[303] However, given the suffering that clinically viable xenotransplantation would be able to obviate, the Committee:

> ... believes that, from a human point of view, xenotransplantation is ethically acceptable. Furthermore, the Committee is of the opinion that the interests of people who might benefit from the technique are sufficient to justify the possible inconvenience to or infringement upon the integrity of the animals concerned and that the breeding of genetically modified animals for xenotransplantation purposes is therefore acceptable.[304]

---

296 At p. 54, paras 2vi, vii.

297 At p. 54, para. viii.

298 Institute of Medicine (1996), *Xenotransplantation: Science, Ethics and Public Policy*, National Academy Press: Washington D.C.

299 At pp. 57ff.

300 At p. 57.

301 At p. 95.

302 Health Council of the Netherlands, Committee on Xenotransplantation (1998), *Xenotransplantation*, Health Council of the Netherlands: Rijswijk, at pp. 9 and 27.

303 At p. 46.

304 Ibid.

The report insists that an examination of the ethical issues raised by xenotransplantation should take place at an early stage in the development of the procedure.[305] Legislation must also be in place before clinical trials take place.[306]

The Committee's examination of the socio-ethical issues raised by xenotransplantation considers questions such as the implications of animal to human transplantation for human identity, the social acceptability of the practice and the impact of successful xenotransplantation on the donation of human organs.[307] It highlights the importance of all patients being properly informed about the procedure, the risks it involves and the obligation to consent to monitoring requirements.[308] During early trials, the report states that it will be necessary to 'restrict the number of people with whom a patient had contact'.[309] In respect of animal welfare, although the report argues that it is acceptable to use animals to support human well-being, there are certain preconditions; namely, that it is necessary to maintain certain standards in respect of animal welfare and the use of non-human primates is prohibited.[310] Given such concerns it is stressed that, while xenotransplantation offers one way to overcome the shortage of organs, the various prevention measures that could be developed should not be overlooked.[311]

The Dutch Committee concurred that an appropriate legislative framework is crucial for the protection of public health, and cites five bodies of legislation as being pertinent to xenotransplantation: law on the use of animals; law on genetically modified organisms; product law; care sector law and patent law.[312] More specifically, the use of animals in research is monitored by the Animal Health and Welfare Act. However, the Act is not applicable to materials that are modified in other countries. In such cases, the Biotechnology in Animals Committee would have to be consulted.[313] Thus, the committee suggested that the Act should be modified to require the Biotechnology in Animals Committee to license procedures using GM material produced outside the Netherlands. As organs from genetically modified animals are covered by legislation on genetically modified organisms (GMOs), recipients of animal organs should technically be regarded as carriers of GMOs and would therefore come within the scope of the Environmentally Hazardous Substances Act. This, it was felt, was undesirable and required amendment. However, the Medical Research Involving Humans Act is now in place and provides a better framework for xenotransplantation.[314] This piece of legislation could, for example, be employed to protect the patient and to set standards in respect of the quality of care that is required.[315] The Infectious Diseases Act allows for diseases

305 At pp. 9 and 46.
306 At p. 47.
307 At p. 30f.
308 At p. 43.
309 At p. 44.
310 At p. 32f.
311 At p. 36.
312 At p. 37.
313 At p. 39.
314 At p. 40.
315 At p. 42f.

that may be associated with xenotransplantation to be named reportable and for carriers to be isolated.

In its September 1999 response to the Council of Europe survey, the Netherlands reported that two clinical trials were under way in its jurisdiction. Both used extra-corporeal liver devices. One was an international study based at University Hospital Rotterdam and the other a local project based at the Hospital of the University of Amsterdam.[316]

In February 2000 the Dutch Parliament debated xenotransplantation and decided to request the Government to prepare a legally binding moratorium on all xenotransplantation clinical research. Parliament also requested that there should be public debate on the topic of xenotransplantation. This public consultation was launched in November 2000 and ran through to April 2001. The results of this debate were published as a report later in 2001, *Xenotransplantation: Is and Should it be Possible?*[317] The introduction to the report clarifies that it is not only concerned with whether the procedure is technically possible but also with whether it should be permitted on ethical grounds.[318] The results show that public opinion on xenotransplantation is divided: some participants did not have strong views on xenotransplantation, while others pointed either to its ability to save lives or the capacity of such an 'unnatural' practice to compromise the integrity of the human body. The issue of most concern to the public was the infection risk posed by xenotransplantation. However, not even this was considered by many to be a reason to reject the procedure. The implications of xenotransplantation for animals led some to reject the practice, while others considered the potential benefits to outweigh the costs to animals. The report concluded that:

> The majority of people do not want the government to encourage research into xenotransplantation. Some of these people would even like government to halt current research. However, the majority of people do not expect it to be possible to stop research. Almost a quarter want the government to actually encourage research.[319]

Thus, the public debate on xenotransplantation in the Netherlands has provided no clear basis on which to build public policy. Furthermore, the report does not attempt to formulate more substantial conclusions of its own that would prove more helpful to policy decisions in the area. In its final *State of the Art Report* the Council of Europe noted that 'in the spring of 2002 an act holding a ban on the clinical use of live animal material was gazetted in the Netherlands'.[320]

Spain In May 1997, the National Transplant Commission approved the creation of a Subcommittee on Xenotransplantation, the Xenotransplantation Committee. The functions of the committee are:

---

[316] Working Party on Xenotransplantation, Questionnaire on Xenotransplantation (1999), p. 9, unpublished – a summary is available in Council of Europe (2003), pp. 76–86.

[317] The Dutch Consumer and Biotechnology Foundation (2001), *Xenotransplantation: Is and Should it be Possible? Final Report in Respect of the Public Debate on Xenotransplantation*, The Dutch Consumer and Biotechnology Foundation: The Hague.

[318] At p. 10.

[319] At p. 34.

[320] Council Of Europe (2003), p. 99, n. 161ff.

- To review and follow-up research on all research projects involving primates and/or humans.
- To follow-up international advances in the field.
- To develop and approve recommendations to be followed by research teams.
- To prepare official reports on xenotransplantation.
- To analyse and eventually approve any clinical research projects on xenotransplantation.
- To oversee the development and maintenance of a registry.[321]

This multidisciplinary committee published a background document on xenotransplantation and *Recommendations for the Regulation of Xenotransplantation Activities in Spain*, in June 1998.[322] The guidelines recommend that in pre-clinical work there should be a strict follow-up of infectious agents and compliance with general animal research and public health regulations. Before clinical trials commence a certain level of success in pre-clinical trials is required. More precisely, cells, tissues and organs should have survived for six months in an animal model and during this time there should be no sign of an infectious disease. There should also be a minimum of a one-year follow-up to check for the transmission of infectious agents.[323] The report outlines the conditions that should be adopted in respect of the housing and movement of animals and the procurement of organs, including the surveillance measures that are necessary to protect public health.[324] In reference to clinical studies, the report regards the post-transplantation screening of transplant recipients as 'critical' to the monitoring of infectious agents. Surveillance and archiving procedures should be carried out by each clinical centre – that is, at a local and not a national level – and the life-long monitoring of xenotransplant recipients is required.[325] The transplant recipient must inform close contacts of infection dangers.[326] These include:

> ... the uncertainty regarding the risks of xenogenec infections, information about behaviours known to transmit infectious agents from human to human (e.g., unprotected sex, intravenous drug use with shared needles, and other body fluids) and methods to minimise the risk of transmission.[327]

This should also include the need to report any unexplained illnesses to their doctor. The standards required for the control of infection in hospital are also outlined.[328]

While there is no legislation specific to xenotransplantation, different aspects of the procedure are covered by animal protection laws and those relating to

---

321 Xenotransplantation Commission of the National Transplant Commission (1998), *Xenotransplantation: Recommendations for the Regulation of Xenotransplantation Activities in Spain*, National Organisation of Transplants: Madrid, p. 5f.

322 Ibid.

323 At p. 7.

324 At p. 7ff.

325 At p. 15.

326 At p. 16.

327 At p. 16.

328 At p. 17.

genetically modified organisms. Clinical trials cannot be carried out on humans without permission from the Xenotransplantation Commission. As of 1999, clinical trials were taking place using extra-corporeal liver devices on humans as a bridge until a suitable human organ became available. There are also general rules in place to cover confidentiality and consent, but they do not address the specific challenges raised by xenotransplantation.[329]

Conclusion

The review of different national regulatory approaches to xenotransplantation reveals both continuity and diversity. Many states discuss similar ethical and regulatory issues. For example, much attention is given to the measures that are needed to protect public health, the ethical legitimacy of restrictive surveillance strategies and the need to protect the welfare of animals as much as possible. However, it is evident from the initiatives of the countries that have been addressed in detail that there is no agreement between states over how, when and in what circumstances to proceed with xenotransplantation.

Most nation states hold that more research in animal models is required before clinical trials should be permitted. Other countries have deemed it acceptable to proceed to clinical trials. In this respect, the cautious approach of countries which have not proceeded to clinical trials – despite their interest in the technique – is arguably negated by those which have begun trials of xenotransplantation in humans using extra-corporeal devices and animal tissue. The potential public health risk associated with xenotransplantation makes this unco-ordinated approach problematic. In respect of legislation, the Council of Europe survey reports that while a minority of countries have legislation in place that applies specifically to xenotransplantation, others rely on general biotechnology laws. Some nations, like the United Kingdom, are reliant on non-statutory guidance documents and others are committed to implementing urgent statutory changes; still others have called for a moratorium.

In the previous section it was noted that the work of European and international agencies on xenotransplantation is united by calls for international co-operation and national regulation. This has not been met in some countries at a national level by the necessary action or commitment. In fact the lack of consensus within and between nation states over the essential elements of an ethically acceptable xenotransplantation surveillance programme suggests that more attention must be given to the fundamental issues the procedure raises. Thus, it is of concern that the ethical issues presented by xenotransplantation are rarely discussed in detail by national or international bodies. Rather, ethical issues are frequently deemed to lie outside the remit of the body concerned, or at least the place for a detailed assessment of the ethical and legal issues is thought to lie elsewhere. The following chapters will conduct a detailed examination of the ethical and legal issues raised by animal to human transplantation.

---

329 Spanish response to the Council of Europe's Working Party on Xenotransplantation, Questionnaire on Xenotransplantation (1999), p. 6, unpublished.

Chapter 6

The Ethical Dimensions of Xenotransplantation

Introduction

In the modern era clinical efforts to transplant animal organs into humans have been driven by a desire to treat critically ill patients for whom no other treatment options have been available.[1] Dedicated researchers and programmes have sought to develop animal to human transplantation into a technique able to overcome the shortfall of organs. In addition, different forms of cellular xenotransplantation are being developed as therapeutic options for a variety of degenerative diseases. Thus, like allografting, the primary aim of xenotransplantation is to improve the quality and length of human life. To be adopted as treatment options, xenogeneic therapies must be ethically acceptable as well as scientifically and medically viable. Previous chapters have shown that the development of xenotransplantation raises a host of ethical concerns. This chapter will focus on a number of these ethical issues; namely the concerns which surround the use and treatment of animals and the potential impact of xenotransplantation on individuals and wider society. A number of preliminary issues concerning the aims and nature of ethics will be addressed before these topics are investigated.

The Role and Nature of Ethics

Our individual and communal (local and global) ethical and moral convictions are statements on the things to which we attribute most value. Importance is attached to these basic values or items such as good health, truth telling and freedom because we sense that they enhance our existence. The aim of ethical analysis is to provide an intellectually rigorous account of 'how we should live'.[2] Ethical work of this kind tests assumptions, hypotheses and arguments to help determine whether a particular action or policy is in keeping with our most basic values, out of step with them or – perhaps – an acceptable development of them. Thus, in seeking to produce an account of how best to live we are investigating fundamental questions concerning the nature of human life. Daniel Callahan notes:

> While bioethics as a field may be understood in different ways and be enriched by different perspectives, at its heart lie some basic human questions. Three of them are

[1] See chapter 2 for a discussion of the historical development of xenotransplantation.

[2] Plato (1987), *The Republic*, Book I, 352d Lee, D. (Trans), Penguin Classics: London.

> paramount. What kind of person ought I to be in order to live a moral life and to make good ethical decisions? What are my duties and obligations to other individuals whose life and well-being may be affected by my actions? What do I owe to the common good, or the public interest, in my life as a member of society?[3]

This particular account of the questions which lie at the centre of bioethics is posed from the perspective of the individual. However as the Kennedy Report emphasized, 'there are not separate public and private areas of ethics'.[4] Thus, it is also desirable that the questions which underpin ethical investigations should be articulated from a societal perspective. In this form, such questions would concern what obligations society has towards it citizens, what social policies say about our society and the things on which it places most value, and how public policies can best promote the common good. An ethical treatment of xenotransplantation which comprehends that its individual and social dimensions are interrelated is able to ensure that both the personal and social aspects of our lives are subject to critical scrutiny.

Keeping such basic moral questions in mind during our examination of the ethical dimensions of xenotransplantation offers a number of benefits. Firstly, much ethical work on xenotransplantation concentrates on issues such as confidentiality and consent.[5] A number of erroneous assumptions can accompany this focus on what are nonetheless admittedly important issues; namely, that ethical work on animal to human transplantation can now safely advance beyond the assessment of the fundamental ethical issues, and that ethical assessments of the procedure should focus on determining how best to proceed with clinical trials, not with reassessing whether such trials should proceed at all. However, the dynamic nature of biomedical science requires that ethical analysis at all levels must be iterative. In order to appreciate this point it is necessary to emphasize the interrelationship between empirical and ethical work.

Although ethical analysis investigates distinctive questions, it requires contributions from other disciplines. The utilization of basic factual information is particularly important when assessing a biomedical issue like animal to human transplantation. It would not be possible to engage in an ethical assessment of the practice without an understanding of the benefits it promises, the burdens it may place on humans and animals, its likely chance of success and whether other ways of providing its promised benefits are realistically possible. Similarly, the aims and methods of science and policy should also be influenced by ethics. Without such ethical oversight, individuals and non-human animals would be offered no protection against others pursuing their own interests. Thus, the

3 Callahan, D. (2004), 'Bioethics', in Post, S.G. (ed.), *Encyclopaedia of Bioethics* (3rd Edn) Macmillan: New York, pp. 278–287, at p. 282.

4 Kennedy Report (Report of The Advisory Group on the Ethics of Xenotransplantation (1997), *Animal Tissue into Humans*, HMSO: London, at p. 4.

5 See for example Barker, J.H. and Polcrack L. (2001), 'Respect for Persons, Informed Consent and the Assessment of Infectious Disease Risks in Xenotransplantation', *Medicine, Health Care and Philosophy*, **4** (1), pp. 53–70; Caulfield, T.A. and Robertson, G.B. (2001), 'Xenotransplantation: Consent, Public Health and Charter Issues', *Medical Law International*, **5** (2), pp. 81–99; Daar, A.S. (1999), 'Xenotransplantation: Informed Consent/Contract and Patient Surveillance', *Biomedical Ethics*, **4** (3), pp. 87–91.

relationship between ethics and these other fields should be mutually informative.

Despite this interdisciplinarity, a number of scholars have highlighted that policy work on xenotransplantation has tended to see ethical issues as being detached from scientific questions and policy decisions.[6] Pierson, for example, has recently commented that '[o]nce the scientific hurdles are surmounted, ethical concerns associated with recipient selection, animal welfare and public health implications will become paramount'.[7] This assumes that no significant issues are raised by pre-clinical research. There are, however, substantial ethical issues raised by the use of animals in research; and, more generally, about whether xenotransplantation is the type of research programme the human community wishes to pursue.

This chapter contends, therefore, that ethical assessments are associated with scientific investigations at all stages and cannot be put off to some future date. Failure to accept this often means that, although considerable time may be devoted to analysing the ethical issues raised by xenotransplantation, the findings of such work are not considered by scientists or applied consistently in social policy. For example, previous chapters have encountered just such failures to incorporate ethics into policy work. In the examination of UKXIRA's Biosecurity and Surveillance Steering Groups it was revealed that ethical issues were often seen as being beyond its remit.[8] Similarly, although the WHO appreciated the importance of ethical issues in its 1998 *Guidance on Infectious Disease Prevention and Management* it also deemed it appropriate to separate its consideration of practical scientific questions from the concerns of ethics.[9] Such assumptions are misguided; as the British Medical Association has said, 'the scientific and practical issues cannot be separated from the ethical issues'.[10]

Finally, another benefit of concentrating on fundamental ethical issues in this chapter is that it will help to avoid an overlap between ethical and legal analysis. There is a close relationship between ethics and law: basic ethical judgements – those on which there is wide agreement – are often supported not only by ethical arguments but also by national and international law.[11] Therefore the legal chapters to follow will concentrate on legal-ethico issues such as consent, confidentiality and liability, while this chapter will focus on what can be termed fundamental ethical issues such as the use of animals and the potential implications of xenotransplantation for individuals and society. Despite this division, some overlap is inevitable – is indeed required – for a thorough and detailed examination of the issues.

---

6 Downie, R. (1997), 'Xenotransplantation', *Journal of Medical Ethics*, **23**, pp. 205–206, at p. 205; Vanderpool, H.Y. (1998), 'Critical Ethical Issues in Clinical Trials with Xenotransplants', *The Lancet*, **351**, pp. 1347–1350, at p. 1348.

7 Pierson, R.N. (2004), 'Xenotransplantation at the Crossroads', *Xenotransplantation*, **11**, pp. 391–392, at p. 391.

8 See chapter 4.

9 World Health Organization (1998a), *Xenotransplantation: Guidance on Infectious Disease Prevention and Management*, WHO: Geneva, at p. 1.

10 British Medical Association (1996), 'The Ethics of Xenotransplantation: The BMA's Views', available at http://www.bma.org.uk/ap.nsf/content/Hubethics.

11 See Dworkin, R. (1998), *Law's Empire*, Hart Publishing: Oxford, at p. 1; Lyons, D. (1984), *Ethics and the Rule of Law*, Cambridge University Press: Cambridge, at p. 61ff.

The Use of Animals

One of the most basic questions that must be addressed in the context of xenotransplantation is whether it employs animals in ways that are considered ethically acceptable and whether it will continue to do so during all stages of development and practice. In this regard it is desirable to ensure that the use of animals in research and any future large scale clinical application of xenotransplantation is, or can become, ethically sound. There are a number of features that require particular attention; namely, the rationale(s) given to justify the use of different animal species for research and clinical practice, the welfare of transgenic animals and whether it is acceptable to use animals to benefit humans in this way.

The selection of source animals for xenotransplantation is an issue that has received considerable attention.[12] The debate has been influenced by a range of practical factors including the need to: use organs that are physiologically capable of supporting human life; choose species that will supply organs and tissue that will minimize the risk of transmitting diseases to humans; and ensure that the chosen species breed in sufficiently large numbers.[13] In fact there is a tension at the centre of efforts to select the most suitable species. That is, whole organs from species that are closely related to humans (non-human primates) are most likely to function physiologically but are also arguably the most likely to transmit diseases. On the other hand, organs from animals distantly related to humans are less likely to transmit infectious disease, but are more likely to have physiological complications.[14] Given these concerns the World Health Organization explains that:

> Pigs have been considered as xenotransplant source animals because of their comparable organ size and general anatomic similarities to humans. The species is currently favoured because of the existent knowledge of its diseases and husbandry requirements. Non-human primates have been considered because of their phylogenetic and therefore expected immunological and physiological similarities to humans. However, animal welfare concerns, zoonosis transmission risks, and animal conservation issues have been greater in the case of non-human primates, and therefore have discouraged the use of these animals as source animals.[15]

The prudent selection of source animals to help avoid disease transmission and the failure of organs could forestall a range of ethical questions which may come to the

[12] Bloom, E.T. (2001), 'Xenotransplantation: Regulatory Challenges', *Current Opinion in Biotechnology*, **12** (3), pp. 312–316; World Health Organization (1998a); Council of Europe (2003), *Report on the State of the Art in the Field of Xenotransplantation*, Council of Europe: Strasbourg, pp. 31–52; OECD (1999), *Xenotransplantation: International Policy Issues*, OECD: Paris, pp. 32–39.

[13] WHO (1998a), at p. 7.

[14] Sykes, M. et al. (2003), 'Position Paper of the Ethics Committee of the International Xenotransplantation Association', *Xenotransplantation*, **10**, pp. 194–203, at p. 196; Engels, E-M. (2000), 'The Moral Status of Animals in the Discussions on Xenotransplantation (Part 1)', *Law and Human Genome Review*, **13**, pp. 165–181, at p. 174.

[15] WHO (1998b), *Report of the WHO Consultation on Xenotransplantation, Geneva, Switzerland 28–30 October 1997*, WHO: Geneva, at p. 6.

fore if patients were given organs that were unlikely to work and xenogeneic diseases emerged in the human community. However, other ethical issues concerning the use of animals in xenotransplantation exist. Most fundamentally, these questions concern whether the animals used in xenotransplantation will suffer harm. Despite the attention that has been afforded to the selection and treatment of source animals, it is important to acknowledge that large numbers of animals have been, and will continue to be, used in research if xenotransplantation is to become a clinical reality. Hence, questions of suffering, selection and usage must be applied to research animals and those intended as source animals. Efforts to address the general concern about suffering must investigate issues such as whether the animal species currently at the centre of xenotransplantation research (non-human primates and pigs) have the ability to experience pain and discomfort, whether some species have the capacity to suffer more than others and, if pigs and non-human primates do suffer, what limits should be imposed on their suffering *vis-à-vis* the benefits which may arise from their use. The central issues in these debates are clearly articulated by the Reports of the Advisory Group on the Ethics of Xenotransplantation (Kennedy Report)[16] and the Working Group of the Nuffield Council of Bioethics.[17] Thus, we will draw on these reports to give an exposition of the ethical issues that exist in this area before advancing to critically evaluate the issues raised.

The Kennedy and Nuffield Reports both state that the use of primates as source animals is unacceptable, but that the use of pigs is ethically acceptable providing their welfare is protected.[18] The explanation given by the Kennedy Report for why it is 'ethically unacceptable' to use non-human primates as source animals is, as has been seen in chapter 3, because they are regarded to have a greater ability to suffer than other animals.[19] The Advisory Group explains, in respect of non-human primates:

> We consider that these animals can be distinguished from other animals not least by virtue of their greater self-awareness and mental capacity. We consider that these features increase their capacity for suffering, particularly given the conditions under which source animals would be kept in order to ensure proper controls (e.g. biosecure and isolated accommodation). To use them for xenotransplantation would therefore, in our view, constitute too great an infringement of their right to be free from suffering.[20]

The Advisory Group continues that the reasons for not using non-human primates as source animals do not apply to pigs. Hence, it is not 'unacceptable in principle' to use pigs as sources for tissue and organs to be transplanted into humans.[21] However, the acceptability of using pigs must be determined by balancing the benefits that humans will gain against the suffering and harms that will be imposed on pigs.[22] Similarly, the Nuffield Report claims that the:

---

16 Kennedy Report (1997).

17 Nuffield Report (Report of the Nuffield Council on Bioethics) (1996), *Animal-to-Human Transplants: The Ethics of Xenotransplantation*, Nuffield Council on Bioethics: London.

18 Kennedy Report, at p. 65; Nuffield Report, at p. 50ff.

19 Kennedy Report (1997), at p. 65.

20 Ibid.

21 Ibid.

22 Ibid.

> ... crucial point is the extent to which animals share the features supposed to be important to human interests and rights. The feature to which most importance has been attached is that of self-awareness. This may be described as the consciousness an individual has of his or her own condition and experiences. To be self-aware requires a high degree of intelligence ... Self-awareness allows individuals to plan, to make choices and to engage in complex social relationships.[23]

The Nuffield Working Group acknowledges that there is growing evidence that some animals, especially non-human primates, have such abilities. If this is so 'these animals should be accorded the same moral status as human beings'.[24] Although pigs are judged to be 'unquestionably intelligent and sociable animals', there is:[25]

> ... less evidence that pigs share capacities with human beings to the extent that primates do. As such, the adverse effects suffered by the pigs used to supply organs for xenotransplantation would not outweigh the potential benefits to human beings.[26]

Thus, both Reports argue that the capacities (self-awareness and intelligence) of non-human primates are so highly developed that using them as source animals would be ethically illicit. However, while pigs are intelligent, their capacities are not thought to be as highly developed as those of non-human primates or humans. On this basis both Reports hold that there is a morally relevant difference between pigs and humans which allows us to treat pigs in a way that we could not ethically treat humans or non-human primates. That said, the intelligence of pigs means that they cannot be used *carte blanche.* Rather, their use must be carefully monitored and regulated to ensure that their suffering is minimized. This argument uses the capacities of different species to determine their moral status and to identify the ways in which they should be treated. It also appeals to the idea that some use of certain animals is not solely reliant on their capacities but on the benefits (consequences) using them will yield for humans.

The Kennedy and Nuffield Reports also argue that a cost-benefit assessment makes it ethically acceptable to use a small number of non-human primates in xenotransplantation research programmes.[27] The rationale they use to justify this position is that harm to the animals will be outweighed by 'the potential benefits if xenotransplantation were to become a successful procedure'.[28] Thus, while the decision that the use of non-human primates as source animals was ethically unacceptable depended on the high moral status and capacities of this species, this judgement prioritizes a cost-benefit assessment. The appeal to cost-benefit analysis and capacities will both therefore be assessed to determine their legitimacy in determining how animals should be used in xenotransplantation.

---

23 Nuffield Report, at p. 39f.

24 Ibid., at p. 40.

25 Ibid., at p. 52.

26 Ibid.

27 Kennedy Report, at p. 65; Nuffield Report, at p. 50.

28 Nuffield Report, at p. 50.

The Use of Animals: Cost-Benefit Analysis

The use of cost-benefit assessment to determine whether animals should be used in xenotransplantation and, if so, to what sort of uses they can be put, encounters a number of difficulties. Most basically, it is possible to contend that we do not have sufficient information about xenotransplantation procedures confidently to calculate the harms and benefits that they may produce.[29] This point has, for example, been made in relation to cost-benefit assessments of xenotransplantation that do not focus specifically on the costs experienced by animals. Thus, in its work on xenotransplantation and public policy, the Institute of Medicine (IOM) has stressed in relation to the potential disease risk posed by xenogeneic procedures to humans that:

> ... quantitative risk characterization is not possible given the current state of knowledge, and risk management will have to proceed in the absence of complete characterization. Risk communication is also difficult because of the lack of data and certainty.[30]

It was the lack of accurate information available on xenotransplantation that led the Kennedy Report to recommend that more research should take place *before* work progressed to clinical trials.[31] This is because, without detailed information on risks and a realistic evaluation of the likely success of a procedure, it is not possible to make an informed cost-benefit analysis nor, therefore, to determine whether a programme is ethically acceptable on this basis.

The accuracy of cost-benefit assessments involving animal interests can also be affected by our limited understanding of what animals actually experience. Amongst the issues that are usually included in efforts to assess the costs experienced by animals is that source animals will be raised in sterile (Qualified Pathogen Free) conditions to prevent the spread of infectious agents. There is concern that such conditions prevent animals from carrying out some of their most basic behaviours and that this imposes costs on animals that are too high. As the Council of Europe states:

> The requirement for S/QPF status, however, immediately imposes limitations on pig husbandry and hence their welfare. Therefore, the provision of appropriate bedding, nesting and rooting material should be taken into account so that animals can have the opportunity, where possible, to perform some of their most important and fundamental natural behaviours. It is clear, however, that the requirements of a xenotransplantation programme may sometimes create a tension with the currently accepted standards necessary to satisfy the requirements of animal welfare.[32]

In addition, we will see in our examination of capacities below that there is also much disagreement over the nature of porcine intelligence. Hence, the costs of this

---

[29] Clark, M.A. (1999), 'This Little Piggy Went to Market: The Xenotransplantation and Xenozoonosis Debate', *Journal of Law, Medicine and Ethics*, **27**, pp. 137–52, at p. 137.

[30] Institute of Medicine (1996), *Xenotransplantation: Science, Ethics and Public Policy*, National Academy Press: Washington D.C., p. 46.

[31] Kennedy Report, at p. xii.

[32] Council of Europe (2003), at p. 72.

practice for pigs could be higher than is acknowledged by policies which permit their use in xenotransplantation procedures. Despite the attention which has been given to such issues, the Royal Society for the Prevention of Cruelty to Animals (RSPCA) has suggested that a cost-benefit assessment of xenotransplantation procedures could be inaccurate because of failures to include the wide range of costs experienced by animals. In this respect, the RSPCA's Research Animals Division states:

> ... it is our view that the nature of the harms – the summation of all the adverse effects – have hitherto not been fully appreciated in terms of understanding and acknowledging what animals really experience. We believe that as a consequence, the harms have not been adequately assessed in the overall harm/benefit evaluation of xenotransplantation ...[33]

It then outlines in detail the different costs that xenotransplantation research animals have experienced, some of which are not always incorporated in cost-benefit assessments. It states:

> ... wild-caught baboons suffer the distress of capture from the wild and confinement in captivity. Both wild-caught baboons and captive-bred macaques have to endure the stress of removal from their social groups, of loading, and of long distance transport from their country of origin. The baboons used by Imutran, for example, endured a journey of 34 hours from their supply centre in Kenya ... Then there is the suffering involved in quarantine and acclimation to an unfamiliar laboratory environment, restrictive housing, social isolation, lack of environmental enrichment, the major surgery itself, post-operative recovery, the immunosuppressive regime, routine procedures, and the inevitable decline into illness due to transplant rejection and eventual death.[34]

Given concerns about the costs or disbenefits which animals experience, caution is required to ensure that policy decisions remain ethically justifiable as our knowledge of animal experience grows and the necessary adjustments are made to cost-benefit assessments. This is not least because it will, arguably, be more difficult to scale-down or stop using animals as a source for organs if the process begins, as society is likely to be reluctant to relinquish any benefits gained from xenotransplantation should it prove to be successful.

Recently the Animal Procedures Committee (APC) which regulates the use of animals in the United Kingdom has pointed to concerns that cost-benefit assessment is more subjective than might be assumed. In relation to the Animals (Scientific Procedures) Act 1986 it emphasizes that:

> ... opinions differ not only on what should count as legitimate benefits and harms under the Act, but also on the relative weights that should be accorded to the different kinds of potential benefits and harms in the cost-benefit assessment. This is because assessments of both costs to animals and benefits are matters of judgement, which, by their nature, are contestable.[35]

---

[33] Jennings, M. et al. (2002), *RSPCA Report: Non-Human Primates in Xenotransplantation Research in the UK*, RSPCA: Horsham, at p. 11.

[34] Ibid., at p. 29.

[35] Animal Procedures Committee (2003), *Review of Cost-Benefit Assessment in the Use of Animals in Research*, APC: London, at p. 35.

This concern over the subjectivity of cost-benefit assessment and the difficulties that exist in humans appreciating what animals actually experience leads to a more theoretical concern; namely, that we do not have the intellectual resources to compare animal and human experience in a meaningful way. That is, their different experiences cannot be weighed: they are incommensurable. Thus, at the very least, assumptions that cost-benefit assessment is reliable should be treated with caution.

Another concern which surrounds cost-benefit analysis is, as Mepham and Crilly point out, that the key to a positive assessment of xenotransplantation rests on the comparatively large benefits it affords to humans and the minor costs to animals.[36] However, in light of the uncertainty that exists about what animals experience it is unclear that animals do experience only minor costs.[37] Yet this concern may be exacerbated by the manner in which the use of animals in biomedical procedures is regulated in the United Kingdom.

In the United Kingdom the use of cost-benefit analysis to determine whether animals can be used in particular biomedical research programmes has statutory backing. That is, the Animals (Scientific Procedures) Act 1986 has at its centre the need for cost-benefit assessment. In this respect Section 5(4) of the Act states:

> In determining whether and on what terms to grant a project licence the Secretary of State shall weigh the likely adverse effects on the animals concerned against the benefit likely to accrue as a result of the programme to be specified in the licence.[38]

The Act provides 'severity limits' to determine the degree of suffering experienced by animals to help judge whether such suffering is acceptable,[39] using the following categories:[40]

> **Unclassified**: procedures are performed entirely under general anaesthesia, from which the animal does not recover consciousness.
>
> **Mild**: procedures give rise to slight or transitory minor adverse effects. Examples include: small infrequent blood samples; skin irritation tests with substances expected to be non-irritant or only mildly irritant; minor surgical procedures under anaesthesia ... However, if used in combination or repeated in the same animal, the cumulative severity may be increased beyond mild.
>
> **Moderate**: procedures include toxicity tests (which do not involve lethal end points) and many surgical procedures (provided that suffering is controlled and minimised by effective post-operative analgesia and care). Protocols that have the potential to cause greater suffering but include controls which minimise severity, or terminate the protocol

---

36 Mepham, T.B. and Crilly, R.E. (1997), 'Transgenic Xenotransplantation: Utilitarian and Deontological Caveats', in van Zutphen, L.F.M. and Balls, M. (eds), *Animal Alternatives, Welfare and Ethics*, Elsevier: New York, pp. 355–360, at p. 356.

37 It is also possible to take issue with the claim that humans will receive substantial benefits from xenotransplantation, an issue to which this chapter will return.

38 Animals (Scientific Procedures) Act 1986 Section 5(4), available at www.archive.official-documents.co.uk/document/hoc/321/321-xa.htm, accessed on 19/9/04.

39 Ibid., para. 5.42.

40 Ibid.

> before the animal shows more than moderate adverse effects, may also be classed within the moderate severity limit.
>
> **Substantial**: procedures may result in a major departure from the animal's usual state of health or well-being. These include: acute toxicity procedures where significant morbidity or death is an endpoint ... major surgery ... If it is expected that even one animal would suffer substantial effects, the procedure would merit a 'substantial' severity limit.

The Act also adopts European policy, which states that animals used in research should not be 'subject to severe pain, distress or suffering'.[41] It is by utilizing these apparently clear requirements and categories that the costs to animals used in research are managed. However, in the context of xenotransplantation research there has been debate over whether these tools have been employed in a manner which allows the costs to animals to be accurately recorded and the ethical use of animals assured.

The catalyst for this debate was the publication of leaked confidential information regarding the xenotransplantation research programmes conducted by Huntingdon Life Sciences, on behalf of Imutran.[42] In *Diaries of Despair* and subsequent publications, Uncaged Campaigns claimed that the costs to animals were underestimated because 'moderate' severity categorizations were used for research protocols which should have been rated as 'substantial'.[43] In addition, the group suggested that the severe suffering endured by animals meant that under Section 10 (2A) of the Animals (Scientific Procedures) Act 1986 the research should have been deemed illegal.[44] To support its case, Uncaged reproduced a substantial amount of material from 39 draft reports on particular xenotransplantation research studies.[45] One section from a reproduced draft report, for example, records the experience of a cynomolgus monkey who had been transplanted with a pig kidney thus:

> 21 [day] am Quiet, huddled on perch, reluctant to move. No reaction to external stimuli, vacant appearance. Clear nasal discharge. Liquid faeces in cage.
> pm Quiet, huddled on perch, reluctant to move. No reaction to external stimuli, vacant appearance. Clear nasal discharge. Liquid faeces in cage. Collapsed following administration of parental dosing. Some recovery, very quiet, sitting holding perch. Little interest in surroundings.
> 22 am Quiet and huddled. Reluctant to move. Constant grinding of teeth[46]

41 Animals (Scientific Procedures) Act 1986 Section 10 (2A), Schedule 2 A, Article 8 of Council Directive No. 86/609/EEC.

42 Lyons, D. (2000), *Diaries of Despair: The Secret History of Pig-to-Primate Organ Transplant Experiments*, Uncaged Campaigns: Sheffield. The confidential and copyright material used within this report was subject to a High Court injunction from 26 September 2000 until April 2003.

43 Lyons, D. (2004), *In a Collapsed State: Imutran Xenotransplantation Research. A Case Study of Home Office Enforcement of Animal Experimentation Legislation*, Uncaged Campaigns: Sheffield, at p. 1ff.

44 Lyons, D. (2000), at pp. 24ff, 147ff; Lyons, D. (2004), at pp. 1ff, 39ff; 'The Legal Battle', all available at www.xenodiaries.org, accessed on 13/11/04.

45 Lyons, D. (2000), at p. 5.

46 Ibid., at p. 8.

Another extract from the leaked material states of a baboon which had a pig heart transplanted into its neck:

12 [day]	am	Quiet and huddled. Holding neck. Appears unsteady.
	pm	Quiet and huddled. Holding neck. Appears unsteady.
13	am	Quiet and huddled. Holding neck. Appears unsteady.
	pm	Quiet and huddled. Supporting neck with left arm. Unsteady when moving.
14	am	Quiet and huddled. Transplanted heart swollen and red, seeping yellow fluid.
	pm	Quiet and huddled. Transplanted heart swollen and red, seeping yellow fluid.
15	am	Quiet and huddled. Transplanted heart appears swollen. Yellow fluid around swelling.
	pm	Quiet and huddled. Transplanted heart appears swollen. Yellow fluid around swelling.
16	am	Quiet and huddled. Transplanted heart appears swollen. Animal picking at transplant site. Yellow fluid around swelling.
	pm	Quiet and huddled. Transplanted heart appears swollen. Animal picking at transplant site. Yellow fluid around swelling.

Finally, on day 21:

21	am	Quiet but alert. Scab on operation site appears clean and dry. Reluctant to move. Marked firm swelling around implant. Animal showing obvious discomfort. Fluid swelling developing in sub-mandibular region.
	pm	Sero-sanguinous fluid drained but no purulent material. Transplanted heart beat barely palpable. Swelling so large animal sacrificed for humane reasons.[47]

In its assessment of *Diaries of Despair*, the Research Animals Division of the RSPCA states that the material found in the report does provide insight into what animals used in xenotransplantation research actually experience;[48] that is, the type of detail that should feature within a cost-benefit assessment, along with details of the costs associated with transportation, confinement and capture.[49] The RSPCA also points out that it is an 'unavoidable conclusion' that research classified as 'moderate' and 'substantial' will result in animal suffering.[50] They continue that:

> ... questions remain as to whether the suffering of these animals was accurately predicted and assessed by the project licensee and how the predicted suffering was weighed. This requires access to the relevant section in the licence applications, which we do not have for the purposes of preparing this report.[51]

---

47 Ibid., at p. 52f.

48 Jennings, M. et al. (2002), at p. 35.

49 Ibid., at p. 12ff.

50 Ibid., at p. 29.

51 Ibid., at p. 35.

In relation to the suggestion that primates used in xenotransplantation research suffer severe (illegal) pain the RSPCA states that confusion over the relationship between 'severe' and 'substantial' terminology means this point cannot be settled, making it 'essential for the Home Office to explain more clearly how these terms are actually applied in practice within the legislation'.[52] This concern points up another obstacle to attaining an accurate cost-benefit assessment. While there may be uncertainty surrounding how to categorize accurately the level of suffering endured by animals used in xenotransplantation research, it seems likely that many animals experience costs which are (to them) considerable and difficult to assess as minor.

The 'severity limits' which are utilized by the Animals (Scientific Procedures) Act 1986 also lead to concerns about what is counted as a cost. This is because the 'unclassified' category implies that, providing that the animals concerned do not suffer pain, their deaths are not considered morally significant. This view is supported by a note from the Chief Inspector of the Animals (Scientific Procedures) Inspectorate on the implementation of the Animals (Scientific Procedures) Act, which states:

> The killing or death of an animal need not, in every case, require a 'substantial' severity limit. Humane killing ... may be performed without specific licence authorities. *It would be difficult to argue that death under general anaesthesia, or lethality testing of anaesthetic agents cause significant suffering.*[53] (emphasis added)

However, it is questionable whether an animal is harmed only when it suffers physical or psychological pain. In this respect the APC has recently agreed that the Home Office requirement – that efforts should be made to reduce the number of animals used in research wherever possible – seems to be required not simply to reduce suffering but because the taking of life in itself is a harm.[54] The APC also suggests that 'an animal is harmed if it is made worse off'.[55] While there are circumstances in which taking the life of an animal would not make it 'worse off' – when animals are suffering considerable pain which cannot be remedied – on other occasions ending the life of an animal painlessly may count as a harm. If we accept that animals such as primates and pigs are intelligent and social creatures, then it follows that their lives and experiences are of some value *to them*. That is, even if their experiences are different from our own it is morally important to acknowledge the loss (harm) that is caused to animals when their lives are ended suddenly, even if this death is painless. Thus, costs to animals should include all relevant harms; including death and other forms of harm and not only the degree of hurt.

---

52 Ibid., at p. 21.

53 A Note by The Chief Inspector 'Cost/Benefit Assessment' Annex 1, pp. 50–59, in The Animal Procedures Committee (1997), *Review of the Operation of the Animals (Scientific Procedures) Act 1986*, which in turn forms part of *The Report of the Animal Procedures Committee for 1997*, The Stationery Office: London, para. 5.5, p. 54.

54 APC (1997), at p. 47. The requirement to reduce the number of animals used in medical research is part of the 'three Rs' requirement of replacement, reduction and refinement outlined in Russell, W.M.S. and Burch, R.L. (1959), *The Principles of Humane Experimentation Technique*, Universities Federation for Animal Welfare: Potters Bar.

55 Animal Procedures Committee (2003), at p. 39.

If painless death were acknowledged as a harm to animals within cost-benefit assessments, more weight would need to be given to those aspects of xenotransplantation which will result in the painless killing of animals. In this respect, the death of source animals under general anaesthetic and of the sows which will be allowed to die once their litter has been harvested must both be counted as costs to animals. In addition, the Council of Europe draws attention to the fact that a substantial number of animals will be killed because they are born without the necessary modified genetic make-up. It states:

> Very large numbers of animals are involved and many are 'wasted' because they do not incorporate the relevant gene. These animals – which may amount to thousands – will just be killed.[56]

It is important to note that it is fundamental to a cost-benefit analysis that the costs are necessitated by the benefits they are intended to support.[57] But this is not the case with the deaths of piglets which have not been successfully genetically modified. This again raises concerns over the ethical acceptability of animal to human transplantation and with the unconsidered manner in which cost-benefit assessments of xenotransplantation are conducted.

Finally, the philosophical foundations of cost-benefit analysis suggest that such an assessment will not necessarily find in favour of human interests. The roots of cost-benefit assessment lie in the utilitarian desire to maximize happiness, or utility.[58] Importantly, within its traditional formulation this framework affords human and animal suffering equal worth. The reason for this is that it focuses solely on ability to suffer, or to experience pain. Jeremy Bentham, the founder of utilitarianism, endeavours to explain the morally relevant features in the assessment of the relative worth of humans and animals thus:

> Is it the faculty of reason, or perhaps the faculty of discourse? But a full-grown horse or dog is beyond comparison a more rational, as well as a more conversable animal, than an infant of a day or a week, or even a month, old. But suppose they were otherwise, what would that avail? The question is not, Can they reason? nor Can they talk? but Can they suffer?[59]

Despite this egalitarianism, as has been seen, contemporary policy decisions based on this theory often prioritize the interests of humans. This situation leads Fox and McHale to insist that 'human needs are rendered paramount' in cost-benefit assessments of xenotransplantation.[60] In response to this concern, contemporary utilitarian theorist Peter Singer has restated the claim that animal pain deserves

---

[56] Council of Europe (2003), at p. 71.

[57] Animals Procedure Committee (2003), at p. 53.

[58] Beauchamp, T.L. and Childress, J.F. (2001), *Principles of Biomedical Ethics*, (5th Ed), Oxford University Press: Oxford, at p. 341.

[59] Bentham, J. (1789), *Principles of Morals and Legislation*, Clarendon Press: Oxford, at p. 310.

[60] Fox, M. and McHale, J. (1998), 'Xenotransplantation: The Legal and Ethical Ramifications', *Medical Law Review*, **6**, pp. 42–61, at p. 44.

equal consideration with that experienced by humans.[61] However, contemporary cost-benefit assessments do not only focus on suffering, but also afford considerable importance to capacities such as intelligence and self-awareness. Appeals to such capacities are assumed to justify using animals in ways in which we would not find it acceptable to use humans. But for this use of 'higher' capacities to act as the trump card in cost-benefit analyses the arguments that are used by drawing on capacities will have to be legitimate. It is to an investigation of such appeals to capacities that the chapter now turns.

The Use of Animals: The Assessment of Capacities

The moral worth afforded to different animal species is often assessed by deciding whether and to what degree they share capacities which are possessed by humans.[62] In this respect the ability to suffer, intelligence and self-awareness are capacities which are often invoked to help identify how animals should be treated. A number of issues are raised by using this approach to determine which animals it is acceptable to use in xenotransplantation. Firstly, it is unclear that a definitive distinction can be drawn between the capacities of non-human primates and those of pigs. That is, the judgement that pigs should not be regarded as highly as primates has been questioned on the basis of growing information on the behaviour of pigs which, it is argued, shows them to be intelligent and social creatures. In this respect, Langely and D'Silva contend that there is 'no scientific or empirical reason for distinguishing between primates and pigs'.[63] They state that:

> Pigs are known to be highly intelligent creatures. They naturally live in family groups; the pregnant sow will build a nest, maybe a metre high, in which to give birth and nurse and protect her piglets. When sows are so closely confined, they display characteristic states of psychological distress, i.e. severe escape reaction followed by inactivity and unresponsiveness, and then the development of stereotypic behaviours such as bar-chewing. These states are similar to those recorded in the development of affective disorders in humans: conflict, learned helplessness and psychoses or neuroses.[64]

If a clear distinction cannot be drawn between the capacities of primates and pigs, the moral distinction between them which allows the use of pigs as source animals but not the use of primates is also eroded. This leads Fox and McHale to state:

> One is left to conclude that the boundaries drawn between humans, primates and pigs in the Kennedy Report may have been dictated by practical concerns rather than compelling moral reasons.[65]

---

61 Singer, P. (1992), 'Xenotransplantation and Speciesism', *Transplantation Proceedings*, **24**, 2 April, pp. 728–732, at p. 729.

62 See, for example, Orlans, F.B. et al. (1998), *The Human Use of Animals: Case Studies in Ethical Choice*, Oxford University Press: Oxford, at p. 17f.

63 Langley, J. and D'Silva, J. (1998), *Animal Organs in Humans: Uncalculated Risks and Unanswered Questions*, British Union for the Abolition of Vivisection & Compassion in World Farming: London, at p. 44.

64 Ibid.

65 Fox, M. and McHale, J. (1998), at p. 48.

Related to this is a second concern; namely, that there is confusion over what characteristics entitle certain animals to special moral consideration. The Animals (Scientific Procedures) Act 1986 states of the animals to which it awards special status:

> The Secretary of State shall not grant a project licence authorising the use of cats, dogs, primates, equidae unless he is satisfied that animals of no other species are suitable for the purposes of the programme to be specified in the licence or that it is not practicable to obtain animals of any other species that are suitable for those purposes.[66]

There is little doubt that all of these species (cats, dogs, primates and equidae) are intelligent and have the ability to suffer physically and psychologically. However, their special status seems to owe less to capacities which separate them clearly from other species and more to the fact that non-human primates are closely related to humans and the other animals are human companions. In fact, the protection of certain species appears to be influenced more by current social mores than by consistent, critical thinking about capacities like sentience and intelligence. In this respect the APC has acknowledged that:

> Evaluating the moral status of different species in this way is clearly difficult and highly contentious; and, moreover, is likely to be influenced by the context in which the animals are encountered and/or used. However, **it is clear that the Act's requirement for special justification for use of certain species should not be taken to imply that the costs of using other species, such as mice, ferrets or pigs for example, are *necessarily* less, all other things being equal.**[67]

This being so, it is unclear how it is possible to state categorically that the capacities of pigs are such that their use in xenotransplantation procedures is less costly than the use of non-human primates. However, despite such muddled thinking there is an even more difficult obstacle for the appeal to capacities to overcome. As Hughes points out:

> The problem is that capacities for pleasure and pain, fulfilment and suffering vary not only between but within species, including humans. So while it is true that the capacities of a normal adult human exceed those of a pig, the same cannot be said for all humans.[68]

Similarly Singer, following Bentham, insists that 'there is no morally important feature which *all* human beings possess, and *no* nonhuman animals have'.[69] Thus, to be consistent and ensure that we do not arbitrarily prioritize the interests of our own species, Singer argues that we must conclude that if it is acceptable to use animals as a source of organs then humans with similar, or lesser, capacities could be used in the same way.[70] This suggestion helps to show that inconsistent appeals

---

66 Animals (Scientific Procedures) Act 1986, chapter 14, para. 5.6.

67 Animal Procedures Committee (2003), at p. 43, emphasis in original.

68 Hughes, J. (1998), 'Xenografting: Ethical Issues', *Journal of Medical Ethics*, **24**, pp. 18–24, at p. 23.

69 Singer, P. (1992), at p. 729.

70 Ibid.

to capacities problematize attempts to justify rationally the use of animals in biomedical research in general, and xenotransplantation in particular. This is because, as the Nuffield Council emphasizes:

> ... if animals are to be used for medical purposes in ways that would not be considered ethically acceptable if applied to human beings, then there must be some basis for drawing the distinction between animals and human beings. If there are no convincing reasons to ascribe to animals a lower moral status than that ascribed to human beings, then the use of animals for medical purposes would be hard to justify.[71]

The Use of Animals: Conclusion

This chapter has suggested that the use of animals in xenotransplantation (for research and clinical purposes) is ethically problematic. In this respect, difficulties have been identified with the main approaches that have been used to support the use of animals in biomedical procedures like animal to human transplantation cost-benefit analysis and the assessment of animal capacities. In respect of cost-benefit assessment it has been seen that lack of information on the nature of animal experience, the incommensurability of human and animal experience and concerns over what constitutes a cost to animals are all areas which problematize this method of assessment.

Arguments based on capacities are undermined by the fact that it is difficult to find a criterion which justifies the use of certain animals (pigs) and excludes the use of other animals, or for that matter the use of certain humans. In addition there is disagreement over the level of capacities of different species. Of particular concern is that judgements using such criteria are often assertions of pre-existing social assumptions rather than the product of critical reflection. Finally, the fact that arguments from capacities are unable to present a clear, morally relevant distinction between animals and humans, or between different animal species, serves further to problematize cost-benefit analysis. This is because cost-benefit assessments are based on the notion that animals are in some way different from humans; for example, that they suffer less or are not sufficiently intelligent to feel fear and other psychological harms. However, if we cannot consistently identify why humans have a higher moral status than non-human animals, then justification for the moral segregation which exists between humans and animals crumbles. This being so, the human use of animals becomes, in the words of Plato's character Thrasyamchus, merely a matter of right being the 'interest of the stronger party'.[72]

In 1997 the Kennedy Report stated that the use of animals was of 'principal concern' in ethical assessments of xenotransplantation.[73] However, in his 1997 paper Daar gave voice to the increasing unease that '... today the main concern is the risk of xenozoonoses and the ethics of controlling that risk'.[74] Indeed the need to focus on the public health issues raised by xenotransplantation has become a central feature in the ethical assessment of the procedure.

---

[71] Nuffield Report (1996), at p. 38.

[72] Plato (1987), at p. 77.

[73] Kennedy Report (1997), at p. 59.

[74] Daar, A.D. (1997), 'Ethics of Xenotransplantation: Animal Issues, Consent, and Likely Transformation of Transplant Ethics', *World Journal of Surgery*, **21**, pp. 975–982, at p. 975.

The Costs and Benefits for Individuals and Society

An assessment of the cost-benefit implications of xenotransplantation for humans is more balanced than a similar assessment of the use of animals, because the procedure actually offers humans potential benefits: the animals involved will only experience harms. The primary benefit associated with xenotransplantation is that it may have the potential to improve human health. This general gain would be felt by critically ill patients who await replacement organs and those with degenerative conditions like Parkinson's disease. It has also been suggested that using xenogeneic replacement organs would offer a number of other benefits. Kress, for example, suggests that xenotransplantation could have advantages over allografts, because it will allow for transplants to be scheduled, for suitable matches to be obtained,[75] and possibly for the transplantation of animal organs and cells that may be immune to certain human diseases.[76] Furthermore, it has been suggested that xenotransplantation would have psychological benefits over allografts because it would reduce the burden on recipients, since their health would not depend on the death of another human being.[77] Other benefits could include relieving the anguish of the relatives of those who require a transplant, whether of cells or a whole organ.

A cost-benefit assessment of the potential impact of xenotransplantation on humans must also consider the negative ramifications of the practice on participants in xenotransplantation trials, their immediate contacts, healthcare professionals involved in the treatment and indeed the global human community. However, the unproven nature of xenotransplantation means that if clinical trials proceed, individuals would be opting for treatments of unknown value. In fact it is likely that in any early trials that take place the transplants will fail; if the treatment in question is the transplant of a whole organ then it is also likely that the patient will die. Of course, for those with end stage organ failure this will be their fate in the immediate future in any event. In the case of cellular grafts, which seem unlikely to result in the immediate death of the patient, it is nonetheless unlikely the patient's condition will improve in the long term.[78] Secondly, another possibility which receives much attention is that animal diseases may be transferred to patients, their contacts (including healthcare professionals) and the wider community. Cellular therapies, not only whole organ transplants, may carry a risk.[79] It is of relevance for an assessment of the harms that the procedures may cause that many zoonoses are

---

75 Kress, J.M. (1996), 'Xenotransplantation: Ethics and Economics', *Food and Drug Law Journal*, **53** (2), pp. 353–384, at p. 365.

76 Starzl, T.E. (1993), 'Baboon-to-Human Liver Transplantation', *The Lancet*, **341** (8837), pp. 65–71; Baker, R. (1995), 'FDA Approves Baboon Bone Marrow Transplant for AIDS Patient', *BETA: Bulletin of Experimental Treatments for AIDS*, September, pp. 7–8.

77 Appel, J.Z. et al. (2000), 'Xenotransplantation: The Challenge to Current Psychological Attitudes', *Progress in Transplantation*, **10** (4), pp. 217–225; National Consultative Bioethics Committee for Health and Life Sciences (1999), *Opinion on Ethics and Xenotransplantation*, National Consultative Bioethics Committee for Health and Life Sciences: Paris.

78 Groth, C.G. et al. (1993), 'Transplantation of Porcine Fetal Islet-Like Cell Clusters into Eight Diabetic Patients', *Transplantation Proceedings*, **25** (1), p. 970; Groth, C.G. (1994), 'Transplantation of Porcine Fetal Pancreas to Diabetes Patients', *The Lancet*, **344**, pp. 1402–1404.

79 Sykes, M. et al. (2003), at p. 198f.

particularly burdensome diseases.[80] While we have seen that it has been suggested that using animal organs will lessen the psychological burdens on patients, a counter argument claims that living with an animal organ could be psychologically problematic for certain patients.[81] Individuals and society may also experience a range of other social and economic costs. That is, individuals with transplants of animal tissue may experience social exclusion, including employment and insurance problems.[82]

These issues encompass a wide range of topics and impact on the interests of various groups. However, underpinning these concerns are a number of fundamental ethical concerns about how best to weigh the interests of individuals against those of society and the extent to which the autonomy of individuals can be restricted by society. A critical assessment of these issues will be the focus of the remainder of this chapter.

Individual Autonomy and Novel Therapies

Autonomy, literally the rule of oneself, has arguably become one of the most important principles in contemporary biomedical ethics.[83] It is invoked to ensure that individuals are not forced to act in ways which they would not choose for themselves. A primary aim of protecting autonomy is to prevent individuals from being abused. However, even if the prospect of such harm is absent, value is placed on individuals having the ability to be self-determining. Thus, as Young explains:

> In a health-care setting, when a patient exercises her autonomy she decides which of the options for dealing with her health-care problem (including having no treatment at all) will be best for her, given her particular values, concerns and goals. A patient who makes autonomous choices about her health care is able to opt for what she considers will be best for her, all things considered.[84]

There are a number of different ways in which it is possible to support an individual's ability to choose; for example, by providing that individual with the resources necessary to empower them or extend their options, and by not blocking or restricting their choices. Beauchamp and Childress explain that autonomy:

> ... can be stated as a negative obligation and as a positive obligation. As a *negative* obligation: *Autonomous actions should not be subjected to controlling constraints by*

---

80 See, for example, Krauss, H. et al (2003), *Zoonoses: Infectious Diseases Transmissible from Animals to Humans*, ASM Press: Washington D.C.

81 Clark, M. (1999), at pp. 137–152; Bigham, D. et al. (1999), 'Xenotransplantation', *Canadian Journal of Surgery*, **42** (1), pp. 12–16.

82 Swiss Science Council (1999), *Xenotransplantation*, Swiss Science Council Assessment Programme; Health Canada (1999), *Proposed Canadian Standard for Xenotransplantation*, Health Canada: Ottawa.

83 Beauchamp, T.L. and Childress, J.F. (2001); Dworkin, G. (1988), *The Theory and Practice of Autonomy*, Cambridge University Press: Cambridge.

84 Young, R. (2001), 'Informed Consent and Patient Autonomy', in Kuhse, H. and Singer, P. (eds), *Companion to Bioethics*, Blackwell: Oxford, pp. 441–451, at p. 442.

> *others*. As a *positive* obligation, this principle requires respectful treatment in disclosing information and fostering autonomous decision-making ... Many autonomous actions could not occur without others' material co-operation in making options available.[85]

In the context of animal to human transplantation – all else being equal – the negative obligations associated with autonomy would, for example, aim to prevent society or other individuals from obstructing an individual's decision to proceed with a transplant; while positive autonomy could demand that patients considering a xenotransplant as a treatment option are supplied with sufficient, accurate information to ensure that the choices they make are really an expression of their wishes.

There are broadly two situations in which an individual could choose to opt for a xenograft.[86] Firstly, in light of the very poor success rate of xenotransplants (particularly of those using whole organs) it is clear that in any early trials individuals are unlikely to benefit from a xenotransplant. However, a patient could still choose to proceed with the transplant on the grounds that the knowledge gained from it would benefit others with a similar condition.[87] Secondly, a patient could choose the treatment as a way to save or improve their quality of life. Both situations could be said to respect the patient's autonomy. However, in the context of xenotransplantation both non-therapeutic and therapeutic research present issues which require further attention.

The Kennedy Report raised concerns over the prospect of xenogeneic non-therapeutic research. It stated:

> We emphasise that at the stage of clinical trials, we are talking about *therapeutic research*. No question arises of *non-therapeutic research* involving xenotransplantation, because the risks are potentially too great. Benefits to patients must be thought possible.[88]

Our historical survey of xenotransplantation has revealed that the vast majority of surgery that has been conducted to date has aimed to benefit the patient who was the subject of the surgery. The primary goal of such surgery has certainly not been to use individuals to gain knowledge that can be applied to help others,[89] although such

85 Beauchamp, T. and Childress, J.T. (2001), at p. 64.

86 Different issues are raised by individuals who are deemed incompetent and not able to decide for themselves. It is widely held that such individuals should not be included amongst the participants in early trials. These issues will be addressed in greater detail in the following chapter.

87 Arnold, R.M. and Dresser, R. (1996), 'Ethical Issues Associated with Xenotransplantation: The Case of Baboon Bone Marrow to Human Transplantation', *Molecular Diagnosis*, **1** (3), pp. 239–242, at p. 240.

88 Kennedy Report (1997), at p. 112, para. 7.5.

89 Reemtsma, K. et al. (1964a), 'Heterotransplantation of the Kidneys: Two Clinical Experiences', *Science*, **143**, pp. 700–702; Reemtsma, K. et al. (1964b), 'Renal Heterotransplantation in Man', *Annals of Surgery*, **160** (3), pp. 384–410; Reemtsma K. et al. (1964c), 'Reversal of Early Graft Rejection After Renal Heterotransplantation in Man', *Journal of the American Medical Association*, **187**, pp. 691–696; Hardy, J.D. et al. (1964), 'Heart Transplantation in Man: Developmental Studies and Report of a Case', *Journal of the American Medical Association*, **188** (13), pp. 1132–1140, at p. 1132; Starzl, T.E. (1993); Groth, C.G. et al. (1993).

knowledge may be gained as a by-product of therapeutic research. It is therefore perhaps unlikely that the topic of non-therapeutic research will emerge as a central issue in the future. Thus, the most likely scenario is that a patient will opt to participate in a trial which may benefit them, but which is also likely to pose them considerable risk.

A number of conditions must be fulfilled for decisions to participate in risky trials to be considered ethically acceptable. Firstly, it will be important that all the conditions which are traditionally associated with the doctrine of consent are fulfilled.[90] Thus, it will be important to ensure that participants in trials are presented with information about the procedure in a form which they find easy to comprehend and assess.[91] This information should include a true assessment of the possibility of the surgery succeeding and the potential psychological, physical and social ramifications of being transplanted with animal tissue. Information must also be given to the patient on the other treatment options which may be available to them. Individuals must be competent to make a decision based on the information with which they are presented,[92] and do so voluntarily; they must not be coerced to participate.[93] The issues raised for xenotransplantation trials by the need to gain legitimate consent from participants will be assessed in detail in the following chapter.

Secondly, in order for it to be ethically licit for individuals to participate in early xenotransplantation clinical trials, it must be deemed acceptable for patients to take part in risky procedures which may be their only hope of survival. In this respect, it is understandable that competent patients, for whom all other treatment options have been exhausted, may decide to accept some risk – however substantial or even unknown – instead of opting to remain without the treatment and the hope it could offer them. As the Council of Europe states:

> The ability to give consent means that patients may accept risky procedures fully understanding those risks and may set limits to other rights or freedoms to which they are entitled.[94]

Perhaps the best-known exponent of the argument that individuals can take such risk on themselves is Joel Feinberg who contends – providing such acts are 'entirely self-regarding and voluntary' – that the 'most plausible' liberal response is to allow individuals to take risk upon themselves.[95] Thus, it may well be ethically acceptable for patients who are able to appraise the risks associated with a novel medical procedure to consent to such treatment. However, xenotransplantation differs from other experimental therapies in that the potential risks associated with it may impact on the wider community as well as on the individuals who choose to receive such therapies. As Bach et al. state:

---

90 Beauchamp, T.L. and Childress, J.F. (2001), at p. 77f.

91 Ibid., at p. 80ff.

92 Ibid., at p. 70ff.

93 Ibid., at p. 93f.

94 Council of Europe (2003), at p. 67.

95 Feinberg, J. (1986), *The Moral Limits of the Criminal Law: Harm to Self*, Oxford University Press: Oxford, at p. 186.

> The right to life is a contradictory and potentially dynamic issue in the context of xenotransplantation. On the one hand, patients pursuing this treatment can make a strong assertion of their right to life, for in many cases xenotransplantation may be their only hope of life. This is an important consideration, but on the other hand, must be placed in the context of the right to life of others, including the general public. The danger to life for a large number of people, in the form of a potential viral epidemic, could tilt the balance against the individual patient's right to life, which cannot be bought at the expense of the right to life of others.[96]

Thus, although autonomy and the associated language of rights may allow individuals to place themselves at risk – either refusing treatment which may save their lives, or choosing treatment which places them at great risk – it would be ethically problematic if their decisions posed a risk to others. Beauchamp and Childress point out:

> Respect for autonomy has only prima facie standing and can sometimes be overridden by competing moral considerations. Examples include the following: If our choices endanger public health, potentially harm others, or require a scare resource for which no funds are available, others can justifiably restrict our exercises of autonomy.[97]

Thus, a patient's right to consent to treatment must be evaluated within the context of the wider community and its right to be protected from potentially harmful diseases which may be transmitted by means of such novel procedures.

The Public Health and Xenotransplantation

Public health medicine differs from other branches of medical practice because it focuses on the health of communities and not primarily on the interests of individual patients.[98] In the words of Dan Beauchamp 'public health is the prevention of disease and premature death through organized community effort'.[99] The conditions for supporting public health can, for example, be fostered by creating an environment in which communities are less likely to contract infectious diseases and by supporting the development of new treatment options for conditions which undermine human health. Thus, animal to human transplantation could either benefit or obstruct efforts to support public health. That is, while it *may* benefit public health by presenting a solution to the shortage of organs and providing new treatment options for degenerative diseases, it *may* also harm public health by introducing new infectious diseases into the human community.

The public health risk associated with xenotransplantation is of such concern that xenotransplantation is usually an issue regulated at a national level, rather than one delegated to local or regional forums. As seen in chapter 5, there are also

96 Bach, F.H. et al. (2001), 'Ethical and Legal Issues in Technology: Xenotransplantation', *American Journal of Law*, pp. 283–300, at p. 295.

97 Beauchamp, T. and Childress, J.T. (2001), p. 65.

98 BMA (2004), *Medical Ethics Today: The BMA's Handbook of Ethics and Law* (2nd Ed), BMA Books: London, at p. 703.

99 Beauchamp, D.E. (2004), 'Public Health: Philosophy (III)', in Post, S.G. (ed.), *Encyclopaedia of Bioethics* (3rd Ed), Macmillan: New York, pp. 2210–2214, at p. 2210.

international proposals to minimize the risks associated with xenotransplantation.[100] Despite the importance of such centralized initiatives, their success will ultimately rely on individuals adhering to national and international policy recommendations; a conclusion which is supported by the suggestion of the OECD/WHO that a xenotransplantation surveillance system should operate via a co-operative network at local, 'intermediate', country-wide and international levels.[101]

There are, of course, disagreements over the most effective way(s) to protect public health in particular circumstances. For example, literature on animal to human transplantation reveals disagreement on whether it is acceptable to begin clinical trials. That is, while some have called for a moratorium to protect the health of the community,[102] others argue that the benefits which xenografting promises to individuals and the community mean that it should be permitted. Cooper et al., for example, contend that there is a:

> ... moral obligation to accept a small risk to the community if the new treatment leads to great benefit to many individuals in that community.[103]

A similar point is made by Vanderpool, who argues that a moratorium would stunt progress and so frustrate any benefits society stands to gain from the development of xenotransplantation.[104] These arguments will be examined in more detail below, but initially the values which underpin public health ethics will be outlined.

A public health ethic aims to resolve disagreements over the best way to promote the common welfare. In performing this task it gives emphasis to principles and frameworks which promote the health of all members of the community. The American Public Health Association (APHA) states in the Preamble to its Public Health Code of Ethics that its efforts to protect public health focus on the:

> ... interdependence of people. This interdependence is the essence of community. Public health not only seeks the health of whole communities but also recognizes that the health of individuals is tied to their life in the community.[105]

---

[100] World Health Organization (2001), *WHO Guidance on Xenogeneic Infection/Disease Surveillance and Response: A Strategy for International Cooperation and Coordination*, WHO: Geneva; WHO (2003), *Human Organ and Tissue Transplantation*, Report by the Secretariat, 27 November, EB113/14; OECD (1999), *Xenotransplantation: International Policy Issues*, OECD: Paris; OECD/WHO (2001), *OECD/WHO Consultation on Xenotransplantation Surveillance: Summary Report*, October, OECD/WHO: Paris; European Commission (2001), *Opinion on the State of the Art Concerning Xenotransplantation*, European Commission: Brussels.

[101] OECD/WHO (2001), at p. 28ff.

[102] Bach, F.H. et al. (1998), 'Uncertainty in Xenotransplantation: Individual Benefit Versus Collective Risk', *Nature Medicine*, **4** (2), pp. 141–144.

[103] Cooper, D.K.C. et al. (2000), 'This New Form of Treatment Might Benefit Millions', *British Medical Journal*, **320**, p. 868.

[104] Vanderpool, H.Y. (1999), 'Commentary: A Critique of Clark's Frightening Xenotransplantation Scenario', *Journal of Law, Medicine and Ethics*, **27**, pp. 153–157, at p. 156.

[105] American Public Health Association, *Public Health Code of Ethics*, at http://www.apha.org/codeofethics/ethics/htm, accessed on 19/9/04.

This emphasis on the community does not mean that the freedom of individuals can be overridden arbitrarily for the good of the community. On this point, for example, the BMA states that the rights of individuals within the community should be respected 'to the greatest extent that is compatible with protecting public health'.[106] The APHA also maintains that prioritizing common welfare does not allow one to disregard the rights and liberties of individuals, but it does stress the difficulty of finding an appropriate balance between individual and community interests, stating:

> There is no ethical principle that can provide a solution to this perennial tension in public health. We can highlight, however, that the interest of the community is part of the equation, and for public health it is the starting place in the equation; it is the primary interest of public health. Still, there remains the need to pay attention to the rights of individuals when exercising the police powers of public health.[107]

Callahan concurs with this, but goes further by suggesting that efforts to protect the well-being of society require a reordering of the importance which is usually given to individual and community interests in healthcare ethics. He claims that we will be unable to overcome:

> ... the problems of our health care system unless we shift our priorities and bias from an individual-centered to a Community-centered view of health and human welfare. We cannot, and ought not to give up a respect for individual needs and dignity, but we can place them within a social perspective and allow that to color our understanding.[108]

All this suggests that an ethical framework which is based on a commitment to protect the health of the community can, under certain circumstances, allow restrictions to be placed on individual freedoms to safeguard the well-being of the wider community. This point is borne out by the fact that public health law is able to restrict the behaviour of individuals with infectious diseases, or of those with communicable diseases who are thought to pose a risk to the general public. As Gostin states:

> Government engages in a broad range of restrictions of the person to reduce the spread of infection – civil confinement (isolation, quarantine, and compulsory hospitalization), mandatory treatment, and criminal penalties for knowing or wilful exposure to disease.[109]

In the United Kingdom the Public Health (Control of Disease) Act 1984 requires certain diseases to be reported to health agencies.[110] If a doctor suspects that a

---

[106] BMA (2004), at p. 705.

[107] American Public Health Association, *Public Health Code of Ethics*, 'Notes on the Individual Ethical Principles', at http://www.apha.org/codeofethics/ethics/htm, accessed on 19/9/04.

[108] Callahan, D. (1990), *What Kind of Life: The Limits of Medical Progress*, Simon and Schuster: New York, at p. 28.

[109] Gostin, L.O. (2000), *Public Health Law: Power, Duty, Restraint*, University of California Press: Berkeley, at p. 203.

[110] Public Health (Control of Disease) Act 1984, para 10. The Public Health (Infectious Disease) Regulations 1988 updated the list of diseases of which health agencies must be notified. In this more recent document notifiable diseases include: anthrax, leptospirosis, malaria, rabies, tuberculosis

patient has a notifiable disease s/he must wave the patient's claim to privacy and confidentiality and inform the relevant authorities – they have a statutory duty to do so.[111] Similarly, an individual with a notifiable disease can also be required to undergo a medical examination; in such circumstances medical staff have the right to override the need for individuals to consent to treatment.[112] Finally, if it is deemed necessary, individuals who have, or are suspected to have, a notifiable disease can be detained in hospital.[113]

In the context of xenotransplantation, the issue which most clearly illustrates the difficulty of balancing the rights of individuals against those of the wider community is disease surveillance. Chapter 4 noted that UKXIRA's draft surveillance document recommended that xenograft recipients should be required – amongst other things – to refrain from having children and to inform all their future sexual contacts of their xenotransplantation status.[114] These recommendations would place considerable limitations on the rights of individuals. However, international agencies like the World Health Organization (WHO) also suggest that it is likely that xenotransplantation surveillance programmes will require participants to be monitored for life and accept the need to adapt their behaviour.[115] The WHO also notes that it is likely that close contacts will be required to participate in surveillance.[116] The Council of Europe has more recently stated that:

> Because of the potential constraints in xenotransplantation, specifically the long term monitoring and surveillance in addition to the curtailment of activities (including procreation), patients are likely to be asked to consent to a very high level of restriction, monitoring and post mortem examination ...[117]

The primary aim of closely regulating clinical trials is to foster an environment in which the health of the community can be protected. However, allied to this is a secondary goal; namely, that permitting closely regulated clinical trials would also allow individuals access to any health benefits that may be associated with animal to human transplantation. In this way, surveillance frameworks which suggest that trials should be permitted if they are rigorously policed, aim to balance the interests of individuals against those of the wider community.

It would be easy to assume that an ethical framework which prioritizes public health would inevitably agree with the strict requirements of xenotransplantation surveillance programmes, but this is not necessarily the case. In fact, there are a number of reasons why the restrictions that may be placed on xenotransplantation

---

(including bovine TB), viral haemorrhagic fever, yellow fever and food poisoning. The status of these diseases was reviewed in July 2003. For up to date information on notifiable zoonoses see: www.hpa.org.uk/infections/topics_az/zoonoses/zoo_noids.htm, accessed on 19/9/04.

111 Public Health (Control of Disease) Act 1984, para. 11.

112 Ibid., para. 35 c.

113 Ibid., para. 38.

114 United Kingdom Xenotransplantation Interim Regulatory Authority (1999c), *Report of the Infection Surveillance Steering Group of the UK*, Department of Health: London, at p. 31ff.

115 World Health Organization (1998b), at p. 3f.

116 Ibid., at p. 4.

117 Council of Europe (2003), at p. 67.

recipients and their close contacts are unsatisfactory from the perspective of a public health ethic. Firstly, there is a logistical concern as to whether the restrictions on individual liberty would actually prevent the spread of an infectious disease. At a practical level, for example, it seems most unlikely that it would be possible to prevent individuals who regained their health following a transplant of animal tissue from having children, or to ensure that they informed all of their future sexual partners of their xenotransplantation status. This being so, it is unclear that it would be possible to protect public health by adopting such surveillance requirements; or in the very least, that trying to do so could create a false sense of security and inadvertently jeopardize public health.

Secondly, many proposed xenotransplantation surveillance frameworks aim to side-step concerns that the measures they recommend to protect public health are too restrictive or coercive, by emphasizing the importance of patients consenting to treatment and any monitoring requirements in advance of their surgery.[118] As the Council of Europe emphasizes, the ability of an individual to consent means that it 'is ethically permissible for patients to choose to set aside such human rights as the right to begin a family or the freedom to donate blood'.[119] But the Council of Europe also states that:

> The risks of xenotransplantation are considered potentially so significant that informed consent should usually be obtained from close contacts such as relatives and family. It is hard to see how such people are able to freely give consent ...[120]

Indeed, the value of consent in the context of xenotransplantation is questionable for a number of reasons. For example, as the following chapter will discuss in more detail, it is difficult to regard the consent of critically ill individuals who are desperate for treatment as being freely given, making it difficult to ensure that consent is legitimate.[121] In addition, the legitimacy of consent also risks being undermined by the likelihood that xenotransplantation recipients will not retain the usual right to withdraw from surveillance programmes.[122] Thus, it seems likely that the fact that individuals who participate in xenotransplantation procedures will be required to consent to surveillance procedures will not prevent such requirements from being coercive.

However, a number of objections can be levelled against suggestions that the risks associated with xenotransplantation are too great from a public health perspective to allow the procedure to go ahead at the present time; these claims will now be examined. Firstly, it is possible to reject the suggestion that xenotransplantation poses a risk to public health and on this basis argue that clinical trials of xenotransplantation should be permitted. In this respect, Rothblatt has

---

118 See, for example, United Kingdom Xenotransplantation Interim Regulatory Authority (1999c), at p. 31ff; OECD/WHO (2001), at p. 21.

119 Council of Europe (2003), at p. 67.

120 Ibid.

121 Beauchamp, T.L. and Childress, J.F. (2001), at p. 79.

122 Council of Europe (2003), at p. 67; OECD/WHO (2001), at p. 21.

recently argued that 'xenotransplantation is unlikely to endanger public health'.[123] In addition, it was noted in chapter 2 that some scholars now think that the risk posed particularly by Porcine Endogenous Retroviruses (PERVs) may have been overstated.[124] However, it has also been established that at the present time national and international regulatory agencies are not satisfied that animal to human transplantation is safe. In April 2004, for example, the Secretariat of the Executive Board of the WHO was still advising that additional research should be done to determine the risks associated with xenotransplantation.[125] Thus, despite Rothblatt's assertion concerning the safety of xenotransplantation, the procedure is still treated with great caution. Therefore, it seems prudent that a public health ethic should also appraise the procedure cautiously while there remains insufficient information to support suggestions that little or no infection risk is posed to the human community by xenotransplantation clinical trials.[126]

Secondly, the suggestion that xenotransplantation is currently ethically unacceptable from a public health perspective must also respond to a more nuanced challenge; namely, the claim that the benefits promised by xenotransplantation to public health mean that the community has a responsibility to accept some risk in order to access these benefits. However, this argument is based on two questionable assumptions: that there will be a 'small risk' to the community and 'great benefit' from xenogeneic techniques.[127] While addressing this point it has been argued that, based on current knowledge, it remains impossible to quantify the infectious disease risk associated with xenotransplantation. Hence it is not possible to ascertain with any certainty that the risks posed to public health will be small. Furthermore, it is also questionable that xenografting will lead to substantial benefits for the human community. As highlighted in chapter 2, immunological and physiological problems must still be overcome. Until such advances are made it could remain the case that animal organs and tissue will not sustain or improve quality of human life. It is this situation which leads Schlaudraff to argue:

> ... from the point of view of individual ethics and of beneficence there is good reason to argue in favour of xenotransplantation. From the point of view of societal or collective

---

[123] Rothblatt, M. (2004), *Your Life or Mine: How Geoethics can Resolve the Conflict between Public and Private Interests in Xenotransplantation*, Ashgate: Aldershot, at p. 134.

[124] Platt, J.L. (2002), 'Knocking out Xenograft Rejection', *Nature Biotechnology*, **20** (5), March, pp. 231–232, at p. 232; Suling, K. et al. (2003), 'Packaging of Human Endogenous Retrovirus Sequence is Undetectable in Porcine Endogenous Retrovirus Particles Produced from Human Cells', *Virology*, **312**, pp. 330–336; Ogata, K. and Platt, J.L. (2004), 'Cardiac Xenotransplantation: Future Limitations', *Cardiology*, **101**, pp. 144–155, at p. 152.

[125] WHO (2004), *Human Organ and Tissue Transplantation*, Report by the Secretariat, 8 April, A57/17 available at http://www.who.int/gb/ebwha/pdf_files/WHA57/A57_17-en.pdf, accessed on 19/9/04.

[126] A similar point is made by those who adopt the 'precautionary principle'. For a discussion of this principle see Darr, A.S. and Chapman, L.E. (2004), 'Xenotransplantation', in Post, S. (ed.), *Encyclopaedia of Bioethics* (3rd Ed), Macmillan: New York, pp. 2601–2612, at p. 2605. It will, however, be referred to in the legal chapters which follow.

[127] Cooper, D.K.C. et al. (2000), at p. 868.

ethics, considering the consequences in an ethical overall assessment, xenotransplantation appears unbalanced. The gains do not clearly outweigh the losses.[128]

Conclusion

An ethical assessment of xenotransplantation which prioritizes public health requires that clinical trials pose a minimal risk to the human community. The primary strategy for reducing the risks which biomedical procedures present to humans is to test such techniques on animals before commencing clinical trials. Thus, a major ramification of the suggestion that research on xenotransplantation should continue until it is safer is that it will increase the burden on animals; a concern that is heightened by the fact that the arguments which are used to justify even the current use of animals do not stand up to scrutiny. This, we have argued, is because the costs to animals are likely to be substantial; to date these costs are not clearly outweighed by large benefits for humans. In addition it is unclear that there is an unambiguous distinction between the capacities of humans, non-human primates and pigs which justifies the distinct moral value and treatment which is afforded to these species.

Given these concerns, if other less costly ways of addressing the shortage of organs and degenerative brain diseases exist, or could be developed within a time-scale similar to that of animal to human transplantation, society would have a moral obligation to re-double its efforts to develop these alternative strategies. The availability of treatment options which are thought to carry less risk for the human community and impose less of a burden on animals would mean that xenotransplantation would cease to have any claim to be ethically justifiable. In this respect, stem cell therapies and artificial organs[129] may well provide preferable treatment options to xenotransplantation.

It could appear that a risk adverse public health ethic might also have a negative attitude towards other avant-garde treatments. Thus, it is important to stress that this cautious approach is specifically concerned with the degree of risk that it is genuinely thought may be associated with transplanting animal tissue into humans. It must be emphasized that it is not medical progress *per se* which a public health ethic seeks to prevent, but the harm which may inadvertently be suffered by the human community as a result of such untried therapies. This means that if safer innovative treatment options were available – all other things being equal – this form of ethical assessment would certainly encourage their development.

A public health ethic has a number of other positive contributions to make to the issues xenogeneic therapies are intended to address. Because public health ethics is driven by the general aim to protect and improve human health, it must conduct a comprehensive assessment of the best way(s) in which to remedy particular concerns. In the context of organ shortage a public health ethic is able to perceive

128 Schlaudraff, U. (1999), 'Xenotransplantation: Benefits and Risks to Society', *Bulletin of Medical Ethics*, March, pp. 13–15, at p. 15.

129 In the United Kingdom the Government has recently announced that it will begin trials of artificial heart pumps in 2005, *Sunday Times*, 23 May 2004, p. 11.

this issue as one which is multi-faceted. Its starting-point is the need to minimize the number of organs that are required and find ways to increase the number of human organs which are donated. While such initiatives would certainly not solve the problem of the shortage of organs, they have the ability to save many lives. They also highlight that *some* of the responsibility for alleviating the current shortage of organs must be taken by community-centred initiatives.

Chapter 7

Legal Issues in Xenotransplantation (Part 1)

Introduction

Although many of the commentaries on xenotransplantation have focused on what might broadly be called ethical issues, there are a number of legal questions which have considerable importance, but have often only been minimally treated. In fact, of course, not everyone would make a clear distinction between law and ethics. Lord Coleridge, for example, suggested that, '[a] legal common law duty is nothing else than the enforcing by law of that which is a moral obligation without legal enforcement'.[1] Others, however, have expressed themselves differently on this matter. For example, in the case of *Law Hospital NHS Trust* v *Lord Advocate*[2] the then Lord President of the Court of Session, Lord Hope, said:

> The law must be guided by moral considerations, but it does not deal only in abstract principles. The right to life and the right to self determination, which are not always capable of being reconciled with each other, must be respected. But in the end of the day the law exists to impose sanctions or to provide remedies. The law becomes relevant to the process of decision taking because a breach of duty is a delict which may give rise to a liability in damages. A deliberate omission which causes death may also expose the medical practitioner to the allegation that his conduct was criminal. Medical ethics must take account of the law on these matters, but it is not a sufficient reassurance for the doctor in the present state of the law to be told that his proposed conduct is medically ethical.[3]

However, as has already been discussed, there are a number of areas in which law and ethics overlap, or complement each other. The concept of consent, for example, can be seen both as a legal and an ethical issue, as indeed might the question of the allocation of resources. In addition to these areas of potential overlap, there are unique stand-alone legal issues which will have significance to the ultimate decisions made in respect of the possibility of accepting xenotransplantation as a research or clinical intervention. As Caulfield and Robertson have said:

> Xenotransplantation gives rise to a number of difficult ethical and legal issues. These are associated not only with the procedure itself, but also with the various strategies which

---

1 In *R* v *Instan* [1893] 1 QB 450, at p. 453.

2 1996 S.L.T. 848.

3 At p. 852.

have been proposed to address the known and unknown health risks which flow from xenotransplantation.[4]

In the following two chapters the main legal issues surrounding xenotransplantation – most particularly solid organ rather than cellular – will be considered in turn. Legal regulation in this area is highly relevant to the future of xenotransplantation, and forms an important strand of the Council of Europe's Convention on Human Rights and Biomedicine,[5] which states:

> Scientific research in the field of biology and medicine shall be carried out freely, subject to the provisions of this Convention *and the other legal provisions ensuring the protection of the human being*.[6] (Emphasis added.)

Consent

It is clear that one of the fundamental issues which must be adequately addressed if xenotransplantation is to move either to clinical trials or into standard medical treatment, is the question of consent. The fundamental legal principle that the free and voluntary consent of an individual is required by law and by ethics before a medical intervention is justifiable, has recently been restated in the Convention on Human Rights and Biomedicine.[7] Article 5 of the Convention says that '[a]n intervention in the health field may only be carried out after the person concerned has given free and informed consent to it'. More recently, Recommendation (2003) 10 of the Council of Europe's Committee of Ministers states that:

> Patients participating in a xenotransplantation should be adequately informed in a comprehensible manner of the nature, objectives, possible benefits, potential risks and consequences of the procedure, as well as of any constrains that may be linked to it.[8]

These commitments restate the terms of the Nuremberg Code,[9] which will be considered in more depth below when we are considering experimentation and research on human beings.

Obtaining a valid consent to any medical intervention is a precursor of the ethical and legal status of the intervention itself; irrespective of the nature of the intervention. However, although central to all medical interventions, it must be said that the obtaining of consent is by no means a straightforward matter.

The Report of the Advisory Group on the Ethics of Xenotransplantation (the Kennedy Report) concluded that:

---

[4] Caulfield, T.A. and Robertson, G.B. (2001), 'Xenotransplantation: Consent, Public Health and Charter Issues', *Medical Law International*, **5** (2), pp. 81–99, at p. 81.

[5] The full title is the Convention for the Protection of Human Rights and Dignity of the Human Being with Regard to the Application of Biology and Medicine, Oviedo, 4.IV.1997, ETS No: 164.

[6] Ibid., Article 15.

[7] Council of Europe (1997), Convention on Human Rights and Biomedicine, Oviedo, 4.IV.1997, ETS No: 164.

[8] Article 13.1.

[9] Derived from the case of *United States* v *Brandt (case no 1)* 1 Trial of War Criminals 3 [1949].

> Consent is an exceptionally complex concept from both an ethical and legal standpoint. We are content to conclude here that the principles ordinarily applied both in the context of therapeutic research and treatment should equally apply to xenotransplantation. However, there are certain particular issues which are raised by xenotransplantation and which call for particular comment. We recommend that they should be incorporated into any consent arrangements, so that the patient may be properly informed.[10]

These were as follows:

- Given the wide variation of views as to the acceptability of xenotransplantation, which may or may not be derived from religious beliefs, consent should always be sought (or in the case of the adult incapable of making a valid decision, the views of those closest to the adult must be sought).
- The current status of xenotransplantation, both as regards the research undertaken and the procedures which had been carried out in humans; including information about how many procedures of the kind being proposed had taken place, what the potential difficulties are (in terms of immunology and physiology) and what the outcomes have been. This would have been particularly relevant during the stage of clinical trials.
- The potential risks of infection, including: what is known and unknown; what is relevant from the outcomes of previous procedures; the form of monitoring that might be required following the procedure, the fact that this may be life-long and the importance of complying with monitoring arrangements; and the implications for patients' close contacts, in particular their partners. Consent should also be sought where access to and appropriate dissemination of certain medical information would be needed for monitoring purposes.
- The alternatives to xenotransplantation; including (for solid organs) the likelihood of receiving an organ in the allotransplantation programme and information about any existing or potential therapies (perhaps, for example, artificial organs, in particular hearts) and the outcomes of these therapies.
- The nature of the procedure; including such information as enables the patient to make a personal decision about the acceptability of xenotransplantation. This should include information which should enable people, including but not limited to those of different faith groups, to make their decision ... this would include information about the source of the tissue; the breeding, genetic modification and raising of animals; and the degree of suffering to which the animals would be exposed.
- The nature of the tissue to be transplanted, including information which addresses particular concerns about the transplantation of certain tissue; for example, that which might be thought to affect personality.
- The potential psychological and social effects that xenotransplantation could have. Allotransplantation has well-documented psychological effects. It is possible that xenotransplantation could also have psychological effects and

---

[10] Kennedy Report (Report of the Advisory Group on the Ethics of Xenotransplantation) (1997), *Animal Tissue into Humans*, HMSO: London, p. 113, para. 7.11.

> this would have to be explained to any potential patient. Given the novel and controversial nature of xenotransplantation and the wide diversions of public views, it would be advisable to point out if people might react in a hostile or uncertain way to a xenotransplant recipient.[11]

Consent in Medicine

It is, perhaps, worth at this point reminding ourselves of the general requirements of the law in respect of consent to treatment, before going on to consider the specific regulation of consent in experimental or research programmes. Simply put, the law requires that there should be no intervention in a human subject unless that individual has agreed to the intervention. The provision of consent is critically dependent on the provision of relevant information to the patient; information is what allows the individual to make a choice.[12] Thus, it might be thought that *all* available information would need to be disclosed about risks, benefits and alternatives before that person's agreement to participation would be deemed to be valid for legal and ethical purposes. As we shall see, however, this is not a standard required in the ordinary medical intervention. In the early part of the twentieth century, the importance of consent was made clear in the American case of *Schloendorff* v *Society of New York Hospital*[13] where Mr Justice Cardozo said:

> Every human being of adult years and sound mind has a right to determine what shall be done with his own body; and a surgeon who performs an operation without the patient's consent commits an assault.[14]

In this section the focus of interest will be on the competent adult human being. The issues surrounding children and the mentally incapacitated have been briefly considered in chapter 1, and will only be touched on briefly again later in this chapter, where relevant. They are not as yet central to this debate, given that – to date at least – it is recommended in the UK that only competent adults will, for the moment, be considered as suitable xenograft recipients.[15]

Although historically failure to obtain a real consent was dealt with under the legal devices of trespass to the person or assault, over the course of the twentieth century courts in many jurisdictions declared themselves dissatisfied with this particular route.[16] One of the reasons for this was almost certainly that the presumption of beneficence which underpins the medical act seemed to sit ill with the hostility which the language of assault denotes. Whatever the reason, it became clear, as the twentieth century progressed, that the appropriate form of action where

---

[11] Ibid.

[12] For a full discussion, see McLean, S.A.M. (1989), *A Patient's Right to Know: Information Disclosure, the Doctor and the Law*, Dartmouth: Aldershot; Mason, J.K, McCall Smith, R.A. and Laurie, G.T. (2002), *Law and Medical Ethics* (6th Ed), Butterworths: London.

[13] 211 NY 125, 105 NE 92 (NY, 1914).

[14] At pp. 126, 93.

[15] Cf, Kennedy Report (1997), p. 112, para. 7.7.

[16] For an excellent discussion, see Schultz, M.M. (1985), 'From Informed Consent to Patient Choice: A New Protected Interest', *Yale Law Journal*, **95**, pp. 219–299.

it was alleged that a proper consent had not been obtained because of a shortfall in the information provided would be negligence rather than trespass/assault. Assault remains a possible option in situations where no information has been provided, or where information is dishonest or fraudulent,[17] but in all other circumstances negligence would be the appropriate form of action.[18]

It is perhaps worth noting at this stage that UK courts do not feel themselves to be bound to the doctrine of 'informed consent', although they occasionally use this language.[19] The concept of informed consent is a specifically American jurisprudential doctrine, designed in large part to expand the liability of doctors in circumstances where it is alleged that inadequate information has been provided.[20] However, the notion that consent should be based on information is one which *has* commended itself in the UK. The presumption legally is that consent is one, but only one, of the possible outcomes of the process of providing information to patients. Strictly speaking, then, the offer of treatment is an invitation to make a judgement based on a risk-benefit analysis by the individual patient him or herself.

Manifestly, if the patient or prospective patient is to reach a conclusion which is both ethically and legally satisfactory, then it is necessary that sufficient, relevant information is disclosed, on the basis of which such a decision becomes possible. Of course, it is also the case that the information which the patient might require will not inevitably be only clinical information. Non-medical considerations which affect the general capacity of individuals to live life as they choose may also be of significance.[21] Caulfield and Robertson suggest that, in addition to the standard clinical information (such as it is) about the medical risks and benefits of xenotransplantation:

> ... some of the 'non-medical' factors that probably warrant disclosure include the possibility of media attention, psycho-social concerns, the risk of compromised confidentiality, the impact of personal and third party surveillance obligations, and an assessment of the patient's post-operative quality of life.[22]

This assertion was endorsed in the Canadian case of *Reibl* v *Hughes*,[23] where the Supreme Court of Canada held that the risk that surgery might affect pension rights should have been disclosed, as it would be relevant to the individual making the decision. UK courts have not directly dealt with this issue, although guidance on their likely approach can be found in the words of Lord Donaldson in the case of *In Re T*:[24]

---

17 For discussion, see Mendelson, D. (1996), 'Historical Evolution and Modern Implications of Concepts of Consent to, and Refusal of, Medical Treatment in the Law of Trespass', *The Journal of Legal Medicine*, **17**, pp. 1–71.

18 This requires the individual to show that there was a duty of care owed, that the duty was breached, and that the harm complained of resulted from the breach of the duty.

19 See, for example, *Hucks* v *Cole* [1993] 4 Med LR 393.

20 For further discussion, see Robertson, G. (1981), 'Informed Consent to Medical Treatment', *Law Quarterly Review*, pp. 102–126.

21 See McLean (1989), for further discussion.

22 Caulfield and Robertson (2001), at p. 83.

23 [1980] 114 D.L.R. (3d) 1 (S.S.C.).

24 [1993] Fam 95.

> Where the patient has unequivocally refused treatment it is not for either the doctor or the court to speculate on the strength of the patient's personal or religious beliefs or the reasons for his refusal. Nor can the court or the doctor speculate on what the patient's decision might have been had he been aware of his present crisis, or more fully informed, or if the implications of his refusal had been more forcefully represented to him. It is no part of the doctor's duty to seek to dissuade the patient from a decision based on non-medical considerations.[25]

Whatever the courts say, the General Medical Council is clear in its advice to doctors:

> When providing information you must do your best to find out about patients' individual needs and priorities. For example, patients' beliefs, culture, occupation or other factors may have a bearing on the information they need in order to reach a decision.[26]

In UK law, the presumption is that a valid consent or refusal can be provided once an individual has been informed in broad terms of the material risks of a particular medical intervention.[27] The extent of the information which it is necessary to disclose to patients is generally bound by the terms of the so-called *Bolam Test*,[28] as modified more recently by the decisions in *Bolitho* v *City and Hackney Health Authority*[29] and *Pearce* v *United Bristol Healthcare NHS Trust*.[30] The so-called *Bolam Test*, which was deemed relevant both to operational negligence and matters of information disclosure by UK courts, dictated that a doctor would not be negligent if he or she acted in a manner deemed appropriate by a responsible body of medical opinion. Such a 'body' of opinion need not be substantial,[31] nor does it matter that other clinicians would have behaved differently. The apparent change resulting from *Bolitho* has been that the behaviour of the doctor must now be considered in terms of the following:

> ... in cases involving, as they so often do, the weighing of risks against benefits, the judge before accepting a body of opinion as being responsible, reasonable or respectable, will need to be satisfied that, in forming their views, the experts have directed their minds to the question of comparative risks and benefits and have reached a defensible conclusion on the matter.[32]

However, it must be said that this apparently strong commitment was somewhat watered down by Lord Browne-Wilkinson's clear expectation that such cases would be 'rare', and that 'it will very seldom be right for a judge to reach the conclusion that views generally held by a competent medical expert are unreasonable'.[33]

[25] At p. 100.

[26] General Medical Council (1998), *Seeking Patients' Consent: the Ethical Considerations*, General Medical Council: London, November, para. 6.

[27] *Chatterton* v *Gerson* [1981] 1 All ER 257.

[28] Derived from the case of *Bolam* v *Friern Hospital Management Committee* [1957] 2 All ER 118.

[29] [1997] 4 All ER 771.

[30] [1999] 48 BMLR 118.

[31] *De Freitas* v *O'Brien* 25 BMLR 51 [1995].

[32] *Bolitho, supra cit.*, at p. 9, per Lord Browne-Wilkinson.

[33] At p. 10.

Research by Maclean,[34] however, suggests that there is room for some scepticism as to the actual impact that *Bolitho* has had on the cases which followed it. Mason, McCall Smith and Laurie, conclude that:

> While it is unwise to generalise from a small number of selected cases, the impression gained is that, while the courts are increasingly determined to see that the *Bolam* principle is not extended, they still have an innate reluctance to abandon it in respect of medical opinion; there is a sense that *Bolitho*, although welcome, is being used mainly in a 'back-up' position.[35]

They do conclude, however, that, '[w]hat seems certain is that *Bolam* can no longer be regarded as impregnable'.[36]

Effectively, therefore, in UK law a certain level of disclosure is required in all medical interventions, although that level of disclosure is by no means full. The law would now seem to be that where there is a dispute about the quality or extent of the information provided, it will generally be resolved by the court on the basis of what a reasonable body of medical opinion would have disclosed in the circumstances, bearing in mind that their decisions must be logical. Unlike some states in the United States, which adhere to a 'prudent patient' test,[37] and also unlike the situation in Australia following the case of *Rogers* v *Whittaker*,[38] United Kingdom courts arguably remain in the thrall of a professional test both in operational matters and in respect of information disclosure.

The amount of information which must be disclosed in general medical practice in the United Kingdom is, therefore, substantially decided upon by clinicians themselves. This was confirmed by the majority decision in the case of *Sidaway* v *Board of Governors of the Bethlem Royal Hospital and the Maudsley Hospital*.[39] However, one caveat is that 'a judge might, in certain circumstances, come to the conclusion that the disclosure of a particular risk is so obviously necessary to an informed choice on the part of the patient that no reasonably prudent medical man would fail to make it ...'.[40] Thus, the second part of the applicable test purports to consider what the individual patient would have wanted to know. However, in fact, courts tend to adopt an objective assessment of this matter, preferring to consider the 'reasonable patient' rather than the individual patient who has raised the complaint. However, in *Pearce* v *United Bristol Healthcare NHS Trust*,[41] the court did recognize that there are some risks which might be so 'significant' to a patient that 'in the normal course it is the responsibility of a doctor to inform the patient of that significant risk, if the information is needed so that the patient can determine for him or herself as to what course he or she should adopt'.[42] However, what is a

---

34 Maclean, A.R. (2002), 'Beyond Bolam and Bolitho', *Medical Law International*, **5**, p. 205.

35 Mason, McCall Smith and Laurie (2002), at pp. 287–288

36 Ibid., p. 288.

37 See, for example, the case of *Canterbury* v *Spence* 409 US 1064 [1972].

38 [1993] 4 Med LR 79.

39 [1985] 1 All ER 643.

40 At p. 663.

41 48 BMLR 118 [1999].

42 At p. 124.

'significant' risk, and who should decide this, is less clear. Significance might be taken to be something calculable statistically, it might be related to gravity of risk or indeed the personal impact of an otherwise small risk. Additionally, as the objective approach has generally been favoured, it remains plausible to conclude that both the significance of the risk and its value in decision-making are unlikely to be personalized to the individual patient.

It also seems that doctors have an obligation to respond honestly to any specific questions from a patient, although case law following the important judgement in *Sidaway* v *Board of Governors of the Bethlem Royal Hospital and the Maudsley Hospital*[43] seems to suggest that even this assertion is not unqualified.[44] However, there has been little judicial activity in this area, and Mason, McCall Smith and Laurie conclude that 'there has been no judicial enthusiasm to follow its line'.[45]

The purpose of obtaining a valid consent to participation in medical treatment in general is twofold. First, and most importantly, the provision of adequate information (unless rejected by the patient) and the reaching of a decision by the patient serve to protect the patient's right to behave autonomously. It is clear from UK law that the patient's decision need not be rational or intelligible to third parties;[46] merely it must be based on appropriate information and taken by a competent, adult human being. The categories of those who are deemed capable of consenting to or refusing medical treatment are relatively wide, and have for example been deemed to include a person suffering from paranoid schizophrenia.[47] Interestingly, such competence has not always been extended to pregnant women making decisions about managing their labour,[48] although it is widely (although not universally[49]) believed that this loophole was closed by the judgement in the case of *Re MB*.[50]

Additionally, the person concerned must be competent to reach a decision, and able to make that decision without duress, undue influence[51] or fraud.[52] If each of these conditions can be satisfied, then the patient is able to act autonomously, and may accept or reject medical interventions. This is so, irrespective of the consequences of the decision. Thus, in the case of *Re T (adult: refusal of medical treatment)*, Lady Butler-Sloss gave this explanation of the basic principles of the law.

> The right to determine what shall be done with one's own body is a fundamental right in our society. The concepts inherent in this right are the bedrock upon which the principles

---

43 1 BMLR 132 (1985).

44 *Blyth* v *Bloomsbury Area Health Authority* [1993] 4 Med LR 151.

45 Mason, McCall Smith and Laurie (2002), at p. 357.

46 *Re T (adult) (refusal of medical treatment)* [1992] 4 All ER 649, per Lord Donaldson at p. 653.

47 *Re C (adult: refusal of treatment)* [1994] 1 All ER 819.

48 For discussion, see McLean, S.A.M. and Ramsey, J. (2002), 'Human Rights, Reproductive Freedom, Medicine and the Law', *Medical Law International*, **5** (4), p. 239.

49 McLean and Ramsey (2002).

50 [1997] 8 Med LR 217.

51 Pattinson suggests that the use of this concept in medical law could well be developed to enhance the protection of the vulnerable patient; see, Pattinson, S.D. (2002), 'Undue Influence in the Context of Medical Treatment', *Medical Law International*, **5** (4), p. 305.

52 *Re T (adult: refusal of medical treatment)* [1992] 4 All ER 649.

> of self-determination and individual autonomy are based. Free individual choice in matters affecting this right should, in my opinion, be accorded very high priority.[53]

Indeed, the Human Rights Act 1998, which incorporates the Council of Europe's Convention on Human Rights into UK law, reinforces the underlying strength of that commitment, perhaps particularly in Article 8. Cases following the passing of the 1998 Act, such as *Ms B* v *An NHS Hospital Trust*,[54] have repeated the right to make such choices, even at risk of loss of one's life.

The second function served by the law of consent is to protect the clinician from allegations of assault or battery, or more commonly from allegations of negligence. If the clinician can demonstrate that adequate information was provided to a patient, and that that patient signified his/her willingness to assume the risks associated with medical treatment, and preferred the recommended treatment to any alternatives which may exist, then the clinician has satisfied the requirements of professional ethics and of the law.

In respect of xenotransplantation, there are two main situations where consent will be relevant. The first will arise when xenotransplantation moves from the laboratory to the clinical trial stage, and the second will occur should xenotransplantation move beyond the clinical trial stage into mainstream medicine. It can be anticipated that, were xenotransplantation to become a standard therapy, the rules of consent which have been described above would apply, albeit that there may be a more complex set of information to be disclosed. The most pressing question, however, relates to consent in clinical trials.

Consent in Experimentation/Research

Were xenotransplantation to be translated from the realms of scientific theory into the arena of scientific fact, this would necessarily be done in the first instance by way of clinical trials (research) or experimental procedures. To an extent, this has already occurred. For example, research on 160 patients who had been treated with various living pig tissues showed that none had contracted Porcine Endogenous Retroviruses (PERVs) – one of the major fears of those who are concerned about the risks of xenotransplantation.[55] Weiss is quoted as saying that these results 'offered some reassurance', but also that 'the ethical and technical problems of maintaining vigilance over xenotransplantation should not be underestimated'.[56]

Before proceeding to consider the question of consent in research and experimentation, it is useful to define our terms. It is often the case that the terms 'research' and 'experimentation' are used as if they were interchangeable. Mason, McCall Smith and Laurie, however, would criticize this, saying:

> Research and experimentation are commonly used as interchangeable terms – we, however, believe that there is a distinction to be made. Research implies a predetermined

[53] [1993] Fam 95, at pp. 116–117.

[54] 65 BMLR 149 (2002).

[55] Weiss, R. (1998), 'Focus on Xenotransplantation', *Nature Medicine*, http://www.nature.com/nm/web_specials/xeno, accessed on 24/04/02.

[56] Ibid.

> protocol with a clearly defined end-point. Experimentation, by contrast, involves a more speculative, ad-hoc, approach to an individual subject. The distinction is significant in that an experiment may be modified to take into account the individual's response; a research programme, however, is, by definition, bound to tie the researcher to a particular course of action until such time as its general ineffectiveness is satisfactorily demonstrated.[57]

The Institute of Medical Ethics Working Party (IMEWP) adopted the definition of research found in the *Shorter Oxford English Dictionary*, namely: 'An investigation directed to the discovery of some fact by careful study of a subject; a course of critical or scientific enquiry.'[58] A research project, then, 'is a systematic enquiry designed to contribute to generalizable knowledge. A speculative or haphazard attempt at a new therapy, for instance, cannot be regarded as a research project.'[59] This distinction is arguably useful both clinically and in terms of the law. In legal terms the distinction is relevant because of the different legal response to each.

Research is governed by the professional rules and regulations of the doctors themselves and their scientific colleagues, and is governed through the scrutiny of research ethics committees. These committees have traditionally formed part of medical self-regulation, but following the terms of a European Directive,[60] statutory regulation of trials of medicinal products is now in place.[61] As this only applies to trials of medical products, it may yet only cover some aspects of xenotransplantation trials. Clinical trials of medicinal products will be subject to the standard of good clinical practice which is described as being a:

> Set of internationally recognised ethical and scientific quality requirements which must be observed for designing, conducting, recording and reporting clinical trials that involve the participation of human subjects. Compliance with this good practice provides assurance that the rights, safety and well-being of trial subjects are protected, and that the results of the clinical trial are credible.[62]

In terms of products developed for xenotransplantation, much will depend on the extent to which they can be said to fit within the proposed statutory regime, although – as will be seen later – it is already recognized in law that blood and blood products will be deemed 'products' for the purposes of the Consumer Protection Act 1987, and their manufacturer will therefore be subject to a strict liability regime.[63] If, on the other hand, material used in xenotransplantation is not deemed to be a medicinal product, its ethical scrutiny – if used in a research project – will not be subject directly to the new regime, even though it can reasonably be assumed that the

---

57 Mason, McCall Smith and Laurie (2002), at p. 573.

58 Report of an Institute of Medical Ethics working group on the ethics of clinical research investigations on children, the discussions and recommendations of which are available as Richard Nicholson (ed.) (1986), *Medical Research with Children: Ethics, Law, and Practice*, Oxford University Press: Oxford, at p. 24.

59 Nicholson, R. (1986), at p. 25.

60 European Parliament and the Council Directive 2001/20/EC, 4 April 2001.

61 The Medicines for Human Use (Clinical Trials) Regulations 2004, Statutory Instrument 2004 No. 1031.

62 Ibid., article 1(2).

63 *A* v *National Blood Authority* 60 BMLR 1 (2001).

proposed change to the authority of research ethics committees will *de facto* affect all research projects. And, of course, this leaves unanswered the question as to whether or not UKXIRA will ultimately assume the full-blown role of research ethics committee for any xenotransplantation-related research.

Arguably, experimentation is slightly better regulated in law for the moment than is research. If by experimentation is meant the adoption of an innovative or novel approach to the circumstances of an individual patient, then the case of *Hunter* v *Hanley*[64] would seem to provide legal regulation. In this case it was said that if a doctor's choice of treatment is challenged as not being the normal treatment – that is, it is experimental treatment – three things must be established. First, in order to establish negligence it must be shown that there is a usual or normal practice; secondly that the doctor deviated from that practice; and thirdly that the deviation was such that no doctor acting with reasonable skill and care would have made it. In other words, although the test is not set particularly high, the law has chosen to intervene in the area of experimentation (for further discussion, see below). Although early attempts at xenotransplantation were probably closer in nature to experimentation rather than research (using these definitions)[65] it is most unlikely in the current climate that the practical application of xenotransplantation would be tested in anything other than the context of clinical trials (research).

The general rules about consent to treatment by and large form the basis of the rules which apply in respect of human experimentation or research. However, although Mason, McCall Smith and Laurie concede that '[t]he principles in relation to experimentation are similar to those governing therapy',[66] they conclude that 'most commentators would hold that the patient's rights are, if anything, greater in the former situation than they are in the sphere of pure patient management'.[67] Thus, it seems that in (experimentation or) clinical trials the amount of information required to achieve a valid consent would be greater than in the standard medical act. This was made very clear by the decision in the Canadian case of *Halushka* v *University of Saskatchewan*[68] where the court said, 'there can be no exceptions to the ordinary requirements of disclosure in the case of research as there may well be in ordinary practice'.[69] Caplan suggests that the following amount to a minimum set of requirements in respect of information to be disclosed:

> Those who will be recruited for clinical trials have the right to know the risks and benefits of the research that can best be inferred from animal and any other relevant studies. They should also know how many subjects should be used before the end-point of this phase of research is reached. The measures taken for coping with any psychological issues raised by the use of animal organs for subjects must be presented. Subjects should also be told about the steps that have been taken to ensure their privacy and confidentiality to the extent that they wish these preserved. It is of special

64 1955 SC 200.

65 See Annas, G. (1985), 'Baby Fae: The "Anything Goes" School of Human Experimentation', *Hastings Center Report*, **15** (1), pp. 15–17.

66 Mason, McCall Smith and Laurie (2002), at p. 586.

67 Ibid.

68 (1965) 53 D.L.R. (2d) 436.

69 At pp. 616–617.

> importance given the high odds of failure in the initial phase of xenografting on human subjects that procedures be in place for ending the experiment if the subject wishes to withdraw from the research.[70]

Thus, if xenotransplantation were to move to clinical trials it is clear that the quality and extent of information disclosed to potential recipients of the xenograft would be required to conform to standards higher than those which would apply in the standard therapeutic interaction.

Although, therefore, there is some law in place which deals with the use of human subjects in research or experimentation, and although the recommendations of the Kennedy Report and the common law itself would seem to demand the fullest possible disclosure of information, it is inadvisable to be complacent about the legal and ethical framework within which experimentation and research take place. As Fox and McHale, for example, point out:

> Safeguards to ensure that research activity is ethical and scientifically valid are particularly important in areas such as this, where immense pressure to produce results exists, not least given the potential to save human lives, and the commercial interests affected. One problem is ensuring accountability in that there is no central regulation of research activity in this country.[71]

While this concern may be in part alleviated by the legislative reform already referred to, the potential consequences of xenotransplantation trials might demand yet further regulation and central control. In the UK this may well be a task for UKXIRA in the future, but the comments made in chapter 4 in respect of this possibility would also need to be borne in mind.

It is extremely important that some central agreement as to the level of risk which is acceptable is in place. This is reinforced by the Nuffield Report's concerns about the feasibility of obtaining any valid consent to inclusion in the early trials of xenotransplantation should they eventuate. As it says:

> Even when the results from animal experiments suggest that xenotransplantation involving human recipients is justifiable, the early clinical trials will involve unknown and unpredictable risks. The question then becomes how best to protect early patients' welfare and interests. It is of the utmost importance that potential patients give free and properly informed consent to participation in the first xenotransplantation trials.[72]

Whatever the ethical or legal difficulties, however, it is clear that research with human subjects has proved beneficial over many years. As the US National Bioethics Advisory Commission puts it:

---

[70] Caplan, A.L. (1992), 'Is Xenografting Morally Wrong?', *Transplantation Proceedings*, **24** (2) (April), pp. 722–727, at p. 726.

[71] Fox, M. and McHale, J. (1998), 'Xenotransplantation: The Legal and Ethical Ramifications', *Medical Law Review*, **6** (1), pp. 42–61, at p. 54.

[72] Nuffield Report (Report of the Nuffield Council on Bioethics) (1996), *Animal-to-Human Transplants: The Ethics of Xenotransplantation*, at p. 118, para. 10.34.

> A wide variety of important research studies using human subjects has long played an essential and irreplaceable role in advancing biomedical and behavioural science, thus enhancing our ability to treat illness and better understand human behaviour.[73]

Indeed, Dickens has suggested that:

> A medical profession which did not seek improved means to conquer disease would be condemned for dereliction of its duty. Members of the public will not accept the current state of the medical arts as finite but feel justified in expecting the development of more effective therapies for illness, and the promotion of improved means of preventive care.[74]

Effectively, Dickens is saying that there are two main reasons for pursuing medical research. First, he suggests that there is a professional failure if clinicians do not seek to pursue new knowledge and new therapies, and second the public themselves drive the demand for progress. Thus, he would conclude that doctors have a responsibility to meet these aspirations. Giesen adds a third element, saying, '... the development of new drugs and medical procedures which will benefit future patients is in the public interest and that freedom of research and scientific enquiry is, in itself, an important aspect of open societies'.[75]

The value of human research, therefore, is not doubted. However, it is also the case that it is bounded by certain imperatives, which in the UK situation are enforced by a variety of ethics committees, made up of professional medical people and lay people. Their job is to scrutinize the ethics and the science of any proposed research project using human subjects. These committees have been widely criticized since their initiation in the 1970s;[76] albeit that it is hoped that some of these criticisms may be reduced or removed by the new regime already referred to. In any event, the Kennedy Report, in agreement with the Nuffield Report, was quite clear that LRECs should not carry the responsibility for judging the ethics of clinical trials of xenotransplantation, and preferred that the recommended national advisory committee should carry that responsibility.[77]

Of more immediate concern, however, are questions surrounding participation in clinical trials themselves. It has already been suggested that a critical component of the lawfulness of any intervention, therapeutic or research based, is that the consent of the subject has been obtained. The issue of consent is generally taken to be of

---

73 National Bioethics Advisory Commission (1998), *Research Involving Persons With Mental Disorders That May Affect Their Decisionmaking Capacity*, December, Volume 1, 1.

74 Dickens, B.M. (1979), 'Human Rights in Medical Experimentation', *Israeli Yearbook on Human Rights*, **9**, pp. 23–57, at p. 23.

75 Giesen, D. (1995), 'Civil Liability of Physicians for New Methods of Treatment and Experimentation: A Comparative Examination', *Medical Law Review*, **3**, Spring, pp. 22–52, at p. 22.

76 Cf Pettit, P. (1992), 'Instituting a Research Ethic: Chilling and Cautionary Tales', *Bioethics*, **6** (2), p. 89; Neuberger, J. (1992), *Ethics and Health Care: The Role of Research Ethics Committees in the United Kingdom*, King's Fund Institute: London; McLean, S.A.M. (1995), 'Research Ethics Committees: Principles and Proposals', *Health Bulletin* **53** (5), September. See, for example, the *Report of the Independent Review Group on the Retention of Organs at Post-Mortem*, Stationery Office: Edinburgh, 2001 and 2003. Also available at http://www.show.scot.nhs.uk/scotorgrev.

77 Kennedy Report, pp. 136–137, para. 8.74.

more importance where the nature of the intervention is as part of a research project. Assuming that sufficient laboratory and animal work has been done, suggesting that it is appropriate to move xenotransplantation into human clinical trials, the critical indicator of the lawfulness of these trials will be the quality of information disclosed, the capacity of individuals to understand the information and the voluntariness of the individual's agreement to participate.

Quality of Information As has already been noted, there is considerable controversy in the standard medical intervention about the type and extent of information that should be disclosed before a patient can reach a judgement on whether or not to participate. It is widely accepted that the situation in respect of experimental or research protocols is even more complex. In the aftermath of the well-documented Nazi atrocities in the Second World War, the Nuremberg Code was drawn up as a template for all experimental or research based interventions in human beings.[78] Article 1 of the Declaration reads as follows:

> The voluntary consent of the human subject is absolutely essential. This means that the person involved should have legal capacity to give consent; should be situated as to be able to exercise free power of choice, without the intervention of any element of force, fraud, deceit, duress, over-reaching, or other ulterior form of constraint or coercion; and should have sufficient knowledge and comprehension of the elements of the subject matter as to enable him to make an understanding and enlightened decision. This latter element requires that before the acceptance of an affirmative decision by the experimental subject, there should be made known to him ... all inconveniences and hazards not reasonably to be expected; and the effects upon himself or person which may visibly come from his participation in the experiment.

The Nuremberg Declaration, therefore, requires a very full disclosure of information before consent to involvement in research will be deemed to be valid. In particular, it explicitly requires the disclosure of the fullest possible information to the research subject in order that he or she can legitimately make a decision about whether or not to be involved in the trial. This commitment to the full provision of information has been taken up by courts throughout the world. In particular, in the case of *Halushka* v *University of Saskatchewan*, the judge made the legal position absolutely clear. As he said:

> The duty imposed upon those who engage in medical research ... to those who offer themselves as subjects for experimentation ... is at least as great as, if not greater than, the duty owed by the ordinary physician or surgeon to his patient. There can be no exceptions to the ordinary requirements of disclosure in the case of research as there may well be in ordinary medical practice. The researcher does not have to balance the probable effect of lack of treatment against risk involved in the treatment itself. The example of risks being properly hidden from a patient can have no application in the field of research. The subject of medical experimentation is entitled to a full and frank disclosure of all the facts, probabilities and options which a reasonable man might be expected to consider before giving his consent.[79]

---

[78] Derived from the case of *United States* v *Brandt (case no 1)* 1 Trial of War Criminals 2 [1949].

[79] (1965) 53 DLR (2d) 436, at pp. 616–617.

It has been said that '... the basic approach to the ethical conduct of research and approval of investigational drugs was born in scandal and reared in protectionism'.[80] Thus, although both *Halushka* and the Nuremberg Code appear unequivocally to demand the fullest possible disclosure of information, since 1949 (when the Code was first promulgated) there have been a number of significant moves which would appear to reduce this absolute commitment. Not least of these is the Declaration of Helsinki,[81] which was first promulgated in 1964 and was most recently updated in Edinburgh in 2000. The primary principles of the Declaration of Helsinki for our purposes are as follows.

- It is the duty of the physician to promote and safeguard the health of the people. The physician's knowledge and conscience are dedicated to the fulfilment of this duty.[82]
- Medical progress is based on research which ultimately must rest in part on experimentation involving human subjects.[83]
- In medical research on human subjects, considerations related to the wellbeing of the human subject should take precedence over the interests of science and society.[84]
- Medical research involving human subjects must conform to generally accepted scientific principles, and be based on a thorough knowledge of the scientific literature, other relevant sources of information, and on adequate laboratory and, where appropriate, animal experimentation.[85]
- Appropriate caution must be exercised in the conduct of research which may affect the environment, and the welfare of animals used for research must be respected.[86]
- Medical research is only justified if there is a reasonable likelihood that the populations in which the research is carried out stand to benefit from the results of the research.[87]
- The subjects must be volunteers and informed participants in the research project.[88]

There are, of course, many other principles contained in the Declaration, some of which will be considered in more depth where appropriate. However, for the moment, it can be seen that the drafters of the Declaration of Helsinki (as amended) did intend that participation should be based on a voluntary agreement, which in itself must follow the adequate disclosure of information about the risks, benefits

[80] Levine, C. (1988), 'Has AIDS Changed the Ethics of Human Subjects Research?', *Law, Medicine and Health Care*, **12**, pp. 167–173, at p. 167.

[81] World Medical Association Declaration of Helsinki (1964), *Ethical Principles for Medical Research Involving Human Subjects* (last revised Edinburgh 2000). Available at http://www.wma.net.

[82] Principle 2.

[83] Principle 4.

[84] Principle 5.

[85] Principle 11.

[86] Principle 12.

[87] Principle 19.

[88] Principle 20.

and alternatives to the treatment. However, although many people might believe that the Helsinki Declaration was substantially a restatement of the principles contained in the Nuremberg Code, it must be borne in mind that it is in fact a set of guidelines drafted by doctors for doctors rather than by law for doctors and research subjects. Garrett, for example, claims that the Helsinki commitments are less stringent than those of the Nuremberg Code, based perhaps on 'the perceived need for more flexible, permissive, and perhaps realistic guidelines for research'.[89] Thus, he concludes that the Helsinki Declaration:

> ... embodies vastly different assumptions about research and experimentation. It promotes a benign rather than a wary view towards science and research. Written by and for physicians, the declaration exudes faith in the methods and goals of medical science and accepts the premise that progress requires human subjects.[90]

Although this may not be the place to consider in depth the Declaration of Helsinki's commitment to the autonomy of the individual, it is worth noting that some at least of the 'scandals' most starkly exposed by Beecher[91] and Pappworth[92] occurred when both the Nuremberg Code and the Declaration of Helsinki were in place. Thus, it would appear that no international declaration has yet managed to ensure that humans are never the subject of research which is based on dubious consent.

However, the fundamental commitment to free and informed consent has subsequently both driven the research agenda and explicated its philosophy. The British Transplantation Society, for example, says that:

> Where the procedure is in any way experimental or where the treatment is part of a clinical trial this must be made explicit and the potential recipient given the right to refuse to take part without prejudice to their treatment.[93]

Moreover, the Convention on Human Rights and Biomedicine expressly requires the consent of the subject,[94] as do all other relevant international statements.[95]

Capacity/Competence One major difference between the Declaration of Helsinki and the Nuremberg Code is the fact that the former permits research to be

---

89 Garrett, R.W. (1995–1996), 'Why Informed Consent? Human Experimentation and the Ethics of Autonomy', *Catholic Lawyer*, **36** (4), pp. 455–512, at p. 473.

90 At p. 474.

91 Beecher, H.K. (1966), 'Ethics and Clinical Research', *New England Journal of Medicine*, **274**; see also, Katz, J. (1987), 'The Regulation of Human Experimentation in the United States – A Personal Odyssey', *IRB: A Review of Human Subjects Research*, **9** (1), January/February, pp. 1–6.

92 Pappworth, M. (1967), *Human Guinea Pigs: Experimentation on Man*, Routledge & Kegan Paul: London.

93 British Transplantation Society (2003), *Standards for Solid Organ Transplantation in the United Kingdom*, para. 2.2.1.5, available on their website at http://www.bts.org.uk.

94 Council of Europe (1997), Article 16.

95 For example, Article 13(1) and (2) of Council of Europe Recommendation (2003) 10 of the Committee of Ministers to member states on xenotransplantation (adopted 19 June 2003).

undertaken on those who are otherwise incompetent.[96] This is not as yet directly relevant in xenotransplantation, as both the Nuffield and the Kennedy Reports recommended that for the present xenotransplantation trials should not include those who are not legally competent to make a decision. However, it is worth briefly exploring this issue, particularly in light of the Council of Europe's recent recommendation that xenotransplantation may be carried out on people unable to consent if: 'there is no effective therapeutic alternative; if the intervention is authorised by an appropriate representative', and where it is expected to produce 'a direct and important benefit for the patient'.[97] Lack of competence may be demonstrated by either mental incapacity (although this does not necessarily exclude decisions made by those diagnosed as mentally ill,[98] even when the treatment is seen by doctors as being in the person's best interests[99]), because of age or potentially because the individual has in some way been subject to a form of undue influence.[100]

The Council of Europe's recommendation firmly requires that there must be evidence, when an individual is incompetent, that there is likely to be a direct benefit for the individual. This is in line with the terms of the Adults with Incapacity (Scotland) Act 2000,[101] and would also conform to the terms of the Mental Capacity Act 2005.[102] Indeed, the recent case of *Simms* v *Simms and another*[103] – which arguably conflated experimentation and research – shows the extent to which pressure to include those who are otherwise incompetent in clinical trials may be recognized, and validated, by the courts.

This case concerned two young people who were thought most likely to be suffering from vCJD. Their current condition was such that they were at risk of early death and were not competent to make healthcare decisions for themselves. An experimental treatment – which had never before been tested on humans – was identified (Pentosan Polysulphate treatment, referred to as PPS). The parents of the patients sought 'declaratory relief that each lacks the capacity to make a decision about future treatment proposed for them and that it is lawful as being in their best interests for them to receive it'.[104] The court concluded, on the available evidence, that each patient was indeed incompetent, and therefore turned its attention to two other questions. First, Dame Butler Sloss addressed the extent to which the *Bolam Test*, referred to above, would be relevant in such circumstances; in other words, was there a responsible body of medical opinion that would offer the treatment in these circumstances. In this case, the judge was content to rely on an even smaller body of expertise than that which was found to be acceptable in *De Freitas*.[105] Effectively,

96 Principles 24–26.

97 Recommendation (2003)10 of the Committee of Ministers to member states on xenotransplantation (adopted 19 June 2003), Article 19.

98 *Re C (adult: refusal of treatment)* 15 BMLR 77 [1994].

99 *H (mental patient)* 9 BMLR 71 [1992].

100 *Re T (adult: refusal of medical treatment)* 9 BMLR 46 [2002].

101 See particularly s. 51, concerning authority for research.

102 Introduced in the House of Commons on 17 June 2004.

103 [2003] 1 All ER 669.

104 Per Dame Butler-Sloss, at p. 670.

105 Supra cit.

she relied on the evidence of one expert ('supported cautiously'[106] by another), whose testimony was that it was indeed in the interest of the patients to proceed with the treatment. Interestingly Dame Butler-Sloss seemed unimpressed with the strict application of the *Bolam Test* in these circumstances, noting that it 'ought not to be allowed to inhibit medical progress'.[107]

The other main question was whether or not the treatment could be conceptualized as being in the patients' best interests. Dame Butler-Sloss regarded her task in this respect as being to:

> Assess the best interests in the widest possible way to include the medical and non-medical benefits and disadvantages, the broader welfare issues of the two patients, their abilities, their future with or without treatment, the views of the families, and the impact of refusal of the applications.[108]

Concluding that '[t]he chance of improvement is slight but not non-existent',[109] Dame Butler-Sloss said that:

> There is sufficient possibility of unquantifiable benefit for me to find that it would be in their best interests to have the operations and the treatment subject to an assessment of the risks. There is no alternative treatment available.[110]

This judgement has two main points of interest. First, it effectively discounts the value of the *Bolam Test* in respect of treatment which – even if unproven – nonetheless seem to offer some hope (however slight) of benefit. Given the criticisms of the *Bolam Test* already highlighted, this will be good news for many. Secondly, of course, it also – and importantly – extends to the incompetent the same rights as the competent to have such treatment. One problem with rigorous application of the rules designed to protect those who are legally incompetent is that they may also be used to prevent them from participating in novel, possibly beneficial, therapies. This judgement seems to remove that paradoxical situation, and will be welcomed by many.

Dame Elizabeth Butler-Sloss then presided over two further decisions, both involving people with vCJD, and reached the same conclusion.[111]

Voluntariness Having established that it is necessary that an informed consent is provided, and that this consent must be based on the provision of information, it is worth turning to the question of voluntariness. This can be taken to encapsulate two main strands; first, that the person truly understands the decision being made and, secondly, that no duress or undue influence is applied (or in existence) which would influence the decision.

---

106 *Simms* v *Simms*, at p. 681.

107 Ibid., at pp. 680–681.

108 Ibid., at p. 683.

109 Ibid.

110 Ibid.

111 *An NHS Trust* v *HM* [2004] Lloyd's Rep Med 207; *EP* v *Trusts A, B&C* [2004] Lloyd's Rep Med 211.

A patient's voluntary participation (with the exceptions already outlined) is generally imperative to a lawful (and ethical) medical intervention. Therefore, a decision purportedly taken by a patient freely, but where in fact there is evidence of strong pressure from other circumstances, will be legally dubious. Such was the court's conclusion in the case of *Re T*.[112] Lord Donaldson summarized the legal situation in this way:

> In some cases doctors will not only have to consider the capacity of the patient to refuse treatment, but also whether the refusal has been vitiated because it resulted not from the patient's will, but from the will of others. It matters not that those others sought, however strongly, to persuade the patient to refuse, so long as in the end the refusal represented the patient's independent decision. If, however, his will was overborne, the refusal will not have represented a true decision. In this context the relationship of the persuader to the patient, for example, spouse, parents or religious adviser, will be important, because some relationships more readily lend themselves to overbearing the patient's independent will than do others.[113]

Pattinson suggests that the doctrine of undue influence 'has a long pedigree as a means of aiding vulnerable persons whose will has been overborne by another ...',[114] but concludes that as yet 'the full potential of the doctrine in the context of medical treatment is only just starting to be realised'.[115]

Of course, it could also be argued that a form of undue influence might arise from the *nature* of the patient's condition itself. Those, for example, faced with the certainty of indignity, pain or imminent death, may make choices based on fear, and may reject treatment even when it is available and potentially effective (to whatever extent). Although this might be conceived as a form of undue influence – to the extent that it directly affects a patient's choice – the courts have been reluctant to conclude that this is so in most cases,[116] preferring instead to endorse the autonomy of the individual rather than inquiring in depth into their decision.[117]

In the absence of questions of undue influence, however, there remain issues about the quality and quantity of available information, as well as issues about the possible limitations on what can lawfully be consented to. Clearly, when an intervention is experimental, there is an inevitable shortfall in the information which can be provided, making understanding of risks, benefits and so on problematic. Thus, it might be asked whether or not a genuine consent is ever possible in research since almost by definition the object of the research is to discover information which is otherwise unknown.[118] This is a matter of some considerable legal interest and is,

112 Supra cit.

113 At p. 62.

114 Pattinson, S.D. (2002), at p. 305.

115 Ibid.

116 Arguably they have been less reluctant in the past to reach this conclusion in respect of decisions of pregnant women about the management of their labour. For discussion, see McLean and Ramsey (2002), at p. 239.

117 Cf *Ms B* v *An NHS Hospital Trust* 65 BMLR 149 (2002).

118 Cf McLean, S.A.M. (2000), 'Informed Consent, Medical Research and the Competent Adult', in Doyal, L. and Tobias, J.S. (eds), *Informed Consent in Medical Research*, BMJ Books: London, pp. 166–172.

of course, open for debate. The decision whether or not a consent offered to research is ever truly competent will likely be one which is taken on consequentialist grounds; that is, the issue of the pressure to accept any intervention that might help (however minimally) when otherwise the person's situation seems hopeless, as in *Simms*,[119] is unlikely to be a real issue. Rather, it will generally be assumed that such a decision (however driven by pressure) is competently within the right of the individual. It is difficult to argue with this approach, given that the alternative would be to deprive very ill people of some hope of benefit. However, as will be seen later, questions remain as to whether or not that situation can or should stand when the treatment under consideration also poses potential risks to third parties.

Although the provision of consent generally is presumed to render an intervention or an action lawful, there is additionally a limit to the kinds of things to which human beings can in fact consent and for some people this might include involvement in some research trials. It is, for example, a standard tenet of criminal law that there are certain kinds of behaviour which even the provision of a consent cannot render lawful.[120] Examples would include murder, and in at least one judgement,[121] which was endorsed by the European Court of Human Rights,[122] involvement in private, consensual sadomasochistic sexual practices. In terms of the civil law, Evans and Evans[123] suggest that there may be doubts about the capacity of the individual to agree validly to involvement in research, particularly where that research involves risks which are more than trivial. They argue that:

> Whilst there are many contexts in which autonomous adults can choose to undertake more-than-minimal risks (sport is an obvious example), clinical research ought perhaps not to be among them. The main reason for thinking this is that we should distinguish between the degree of risk someone might privately undergo in an activity of his choice and the degree of risk that is appropriate for a professional or other public figure to **invite** a patient to contemplate.[124]

Thus, it is possible that not every apparent exercise of autonomy will be validated by the law. Having said this, however, it is clear that it is generally conceded that people, whether sick or healthy, do have the right to enter into respectable clinical trials even if in so doing they assume a degree of risk. What we can learn from the comments of Evans and Evans, and the case referred to, is that there may be a limit to the kind of risk – or the gravity of risk – which people can lawfully assume.

It is also worth noting that the question of understanding may be complicated in clinical trials by the fact that part of the information that must be disclosed to the individual is information about what people do not know. Thus, although in the standard medical intervention risks and side effects are relatively well known, in the case of research it is almost always the case that it is in part to identify these risks

---

119 Supra cit.

120 See for example the case of *R* v *Donovan* [1934] 2 KB 498.

121 *R* v *Brown* [1966] 1 All ER 545.

122 *Laskey, Jaggard and Brown* v *United Kingdom* [1997] 24 EHRR 39.

123 Evans, D. and Evans, M. (1966), *A Decent Proposal: Ethical Review of Clinical Research*, John Wiley & Sons: Winchester.

124 At p. 66 (emphasis in original).

and benefits that a trial is being conducted in the first place. It is perhaps for this reason that the common law has been so stringent in its requirements about the fullness of disclosure required in the research setting.

Equally, the question of voluntariness depends on the condition of the individual. Daar has suggested that:

> In the case of xenotransplantation clinical trials, particularly for the early patients, a number of those provisos [about consent] will need to be compromised. The likely subjects will probably be very sick and voluntariness will be questionable because, especially in the case of liver and heart subjects, the alternative may well be death. The risks from the point of view of rejection and the potential benefit can be vaguely estimated, but not the risk from the xenozoonoses, because we will not know which viruses, for example, will be more pathogenic in man, or will mutate and recombine in the host. We will in fact not know if the source animal has any viruses we know nothing about.[125]

This cautionary statement requires consideration not just of the question of voluntariness, but also of the significance of the risk(s) of a given intervention. Although it might be argued that the possibility of risks eventuating could be small (although we don't know this) it seems likely that their potential gravity would make them significant to the individual and also potentially to the community, (a consideration to which the chapter will return below). This notion of 'significant' risk also has legal import. In the case of *Sidaway* v *Board of Governors Bethlem Royal Hospital and the Maudsley Hospital*[126] it was made clear that the doctor's duty is 'to provide the patient with information which will enable the patient to make a balanced judgment'.[127] *Pearce* v *United Bristol Healthcare NHS Trust*,[128] further explicated this statement by adding that a 'significant risk which would affect the judgment of a reasonable patient'[129] should 'in the normal course'[130] be disclosed.

Additionally, it must be conceded that any early clinical trials will have as their primary function not simply the well-being of individual patients, who will almost certainly be very sick, but also 'to address unforeseen medical complications that arise, to accumulate experience, and to gather information that is simply unavailable from the laboratory'.[131] In other words, even when the decision has been made to move xenotransplantation to the clinical trial stage, it might still reasonably be anticipated that many of those who would be recipients would not be sure of individual benefit. This is what would classically be called non-therapeutic research.

---

125 Daar, A.S. (1999), 'Xenotransplantation: Science, Risk and International Regulatory Efforts', in Caulfield, T. and Williams-Jones, B. (eds), *Commercialization of Genetic Research: Ethical, Legal and Policy Issues*, Kluwer Academic: New York, pp. 129–155, at p. 133.

126 1 BMLR 132 (1985).

127 At p. 159, per Lord Templeman.

128 48 BMLR 118 (1999).

129 At p. 124.

130 Ibid.

131 Appel, J.Z. et al. (2000), 'Xenotransplantation: The Challenge to Current Psychosocial Attitudes', *Progress in Transplantation*, **10** (4), December, pp. 217–225, at p. 222.

As we have already seen, the Kennedy Report has indicated that research should not be conducted unless it is therapeutic in nature,[132] but with respect this seems highly unlikely to be clear-cut, especially in the early stages.

Arnold and Dresser say:

> It is always difficult to know when it is appropriate to move from animal to human studies. Bench research and animal studies are required both to establish biologic plausibility for human experiment and to lay an adequate scientific foundation for learning from the experiment.[133]

In respect of xenotransplantation, it will be no less difficult to make such a decision. Indeed, one commentator has suggested that clinical trials of xenotransplantation, at least in the early stages, are doubly problematic. As he says:

> Transgenic transplants actually represent one experimental technique (the production of transgenic animals) superimposed on another (the transplantation of transgenic animal organs into human beings). Attempts to analyse the possible outcome of this situation lead to a statistical nightmare, since there is an exponential increase in unknown risk.[134]

Arguably, then, the decision to move from animal and laboratory work to the clinical setting is compounded in its complexity, and may require additional stringency of regulation. Welin concludes that:

> Given that stringent safeguards are introduced, a cautious start to the clinical trials of xenotransplantation is consistent with a cautious approach with regard to the risk of viral infections ... the use of new experimental procedures goes on all the time and many of the early xenotransplantations took place in this way. The regulation of clinical research by the Helsinki Declaration allows for experimental procedures to be tried in the clinic without prior consultation with an ethics committee. This clinical freedom must be withdrawn for xenotransplantation procedures – otherwise regulation will be ineffective.[135]

Welin's call for adequate regulation is echoed by Melo et al.,[136] who suggest that, before any clinical trials of xenotransplantation are undertaken, it is necessary that an adequate regulatory framework is devised so that the human rights of those who are likely to be involved can be protected, as well as ensuring the quality of the animal organs or tissue which would be used for transplantation. Again, the most recent recommendations on xenotransplantation emphasize the importance of

---

[132] Kennedy Report (1997), at p. 112, para. 7.5.

[133] Arnold, R.M. and Dresser, R. (1996), 'Ethical Issues Associated with Xenotransplantation: The Case of Baboon Bone Marrow to Human Transplantation', *Molecular Diagnosis*, **1** (3), pp. 239–242, at p. 239.

[134] Menache, A. (1999), 'Stop Now Before it's Too Late', *Bulletin of the World Health Organization*, **77** (1), pp. 76–77, at p. 76.

[135] Welin, S. (2000), 'Starting Clinical Trials of Xenotransplantation – Reflections on the Ethics of the Early Phase', *Journal of Medical Ethics*, **26**, pp. 231–236, at p. 232.

[136] Melo, H. et al. (2001), 'Ethical and Legal Issues in Xenotransplantation', *Bioethics*, **15** (5/6), pp. 1427–1442.

adequate regulation. The World Health Organization, for example, notes the potential risks of xenotransplantation in this way:

> Xeonotransplantation has the potential to supplement the limited supply of human material for transplantation and may even become an alternative. However, xenotransplantation (including the use of living xenogeneic cells, tissues or organs, as well as human bodily fluids, cells, tissues or organs that have had *ex vivo* contact with living xenogeneic material) presents specific immunological problems for recipients. It also may transmit pathogens from the animal source to the recipient and, hence, possibly to the general public; recent instances of human epidemics/pandemics arising from cross-species infections, such as severe acute respiratory syndrome, underline the public health risks of xenotransplantation. These risks are compounded by immunosuppression, nonexistent or inadequate diagnostic tools, and an absence of effective therapy.[137]

In light of this, the WHO:

> 1 URGES Member States:
>
> (1) to allow xenotransplantation *only when effective regulatory control and surveillance by national health authorities are in place*;
> (2) to draw up protective measures to prevent the potential secondary transmission of any xenogeneic pathogen that could have infected recipients of xenotransplants;
> (3) to support international collaboration for the prevention and surveillance of infections resulting from xenotransplantation;[138] (emphasis added)

The regime established in the United Kingdom to date has already been considered, and will be returned to briefly in the concluding chapter.

In addition – and this is vital to the question of voluntariness – questions will arise about who should be recruited into such trials. Although in the United Kingdom it is generally for the moment presumed that there will be no trials conducted on anyone who lacks the capacity to consent,[139] this does not finally resolve the question of who should be involved. Caplan, for example, suggests that a difficult question will be:

> ... who ought to be the first subjects in clinical xenografting trials ... perhaps adults who would not otherwise be eligible for transplants under existing exclusion criteria, the imminently dying, terminally ill volunteers who agree to serve, those who are brain dead, or those needing a second or third transplant when scarcity and prognosis would make it most unlikely that they would receive another human organ or tissue.[140]

Although this might at first sight seem to be counter-intuitive – even in complete opposition to the current recommendations in the UK – the involvement of such people would seem, at least in part, to meet the criteria derived from *Simms*.[141] On the other hand, the complexities of the information which it will be necessary for

137 WHO (2003), *Human Organ and Tissue Transplantation*, EB113/14, 27 November, para. 11.

138 P. 6.

139 But see the brief discussion above.

140 Caplan (1992), at p. 726.

141 Supra cit.

individual research subjects to comprehend in respect of xenotransplantation trials is arguably considerably greater than that which is involved in other trials. Equally, those in imminent fear of death may be subject to psychological pressures and might, therefore, be least likely to be able to assimilate and freely involve themselves in trials of xenotransplantation, as discussed above.

There are a number of reasons why information about xenotransplantation is particularly difficult. First, xenotransplantation represents a major deviation from standard medical practice. Although porcine cells have been used in human subjects before,[142] the possibility of transplantation of large segments of tissue or whole organs poses an entirely novel set of considerations which it would be necessary for the subject to understand. Thus, it will be necessary that potential human subjects are informed of a wide range of potential, but by no means predictable, consequences of their involvement. Additionally, as we have suggested, it is likely that those being considered for inclusion in the early clinical trials will be particularly vulnerable because of their medical condition, and potentially easily influenced by the enthusiasm of the researchers. Of course, as we have also noted, this may be true in other circumstances, and in itself may not be sufficient to affect the quality of an agreement to participate. However, there is a crucial difference with xenotransplantation; namely its potential impact on others.

The nature and extent of that impact are unclear at present. For some the possibility of risk is so significant as to merit reconsideration of xenotransplantation itself. Incorvati, for example, says:

> As a rule, before proceeding with any clinical trial the informed consent of the participant is required. But in xenotransplantation research, individual consent is not the sole requirement. Risks exist not only for the immediate individual subjects of the research, but also for third parties or for the public at large.[143]

On the other hand, Chae and Cooper suggest that although the potential risk to the public is '[t]he most significant legal issue'[144] in this area:

> ... this is not a unique problem. The potential for the transfer of infection for allotransplantation arises daily. Moreover, the risk of the transfer of known microorganisms would appear to be significantly less than in allografting if quality-controlled animal organs are utilized.[145]

Although their reasoning is persuasive to an extent, the reality of the scale of the potential risk in xenotransplantation is seen by many as requiring its differentiation from allotransplantation. *Nature Medicine*, for example, reports that:

---

[142] Bach, F.H. et al. (1998), 'Uncertainty in Xenotransplantation: Individual Benefit Versus Collective Risk', *Nature Medicine* **4**(2), pp. 141–144, at p. 141.

[143] Incorvati, G. (2003), 'Xenotransplantation, Public Responsibility and Law', *European Journal of Health Law*, **10**, at p. 299.

[144] Chae, S.J. and Cooper, D.K.C. (1997), 'Legal Implications of Xenotransplantation', *Xenotransplantation*, **4**, at p. 139.

[145] Ibid.

> With this great potential for medical advance comes an undefined but nonetheless very real risk that the transplanted tissue may carry unknown latent infections that, once introduced into the recipient, could be activated and give rise to infection. As a worst case scenario it is possible that such a new infectious agent could sweep through human populations giving rise to a life-threatening pandemic. Such an event has never been documented and there simply are not the data available to address the extent of the risk.[146]

We have already suggested that in any research – given that it should start with a null hypothesis[147] – there are always questions which cannot be answered. If not, there would be no justification for doing the research at all. Arguably there is much more that is unknown in xenotransplantation than is normal in clinical research, making the provision of a meaningful consent particularly problematic. Of course, it is the nature of research that less is known at the beginning of the enterprise, and more later. In this respect, research on xenotransplantation may eventually be able to answer some of the postulated problems, and adequately quantify the level of risk. However, one additional consideration arises in xenotransplantation; namely, that even if this is so, the attitudes of the public may need to be taken into serious account.

Even assuming that the individual prospective participant in clinical trials of xenotransplantation can satisfy the requirements of autonomy, and is deemed to have been provided with adequate information, virtually all commentators on xenotransplantation have introduced a further element into the consent process; namely the agreement of the community. Standard consent rules relate to the individual patient/participant, and are based on the presumption of the individuality *of* that person and the limitation of the impact of involvement *to* that person. However, the potential risks associated with xenotransplantation will affect the rest of the community (local, national and international) unusually acutely were they to arise. Thus, it has been argued, it is necessary not only to obtain the consent of the individual; it is also vital that the community endorses the use of xenotransplantation.

The involvement of the public is said to be necessary because '[i]t is no longer the individual or society that may be at risk but the human species itself'.[148] The engagement of the public is further reiterated by the Council of Europe.[149] Article 30 states that:

> In accordance with the principles stated in Article 28 of the Convention on Human Rights and Biomedicine, member states should take active steps to ensure that the fundamental questions raised by xenotransplantation are the subject of appropriate public discussion particularly in light of relevant medical, psychological, cultural, ethical, legal, social and economic implications.

These fundamental questions are also noted by Clark, who says:

---

146 'Focus on Xenotransplantation' (1998), *Nature Medicine*, available at http://www.nature.com/nm/web_specials/xeno, accessed 24/04/02.

147 McLean (2000).

148 Incorvati (2003), at p. 300.

149 Recommendation (2003) 10.

> Ethical issues concerning xenotransplantation include animal rights, allocation of resources, and distributive justice. In addition to obtaining consent for xenotransplants from individual patients, consent is also necessary from the populace, given the public health risks.[150]

Of course, it could be argued that Clark's concerns would be minimized were it to be clear that the public health risks are overstated. However, it seems likely that at least some of them would be in large part unknown and unknowable at the point at which early clinical trials might commence, and therefore this concern is likely to remain and carry weight. Involving society in individual decisions is, however, by no means straightforward, and the implications of giving community consent a major role are that the meaning of consent in the law is modified, as well as requiring creative thinking on precisely how the views of the public are to be obtained, evaluated and utilized.

In approaching this question, Bach et al. analysed the problems from the basis of four ethical principles:

> First, a risk to the public requires a public mechanism for determining the acceptability of, and method of consent to, the risk. Second, since the risk to the public is not a 'one time only' event, its assessment and regulation must be iterative. Third, the standard model of individual consent to medical interventions must be modified, since risks involve third parties, requiring that patients and close contacts are carefully monitored. Fourth, the possibility that a new infectious agent with altered passivity will arise within the xenograft recipient may represent a danger to the pig population. Because of these four considerations, xenotransplantation requires a novel process of evaluation at the national level with novel institutional guidelines, responsibilities and resources.[151]

Taking the human concerns from their four ethical principles, it is clear that society has a direct interest in the individual decision whether or not to participate in xenotransplantation. Yet, as Daar points out, taking account of the interests of society will prejudice the interests of the individual subject.[152] As he says, 'generally, consent has nothing to do with protection of contacts or of society, it requires that the subject be made aware of the risks involved, the potential benefits to the subject, and all the alternatives available'.[153] Thus, a new model of consent would be required if the interests of society were to be taken into account, as many commentators feel they must be.

However, it is unclear precisely how the public's views can be effectively obtained, nor is it clear what impact the public's views should have on the 'rights' of individual patients to make decisions to participate in xenotransplantation. As has been said:

> The history of xenotransplantation is replete with daring clinical experiments justified by imminent death. Such experiments were acceptable at the time, but now they would be

150 Clark, M. (1999), 'This Little Piggy Went to Market: The Xenotransplantation and Xenozoonosis Debate', *Journal of Law, Medicine and Ethics*, **27**, pp. 137–152, at p. 141.

151 Bach et al. (1998), at p. 142.

152 Daar (1999), at p. 133.

153 Ibid.

> viewed as overly unbalanced in terms of risk benefit ratio. This ratio was traditionally evaluated by considering the interests of the patient being experimented on. However, over the past two to three years the evaluation has had to be extended to include the interests of the public – and here we have floundered because we have no experience of evaluating this component.[154]

It is clear that obtaining any kind of societal consensus or consent will be problematic. As Caulfield and Robertson say:

> Factors which make this process difficult include: the scientific complexity of the topic, the probabilistic nature of many of the associated risks, the context-dependent nature of the issue, and the inherent difficulty of designing a process which can obtain an accurate picture of a given community's opinion.[155]

But the issue of societal consent is not the only characteristic of consent to xenotransplantation which differentiates it from the more common form of consent recognized by law. Each of the Reports referred to earlier in this review has made it clear that a mandatory system of post-transplant surveillance is essential if the benefits and risks of xenotransplantation are to be adequately identified and monitored. Indeed, as we have already seen, the United Kingdom Xenotransplantation Interim regulatory Authority (UKXIRA) produced a consultation document on surveillance as a critical part of its early work.

Monitoring and Surveillance

The requirement for surveillance and monitoring is endorsed by the major international statements on xenotransplantation. Article 13 of the Council of Europe Recommendation (2003) 10 reads as follows:

> Article 13
> 1. Patients participating in a xenotransplantation should be adequately informed in a comprehensible manner of the nature, objectives, possible benefits, potential risks and consequences of the procedure, as well as of any constrains that may be linked to it.
> 2. In particular patients should also be made aware of the constraints of monitoring and precautionary measures that may become necessary subsequent to xenotransplantation. Such measures will, according to the principles of necessity and proportionality, be adapted to the circumstances and adjusted in accordance with the assessment, based on current scientific and medical knowledge, of the risks generated by each of the procedures involved, and may in particular include:
>   a) the collection of personal data and inclusion in a register;
>   b) the provision by the medical team, in accordance with Article 14, of information concerning the risks of infection and the constraints associated thereto;
>   c) long-term medical monitoring including repeated biological samples being taken and archived;
>   d) reporting any significant unexplained symptoms or illness that may arise after the xenotransplantation;

[154] Ibid., at p. 129.

[155] Caulfield and Robertson (2001), at p. 90.

e) maintaining contact with the medical team;
f) taking precautions with respect to sexual activity;
g) the need for the patient to agree that information is provided by a medical team to any future close personal contacts, in accordance with Article 14, concerning the risks of infection and the constraints associated thereto;
h) the other constraints which might be applicable if circumstances so require, in particular the possibility of isolation which may become necessary in the event of a contagious or previously unknown illness occurring.

3. Patients should be informed that, in accordance with Article 21, constraints mentioned hereinabove may be imposed if the person concerned refuses to comply with them.

These recommendations are entirely in line with the thinking of the reports which preceded the establishment of UKXIRA in the UK. For example, the Nuffield Report concluded that:

> The Working Party recommends that standards and mechanisms for monitoring xenograft recipients and for the action to be taken in case of disease transmission should be in place before human trials begin. It should be a requirement of clinical trials that the need for monitoring is explained to the patient and that it is made clear that consent to the operation also implies consent to subsequent monitoring.[156]

Likewise, the Kennedy Report appreciated the need to monitor xenotransplantation should it be ethically acceptable. As it said:

> We conclude that, at the stage where it is considered that a full investigation of potential infection risks has been carried out, and the risks have been shown to be within tolerable margins, it would be ethically acceptable to proceed. This is subject to there being a system in place to monitor the emergence of any unusual disease or any unknown pathogens and to require, as a consequence, that appropriate additional research be completed in a proper fashion.[157]

The need for monitoring and surveillance, then, formed an important element of the consideration of consent in both Reports. Given the concerns they expressed, it is unsurprising that one of the earliest initiatives of UKXIRA was to consider the question of surveillance. In addition to the production of the consultation document, a public meeting to discuss its terms was held, emphasizing the importance that the UKXIRA places on the issues raised by infection surveillance and monitoring.[158] The surveillance document was designed to provide 'a draft model framework to implement infection surveillance, initially for clinical trials'.[159] The Working Party defines surveillance as the 'ongoing systematic collection, analysis, and interpretation of relevant data, closely integrated with the timely dissemination of these data to those responsible for control and prevention'.[160] In their view there are

---

156 Nuffield Report (1996), p. 117, para. 10.28.

157 Kennedy Report (1997), p. 74, para. 4.63.

158 See chapter 3, above.

159 UKXIRA (1999c), *Draft Report of the Infection Surveillance Steering Group of the UKXIRA* (Draft for Consultation).

160 Ibid., para. 1.1.

a number of underlying principles which need to be in place to inform the development of any surveillance system put in place in respect of xenotransplantation. These principles are as follows:

> *One*: Successful outcomes will depend on integrated approaches across all areas of health care delivery, surveillance and policy.
> *Two:* All patients must have access to a uniformly high quality of infection diagnosis.
> *Three:* Clear and accurate information should be readily available to patients about how they can play their role in their treatment, including issues of consent, and how they can help recognise and prevent potential infections.
> *Four:* The development of infection surveillance should take account of the views of patients and professionals.
> *Five*: Infection surveillance should be based on the best available evidence and this evidence should be shared with patients and the public.
> *Six*: There should be explicit minimum standards to ensure effective infection surveillance and auditing to those standards.[161]

Section 2 of the draft report indicates that the aim of infection surveillance would be '[t]o inform strategies to prevent and reduce the risk of xenogeneic infections in recipients, their contacts and the public'.[162] The objective of surveillance and monitoring would be to ensure that there is prompt recognition, investigation and management of any suspected or confirmed infections which arise in recipients of xenografts or their close contacts, or in healthcare and animal workers.[163] In addition, the surveillance should ensure that 'the rapid and appropriate control measures are monitored to prevent spread of infection'.[164] Additional benefits to be gained from surveillance would be prompt feedback of information to all of those concerned in xenotransplantation, professionals and patients, and the provision of information which is appropriate to evaluate and review the system.[165] The report encourages the collection of data both locally and nationally and indicated that such data should be actively collected, for example by a dedicated co-ordinator making regular requests for information from data contributors.[166] In addition, the benefits of collecting such information would be both national and international.[167] In this way, any apparent threat to international health would be minimized and any untoward events arising in other countries would be able to inform national policy.[168]

The Working Party envisages that the main sources of data would be animals, animal workers, recipients of xenotransplantation, recipients' household/close contacts and recipients' healthcare workers.[169] The report makes it clear that a considerable amount of data would need to be recorded and stored for the duration

161 Para. 1.3.
162 Para. 2.1.
163 Para. 2.2.
164 Ibid.
165 Ibid.
166 Para. 2.4.
167 Ibid.
168 Ibid.
169 Para. 2.5.

of human surveillance – effectively indefinitely.[170] The mechanics of how this would be done are outlined in the report.[171] For our purposes, however, the significant issues relate to how the recipients of xenotransplantation and their household/close contacts are to be managed. We are less concerned with problems associated with those who are involved professionally, as their involvement is likely to be clearly both voluntary and understanding. However, they would require to have access to occupational health services and it is recommended that they should have baseline blood samples taken for archiving before the xenotransplant is carried out.[172]

In an effort to ensure that any adverse effects of xenotransplantation do become known, it is necessary in the view of the Working Party that recipients of xenotransplants should be monitored both before and after xenotransplantation, with life-long follow-up.[173] In order to achieve the purposes of the surveillance regimen, it would also be necessary that the recipient agreed to make any untoward event known.[174] As for household or close contacts, which UKXIRA defines as 'household members and sexual partners and others with whom the xenotransplant recipient may engage in activities in which bodily fluids may be exchanged',[175] again it is recommended that all close contacts should be seen by the transplant team before xenotransplantation. This would be to ensure that they are aware of the possible risks and how to minimize them, as well as having base line blood samples taken for archiving.[176] These requirements further emphasize the difference between xenotransplantation and other forms of medical intervention. It is unusual for any patient to be required to agree to life-long and highly intrusive monitoring – although the rationale for so doing in xenotransplantation is clear – but it is even more unusual that contacts should effectively be subject to intrusion into what would otherwise be private matters, because of treatment being carried out on a third party.

Of significance in these recommendations are the considerations which informed the Working Party's approach to consent in this area. In Annex 5 to the document, the Working Party lays out some of the considerations that influenced its thinking. Unsurprisingly, a primary consideration was to reduce risk to all of those involved in xenotransplantation, both recipients and those closely related to them, as well as society as a whole.[177] Given that it is uncertain whether or not there is any risk of xenozoonosis, it was felt necessary to maximize the amount of information which was obtained, in order that any adverse effects could be identified and acted on immediately.[178]

The Working Party notes that those who are involved in allotransplantation are in any event subject to regular check-ups throughout their lives.[179] However, in respect

170 Ibid.
171 Section 2.
172 Introduction.
173 Section 4.
174 Introduction.
175 Ibid.
176 Ibid.
177 Para. A.5.1.
178 Ibid.
179 Para. A5.2.

of xenotransplantation it seems likely that the need for monitoring will be more acute and not related only or primarily to the health of the transplanted organ. Thus, the Working Party recommends that the recipient would need to agree to a number of additional conditions, which they list as follows:

- to remain in the surveillance programme whether or not the xenotransplantation was successful
- to have samples taken at specified intervals
- to use barrier contraception consistently and for life
- to refrain from pregnancy/fathering a child
- to undertake to be contactable
- to allow the relevant health authorities to be notified when moving abroad
- to be willing to identify possible contacts beyond known *close contacts* in case of adverse events
- to storage of data and storage of samples indefinitely
- to divulging of anonymised information to others for research/analysis
- that any doctor they register with will be told of their status as a xeno–recipient
- that they should declare their status to any doctor of whom they might seek emergency advice.[180]

In addition, recipients of xenotransplantation would be required to agree to refrain from donating blood or organs; to have a post-mortem undertaken on their death and to ensure that their families are aware of this agreement.[181] Additionally, they would need to agree that samples could be stored following the post-mortem examination.[182] Moreover, recipients would need to agree that their contacts could be informed about their condition, the procedure itself, any subsequent treatment, any possible side-effects and any symptoms that they might identify in themselves.[183] Recognizing the breadth of these requirements, the Working Party notes that the personal and family relationships of any xenotransplantation recipient would not stay static, and that counselling might be needed to inform future sexual partners about their status as xenotransplant recipients.[184]

In addition to the requirements imposed on xenotransplantation recipients themselves, the close contacts, as defined by UKXIRA, would also need to agree to: a check-up and testing schedule; the giving of samples; and an undertaking to be contactable by keeping their name and address on the register.[185] Additionally, they would be required to agree to the storage of data and samples indefinitely.[186] Moreover, as with the recipient, they would be required to agree to the divulging of anonymized information for research or analysis, and should be informed that their general practitioner would be made aware of their status, because they need to have information about the tests undergone by their patients.[187] Not only

180 Ibid.
181 Ibid.
182 Ibid.
183 Ibid.
184 Ibid.
185 Ibid.
186 Ibid.
187 Ibid.

xenotransplantation recipients themselves, but close contacts would be required to refrain from donating blood or organs.[188] Overall, these requirements are designed to ensure that the necessary caution at the beginning of clinical trials is exercised, and of course to provide a mechanism for monitoring the possibility of the emergence of xenozoonoses.

It is both responsible and unsurprising that UKXIRA has attempted to lay down such stringent conditions, should xenotransplantation proceed to clinical trials. It is equally clear, following our analysis of the law of consent, that the outcome of this responsible caution is to extend the information required to be provided even further than that which would be required in the normal experimental or research situation. This is, of course, as much in the interests of the community as it is in the interests of the individual recipient. Additionally, however, the stringency of the surveillance programme requires of xenotransplantation recipients and their contacts an unusually high level of restriction on their capacity to make life choices. This naturally poses additional matters of concern, even if this is ultimately held to be acceptable to the community. Rothblatt seems sure that there will indeed be no problems, saying:

> Unlike the emotion-driven public opposition that suppresses commerce in human organs and compulsory cadaveric transplants, there is little emotive basis for public opposition to xenotransplant safeguards.[189]

Two things need to be said about her assertion, however. First, it is not clear on what evidence she bases it; and second, even if it is true, that does not mean that there may not be forceful objections to the very nature of xenotransplantation itself. In any event, the Working Party itself was concerned about how such intrusive requirements could be imposed. As they note, '[t]here is no current legislation that would require or force patients to comply with surveillance requirements',[190] but they also conclude that this is probably not necessary.[191] In their view, patients would normally be willing to co-operate with any surveillance put in place in order to maintain their own health. They also note, however, that any attempt to require – rather than invite – patients to agree to all of the limitations to be imposed on their future life would be likely to run contrary to the terms of the Human Rights legislation, in particular Article 8. They note that Article 2 of the Human Rights Act does provide the state with certain justifications for breaching Article 8, but conclude that the introduction of legislation for routine surveillance, even for the protection of health, could fall outside the scope of the justifications for derogation which Article 2 permits.[192] In any event, as they note, even if it were possible to utilize Article 2 as a justification for derogating from Article 8, 'it is hard to see how compliance could be fully enforced'.[193]

---

188 Ibid.

189 Rothblatt, M. (2004), *Your Life or Mine*, Ashgate: Aldershot, at p. 62.

190 UKXIRA (1999c), para. A5.3.

191 Ibid.

192 For a brief additional consideration of this issue, see below.

193 UKXIRA (1999c), para. A5.3.

In support, however, of the imposition of certain mandatory requirements, the Council of Europe Recommendation states that:

> If, after the xenotransplantation has been carried out, the recipient or his or her close personal contacts refuse to comply with the constraints associated with xenotransplantation, public authorities should intervene and take appropriate measures, where public health protection so requires, in conformity with principles of necessity and proportionality.
>
> Depending on the circumstances and in accordance with the procedures provided for by national law, such measures might include registration, compulsory medical follow-up and sampling.[194]

Whether or not it is envisaged that constraints on individuals may need to be considerably more forceful than those described above, however, is an important, and currently moot, question. Indeed, although generally welcoming xenotransplantation, Rothblatt makes the point that:

> With a conception of autonomy – including informed consent – in mind, the issue that must be addressed head-on is the possibility of reconciling the necessity for effective surveillance ... with legitimate constraints on autonomy. There can be no question that a dramatic threat is indeed potentially posed by the type of surveillance widely regarded as required to avert a xenogeneic pandemic.[195]

In terms of consent, the Working Party agrees that no xenotransplantation can proceed unless a valid agreement is obtained from the patient that they will comply with the surveillance regimen.[196] This, therefore, requires that the full extent of the regimen be explained to people before they are asked to consent, and that they 'have the commitment to comply'.[197] As the Working Party says, 'UKXIRA would expect to see a very high standard of information supplied to the patients to ensure they are advised about all the material foreseeable risks in a way that they can use in their decision making'.[198] It also notes that patients who give their consent must, as is common in all clinical trials, be told that they can withdraw from the trial at any stage.[199] However, naturally, this is problematic. If the surveillance regimen is in fact essential, then the patient who gives an agreement to conform to the regimen and then subsequently withdraws it could become a risk to themselves or to the public. Additionally, any such withdrawal of conformity with the regimen would also potentially mean that:

> A patient who has withdrawn consent for participation in the protocol and surveillance program may also be able to withdraw consent in relation to the banking and sharing of identifiable health information.[200]

194 Council of Europe Recommendation (2003) 10, Article 21.

195 Rothblatt (2004), at p. 58.

196 UKXIRA (1999c), para. A5.4.

197 Ibid.

198 Ibid.

199 Ibid.

200 Caulfield and Robertson (2001), at p. 88.

If so, and it must be said that this is an assertion difficult to disagree with, then there would inevitably be serious consequences for the research/therapeutic programme itself, as the retention, analysis and use of such data would be vital to compliance with best practice, as well as with the clear urging of the World Health Organization.[201]

Following the general provisions of the Nuffield and Kennedy Reports, the Working Party also concludes that:

> The UKXIRA will need to be satisfied that arrangements allow for consent to be given genuinely freely and that the assessment of the competence of the patient or contact has been properly carried out. The UKXIRA would expect patients to be informed about the procedures by, and to discuss consent with, a suitably qualified person who is independent of the xenotransplantation team. A suitably qualified person (also independent of the xenotransplantation team) should assess the competence of the patient and/or his close contacts. The UKXIRA would probably not agree to the inclusion in early trials of a patient who had a close contact ... incapable of giving valid consent to be included in the surveillance programme.[202]

Finally, the Working Party concludes that the quality of information, as well as the skill of the person providing that information, will affect the willingness both of patients and of their contacts to comply with the regimen. Thus, any applicant who intends to carry out xenotransplantation clinical trials would have to produce a well-prepared programme in order to ensure that adequate information is given to patients and their contacts, both about the transplant itself and about the follow-up programme.[203] And, of course, no decision should be taken as a matter of urgency, but rather time should be given to individuals and their contacts to consider the gravity both of the operation itself and of the requirements which are imposed by the surveillance regimen.

The impact of xenotransplantation on individual recipients of xenografts and those closely associated with them requires an adequate evaluation of the extent to which the potential benefits of xenotransplantation might outweigh the risks, which in this case must include the risk of dramatically restricted life choices. There are a number of important questions raised by the widely accepted need for surveillance – questions which, if not capable of satisfactory resolution, might place the legal basis of surveillance in doubt. These will be considered briefly in turn.

Surrendering Life Choices

As Bach et al. say:

> Xenotransplantation informed consent goes beyond fully explaining the risks and experimental nature of the procedure itself. Due to the unknown risk of cross-species viral infection, patients must agree to an unprecedented variety of restrictions on their individual freedom. These include restrictions in relation to freedom of association,

201 WHO (2003), at p. 6.

202 UKXIRA (1999c), para. A5.5.

203 Para. A5.8.

> freedom of movement, freedom of international travel, sexual freedom and privacy. The restrictions will need to be of unlimited duration because of the impossibility of predicting the period in which a possible infection might manifest itself. A patient consenting to such conditions would in effect be giving away important aspects of his or her freedom for life.[204]

Thus, the individual invited to participate in a trial of xenotransplantation is being asked to agree to adopt a heavily restricted lifestyle for as long as they survive. In addition, as Caulfield and Robertson point out, there are other potential impacts on the life of xenotransplantation subjects which would also require to be disclosed, including, for example, the possibility of the media attention which seems likely to follow.[205] Indeed, it must be questioned whether or not any purported consent to participation in a surveillance programme, such as that proposed by UKXIRA, could in fact be deemed legally valid. This is because, as has been pointed out:

> From a legal standpoint consent to medical treatment is characterised not as a *contract* but as a *permission*. It protects the treating physician from an allegation of assault and battery, but it does not bind the patient to continue with the treatment ... moreover, there may well be compelling policy reasons which militate against characterising the patient's consent as an irrevocable agreement including the importance of protecting patient autonomy and bodily integrity, the asymmetry of power and knowledge between doctor and patient, the fiduciary obligations which arise from that relationship and the vulnerability of the patient (particularly in a research setting).[206]

Thus, the patient's purported consent to surveillance or monitoring is unlikely to be either legally binding or legally enforceable, unless specific legislation is introduced to render it so. Under current law, therefore, it would be impossible to impose such a regimen on individuals. Equally, to change the law of consent to account for surveillance regimens would touch at the very heart of the voluntariness which is central to the concept itself. This assertion is, however, rejected by Rothblatt, who says:

> ... the law has been clear for a century or more that it is acceptable to withdraw respect from autonomy rights in the face of circumstances where there is wide agreement that respecting them potentially undermines the health and safety of others – including, in the US, mandatory vaccination ... Given the dramatic threat to public health potentially posed by xenotransplantation, and the minimal inconvenience of biomonitoring, it is not unreasonable to require the modest impingement on autonomy of non-cancellability of informed consent to bio-monitoring.[207]

We, however, find there to be more validity in the suggestion that '[e]nforcement of guidelines/regulations on individual patients and their many human contacts may prove controversial and sometimes difficult, if not impossible'.[208] In any event, there

---

204 Bach et al. (2001), 'Ethical and Legal Issues in Technology: Xenotransplantation', *American Journal of Law and Medicine*, **27** (2 and 3), pp. 283–300, at p. 293.

205 Caulfield and Robertson (2001), at p. 83.

206 Caulfield and Robertson (2001), at p. 86.

207 Rothblatt (2004), at p. 60.

208 Chae and Cooper (1997), at p. 139.

are further reasons to question Rothblatt's position. In support of her claim, she calls into service the case of *Jacobson* v *Massachusetts*.[209] However, not only was this case concerned with the issue of mandatory vaccination (surely less intrusive or risky than trials of xenotransplantation), but it was also decided at a time when the US was unconcerned about some matters which we would now regard as fundamental to human rights. For example, the analogy of compulsory vaccination was used in the case of *Buck* v *Bell*[210] in support of the compulsory sterilization of the 'feeble minded'. In this case the judge said, '[t]he principle that sustains compulsory vaccination is broad enough to cover cutting the Fallopian tubes'.[211] It is surely not seriously suggested that such decisions are likely to commend themselves to contemporary judges? Although Rothblatt may be correct to state that 'when a representative government decides ... to authorise the [xenotransplantation] procedure within its jurisdiction, it can consent to biosurveillance on behalf of the population it represents',[212] this does not mean that the limits it imposes on individuals can be endless, nor that any such limits would not be the subject of a successful human rights challenge.

If surveillance is necessary – either to obtain information about the benefits and risks of xenotransplantation or to monitor the health of the individual or the risks to the public – then two questions arise. First, it must be asked whether or not we should proceed to trials of xenotransplantation at all, at least until better information about risks is available; and second, a decision is needed on whether or not we are prepared to sacrifice the basic consent rules, which protect present and continuing autonomy, in order to proceed with this particular intervention.

If we answer the first question in the affirmative, then we risk causing harm at a local, national or international level. The model of consent which is traditionally used, and which has been referred to above, is a model which hinges on the intimate nature of the relationship between the doctor/researcher and his or her patient/research subject. The primary principles of biomedical ethics, as we have suggested, describe the ideal relationship between an *individual* doctor and an *individual* patient. This model of consent is the one traditionally endorsed by the law. Yet, arguably, the accepted concept of consent would need to be radically modified if it were to take account of the possibility that involvement (even it if could be informed and voluntary) in trials of xenotransplantation will have a negative impact on the community. Reiss, for example, has suggested that 'until widespread agreement as to the acceptability or otherwise of xenotransplantation is reached, a considerable amount of work needs to be done on its ethics'.[213] It is manifestly the case that a considerable amount of work also remains to be done on the law surrounding consent in this area.

If we answer the second question in the affirmative, then legislation would be needed which would fundamentally affect the accepted concept of consent in law.

---

[209] 197 US 11 (1905).

[210] 274 US 200 (1927).

[211] Ibid., at p. 207.

[212] Rothblatt (2004), at p. 65.

[213] Reiss, M.J. (2000), 'The Ethics of Xenotransplantation', *Journal of Applied Philosophy*, **17** (3), pp. 253–262.

In other words, to legislate to force patients to agree to stringent surveillance requirements would be to turn the notion of consent on its head. Indeed, Bach et al. say:

> It is a basic legal principle that one cannot by sale or contract surrender or give away one's fundamental freedoms or human dignity. This would be regarded as contrary to public policy. Consequently, if a patient consents to restrict his or her freedom of movement or of association for life, and thereafter seeks to withdraw that consent, it is possible that courts may uphold that withdrawal.[214]

Submission to life-long surveillance, then is 'a critically unique component of xenotransplantation research trials ...'.[215]

Mandatory Autopsies

One final aspect of surveillance that is required by the draft report from UKXIRA, and which is widely regarded as an important characteristic of all surveillance programmes, is the need for a mandatory post-mortem examination to be carried out on any xenograft recipient. This, of course, is entirely intelligible in terms of the scientific endeavour that will be the monitoring process of those who receive a xenograft, either in clinical trials or as part of standard healthcare therapy. This requirement, however, seems to stand in stark contrast to the reports recently produced in relation to the removal and retention of organs at post-mortem examination. Each of the reports, in Bristol,[216] Alder Hey[217] and Scotland,[218] emphasized the importance of the voluntary wishes of the deceased person being carried out after his or her death. It could be argued that the pressure, both physical and psychological, to agree to receive a transgenic organ renders the inevitable mandating of a post-mortem examination less than voluntary, and subject to the same criticisms raised in the reports mentioned above. The Human Tissue Act also endorses the role of consent in post-mortem examinations, and the use of tissue (although it does permit certain exceptions).

Withdrawal of Consent

It is a fundamental cornerstone of the Declaration of Helsinki, which governs clinical trials and research in general, that an individual is free at any stage to withdraw from a research programme.[219] This right to withdraw has already been touched on briefly, and is endorsed by the Council of Europe.[220] Yet it is inherent in

---

214 Bach et al. (2001), at p. 291.

215 Caulfield and Robertson (2001), at p. 85.

216 HMSO (2001a), *Learning from Bristol: The Report of the Public Inquiry into Children's Heart Surgery at the Bristol Royal Infirmary 1984–1995*, Cm 5207, HMSO: London.

217 HMSO (2001b), *The Royal Liverpool Children's Inquiry Report*, HC12, HMSO: London.

218 Independent Review Group on Retention of Organs at Post-Mortem (2001), HMSO: Edinburgh.

219 World Medical Association Declaration of Helsinki (1964).

220 Council of Europe Recommendation (2003) 10, Article 16.2.

the surveillance programme that any such withdrawal is to be discouraged – even prevented if possible. Thus, added to the problem that people are generally precluded from dispensing in advance with fundamental freedoms is the concern that they are also precluded from withdrawing from the full trial by the nature of their earlier agreement. As we have seen, any such agreement would be unlikely to have legal force, and it flies in the face of the Helsinki requirements. Of course, it could be said, these requirements can – perhaps should – change to take account of novel situations, but we would conclude that this can only be seriously considered when the risk/benefit analysis has been undertaken and has come down firmly on the side of benefit.

Principle 22 of the Declaration of Helsinki reads as follows:

> In any research on human beings, each potential subject must be adequately informed of the aims, methods, sources of funding, any possible conflicts of interest, institutional affiliations of the researcher, the anticipated benefits and potential risks of the study and the discomfort it may entail. *The subject should also be informed of the right to abstain from participation in the study or to withdraw consent to participate at any time without reprisal.* (Emphasis added)

As Welin says, demanding adherence to a life-long surveillance agreement 'in order to protect the public from xenotransplantation-induced viral infections might conflict with the exit clause [of the Declaration of Helsinki]'.[221] Indeed, Caplan argues that:

> It is of special importance given the high odds of failure in the initial phase of xenografting on human subjects that procedures be in place for ending the experiment if the subject wishes to withdraw from the research.[222]

However, it will be technically very difficult, if not impossible, for this to be done in xenotransplantation trials, since information will already have been collected, stored and probably used, and the transplant may well already have taken place. If it is the case that there are risks to the public potentially associated with xenotransplantation, then they will already have been created. Effectively, therefore, the clinical trial must be seen not only as the transplantation of the organ, but the whole life-long process of surveillance, from which withdrawal could have enormously serious consequences.

The Role of Relatives/Contacts

As has been seen, relatives or contacts of the potential xenograft recipient will also be required to be involved in the decision-making process. This raises a number of issues about privacy and confidentiality which will be discussed in the next chapter, but it also adds one further anomaly to the consent issue. It is a general rule of consent law that the intervention or opinion of a third party is irrelevant to the authority vested in the competent, adult individual to agree to or refuse medical

221 Welin (2000), at p. 233.

222 Caplan (1992), at p. 726.

interventions.[223] Indeed, even where the adult is incompetent, there is no common law provision for a third party to agree on their behalf to treatment,[224] although statutory authority now exists following the passing of the Adults with Incapacity (Scotland) Act 2000 (and the Mental Capacity Act 2005). Each of these legislative interventions, however, requires that a benefit derives from or best interests are served by the research or treatment, and the question as to whether or not xenotransplantation would satisfy these requirements cannot as yet be answered in the affirmative.

Assuming the recipient of a xenograft to be competent, the involvement of relatives and close contacts takes on a new significance. If close contacts are unable or unwilling to offer a legally valid consent then it seems likely that the individual will not be considered for transplantation, even if they would otherwise qualify clinically. Equally, if relatives/contacts refuse to agree to the intrusions required by the surveillance programme, this too would be likely to result in deselection of the individual who would potentially have received a xenotransplant. The question, therefore must be asked, '[i]f family members or other close contacts are not in agreement with the patient's decision to have the transplant, can they prevent it?'[225]

Technically, in law, they have no standing to do so, since – as has been seen – their views are generally irrelevant.[226] However, practically, the refusal of the relatives or contacts to participate in the surveillance programme would deny the patient the ability to participate. Functionally then, relatives and contacts are being given an authority which they have always lacked in law, thus further skewing the legal understanding of consent as authorization.

Conclusion

It is clear that moving to clinical trials of xenotransplantation would pose considerable challenges to the current law of consent. Not only do we doubt the capacity of the individual to agree to participation in clinical trials of xenotransplantation given the current state of knowledge, but the interests of third parties are given an unusual significance. If xenotransplantation is to proceed, therefore, either to clinical trials or beyond them into part of the lexicon of medical treatment, arguably a new model of consent which engages third parties and the public, as well as the patient, would need to be developed. How this *would* be achieved is, however, every bit as problematic as whether it *should* be, and its impact on the general rules about consent to medical treatment can only be guessed at. Alternatively, a point in the research spectrum must be reached where the questions remaining to be answered about xenotransplantation are considerably less critical than they currently seem to be. Even then, we remain concerned about the

---

223 For a full discussion, see Mason McCall Smith and Laurie (2002), chapter 10.

224 See discussion in *Airedale NHS Trust* v *Bland* [1993] 1 All ER 821; *Re T (adult: refusal of medical treatment)* [1992] 4 All ER 649.

225 Caulfield and Robertson (2001), at p. 89.

226 See, for example, the statement of Lord Donaldson in *Re T (adult: refusal of medical treatment)*, at p. 50.

freedoms which would be required to be surrendered by recipients and their relatives/close contacts, and the standing of any purported agreement to participation.

It follows that if it is impossible to bind the patient or immediate family members, then it is even more difficult to imagine how one could bind the community. Equally, it is very difficult to imagine a mechanism whereby community involvement could be sufficiently robust as to guarantee or reassure that the community is in fact willing to take the kind of risks xenotransplantation might present.

Finally, there are concerns about the impact which xenotransplantation trials may have on future generations. The concept of intergenerational justice is gaining credibility in biomedical discourse, particularly in light of the so-called genetics revolution.[227] Indeed, UNESCO has formulated a code on the responsibilities of current generations to future generations,[228] and it is clear that, if the risk of the transmission of unknown or untreatable viruses is a potential consequence of xenotransplantation, then both moral and legal liability may lie. As Bach et al. point out:

> If one generation through an excess of scientific zeal or curiosity investigates or uses a procedure which could damage the environment or specific living species in a manner which would carry over to future generations, then those actors could face international sanctions. Previous cases discussing this principle dealt with nuclear testing and the resulting and essentially permanent damage caused by the radioactive contamination of the area. An outbreak of a deadly new virus caused by xenotransplantation could be easily analogised to these cases.[229]

We are, thus, driven to disagree fundamentally with Rothblatt's assertion that: '[i]nformed consent turns out not to be an obstacle to xenotransplantation'.[230] The complexities surrounding agreement to participate in clinical trials of xenotransplantation are such that there remain more questions than there are answers. Further, even if the requirement to provide potential recipients with adequate information becomes a reality, concerns remain about the impact of an individual's choice for therapy on third parties; not just their contacts, who will be required to adopt a constrained lifestyle in perpetuity, but also the wider community.

However, the legal matters which are relevant to xenotransplantation do not end with the issue of consent. The very risks, the scale of which we do not yet know, which provoke dubiety about the validity of any purported consent will potentially place incalculable liability on states, challenge the medical profession's commitment to confidentiality and may be in danger of conflicting with internationally agreed norms of behaviour. These issues will be considered in the following chapter.

---

227 For discussion, see McLean, S.A.M. (2000), 'Intergenerational Justice: A Brave New World or a Leap in the Dark?', *Genetics Law Monitor*, **1** (1), July/August, pp. 1–3.

228 UNESCO (1997), *Declaration of the Responsibilities of the Present Generations Towards Future Generations*, UNESCO: Paris.

229 Bach et al. (2001), at p. 297.

230 Rothblatt (2004), at p. 60.

Chapter 8

Legal Issues in Xenotransplantation (Part 2)

In addition to the – admittedly critical – issue of consent, there is a range of other additional legal matters which also impact on xenotransplantation. The complexity of the entire plethora of legal issues involved reinforces the need to consider the (non-scientific) viability of xenotransplantation at the earliest possible stage; certainly before contemplating proceeding to clinical trials or investing significant sums of money in continued scientific research in this area.

Confidentiality

It is widely accepted that medical information is amongst the most confidential which can be held in respect of an individual, and as Gillon points out confidentiality 'is one of the most venerable moral obligations of medical ethics'.[1] Information is generally in law held to be confidential if it is provided in a situation where it is anticipated that the person receiving it will treat it in confidence and where a breach of that confidence may cause harm to the party confiding the information.[2] Although Mason, McCall Smith and Laurie[3] express themselves as not entirely clear what is the legal basis for the duty of confidentiality, they nonetheless reaffirm that '[a] general common law duty is imposed on a doctor to respect the confidences of his patients'.[4] Certainly, case law has made it clear over a long period of time that if a harm results from breach of confidence where that duty of confidence is owed, then damages may be recoverable. In the case of *A-G* v *Guardian Newspapers Ltd (No 2)*[5] the Court of Appeal recognized the public interest associated with legally enforceable protection of confidential information. Subsequently, this was restated in cases such as *X* v *Y*[6] and *W* v *Edgell*.[7]

Confidentiality is often described as the cornerstone of the doctor/patient relationship and this is arguably no less true when the healthcare worker is not a

---

1 Gillon, R. (2001), 'Telling the Truth, Confidentiality, Consent, and Respect for Autonomy', in Harris, J. (ed.), *Bioethics*, Oxford University Press: Oxford, at p. 512.

2 *Coco* v *A N Clark (Engineers) Ltd* [1969] RPC 41.

3 Mason, J.K., McCall Smith, R.A. and Laurie, G.T. (2002), *Law and Medical Ethics* (6th Ed), Butterworths: London, at pp. 240, 241.

4 At p. 239.

5 [1990] AC 109.

6 [1998] 2 All ER 648.

7 [1989] 1 All ER 1089.

treating physician but rather a doctor or scientist engaged in a research project. Indeed, Principle 21 of the Declaration of Helsinki says:

> The right of research subjects to safeguard their integrity must always be respected. Every precaution should be taken to respect the privacy of the subject, the confidentiality of the patient's information and to minimize the impact of the study on the subject's physical and mental integrity and on the personality of the subject.

However, consent and surveillance requirements, such as those drafted by UKXIRA, require *ab initio* that the confidentiality of the patient be breached. In other words, in order to involve the family and contacts in the process of consent and continued surveillance, it is necessary that that they are made aware – as are a number of third parties – of the health status of the actual or potential recipient of a xenograft. It is, as would be expected, unusual for any medical intervention to start from the presumption that confidentiality is irrelevant, or must be disregarded. Gillon – while restating the value of confidentiality in medical practice – does make the point that it is not an absolute principle. Nonetheless, he also claims that 'exceptions to medical confidentiality need to be not merely specified ... but also justified'.[8] He continues, 'I have argued against accepting exceptions that are justified by appeals to medical paternalism or medical research.'[9] At least in the early stages, as we have already argued, the introduction of xenotransplantation will be classifiable as either research or experimentation, and Gillon's caveat must, we believe, be taken seriously. Confidentiality is based on the rights of individual patients to manage their own private medical information, and breaches in the interests of anything external to that require justification, rather than simple assertion.

The General Medical Council has drawn up guidelines which inform clinicians as to when it is permissible to disclose information.[10] These may be broadly categorized as being in situations where the patient consents to it, where anonymized information is required for medical research or where the public interest demands disclosure. In its recently published report on confidentiality, the Department of Health reaffirms the extent to which the obligation is based firmly on patient control, requiring consent for disclosure in most situations, even where refusal to permit wider dissemination of information risks treatment options. The report says:

> Patients generally have the right to object to the use and disclosure of confidential information that identifies them, and need to be made aware of this right. Sometimes, if patients choose to prohibit information being disclosed to other health professionals involved in providing care, it might mean that the care that can be provided is limited and, in extremely rare circumstances, that it is not possible to offer certain treatment options. Patients must be informed if their decisions about disclosure have implications for the provision of care or treatment.[11]

---

[8] Gillon (2001), at p. 518.

[9] Ibid.

[10] For further discussion, see Mason, McCall Smith and Laurie (2002), chapter 8.

[11] Department of Health (2003), *Confidentiality: NHS Code of Practice*, HMSO: London, November, p. 8, para. 14.

Obviously, in the case of xenotransplantation, it may be argued that the patient, in agreeing to all of the implications of accepting a xenograft, will also have consented to their confidentiality being breached; particularly to those who are providing the treatment and care. Equally, they will doubtless also have been informed of the need for otherwise personal information to be provided to relatives and close contacts. Again, therefore, they might be said to have agreed to the disclosure; thus, any such disclosure would fit within the general exceptions to the rule of confidentiality. Additionally, in terms of section 60 of the Health and Social Care Act 2001 (England and Wales) exception may be made to the general obligation of confidentiality; for example, the Health Service (Control of Patient Information) Regulations 2002 support the workings of cancer registries.[12] The Secretary of State's discretion under the 2001 Act has, however, been criticized as being too concerned with the 'public interest' and less observant of patients' rights.[13] Furthermore, developments in the common law of confidentiality have been described as challenging 'the law of confidence at its very core'.[14] In the case of *R* v *Department of Health, ex p Source Informatics Ltd*,[15] the question at issue was whether or not it was lawful for pharmacists to sell anonymized prescribing data to a firm which intended to sell the information on to a pharmaceutical company. In deciding that such activity was not unlawful, in that it did not represent a breach of confidentiality as the information would not identify individual patients, the Court of Appeal, '[o]n extremely uncertain legal authority ... [shifted] the basis of the duty of confidence from the public interest to the question of fairness of use'.[16] Mason, McCall Smith and Laurie[17] argue that this decision reduces the individual's interest in their own private information and implies that the burden of proving the appropriateness of the disclosure shifts from the person seeking to make the disclosure to the individual who wishes to prevent it. Whether or not the consequences of this decision will in fact be this far reaching is not yet clear, but it clearly has the potential to impact on the rights of individuals to maintain personal information in privacy.

However, apart from specific situations (which may or may not cover surveillance regimens in xenotransplantation clinical trials) consent still seems to be regarded as an important predictor of the lawfulness of disclosure. The existence of a consent to disclosure hinges, as we have already seen, on both the quality of information provided and evaluation of the subject of voluntariness which we have also already discussed. However, a brief reconsideration is appropriate here. If it is the case that those who would be likely to be involved in xenotransplantation, especially at the clinical trial stage, are likely to be particularly vulnerable, and therefore potentially willing to consent to anything which appears to hold out hope for them, then their voluntariness may be in doubt; in other words, consent to

---

12 See DoH (2003), at p. 37, para. 45.

13 See, Beyleveld, D. (2001), 'How Not to Regulate in the Public Interest', *Genetics Law Monitor*, **2** (5).

14 Mason, McCall Smith and Laurie (2002), at p. 258.

15 52 BMLR 65 (2000).

16 Mason, McCall Smith and Laurie (2002), at p. 258.

17 At pp. 258–259.

disclosure of confidential information may suffer from the same inherent flaws as those discussed in the previous chapter. An 'informed' consent to disclosure is, however, of particular relevance in clinical trials in general and, we would argue, in trials of xenotransplantation in particular. Caulfield and Robertson explain its significance in this way:

> Before a research participant's health information is shared (even with family members or close contacts) the patient's consent must be obtained. This consent must be fully informed. As such, in the present context the patient must be made aware that a robust surveillance scheme will require comprehensive data banks and a sharing of information between a variety of interested parties on an international level. The long term nature of the need for access to the patient's records must also be made clear.[18]

Finally, there may be some relevance for xenotransplantation in the GMC's advice to clinicians in respect of HIV. Although committed to the concept of confidentiality, the GMC has concluded that doctors 'may disclose information about a patient ... in order to protect a person from risk of death or serious harm'.[19] However, it is not clear that this exception can simply be transferred to third parties in xenotransplantation trials, where the nature and extent of the risk to them is less obvious than it is to the sexual partner of people who are HIV positive. In any event, any obligation to disclose to third parties (who are not patients of the individual doctor) is generally refuted by the fact that no duty to rescue exists in Scottish or English law.

Despite the concerns generated by statute and case law described above, the importance of confidentiality and its allied value of privacy has, if anything, been re-emphasized by the absorption into UK law of the European Convention on Human Rights, Article 8 of which guarantees people the right to respect for private and family life. Article 8 states:

> 1. Everyone has the right to respect for his private and family life, his home and his correspondence.

Any regime which dispensed with the value of confidentiality and privacy without good cause would undoubtedly be subject to legal challenge. It might be argued, for example, that the exception to the general rule – which permits the passing on of information for research purposes – would apply in respect of clinical trials of xenotransplantation, irrespective of the terms of the Human Rights Act 1998. However, it is generally assumed that the scope of legitimate disclosure should be restricted to those with a professional role in the research. In xenotransplantation, the research exception, therefore, would cover the transfer of clinical information between health professionals but would not necessarily include information being passed to others.

Finally, it might be thought that the public interest exception is particularly relevant here. The Convention on Human Rights in Article 8.2 permits derogation from the general principle on the following grounds:

---

[18] Caulfield, T.A. and Robertson, G.B. (2001), 'Xenotransplantation: Consent, Public Health and Charter Issues', *Medical Law International*, **5** (2), at p. 88.

[19] General Medical Council (1997), *Serious Communicable Diseases*, General Medical Council: London, para. 22.

> There shall be no interference by a public authority with the exercise of this right except such as is in accordance with the law and is necessary in a democratic society in the interests of national security, public safety or the economic well-being of the country, for the prevention of disorder or crime, *for the protection of health or morals, or for the protection of the rights and freedoms of others.* (Emphasis added)

As we have said, the public is uniquely involved in xenotransplantation because of the risks which it also may run. There is a certain amount of case law concerning situations where it is permissible or desirable that confidentiality should be breached in the interests of third parties. In the US case of *Tarasoff* v *Regents of the University of California*,[20] it was held that there was an obligation to disclose otherwise confidential information where a specific individual was put at risk by failure to do so. This judgement has not been directly followed in UK courts, but the case of *W* v *Edgell*[21] shows that a justification can be found for making disclosure where there is a threat to unspecified members of the public, assuming that the disclosure is made to those with a right to know. In other words, the disclosure may be acceptable, but it must be made to appropriate persons. Thus, confidentiality is not absolute, but a breach must be made with the genuine consent of the individual, or to those with responsibility for securing public health (assuming that this is 'in for the protection of health ... or for the protection of the rights and freedoms of others') or on an anonymous basis for research purposes. Whether or not the kinds of disclosure contemplated by UKXIRA's surveillance document can satisfy any of these criteria remains to be seen, although it is likely that the public interest exception would be brought in aided by those seeking to commence trials, and this may very well be accepted. After all, if there is a risk of public health being adversely affected by xenotransplantation, is this not the clearest of possible examples of why this exception exists? However, this simplistic assumption is based on one fundamental flaw. Disclosure 'in the public interest' is permissible to prevent avoidable harm; the whole point in xenotransplantation, however, is that the harm is generated by those who then seek to make the disclosure. Simple application of the 'public interest' exception cannot, therefore, be easily justified.

In addition, information stored in respect of xenotransplantation recipients and their contacts will need to be managed within the terms of the Data Protection Act 1998 (which came into force in March 2000). Amongst other things this requires that data are processed lawfully, and conform to the data protection principles, as follows:

1. Personal data shall be processed fairly and lawfully and, in particular, shall not be processed unless
   (a) at least one of the conditions in Schedule 2 is met, and
   (b) in the case of sensitive personal data, at least one of the conditions in Schedule 3 is also met.
2. Personal data shall be obtained only for one or more specified and lawful purposes, and shall not be further processed in any manner incompatible with that purpose or those purposes.

---

20 551 P 2d 334 (1976).

21 [1989] 1 All ER 1089.

3. Personal data shall be adequate, relevant and not excessive in relation to the purpose or purposes for which they are processed.
4. Personal data shall be accurate and, where necessary, kept up to date.
5. Personal data processed for any purpose or purposes shall not be kept for longer than is necessary for that purpose or those purposes.
6. Personal data shall be processed in accordance with the rights of data subjects under this Act.
7. Appropriate technical and organisational measures shall be taken against unauthorised or unlawful processing of personal data and against accidental loss or destruction of, or damage to, personal data.
8. Personal data shall not be transferred to a country or territory outside the European Economic Area unless that country or territory ensures an adequate level of protection for the rights and freedoms of data subjects in relation to the processing of personal data.[22]

Resources

For present purposes there are two aspects to the resource issue which are worthy of consideration. The first relates to the costs (in healthcare terms) likely to be associated with xenotransplantation and the second to the rights of individuals to have resources allocated to them should they have a need for them. Although the question of allocation of resources both into and within the healthcare system is one which may be described as ethical, it clearly also has legal implications and therefore merits consideration in this chapter. As Melo et al. have said, '[t]he implementation of any care system requires that a resource allocation policy must be regulated by explicit criteria. These criteria are associated with the management of both technological and human resources.'[23] To an extent, therefore, an important issue will be the costs associated with xenotransplantation.

Costs to the Healthcare System

It is, for the moment, difficult to evaluate accurately the economic costs to the health service of engagement in xenotransplantation. However, it is clear that the development of the organs which would be used in these procedures is likely to be dominated by private companies, and that cell-based products will also become the primary responsibility of private enterprise. As has been suggested, '[t]he biotechnology companies are likely to control the cost of the organs and, in the absence of real competition, will want to keep this as high as the market will tolerate'.[24] Barker and Polcrack also conclude that '[w]e believe it very likely that the development of transgenic xenotransplant technology will increase economic and other pressures to begin clinical trials of in vivo solid organ transplants sooner

[22] Data Protection Act 1998, Schedule 1 The Data Protection Principles, Part I The Principles.

[23] Melo, H. et al. (2001), 'Ethical and Legal Issues in Xenotransplantation', *Bioethics*, **15** (5/6), pp. 1427–1442, at p. 1434.

[24] Daar, A.S. (1999), 'Xenotransplantation: Science, Risk and International Regulatory Efforts', in Caulfield, T.A. and Williams-Jones, B. (eds), *The Commercialization of Genetic Research: Ethical, Legal and Policy Issues*, Kluwer Academic/Plenum Publishers: New York, pp. 129–155, at p. 136.

rather than later'.[25] They therefore 'urge caution in the face of uncertainty, democratic decision making in the face of for profit technological development, and in instituting this cautious democratic process, the creation of a system that engenders increased respect for all persons'.[26]

It is unarguable that, were states to approve xenotransplantation, those companies which have developed the transgenic animals, and which provide the tissue, cells or organs, stand to gain much, both from their capacity to patent their products[27] as well as from their capacity to sell them to the healthcare system. Considerable profit therefore stands to be made by those companies who are effectively leading the agenda. This is not to say that the intervention of companies in this area is wrong – it is in fact something with which we are very familiar in respect of pharmaceutical and biotechnology companies. As Daar says:

> There can be little doubt that the primary motive of these companies is profit. This does not necessarily mean that their input is tarnished – it simply means that, on the scale envisaged, and given today's realities of funding and organising clinical research, this is a new dimension with predictable consequences and it warrants further discussion.[28]

As the Nuffield Council Report notes, if the fundamental ethical problems of xenotransplantation can be overcome, then it is likely that the National Health Service would see some value in introducing it as a treatment of choice in certain circumstances.[29] This assumption is also based on the Nuffield Council's assertion that, even if all cadaveric or live human tissue that was available could be utilized, there would still be a shortfall in the numbers of organs available for transplantation. Thus, the National Health Service would be justified in looking at alternative ways of managing this. One possible option would be the use of xenotransplantation. Noting that the introduction of any innovative treatment must at least in part be considered against the backdrop of resources, the Nuffield Council states that '[t]he allocation of resources within the NHS is currently a matter of intense debate and widespread concern. Xenotransplantation, like any expensive new technology, will intensify this wider problem.'[30]

At present, it is of course very difficult to estimate what the actual costs of xenotransplantation procedures would be. This is because for the moment xenotransplantation has been performed relatively rarely, and in terms of solid

---

25 Barker, J.H. and Polcrack, L. (2001), 'Respect for Persons, Informed Consent and the Assessment of Infectious Disease Risks in Xenotransplantation', *Medicine, Health Care and Philosophy* **4** (1), pp. 53–70, at p. 67.

26 Ibid.

27 For discussion of the patenting of animals, see *Harvard/Onco-Mouse* [1990] EPOR 501; *R* v *Leland Stanford/Modified Animal* [2002] EPOR 2; for a full discussion of the issues involved, see Cornish, R. (1999), *Intellectual Property*, (4th Ed), Sweet & Maxwell: London; Sterckx, S. (ed.) (1997), *Biotechnology, Patents and Morality*, Ashgate: Aldershot.

28 Daar (1999), at pp. 134–135.

29 Nuffield Report (Report of the Nuffield Council on Bioethics) (1996), *Animal-to-Human Transplants: The Ethics of Xenotransplantation*, Nuffield Council on Bioethics: London, p. 121, para. 10.46.

30 Nuffield Report (1996), p. 96, para. 8.5.

organs not at all, within the National Health Service. If this were to change, particularly in the latter case, it would – as we have already noted – involve two distinct stages. The first would be as part of clinical trials, which are likely to be limited. Second, were these trials to prove the efficacy of xenotransplantation, the National Health Service itself may have to take over the costs of routine xenotransplantation procedures. The Nuffield Council notes that the:

> cost of present transplant procedures is not that high, when compared with other types of treatment. ... the present cost of transplantation is due, largely, to the cost of transplant operations and the cost of drugs for preventing the rejection of transplanted organs. In addition, there are costs that arise from the system used to obtain organs from human donors. These include the costs associated with contributing to the maintenance of intensive care units and the costs of co-ordinating the supply of organs.[31]

As the Report also notes, it is unlikely that xenotransplantation would reduce many of these costs. One potential additional cost, of course, is that, whereas at present human organs are freely given, xenografts would almost certainly require to be purchased as the generation of transgenic animals which will be suitable for organ donation will undoubtedly be the monopoly of the private sector, at least initially. Even were transgenic animals to be bred in large numbers, it remains the case that there would be no free delivery to the Health Service. The Nuffield Report's view is that, even though there are costs associated with the maintenance of human organs for transplantation, it is likely that there would be an increased cost, at least initially, to the Health Service from xenotransplantation.[32] However, they also claim that if xenotransplantation were to become a common and successful procedure, some costs should fall.[33] However, this conclusion, as they note themselves, is speculative, and in any event there would be additional costs associated not just with the new cost of purchasing organs rather than having them donated, but also with any of the consequences of the surveillance programme which has been proposed for recipients of organs and their contacts.[34]

The Nuffield Report also concludes that there might be some reductions in cost, not least in respect of immunosuppression, since, if the transgenic animals provided organs and tissue that were easily compatible with human beings, then the range and volume of drugs required to prevent rejection would be reduced.[35] However, it is clear that the question of health costs in this area cannot as yet be answered. The Kennedy Report, although agreeing that this is essentially speculation, nonetheless feels that:

> Xenotransplantation has the potential to impose a large financial burden on the National Health Service. It is a fact that scientific and medical developments can often cost money rather than save it. A much greater (perhaps unlimited) supply of solid organs could mean that many people could receive transplants who would have otherwise received little more

[31] Ibid., at p. 96, para. 8.6.

[32] Pp. 96–97, para. 8.7.

[33] P. 97, paras 8.7 and 8.8.

[34] Ibid.

[35] P. 97, para. 8.8.

> than palliative care and, who would have, as a consequence, a short life expectancy. Furthermore, new therapies are being developed based on xenotransplantation which are not commonly available as allotransplantation (for example the transplantation of pancreatic islet cells to treat diabetes and the transplantation of foetal cells to treat Parkinson's disease). This could mean that a large number of people could receive new treatments.[36]

The Report concludes, 'we cannot begin to reach any plausible views on the impact which the development and introduction of xenotransplantation could have on the resources of the NHS'.[37] The Committee recognized that some kind of balancing act would need to be undertaken between the benefits, however they are quantified, of successful xenotransplantation, versus the actual costs, however they are calculated.[38] In the long run, they concluded that the National Specialist Commissioning Advisory Group should be involved in addressing the question of costs should xenotransplantation become at any stage available as a realistic treatment option,[39] and doubtless the National Institute for Clinical Excellence[40] would have a powerful voice in deciding on the cost-effectiveness of xenografting.[41]

There are, of course, questions about how, and to what extent, resources are allocated into healthcare. By far the majority of legal activity in the area of resource allocation has concentrated on macro-allocation issues. The fundamental principles can be found in the National Health Service Act 1977,[42] which in s. 1(1) makes it the duty of the Secretary of State to 'continue the promotion ... of a comprehensive health service designed to secure improvement – (a) in the physical and mental health of the people ... and (b) in the prevention, diagnosis and treatment of illness, and to provide or secure the effective provision of services ...'. S. 3(1) creates a duty on the Secretary of State 'to such extent as he considers necessary to meet all reasonable requirements' to provide, inter alia, hospital accommodation, medical, dental, nursing and ambulance services, maternity and child care, and facilities for the prevention and after-care of illness.

It is clear that the most difficult decision facing those committed to delivering on the ideology of the National Health Service has been to confront the reality that resources will seldom – if ever – meet demand. In July 2000, the General Medical Council published its Report, *Priorities and Choices.*[43] In paragraph 1 of the Report it states:

---

[36] Kennedy Report (Report of the Advisory Group on the Ethics of Xenotransplantation) (1997), *Animal Tissue into Humans*, HMSO: London, p. 82, para. 4.101.

[37] Ibid., at p. 82, para. 4.103.

[38] Ibid.

[39] Ibid., at p. 83, para. 4.106.

[40] National Institute for Clinical Excellence (Establishment and Constitution) Order 1999 SI 1999/220.

[41] The Scottish equivalent is the Health Technology Board for Scotland, information on which is available at http://www.htbs.org.uk/home.htm.

[42] Although there has been considerable legislative activity since then; see also the National Health Service (Scotland) Act 1978, ss. 36–38; the Health and Community Care Act 1990; the Scotland Act 1998.

[43] This report can be found on the GMC's website at http://www.gmc-uk.org.

> Before the advent of the NHS, therapeutic options were often limited to what the patient could afford. The introduction of comprehensive universal healthcare, funded through taxation, as in the case of the NHS, or by social insurance, served to ameliorate these problems. More recently, the rapid advances in medical technology, combined with the increased demands of an ageing population, have once more exposed an increasing level of unmet need. This dilemma is not unique to the National Health Service, but exists in all countries, including the most wealthy. In effect, healthcare is now rationed in all countries by restricting the availability of what is provided or when it is available or to whom.

When disputes over allocation arise outside of the parliamentary arena, it is to the courts that we turn for resolution, and indeed they have been relatively active in this area. In the case of *R* v *Secretary of Social Services, ex p Walker*,[44] the court was quite clear as to its capacity to examine decisions concerning the availability of funding in the health service. The judge said:

> I detect a general criticism of the decisions as to staffing and financing of the National Health Service and of those who provide its funds and facilities. It has been said before, and I say it again, that this court can no more investigate that on the facts of this case than it would do so in any other case where the balance of available money and its distribution and use are concerned. Those, of course, are questions which are of enormous public interest and concern – but they are questions to be raised, answered and dealt with outside the court.[45]

In the Court of Appeal, Lord Donaldson, MR reiterated this position, saying that, '[i]t is not for this court, or indeed any court, to substitute its own judgement for the judgement of those who are responsible for the allocation of resources'.[46] In *R* v *Central Birmingham Health Authority ex p Collier*,[47] although the treatment in question could have been said to be more urgent, Stephen Brown, LJ repeated that '[t]he courts in this country cannot arrange the lists in the hospital ... and should not be asked to intervene'.[48]

In *R* v *Secretary of State for Social Services, West Midlands Regional Health Authority and Birmingham Area Health Authority (Teaching) ex p Hincks*[49] four orthopaedic patients had been on a waiting list for a number of years. They challenged this, claiming that the waiting was the result of the inadequacy of relevant services in their area, and in particular that the Secretary of State had failed to meet his obligations under s. 3(1) of the National Health Service Act 1977. The Court of Appeal, however, concluded that the Secretary of State's responsibility is to do the best he can with the resources made available. In other words, the duty was not an absolute one to meet every demand placed upon him, but rather was constrained by the budget voted to him.

One further case can be considered; namely that of *The Queen* v *NW Thames RHA; Riverside Health Authority; Secretary of State for Health, Ex parte Daniels*.[50]

---

44 [1992] 3 BMLR 32.
45 Per Macpherson, J., at p. 34 (QBD).
46 Ibid., at p. 35.
47 Unreported, 6 January 1988.
48 Ibid.
49 1 BMLR 93 (1980).
50 [1993] 4 Med LR 364.

In this sad case, the facts were as follows. The applicant was diagnosed as suffering from Batten's disease when he was two years old. If he received a bone marrow transplant before the age of three, there was a chance that he might live beyond the age of seven. In 1992, he was examined at the Bone Marrow Transplant Unit at Westminster Children's Hospital in London. This Unit, partly funded by charity and partly by the Riverside Health Authority, had performed a number of similar operations and was shown to have a reasonable success rate. The Hospital Ethics Committee approved the operation in November 1992, and a donor was found in February 1993.

However, in 1988, a proposal to close the Unit and transfer its services to another hospital had been made by Riverside Health Authority and approved by the Secretary of State. In April 1992, a review team had published a report which was critical of the Unit and doubted its viability. Because of the uncertainty over the future of the Unit, the applicant was placed at the top of the list for transplantation in 1992, but subsequently the applicant's father was informed that the operation could not go ahead because of the number of staff who had left the Unit (presumably because it was destined for closure). The Unit finally closed on 1 April 1993.

The applicant challenged the closure of the Unit on two grounds. First, that there had been a failure to comply with a statutory duty to consult under the Community Health Council Regulations 1985, and second, that the decision to close the Unit was irrational. In this case, the court held that the first ground could indeed be upheld, in that proper procedures had not been gone through. However, they declined to hold that the decision to close the Unit was irrational, saying that it had insufficient information before it to make such a decision. In the long run, sadly, it is clear that – no matter what conclusion the court might have reached in this case had it been in possession of the full facts – it would have been of no benefit to the applicant and his family, as the Unit had already closed by the time the case was brought, and the window of opportunity for optimal treatment had already passed.

Decisions taken at national level clearly impact on all other decisions down the line. As the health service will almost certainly never receive sufficient share of the national purse to meet every demand made on it, hard choices have to be made by those charged with the responsibility of providing healthcare. Initially, the question as to whether or not funding will, or should, be found for xenotransplantation trials may fall to grant-giving research bodies, but were it to become a therapy with real potential, it would be for Ministers to decide whether or not it should be taken account of in healthcare funding allocation decisions. Thus, the expense of xenotransplantation has far-reaching consequences, mandating some attempt at assessing it.

The Individual and Healthcare Resources

Assuming that central funding is made available for xenotransplantation, there are additional resource decisions which will be taken at the level of health authorities and boards, and within them. These decisions too have been the subject of legal scrutiny on occasion. For the individual patient, the fact that a treatment is available, and has been shown to be valuable, can generate the demand for it. Yet, even in standard medical treatment, choices have to be made about how limited resources are to be managed, and to whom they should be distributed. James and Longley,[51] for example, say:

> Tragic choices are inherently ethical in nature based on matters of value rather than fact, and operating in a field of palpable uncertainty. Because values are involved there may be a number of reasonable policy alternatives which the public authority may adopt from any given set of circumstances ... Inevitably in this process trade-offs occur which may have the effect of down-grading or marginalising more fundamental concerns such as fairness.[52]

Yet fairness is arguably what patients believe themselves to be seeking when they wish certain therapies to be made available to them, and patient choice (or autonomy) is a fundamental guiding principle of contemporary medical law and ethics. However, if patient choice totally governs the interaction between doctor and patient, what of the patient who demands treatment which the doctor does not feel to be appropriate? As has been said:

> Only in medicine do patients sometimes claim an entitlement to receive whatever medical treatment they wish, regardless of the likelihood of success and regardless of the quality of outcome to be achieved. This expectation must be revisited or the integrity of the medical profession will not remain intact.[53]

There are a number of reasons for endorsing this conclusion. The first relates to the responsibility of the physician to husband resources – not in a cynical but in a realistic way. As The President's Commission for the Study of Ethical Problems in Medicine and Biomedical and Behavioral Health[54] (US) put it, '[t]he care available from health professionals is generally limited to what is consistent with role-related professional standards and conscientiously held personal beliefs'.[55] Pressure for the last chance option of a xenograft may challenge this. Commentators have even suggested that:

> ... physicians who prescribe treatments that they are reasonably confident will not improve patients' conditions break trust with patients and denigrate the practice of medicine. Their conduct allies medicine with quackery and physicians with charlatans.[56]

Moreover, there is a further matter which must be taken into account, and that is the autonomy of the doctor him or herself. Absolute concentration on patient demand could require doctors to act against their best clinical judgement and/or their conscience. In one US case it was said that there was nothing in the law 'which would justify compelling medical professionals ... to take active measures which are

---

51 James, R. and Longley, D. (1995), 'Judicial Review and Tragic Choices: Ex Parte B', *Public Law*, Autumn, p. 367.

52 Ibid., at p. 372.

53 Jecker, N.S. and Schneiderman, L.J. (1993), 'Medical Futility: The Duty Not to Treat', *Cambridge Quarterly of Healthcare Ethics*, **2** (151), at p. 152.

54 The President's Commission for the Study of Ethical Problems in Medicine and Biomedical and Behavioral Health (1983), Government Printing Office: Washington, D.C.

55 Ibid., at p. 44.

56 Jecker and Schneiderman (1993), at p. 153.

contrary to their view of their ethical duty towards their patients'.[57] The decision whether or not to provide treatment, therefore, is one which must respect both doctor and patient, and this is the approach which has also been traditionally taken by UK courts.[58] However, the recent case of *R(on the application of Burke)* v *General Medical Council*[59] may impact on this conclusion.

In this case, a patient was given authority by the court effectively to make an advance statement that, when his condition deteriorated to the point at which doctors would normally consider removing assisted nutrition and hydration, he should nonetheless continue to be provided with it. As the case has been appealed, no definitive conclusions can be drawn from it, but it is worth noting the views of Mr Justice Munby on the issue of patients seeking treatment which doctors would not normally wish to provide:

> I am quite prepared to accept for present purposes that the court will not grant a mandatory order requiring an individual doctor to treat a patient. But this does not mean that a doctor can simply decline to go on treating his patient merely because his views as to what is in his patient's best interests differ from those of the patient or the court ... A doctor is no doubt under a duty at all times to *advise* in accordance with his best clinical judgment, but it can now be seen to be over-simplistic to say that a doctor is always required to *act* in accordance with his best clinical judgment.[60]

Were xenotransplantation to become an established treatment within the Health Service, it is likely that potential recipients might seek to claim a right of access to the treatment, particularly since it may be a treatment of last resort. As we have seen, courts are very reluctant to interfere in clinical decisions as to what treatment to provide, although it is clear that once a condition is recognized as such, any refusal to fund treatment requires taking account of the individual's condition; blanket bans would be unacceptable.[61]

Perhaps the case which brought resource allocation most acutely to the attention of the public was the case of *R* v *Cambridge Health Authority, ex parte B*.[62] In this case, the Health Authority refused to make financial support available for a 'last chance' treatment for a young girl in imminent likelihood of dying from leukaemia. At the Queen's Bench Division, Laws J was moved to say that the decision not to provide the treatment for Jaymee was an assault on her right to life,[63] concluding that '[w]here the question is whether the life of a 10 year-old child might be saved ... the responsible authority must ... do more than toll the bell of tight resources'.[64]

Although considering macro-allocation questions, this judge based his decision on the personal impact of resource allocation decisions, directly tackling not just the macro issue but challenging also the clinical decision that the therapy would not

---

57 *Brophy* v *New England Sinai Hospital* 398 Mass., 417, 497 N.E. 2d 626 [1986].

58 See, for example, the case of *Re J (a minor) (medical treatment)* [1992] 4 All ER 614.

59 [2004] EWHC 1879 (Admin).

60 Para. 191.

61 *R* v *North West Lancashire Health Authority, ex p A, D and G* 53 BMLR 148 (2000).

62 (1995) 25 BMLR 5 (QBD), (1995) 23 BMLR 1 (CA).

63 At p. 6.

64 At p. 17.

serve Jaymee's interests as it was essentially unproven. In the Court of Appeal, a different decision was reached. Sir Thomas Bingham, MR indicated that the court was not entitled to decide upon the (clinical) merits of such cases, but rather to ask whether or not they were lawfully taken.[65] At the micro allocation level, therefore, clinicians and other healthcare providers are constrained substantially, if not solely, by the limits of their professional competence and ethics. The courts will generally be prepared to do no more than endorse clinical decisions where they have been adequately or appropriately taken; that is, where they can be shown to follow accepted clinical practice.[66]

If an individual is denied access to treatments which potentially hold out benefits as a result of resource allocation decisions, it is possible for them to challenge such decisions. The vehicle for challenge is known as judicial review. Essentially, judicial review is an administrative (public) law remedy, although it is increasingly used as a means of seeking to vindicate individual rights. One major criticism of the mechanism of judicial review has been that it is, however, an inappropriate – and therefore largely unsuccessful – basis on which to seek a remedy for a perceived infringement of individual rights.

There are, for the purposes of this discussion, two separate possible groups or individuals who may be challenged using this remedy. First, the relevant Secretary of State or Minister may find him or herself challenged for a failure to act appropriately or 'reasonably' in the exercise of his/her statutory powers. The basis on which such actions may succeed is succinctly outlined by Lord Emslie in the case of *Wordie Property Co Ltd* v *Secretary of State for Scotland*: [67]

> A decision of the Secretary of State acting within his statutory remit is *ultra vires* if he has improperly exercised the discretion confided to him. In particular it will be *ultra vires* if it is based upon a material error of law going to the root of the question for determination. It will be *ultra vires*, too, if the Secretary of State has taken into account irrelevant considerations or has failed to take account of relevant and material considerations which ought to have been taken into account. Similarly it will fall to be quashed on that ground if, where it is one for which a factual basis is required, there is no proper basis in fact to support it. It will also fall to be quashed if it, or any condition imposed in relation to a grant of planning permission, is so unreasonable that no reasonable Secretary of State could have reached or imposed it.[68]

In addition, Lord Diplock describes three bases on which judicial review may be brought in the case of *Council of Civil Service Unions* v *Minister for the Civil Service* (the GCHQ Case).[69] His views have been significantly endorsed in most subsequent cases and bear (somewhat lengthy) quotation:

> Judicial review has I think developed to a stage today when, without reiterating any analysis of the steps by which the development has come about, one can conveniently

65 CA, at p. 7.

66 See the case of *Bolam* v *Friern Hospital Management Committee* [1957] 2 All ER 118. But see also *Bolitho* v *City and Hackney Health Authority* [1997] 4 All ER 771.

67 1984 S.L.T. 345.

68 At p. 347.

69 [1985] A.C. 374.

> classify under three heads the grounds on which administrative action is subject to control by judicial review. The first ground I would call 'illegality' the second 'irrationality' and the third 'procedural impropriety' ... By 'illegality' as a ground for judicial review I mean that the decision-maker must understand correctly the law that regulates his decision-making power and must give effect to it. Whether he has or not is, par excellence, a justiciable question to be decided, in the event of dispute, by those persons, the judges, by whom the judicial power of the state is exercisable.
>
> By 'irrationality' I mean what can by now be succinctly referred to as 'Wednesbury unreasonableness' (see *Associated Provincial Picture Houses Ltd* v *Wednesbury Corp* [1947] 2 All ER 680, [1948] 1 K.B. 223). It applies to a decision which is so outrageous in its defiance of logic or of accepted moral standards that no sensible person who had applied his mind to the question to be decided could have arrived at it. Whether a decision falls within this category is a question that judges by their training and experience should be well equipped to answer, or else there would be something badly wrong with our judicial system ...
>
> I have described the third head as 'procedural impropriety' rather than failure to observe basic rules of natural justice or failure to act with procedural fairness towards the person who will be affected by the decision. This is because susceptibility to judicial review under this head covers also failure by an administrative tribunal to observe procedural rules that are expressly laid down in the legislative instrument by which its jurisdiction is conferred, even where such failure does not involve any denial of natural justice.[70]

It should be clear that this description could also apply to decisions taken by the second party concerned – namely the Health Authority or Board, or any other corporate decision maker, such as a Trust. Essentially any body which exercises a discretion may find its decisions subject to challenge. As Mullen notes:

> Discretion must always be exercised properly, and if exercised improperly may be open to judicial review. Review of discretionary decisions has two purposes. The first is to ensure that discretionary decisions are influenced only by factors which it is proper for public authorities to consider. The second is to ensure decisions are truly discretionary and that discretionary powers are exercised by the appropriate person. These two purposes may be described as preventing abuse of discretion and ensuring retention of discretion. The former provides control of the substantive content of discretionary decisions, the latter provides some control over the process.[71]

The seminal case, in this area was that of *Associated Provincial Picture Houses Ltd* v *Wednesbury Corpn.*[72] In this case Lord Greene, MR discussed the basis for judicial review at some length, saying:

> When an executive discretion is entrusted by Parliament to a body such as the local authority in this case, what appears to be an exercise of that discretion can only be

[70] At p. 410 D.

[71] Mullen, T. (1999), Judicial Review of Administrative Action (unpublished paper prepared for Central Law training, and delivered on 1 December 1999). We are most grateful to Professor Mullen for allowing us access to the paper, which has been of vital importance in our consideration of judicial review.

[72] [1947] 2 All ER 680.

> challenged in the courts in a strictly limited class of case. As I have said, it must always be remembered that the court is not a court of appeal. When discretion of this kind is granted the law recognises certain principles upon which that discretion must be exercised, but within the four corners of these principles the discretion, in my opinion, is an absolute one and cannot be questioned in any court of law. What then are those principles?
>
> They are well understood. They are principles which the court looks to in considering any question of discretion of this kind. The exercise of such a discretion must be a real exercise of the discretion. If, in the statute conferring the discretion, there is to be found expressly or by implication matters which the authority exercising the discretion ought to have regard to, then in exercising the discretion it must have regard to these matters. Conversely, if the nature of the subject-matter and the general interpretation of the Act makes it clear that certain matters would not be germane to the matter in question, the authority must disregard those irrelevant collateral matters. There have been in the cases expressions used relating to the sort of things that authorities must not do, not merely in cases under the Cinematography Act but, generally speaking, under other cases where the powers of local authorities came to be considered. I am not sure myself whether the permissible grounds of attack cannot be defined under a single head. It has been perhaps a little bit confusing to find a series of grounds set out. Bad faith, dishonesty – those of course, stand by themselves – unreasonableness, attention given to extraneous circumstances, disregard of public policy and things like that have all been referred to, according to the facts of individual cases they cannot all be confined under one head, they at any rate, I think, overlap to a very great extent. For instance, we have heard in this case a great deal about the meaning of the word 'unreasonable'.
>
> It is true the discretion must be exercised reasonably. Now what does this mean? Lawyers familiar with the phraseology commonly used in relation to exercise of statutory discretion often used the word 'unreasonable' in a rather comprehensive sense. It has frequently been used and is frequently used as a general description of the things that must not be done. For instance, a person entrusted with a discretion must, so to speak, direct himself properly in law. He must call his own attention to the matters which he is bound to consider. He must exclude from his consideration matters which are irrelevant to what he has to consider. If he does not obey those rules, he may truly be said, and often is said, to be acting 'unreasonably'. Similarly, there may be something so absurd that no sensible person could ever dream that it lay within the powers of the authority. Warrington L.J. in *Short* v *Poole Corporation* gave the example of the red-haired teacher, dismissed because she had red hair. That is unreasonable in one sense. In another sense it is taking into consideration extraneous matters. It is so unreasonable that it might almost be described as being done in bad faith; and, in fact, all these things run into one another.[73]

As can be seen, these principles are essentially rule dominated. Manifestly, this is much more legalistic than the endeavour to find ethical principles on which to base a reasonable exercise of discretion. But it suggests that a failure to perform a duty laid down in statute (such as the provision of healthcare) would readily be the subject of a judicial review. For example, in the case of *Walker* v *Strathclyde Regional Council (No 1)*[74] a parent was held competent to enforce against the education authority their statutory duty '... to secure that there is made for their area adequate and efficient provision of school education ...'.[75] Thus, the powers

73 At p. 682 E.

74 1986 S.L.T. 523.

75 At p. 523 I quoting s. 1(1) The Education (Scotland) Act 1980.

delegated to health authorities or boards to provide healthcare could be successfully challenged by anyone having a legitimate interest in the exercise of their powers.

For health authorities, boards or individual hospitals, it seems likely that the real question will relate to funding. As Mullen notes:

> Several recent cases have considered whether financial considerations are relevant in deciding whether a duty is owed – to put it bluntly, is lack of money an excuse for not giving someone a benefit or assistance. There is no general principle, and everything depends on the construction of the particular statutory scheme.[76]

Traditionally, as suggested, it has been felt that the remedy of judicial review is less than satisfactory in the resolution of disputes about individual rights, and it was postulated that the incorporation of the European Convention of Human Rights into UK law, which occurred as a result of the passing of the Human Rights Act 1998, might make judicial review more 'user friendly'. This has, indeed, apparently occurred following the judgement in the case of *Smith and Grady* v *the United Kingdom.*[77]

The facts of the case are not particularly relevant here, but, briefly, two individuals were discharged from the Royal Air Force on the sole basis that they were homosexual. They argued before the Court of Human Rights that this constituted a violation of Article 8 of the Convention and also of Article 14. They also invoked Articles 3 and 10 of the Convention, and Article 13, in that they claimed that they did not have an effective domestic remedy for these violations. For our purposes, it is the question of the effective domestic remedy that is relevant. On 7 June 1995, the High Court in England dismissed the application for judicial review, considering that the *Wednesbury* principles should be applied, albeit adapted to a Human Rights context. In the view of Simon Brown LJ, 'where fundamental human rights were being restricted, the Minister of Defence needed to show that there was an important repeating interest to justify the restriction'.[78] He also indicated that: '[w]hen the most fundamental human rights are threatened, the Court would not, for example, be inclined to overlook some minor flaw in the decision making process, or to adopt a particularly benevolent view of the Minister's evidence, or to exercise its discretion to withhold relief'.[79]

He emphasized that, even where the most fundamental human rights were being restricted, 'the threshold of unreasonableness is not lowered'.[80] The judge also indicated that had he been expected to make this decision were the European Convention on Human Rights part of UK law, 'the constitutional balance would shift'.[81] On 3 November 1995, the Court of Appeal dismissed the applicants'

[76] Mullen, T.J. (2000), 'The Human Rights Act 1998 and the Incorporation of the European Convention on Human Rights Into Domestic Law, unpublished paper for Legal Services Agency, 20 March.

[77] Application nos 33985/96 and 33986/96, Judgment, Strasbourg, 27/09/99. All quotations are taken from a transcript of the case.

[78] *R* v *Ministry of Defence, ex parte Smith and Others* 2 WLR 305, referred to at transcript para. 31.

[79] Ibid.

[80] Ibid.

[81] Ibid.

appeal. Sir Thomas Bingham, Master of the Rolls, delivered the main judgement and said:

> ... the Court may not interfere with the exercise of an administrative discretion on substantive grounds save where the Court is satisfied that the decision is unreasonable in the sense that it is beyond the range of responses open to a reasonable decision-maker. But in judging whether the decision-maker has exceeded this margin of appreciation the human rights context is important. The more substantial the interference with human rights, the more the Court will require by way of justification before it is satisfied that the decision is reasonable in the sense outlined above.[82]

In addition, the judge indicated that under the non-Convention domestic law of the United Kingdom at the time of the original case being heard, 'the threshold of irrationality was "a high one"'.[83] A different approach might therefore be taken when the case reached Strasbourg and Convention rights were directly considered.

In respect of Article 13 breaches, the applicants argued that there were two minimum requirements. First, that the relevant national authority had jurisdiction to examine the substance of the complaint, and secondly, the authority had to have jurisdiction to grant a remedy if the complaint was deemed to be well-founded. In their view, the judicial review remedy did not meet the first of these requirements for two reasons. First of all, because the Ministry of Defence policy was a blanket policy which did not allow for exceptions, it was 'impossible for the domestic Courts to consider the merits of the applicants' individual complaints'.[84] It was also contended that judicial review proceedings did not comply with the second requirement of Article 13, in that the domestic courts were not able to provide a remedy, even though, as they noted, the majority of judges who had heard their case considered the policy not to be justified.[85]

Although the Court of Human Rights believed that the Article 8 rights were the critical issue, they nonetheless commented on the general question of judicial review. As was said:

> In such circumstances, the Court considers it clear that, even assuming the essential complaints of the applicants before this Court were before and considered by the domestic Courts, the threshold which the High Court and the Court of Appeal could find the Ministry of Defence policy irrational was placed so high that it effectively excluded any consideration by the domestic Courts of the question of whether the interference with the applicants' rights answered a pressing social need or was proportionate to the national security and public order aims pursued, principles which lie at the heart of the Court's analysis of complaints under Article 8 of the Convention.[86]

In other words, the Court of Human Rights concluded that there had been a violation of Article 13 of the Convention.

---

82 Ibid.

83 Para. 35.

84 Para. 37.

85 Para. 132.

86 Para. 138.

In terms of the potential recipient of xenotransplantation, this case has interesting and potentially far reaching consequences, particularly where the proposed xenograft is the only treatment which seems likely to succeed. What can be deduced from the case of *Smith and Grady* is that challenges to any blanket decision not to offer funding for xenotransplantation (say, because of its expense) or not to provide it to a particular individual (perhaps because third parties object) could breach Convention rights. The erosion of the *Wednesbury* principles might therefore make judicial review in such cases more likely to be successful. Of course, it remains speculative precisely what impact this will have on the provision of healthcare in general and xenotransplantation in particular.

Dyer suggested that the incorporation of the Convention would 'bring issues of NHS resources and healthcare rationing to the fore'.[87] What is certain is that:

> ... wherever a public authority exercises a statutory power, or performs a statutory duty which is to some degree discretionary, the discretion must be exercised in a manner consistent with the Convention. It is only where the public authority has no discretion that the performance of statutory functions can override Convention rights.[88]

Human Rights and International Law

The United Kingdom government signed up to the European Convention on Human Rights as long ago as 1951. Since that date, British citizens have had the right to take certain grievances to the Court of Human Rights in Strasbourg, and that Court may declare specific legal provisions to be in breach of the terms of the Convention. We have already seen that the Human Rights Act may make some differences in the area of medicine, but some additional general points are also worth mentioning at this point.

The essential difference is that, since 2 October 2000, United Kingdom courts have had to take account of the jurisprudence emanating from Strasbourg in reaching their decisions. As Travis and Dyer say:

> ... for the first time government ministers and public bodies will find themselves having to operate within a set of agreed minimum standards which can be enforced by British judges. The courts will have much more power than before to hold the government and public bodies to account.[89]

Or as Carlisle puts it:

> The Act writes into UK domestic law the European Convention on Human Rights. Public authorities, including the NHS, will for the first time have to respect and protect citizens' human rights. The DoH, health authorities, trusts, primary care groups and even individual doctors all come within the definition. Managers will have to consider matters such as the

87 Dyer, C. (1998), 'UK Human Rights Act will Allow Challenges to Treatment Refusals', *British Medical Journal*, **317**, p. 1339.

88 Mullen (2000).

89 Travis, A. and Dyer, C. (2000), 'Power Shifts to the Judges', *The Guardian*, 11 September, pp. 6–7, at p. 6.

> right to life, freedom from inhuman or degrading treatment, respect for privacy and family life, the right to a fair hearing and the right to freedom of expression.[90]

What the Human Rights Act does not do is to create new rights as such; rather it allows people to enforce existing rights in domestic tribunals without the need to go to the Strasbourg court, although recourse to that Court will still be available if the domestic courts fail in their new responsibilities.

In addition to the specific concerns of the Human Rights Act 1998, there are more general international human rights which might be threatened by xenotransplantation. Bach et al. suggest that these include 'the right to life, health, a pure environment, human dignity, privacy and freedom of movement'.[91] As they note 'most of these rights are embodied in binding treaties to which most governments of the world are parties which impose legal obligations upon those governments to assure those rights to their people'.[92]

Thus, international humanitarian law, designed as it is to protect fundamental rights and freedoms, might well be in conflict with the practice of xenotransplantation. The World Health Organization highlights the potential global consequences of xenotransplantation in this way:

> Xeonotransplantation has the potential to supplement the limited supply of human material for transplantation and may even become an alternative. However, xenotransplantation (including the use of living xenogeneic cells, tissues or organs, as well as human bodily fluids, cells, tissues or organs that have had *ex vivo* contact with living xenogeneic material) presents specific immunological problems for recipients. It also may transmit pathogens from the animal source to the recipient and, hence, possibly to the general public; recent instances of human epidemics/pandemics arising from cross-species infections, such as severe acute respiratory syndrome, underline the public health risks of xenotransplantation. These risks are compounded by immunosuppression, nonexistent or inadequate diagnostic tools, and an absence of effective therapy.[93]

Additionally, the British Transplantation Society says:

> A major concern about xenotransplantation is the potential risk of transmission of infectious agents. Of these, porcine endogenous retrovirus, which is embedded within the pig genome and cannot, therefore, be eliminated as a potential hazard, is the most important. Infection by porcine endogenous retrovirus could pose a potential risk not only to the recipient of a porcine graft, but also to those in close contact with the recipient and perhaps even the wider population ... It is likely that any future trials of organ transplantation will be preceded by clinical trials of cell (eg neural cells) and tissue (eg pancreatic islets) based xenotransplantation therapies.[94]

---

90 Carlisle, D. (2000), 'News Focus', *Health Services Journal*, 27 April, pp. 10–11, at p. 10.

91 Bach et al. (2001), 'Ethical and Legal Issues in Technology: Xenotransplantation', American *Journal of Law and Medicine*, **27**, pp. 283–300, at p. 293. This article is of particularly high quality and has informed much of our consideration of international humanitarian law.

92 Ibid.

93 WHO (2003), *Human Organ and Tissue Transplantation*, EB113/14, 27 November.

94 British Transplantation Society (2003), *Standards for Solid Organ Transplantation in the United Kingdom*, para. 10.1; available on their website http://www.bts.org.uk, accessed on 20/01/2004.

The question to be posed, therefore, is whether or not it is worth running these risks in order to advance this particular innovative treatment. To an extent, this question has been answered by the fact that limited options are already available. We have already referred to the research on 160 patients treated with living pig tissues,[95] and the drive – especially to develop new cell-based treatments – is very much on.[96] However exciting these possibilities, at a national level the state has an obligation to protect its citizens, and at an international level, states like the UK have entered into agreements concerning the extent to which their behaviour can legitimately impinge on others. With xenotransplantation, this forms a major part of the arguments for caution. *Nature Medicine*, for example, has said that:

> As a worst case scenario it is possible that such a new infectious agent could sweep through human populations giving rise to a life-threatening pandemic. Such an event has never been documented and there simply are not the data available to address the extent of the risk.[97]

Additionally, of course, the fact that international humanitarian law is potentially involved also means that there are direct responsibilities imposed upon states. The relevant obligations of states are based 'on certain general and well recognised principles, namely elementary consideration of humanity'.[98] The possibility of the spread of unknown and undetectable viruses as a result of xenotransplantation programmes, even if they are only at the research stage, is one which states themselves would have to take seriously, having regard to their obligations under international law. As has been said:

> It is a principle of customary international law that no state is entitled to conduct itself as to create a foreseeable danger to other states ... conduct, of course, comprises both acts and omissions. Inaction, where action is called for to avert a foreseeable danger, is no less culpable than action. Consequently, if xenotransplantation takes place in a state that has taken no steps to restrict or control that activity and an epidemic arises which spreads to another state, the latter state may well be entitled to claim damages against the state which permitted such activity.[99]

Indeed, international environmental law is also potentially implicated in the practice of xenotransplantation. Both the Stockholm Declaration of 1972 and the Rio Declaration of 1992 have imposed obligations on individual states to take positive action to protect the environment. Principle 21 of the Stockholm Declaration and Principle 22 of the Rio Declaration impose on states which have signed these declarations an obligation 'to ensure that activities within their jurisdiction of control do not cause damage to the environment of other states or areas beyond the limits of national jurisdiction'. Manifestly the spread of dangerous pathogens,

---

95 http://www.news.bbc.co.uk, accessed on 26/05/2002.

96 For further discussion, see chapter 2.

97 'Focus on Xenotransplantation', available at http://www.nature.com/nm/web_specials/xeno, accessed on 24/04/2002.

98 *The Corfu Channel Case* 1949 1 I.C.J. 4, at pp. 22–23.

99 Bach et al. (2001), at p. 298.

which may be a consequence of xenotransplantation, would appear to fit within the prohibition contained in these principles.

Of course, the activities of states will be judged against certain accepted principles. A variety of these exists, which it is not necessary to elucidate on at length here, but a brief discussion might be of value. One commonly used guiding principle is known as the precautionary principle, which 'suggests that the burden of proof should lie with those developing the technology to demonstrate that it will not cause serious harm'.[100] Resnik highlights the implicit value of the application of this principle by noting that 'we often need to make important decisions even though we lack scientific certainty'.[101] However, he also notes that there are arguments against its use; for example, that it 'is a highly conservative, risk-aversive rule that can stifle progress, change and growth'.[102]

Other relevant models include risk management strategies, which garner some support. Using this approach, 'one should develop strategies to manage risks based on a quantitative assessment of those risks. Risk assessment classifies and describes various risks and estimates the probability that they will occur, based on empirical evidence.'[103] This model equates closely to that traditionally applied in scientific research, and seems also to have commended itself to the Council of Europe.[104] Article 12 of its Recommendation on xenotransplantation reads as follows:

> No xenotransplantation should be carried out unless the following specific conditions are fulfilled:
> i) There is no other appropriate therapeutic method of comparable effectiveness available for the patient.
> ii) The data resulting from pre-clinical research suggest or, where appropriate, the data resulting from prior clinical research indicate a clear therapeutic benefit for the xenotransplantation patient. In particular these data should:
>   - have demonstrated an adequate function of the xenotransplant in relevant models for an appropriate period of time through a clinically applicable methodology,
>   - provide sufficient reasons to believe that rejection can be overcome and that the xenotransplant can function adequately in humans.
> iii) The risks which may be incurred by the patient are not disproportionate to the potential therapeutic benefit of the procedure.
> In particular, the evaluation through pre-clinical research of the risks for adverse events and transmission of infectious agents to the recipient, as based on international standards for laboratory results and diagnostic assays, should have demonstrated sufficient safety.

However, risk management is also not without its critics. Starr, for example, says that '[g]overnments asked to regulate exposure to risks from man-made sources ...

---

[100] Incorvati, G. (2003), 'Xenotransplantation, Public Responsibility and Law', *European Journal of Health Law*, **10** (295), at p. 301.

[101] Resnik, D.B. (2003), 'Is the Precautionary Principle Unscientific?', *Studies in History and Philosophy of Biological and Biomedical Sciences*, **34** (329), at p. 330.

[102] Ibid.

[103] Ibid., at p. 333.

[104] Recommendation (2003) 10 of the Committee of Ministers to member states on xenotransplantation (adopted 19 June 2003).

face a tortuous decision process because of the ... uncertainties of risk analysis'.[105] Equally, however, Starr points to the fact that use of the precautionary principle is by no means uncontroversial. As he says, '[p]rotection from a risk that may be nonexistent or trivial may deprive the public of attractive and valuable lifetime choices'.[106]

Irrespective of the principle applied to the calculation of the risks, benefits and consequences of xenotransplantation trials in particular, it is clear that governments will have to address some very complex decisions. The use of the precautionary principle seems to sit comfortably with the requirements of international humanitarian law, whereas the risk management strategy is more familiar in medical research. Given the current uncertainties as to the risks actually posed by xenotransplantation, it might be felt that the precautionary principle holds out more hope of preventing the kind of pandemic to which the WHO refers; yet it might equally be criticized as stifling or delaying the development of legitimate and beneficial therapies. Clearly, this is not a matter which will be easily resolved.

Legal Liability for Harm

One further important matter must be considered. It is, of course, not only states which may find themselves in breach of their legal obligations or duties. Both in terms of national and international law, where a harm is caused, the individual who is responsible for it would normally be called upon to pay compensation. Thus, in the case of xenotransplantation, the person or organization producing or providing the products or organs which generate the risk may find themselves liable both at common law and in terms of statute for any harm that occurs.

Legal liability under the common law would arise in terms of the doctrine derived from the case of *Donoghue* v *Stevenson*.[107] This case, which has been highly influential throughout the world, indicates two things of particular relevance to xenotransplantation. First, it indicates that negligence is a developing legal concept. The fact that something has not been done before, and that the question of liability has not therefore been previously considered, does not mean that the law cannot take account of it. Second, the case developed the famous 'neighbour principle', which indicates that liability for harm can extend to anyone who ought reasonably to have been in the contemplation of the actor. Thus, the novelty of xenotransplantation and the legal issues it raises will be no barrier to a finding of liability at common law.

However, the basis for any legal action requires some consideration here. Litigation might proceed on the issue of operational negligence or on the basis of lack of consent. We have already seen that – unless there is a major failure to disclose or a consent is obtained by fraud or undue influence[108] – alleged failure in the information disclosure process will be dealt with under the law of negligence

105 Starr, C. (2003), 'The Precautionary Principle Versus Risk Analysis', *Risk Analysis*, **23** (1), at p. 2.

106 Ibid.

107 1932 SC (HL) 31.

108 See chapter 7.

(even if the standard for disclosure is set higher in the clinical trial phase). Thus operational and consent-based actions can for the present be discussed together.

The rule of the common law is that, in order for negligence to be established, it must be established that a duty of care existed, that the duty was breached and that harm followed from that beach, such harm being of the type that can be compensated for in law.[109] Space does not permit, nor arguably require, a full discussion of the rules of negligence, but they are important to the extent that harm caused by xenotransplantation (whether involving cells or organs), if proved to have been caused by the transplant, can and should be compensated. This will need to be taken account of when calculating potential costs to the health service, as discussed below.

Where an individual has given a valid consent to participation in xenotransplantation the normal rule would be that, if one of the disclosed risks eventuates, they would be unable successfully to sue. Triller and Bobinski also consider that consent would amount to a form of waiver both for the recipient and their close contacts, and agree that it is unlikely (always assuming that the question of the quality of consent has been satisfactorily resolved) that litigation would succeed.[110] Therefore, 'the most likely person to succeed in such a suit would be a third party who was unaware of the risks of close contact with the patient'.[111] Indeed:

> When unknown or untreatable infectious disease is transmitted to a member of the public, who was not required to sign an informed consent form, the court might find that the transplant hospital owes a legal duty to the public not to introduce infectious diseases into the public domain.[112]

Although possibly precluding successful litigation on the part of the patient and the notified close contacts, the risk of litigation following the spread of disease into the rest of the community could seriously question the merit of commencing clinical trials until pre-clinical work produces a high level of certainty on this point. Article 33 of the Council of Europe's Recommendation referred to above also addresses the question of compensation, asserting that '[t]he person who has suffered undue damage resulting from a xenotransplantation is entitled to fair compensation according to the conditions and procedures prescribed by law'. This provision is echoed in the Convention on Biomedicine and Human Rights.[113] Equally, the Convention on Civil Liability for Damage resulting from Activities Dangerous to the Environment sought to establish a clear liability to compensate in a variety of circumstances, including in respect of genetically modified organisms.[114]

---

109 For a full discussion of the law of negligence, see Mason, McCall Smith and Laurie (2002), chapter 9; Brazier, M. (2003), *Medicine, Patients and the Law* (3rd Ed), Penguin Books: London, Part 2.

110 Triller, K. and Bobinski, M.A. (2004), 'Tort Liability of Xenotransplantation Centers', *Xenotransplantation*, **11**, pp. 310–314.

111 Chae, S.J. and Cooper, D.K.C. (1997), 'Legal Implications of Xenotransplantation', *Xenotransplantation*, **4** (132), at p. 136.

112 Triller and Bobinski (2004), at p. 310.

113 Convention for the Protection of Human Rights and Dignity of the Human Being with Regard to the Application of Biology and Medicine, Oviedo, 4.IV.1997, ETS No: 164, Article 24.

114 CETS No: 150, Council of Europe, Opened for signature, Lugano 21/6/1993. Three ratifications are needed to bring this convention into force, but as at 16/02/04 no ratifications had been received.

The importance of ensuring that adequate means of compensation are available, therefore, seems to be clear. Whether or not the current common law is sufficiently robust to achieve this is for another discussion. However, in addition to the common law, other specific legal remedies may be available. It has already been noted that the relationship between those providing xenotransplantation products or organs and the NHS/final recipient will essentially be commercial. Thus, two main additional areas of law become relevant: namely, sale of goods and the consumer protection legislation.

Contract/Sale of Goods Legislation

Sale of goods legislation, most notably the Sale of Goods Act 1979 as amended in 1994, covers all products and: 'implies certain conditions into contracts of sale which cannot be excluded in the case of consumer sales and can only be excluded in commercial sales if the exclusion is "reasonable"'.[115] Purchasers of products, therefore, can expect that any goods purchased are of 'satisfactory quality'. The Act defines 'satisfactory quality' as being of a standard 'that a reasonable person would regard as satisfactory, taking account of any description of the goods, the price (if relevant) and all the other relevant circumstances'.[116] The legislation is an example of a strict liability regime, in that:

> ... where goods supplied under contract are 'defective', in the sense of either being of inadequate quality or unfit for purpose, it is no defence for the seller to argue that he has exercised all reasonable care in the supply of such goods. Such liability has always been 'strict'. It is the existence of, and not the discoverability of or the reason for, the defect in the product which renders the seller liable for the resulting damage caused. Moreover, there is no doubt that such liability may arise out of the inadequate nature of the labelling or instructions for use rather than the inherent design of the product itself.[117]

Sale of goods legislation depends on the existence of a contract between the supplier/manufacturer and the person harmed. Therefore, liability under this legislation will be limited by the fact that there must be a contract between the person allegedly causing the harm and the person harmed. In *Pfizer Corpn* v *Ministry of Health*[118] and *Appleby* v *Sleep*,[119] for example, it was held that a pharmacist did not enter into a contract with a person to whom he or she prescribes a drug under the National Health Service. Thus, only over-the-counter products and those supplied privately would be covered by this legislation. Thus, the NHS may have a claim against the 'manufacturers' but the patient who suffered as a result would not. Of more relevance to the ultimate consumer would be the terms of the Consumer Protection Act.

---

[115] Dodds-Smith, I. and Spencer, M. (1994), 'Product Liability for Medicinal Products', in Powers, M. and Harris, N., *Medical Negligence* (2nd Ed), Butterworths: London, at p. 505.

[116] S. 14(2A).

[117] Dodds-Smith and Spencer (1994), at p. 505.

[118] [1965] 1 All ER 650 (HL).

[119] [1968] 2 All ER 265.

The Consumer Protection Act 1987

Deficiencies in the traditional remedies in product liability became the subject of European Community interest in the aftermath of a number of failed claims, perhaps particularly the thalidomide tragedy.[120] Council Directive No 85/374/EEC was the culmination of debate and discussion throughout Europe on the appropriate regime to be applied to allegedly defective products. In the Preamble to the Directive, it is clearly stated that 'liability without fault on the part of the producer is the sole means of adequately solving the problem, peculiar to our age of increasing technicality, of a fair apportionment of the risks inherent in modern technological production'. Effectively, this legislation introduces a strict liability regime. The difference between fault-based systems and those which rely on strict liability was described in one US case as follows: 'in a strict liability analysis the *defendant* is *assumed* to know of the dangerous propensity of the product, whereas in a negligence case, the *plaintiff* must *prove* that the defendant knew or should have known of the danger.'[121] (Emphasis added.)

European Member States were given until 1988 to enact legislation incorporating the Directive into domestic law. The Directive was absorbed into UK law in 1987 with the passing of the Consumer Protection Act 1987. Thomson says:

> The general idea of the Act is simple: it is to place the primary responsibility for injury or damage caused by a defective product on the producer and to enable the consumer who has been injured by the defective product or whose property has been damaged by the defective product to obtain compensation from the producer without having to prove fault.[122]

Or as Brahams puts it, '[t]he Consumer Protection Act 1987 shifts the burden of defending a product on to the manufacturer or producer once a plaintiff has prima facie evidence that his or her injury was caused by a "defect" in the product as defined by the Act'.[123] That being said, '... the provisions of the statute are hideously complex'.[124]

A full description of the legislation will not be undertaken here. Rather, some of the difficulties which the Act raises for consumers will be highlighted in order to reach an overall impression of its likely impact in relation to xenotransplantation. It should be remembered that the intention of the legislation was to provide a 'fair' distribution of responsibilities, and to ease the burden of proof on the consumer, who will generally have less expertise and fewer resources than his or her opponent when challenging a manufacturer or supplier of a product. S. 1(2) of the Act defines its terms, including providing definitions of 'product', 'producer' and so on. S. 2 describes the liability of individuals or companies for any defective product (initially excluding game or primary agricultural produce, although this section was later modified to take account of the BSE crisis).

---

120 For a discussion of this case, see Teff, H. and Munro, C. (1976), *Thalidomide: The Legal Aftermath*, Saxon House: Farnborough.

121 *Feldman* v *Lederle Laboratories* 479 A 2d 374 (1984), at p. 385.

122 Thomson, J. (1994), *Delictual Liability*, Butterworths: London, at p. 138.

123 Brahams, D. (1994), 'Advantage to the Plaintiff', *Gazette*, **91** (27), 13 July, at p. 23.

124 Thomson (1994), at p. 138.

A producer of a product is:

> (a) the person who manufactured it;
> (b) in the case of a substance which has not been manufactured but has been won or abstracted, the person who won or abstracted it;
> (c) in the case of a product which has not been manufactured, won or abstracted but essential characteristics of which are attributable to an industrial or other process having been carried out (for example, in relation to agricultural produce), the person who carried out that process.[125]

Thus, as Thomson notes, '... all parties in the distribution chain from the producer, to the own brander or importer are potentially liable under the Act ...'.[126]

A product is defined in s. 1(2) as being 'any goods or electricity and....includes a product which is comprised in another product whether by virtue of being a component part or raw material or otherwise ...'. Human products, such as blood, can reasonably be taken to count as products following the case of *A and Others* v *The National Blood Authority and Others.*[127] By analogy, therefore, organs and tissue in this context could amount to products for the purposes of the legislation.

The meat of the legislation is contained in the following two sections which explain what is meant by a defective product and list a series of defences available to the producer. For the purposes of the Act, there is:

> ... a defect in a product ... if the safety of the product is not such as persons generally are entitled to expect; and for those purposes 'safety', in relation to a product, shall include safety with respect to products comprised in that product and safety in the context of risk of damage to property, as well as in the context of risks of death or other personal injury ...[128]

Liability in terms of this section hinges to a large extent on what persons are 'generally entitled to expect' in terms of safety. It has been pointed out that:

> ... the expression in s 3 'safety ... such as persons generally are entitled to expect' utterly fails to provide the interpreter with an autonomous standard. Indeed, it has been forcefully argued that in anything resembling a difficult case, the consumer expectations test will be unable to stand of its own and will necessarily fall back on a risk-utility analysis.[129]

The legislation does, however, attempt an explanation of what persons are generally entitled to expect in s. 3(2). This section states that:

> ... all circumstances shall be taken into account, including –
> (a) the manner in which, and the purposes for which, the product has been marketed, its get-up, the use of any mark in relation to the product and any instructions for, or

125 Consumer Protection Act 1987 s. 1 (2).

126 Thomson, J. (2004), *Delictual Liability* (3rd Ed), Butterworths: London, at pp. 167–169.

127 [2001] 3 All ER 289.

128 S. 3(1).

129 Stoppa, A. (1992), 'The Concept of Defectiveness in the Consumer Protection Act 1987: A Critical Analysis', *Legal Studies*, **112** (2), at p. 215.

warnings with respect to, doing or refraining from doing anything with or in relation to the product;
(b) what might reasonably be expected to be done with or in relation to the product; and
(c) the time when the product was supplied by its producer to another;
and nothing in this section shall require a defect to be inferred from the fact that the safety of a product which is supplied after that time is greater than the safety of the product in question.

It is worth, therefore, addressing what might amount to defect for the purposes of the legislation. This can be undertaken by a brief review of some recent cases. In *Richardson* v *LRC Products Ltd*,[130] the claimant failed in her attempt to argue that a fractured condom was defective for the purposes of the Act. In *Foster* v *Biosil*,[131] a similar decision was reached in respect of a ruptured silicone breast implant. In both cases, identification of the cause of the alleged defect was necessary if they were to establish that the product was defective.

However, defectiveness was established in the case of *Abouzaid* v *Mothercare (UK) Ltd*,[132] the court saying:

> The product was defective because it was supplied with a design which permitted the risk to arise and without giving a warning that the user should not so position himself that the risk arose.[133]

Although there were clearly problems associated with establishing the defectiveness of a product, the law has been clarified by the case of *A* v *National Blood Authority and another*.[134] In this case a number of individuals raised an action based on the fact that they had contracted Hepatitis C following the use of blood and blood products. In this case, Burton, J drew a distinction between standard and non-standard products, concluding that the products in this case were non-standard. Thus, he explicated the test for defectiveness in respect of non-standard products as follows:

> ... the primary issue in relation to a non-standard product may be whether the public at large accepted the non-standard nature of the product – i.e. they accepted that a proportion of the products is defective ... That ... is not of course the end of it, because the question is of *legitimate* expectation, and the court may conclude that the expectation of the public is too high or low. But manifestly questions such as warnings and presentations will be in the forefront. However, I conclude that the following are not relevant: (i) avoidability of the harmful characteristic – i.e. impossibility or unavoidability in relation to the precautionary measures; (ii) the impracticability, cost or difficulty of taking such measures; and (iii) the benefit to society or utility of the product (except in the context of whether – with *full information and proper knowledge* – the public does and ought to accept the risk.[135]

---

130 (2000) 59 BMLR 185.
131 (2000) 59 BMLR 178.
132 2000 WL 1918530.
133 Ibid., at p. 5.
134 (2001) 3 All ER 289.
135 Ibid., at pp. 339–340.

From the point of view of xenotransplantation, this dictum is clearly extremely important. If transgenic organs are deemed to be non-standard products (that is, products which deviate in some way from the standard product) then it would appear that neither the impossibility of rendering them risk-free nor any cost implications of making them so will be relevant to avoid liability, unless – it would seem – the risks are judged to have been agreed to by the public. It is a recurrent theme in this analysis of xenotransplantation that the questions of social utility and public consent have not yet been resolved. Therefore, if organs were deemed to be non-standard products then liability could not be avoided since significant parts of the test have not been met.

In respect of xenotransplantation, it may be that it is impossible to be certain that the product or organ is 'safe', particularly given the uncertainties about the risks of infection, and the possibility that even the most thorough scientific tests could fail to find an unknown virus in source animals, or eradicate it in the development process. It might be thought unreasonable to find a producer liable for every possible side-effect, but liability will be imposed where the manufacturer should have foreseen a real risk, and will cover all of the consequences.

It is well established at common law that manufacturers have a duty to warn of possible risks associated with their products. In *Donoghue* v *Stevenson*, for example, it was said that:

> ... the general rule at common law is that the manufacturer of ... drugs, like the manufacturer of other products, has a duty to provide consumers with adequate warning of the potentially harmful side-effects that the manufacturer knows or has reason to know may be produced by the drug.[136]

This duty to warn is also clearly encapsulated in the Consumer Protection Act 1987. In fact, one author suggested that 'there is not, apparently, a definite conceptual distinction between failure to warn and design defect cases, and warnings and instructions may be properly viewed as components of a product's overall design'.[137]

In proving failures under the 1987 Act, the consumer is required only to establish what would be necessary in a strict liability scheme. Thus, there is technically no need to establish that the producer was at fault in any such alleged failure. Rather, the only hurdle is the establishing of a link in causation between the defect or failure and the harm allegedly resulting from it. However, changing the standard of liability from fault to strict may not, in reality, have made a significant contribution to the likelihood of successful actions. For example, where the allegation that a product was defective is raised, it has been suggested that '... notwithstanding that the test is couched in terms of consumer expectations, in many cases the defective nature of a product will probably have to be assessed by means of a risk-utility analysis, an approach which has been inherited from the law of negligence'.[138] This is of particular interest, given what has been said about consent where failure to warn is

136 [1932] AC 562 (HL), at p. 697.

137 Stoppa (1992), at p. 222.

138 Stoppa (1992), at p. 218.

at the heart of the litigation. In this situation, the producer's liability will be measured against other producers. In other words, liability is not absolutely strict – it will also depend on judgement, in a similar manner to actions heard under the tort/delict system.

Defences The impact of the 1987 Act will also be affected by the defences which are available to manufacturers or producers of products. In the United Kingdom, although not in some other European countries, the Government built into the legislation the 'state of the art' or development risks defence. This defence allows manufacturers to escape liability where:

> ... the state of scientific and technical knowledge at the relevant time was not such that a producer of products of the same description as the product in question might be expected to have discovered the defect if it had existed in his products while they were under his control ...[139]

Interestingly, the Royal Commission on Civil Liability and Compensation for Personal Injury (Pearson Commission),[140] the Law Commission[141] and the Scottish Law Commission[142] were all opposed to the incorporation of this defence, substantially because:

> To allow a defence to strict liability on the ground that there is no way, either practical or theoretical, for a defendant to ascertain the existence of impurities in his product would be to emasculate the theory and in a very real sense would signal a retreat to negligence theory.[143]

And, as the Pearson Commission said, 'to exclude development risks from a regime of strict liability would be to leave a gap through which, for example, the victims of another thalidomide disaster might easily slip'.[144]

The burden on producers is limited by this defence to showing that they took reasonable care – a basis under which they have traditionally escaped liability in negligence analysis. The wording of this defence was as controversial as its outcome, and was indeed challenged in the European Court of Justice.[145] The allegation laid at the door of the British Government was that it had failed to fulfil its obligations under the Directive by the manner in which it enacted the development risks defence. The Commission of the European Community sought a ruling from the Court concerning the compatibility of Article 7 of the Directive and section 4(1)(e) of the Consumer Protection Act 1987.

In the event, the Court found in favour of the United Kingdom, arguing that:

---

139 Consumer Protection Act 1987, s. 4(1)(e).

140 Cmnd 7054 -1 (1978).

141 Law Com. No 82; Cmnd 6831 (1977).

142 Scot. Law Com. No 45; Cmnd 6831 (1977).

143 *Cunningham* v *MacNeal Memorial Hospital* 226 NE 2d 897 [1970], at p. 902.

144 Pearson Commission, para. 1259.

145 *Commission* v *United Kingdom (Re the Product Liability Directive)* [1997] 3 CMLR 923.

> The Court has consistently held that the scope of national laws, regulations or administrative provisions must be assessed in the light of the interpretation given to them by national courts. Yet in this case the Commission has not referred in support of its application to any national judicial decision which, in its view, interprets the domestic provision at issue inconsistently with the Directive.[146]

In other words, since there had been no case in which this issue had been considered, the Commission was disinclined to speculate about what UK courts would do. In addition, the Court felt that there was nothing in the wording of the relevant UK law which would preclude its courts from interpreting the defence in line with the Directive. However, the Court did restate the fact that the test is objective; that is that it 'does not contemplate the state of knowledge of which the producer in question actually or subjectively was or could have been appraised, but the objective state of scientific and technical knowledge of which the producer is assumed to have been informed'.[147]

Thus, the test is described as follows:

> In order to have a defence under Article 7(e) of the Directive the producer of a defective product must prove that the objective state of scientific and technical knowledge, including the most advanced level of such knowledge, at the time when the product in question was put into circulation was not such as to enable the existence of the defect to be discovered. Further, in order for the relevant scientific and technical knowledge to be successfully pleaded against the producer, that knowledge must have been accessible at the time when the product in question was put into circulation.[148]

The move to strict liability was widely welcomed as a means of redressing the imbalance between producer and consumer. It offered the theoretical possibility of shifting the burden of proof onto those who generate risk – in much the same way as the New Zealand and other no fault systems tried to do.[149] However, like these systems, and particularly the New Zealand scheme,[150] sufficient caveats were introduced to make the impact of legal change ultimately less impressive than the rhetoric of radical reform. Despite the claims made for strict liability, UK law retains significant and critical conceptual remnants of the system it purported to replace and on which it sought to improve.

However, it seems that – for the individual harmed as a result of unconsented to risks in xenotransplantation – there is *some* legal mechanism available to ensure that a claim for compensation may succeed. Given what has been said about liability for defective products, it is perhaps scarcely a surprise to note that even the Consumer Protection Act provides that a residual right of action remains. Thus, if a person cannot or does not succeed under the strict liability scheme, he or she may still sue using the common law as described above. How successful the consumer would be under the common law remains moot.

---

146 Ibid., Transcript, p. 2.

147 Ibid., p. 940.

148 Ibid.

149 For further discussion of no fault liability schemes, see McLean, S.A.M. (ed.) (1995), *Law Reform and Personal Injury Litigation*, Dartmouth: Aldershot.

150 For discussion, see Mahoney, R. (1995), 'Trouble in Paradise', in McLean (ed.) (1995), note 145.

Conclusions

As can be seen, there are a number of legal questions which arise directly or tangentially from xenotransplantation. Unarguably, the major problems will be those which relate to consent issues in either clinical trials or the use of xenografting as standard medical treatment in the future. There must, therefore, remain a question as to whether or not the practice of xenotransplantation, given the current state of knowledge, allows potential recipients the protection of the general rules of consent, and whether harm caused will be compensated under any of the legal regimes in place. Additionally, there are consent-based questions which go beyond the individual, and which severely test the accepted legal understanding of consent. Not only would individuals be expected to submit to unusual limitations on their basic freedoms, but others would have a direct impact on the availability of the treatment, and would also be required to make significant modifications to their lifestyles.

Moreover, in the case of xenotransplantation, it seems likely – in the early stages at least – that those considered as possible participants will be those who are the most critically ill and therefore, arguably, the most vulnerable to the pressures associated with that illness. Thus, they may agree to try virtually anything in order to restore their health. This fact, while it makes patients more vulnerable, may also affect their ability to succeed under the common law, particularly in respect of proof of causation. As Caulfield and Robertson say:

> Patients may have few options available so a court may be inclined to find that no amount of information about the risks would have swayed a reasonable person from proceeding with the xenotransplantation. On the other hand, if a research participant had a number of more conventional treatment options available at the time the xenograft was proposed, the extreme nature of this procedure may actually make it easier for plaintiffs to clear the causation hurdle.[151]

However, the assessment of competence to consent remains highly significant. The potential for pressures to be brought to bear – on all of those involved – is sufficiently great to merit concern about the element of voluntariness which is essential to a valid consent.

As we have seen in this chapter, however, difficult issues arise not only from the question of consent. Wider accountability issues must also be recognized, and relevant problems addressed. Many of these raise direct challenges to fundamental concepts such as confidentiality and accountability which are by no means trivial.

The impact of human rights legislation and international humanitarian law must also be taken account of in any evaluation of xenotransplantation. As has been said, states do not have unequivocal rights under international law to engage in practices which may have unforeseen harmful consequences for the rest of the world, and liability may well follow any such venture. Thus, the United Kingdom, in common with other states, must carefully consider its potential global liability. The Human Rights Act will also directly impact on some of the proposed restrictions on individual recipients and their families, and the state may well find itself

[151] Caulfield and Robertson (2001), at p. 85.

successfully challenged even when the regime imposed makes apparently perfect practical sense. Additionally, the internationally agreed standards to which healthcare professionals subscribe, for example the Declaration of Helsinki, also pose some problems in respect of clinical trials of xenotransplantation.

Resource allocation decisions will require careful scrutiny, both at macro and at micro level, particularly given the judgement in the case of *Smith and Grady*.[152] Liability will also devolve onto those who produce the organs for xenotransplantation or associated products. Either under sale of goods or consumer protection legislation, where there is a defect or inherent danger in the product, either the NHS or the producer will have liability. Successful litigation, or its prospect, will inevitably require to be considered when evaluating the costs likely to be associated with xenotransplantation.

This review of the ethical and legal considerations in xenotransplantation leads, we believe, inexorably to the conclusion which now follows.

---

152 Supra cit.

Chapter 9

Xenotransplantation: What Next?

The impetus to consider xenotransplantation as a viable treatment option in the future remains clearly grounded in the possibility that, even were less controversial sources of organ transplantation to be maximized, there would still remain a shortage of organs for transplantation. On the plus side, xenotransplantation has a number of immediate attractions; not least that, were it possible to breed sufficient numbers of transgenic animals, and were we able to overcome immunological and physiological problems, it would provide a ready supply of organs, permit the planning of surgery and perhaps reduce the need for expensive immunosuppressive regimes. Equally, the development of cellular xenografting is potentially of benefit in respect of certain degenerative conditions, such as Parkinson's disease. However, the promise of xenotransplantation, even if established, would not be without costs, both ethical and legal.

Ethical Issues

To determine the ethical standing of different aspects of animal to human transplantation it is imperative that ethical work is based on the most up to date empirical information. This necessitates that the ethical analysis of xenotransplantation is a dynamic enterprise. In order for this type of iterative ethical assessment to take place, both the inclination and the mechanisms to support this must exist. However, we have suggested that current efforts to assess xenotransplantation in the United Kingdom are heavily dependent on the now largely outdated Kennedy Report. Furthermore, the agency that regulates xenotransplantation in the UK – UKXIRA – does not have an explicitly ethical component within its remit. As a result, the ethical implications of contemporaneous scientific work are not being assessed in a thoroughgoing manner. It is important that this concern is remedied if policy decisions are to be valid and ethically legitimate.

The ethical acceptability of xenotransplantation is dominated by two issues: whether its use of animals is acceptable and whether its contribution to public health is likely to outweigh any harm it may cause. The public health issues raised by animal to human transplantation are not easily addressed within a framework that is primarily concerned with the interests and rights of individuals. Thus, this book has suggested that it is preferable to utilize an ethical approach which gives priority to the interests of the whole community and which will also respect the autonomy of individuals, unless public health issues make this impossible. This led to the conclusion that although individual patients are able to consent to some treatments which may pose a risk to them, the public health implications of xenotransplantation appear sufficiently serious to make it necessary for public health to trump individual choice on this issue. Importantly, at the present time a public health ethic would support a moratorium on xenotransplantation clinical trials until more information is available on the procedure.

In respect of animals, although it seems likely that animals experience considerable harm from xenotransplantation procedures, currently there is insufficient information regarding animal experience to identify the costs to animals accurately. That said, this book has contended that the arguments that are commonly employed to justify the use of certain animals (pigs) and restrict the use of others (non-human primates) in xenotransplantation procedures have been found wanting. This is partly because the consideration of the different components of cost-benefit assessment suggested that it is likely that the costs to animals are underestimated. The RSPCA, for example, has raised concerns that cost-benefit assessments do not consider all of the different components of xenotransplantation which may result in costs to animals. That is, the omission of issues like capture from the wild and transportation from any cost-benefit assessment will result in the degree of harm caused to animals being underestimated. The book has also argued that cost-benefit analysis should include harms other than those which involve physical and psychological pain. That is, one of the greatest costs to animals is that huge numbers of animals will have their lives ended; even if this loss of life is painless, it has been argued that it must nonetheless be incorporated within a cost-benefit assessment. However, even more ethically problematic is that many animals involved in xenotransplantation procedures will die needlessly. In this respect, the large-scale slaughter of piglets born without the required modified genetic make-up will be conducted only for economic reasons; that is, so that the costs of raising the animals can be avoided. This unnecessary killing points to a complete disregard for the value of animal life and the instrumentalization of non-human life.

Additionally, we have has argued that the use of capacities (animal and human) to determine the ethical legitimacy of xenotransplantation procedures is also problematic. This is because it is not possible to forge a consensus on the intellectual and social abilities of different non-human species. Furthermore, it is not true that all members of a particular species share, or will come to attain, the same intellectual and social capacities. Thus, capacities cannot be employed as a yardstick to support the differential treatment of all members of particular species, without allowing for the instrumental use of certain members of our own species.

Legal Issues

The legal problems can be summarized briefly, but their impact is significant. Starting with probably the least problematic, there are issues concerning the liability of industry, the National Health Service and the state itself which were inadequately scrutinized in the past. Although one does not always need to approach innovation by making the assumption that something will go wrong, in the case of xenotransplantation the possibility of something going wrong is a central aspect of concerns about its viability and appropriateness. Not only might the costs of xenotransplantation failures, or side-effects, significantly affect the resources of the

NHS, but the potential costs to the individual would be dramatic. Thus, not only might the NHS be liable to compensate anyone harmed as a result of a xenotransplant, but it would also have potentially unlimited liability for caring for the individual who has been harmed. The responsibility of the state to meet its international obligations must also be borne in mind.

Equally the Human Rights Act 1998 commits the UK to the maintenance of privacy except in certain (probably exceptional) circumstances. Xenotransplantation, on the other hand, is one of the few interventions (if not the only one) which has built into its very design the imperative of a fundamental breach of privacy, requiring the potential recipient to waive his or her right to confidentiality. Should clinical trials show xenotransplantation to be safer than is anticipated at present, this may become less significant, but taken together, the issues just raised seem to militate against an early resort to clinical trials.

Perhaps a more problematic legal issue is the question of consent to involvement in xenotransplants. This can be considered in two stages. For present purposes, the question of consent should xenotransplantation become part of standard therapy is less important than is the question of consent to clinical trials. In the research phase, issues surrounding the selection of patients, the capacity of those selected to provide a valid consent and the general question as to whether or not it is either possible to agree to surrender basic human rights or to enforce the recommended surveillance and monitoring requirements are of considerable importance. In the view presented here, and despite contrary opinions expressed by others, compliance with the surveillance and monitoring regimes cannot be enforced under the present legal regime and doubts must be raised about the capacity of individuals to surrender fundamental rights. Equally, research concerning the social and psychological potential of xenotransplantation would need to be undertaken before proceeding to trials so that, in as much as this is possible in any experimental situation, the fullest possible information – as required by law – can be made available to potential recipients. Moreover, it is internationally accepted that involvement in clinical trials must be subject to the right to withdraw at any stage. It is, however, inherent in the surveillance requirements of xenotransplantation that such withdrawal should be actively discouraged, if not enforced. Also, the need for third party agreement and involvement in life restricting surveillance is of highly dubious legal standing and is certainly unenforceable. In addition, third parties are given an indirect ability to prevent treatment of the prospective participant, even if they are clinically suited and willing; a power which is virtually unheard of in current law, and which may result in refusing someone potentially life saving treatment because of a third party's refusal to participate in the surveillance regimen. Finally, there is wide agreement amongst commentators that no trials should take place until the community as a whole has agreed to this, because of the potential effect on other members of society should the infection risk manifest itself in reality. Identifying public opinion – particularly as this might involve a global consensus – is likely to be difficult to achieve, and commentators have reached conflicting conclusions on how this could be done. Of course, consultation is a relatively common characteristic of law reform, but it is unclear how widely different opinions can be married. For example, a recent report submitted to the House of Lords suggests that:

> ... people see all biotechnology applications as potentially useful, but those involving crop plants, food production, the use of transgenic animals for research and xenotransplantation ... are seen to involve risks; whereas only the use of transgenic animals for research and xenotransplantation are thought of as morally unacceptable.[1]

On the other hand, a paper by Arundell and McKenzie found a relatively equal balance between those who would accept an animal organ and those who were unsure.[2] For the moment, therefore, it seems difficult to identify any consensus on the development of xenotransplantation, and difficult to imagine how precisely one would elucidate the views of members of this or any other committee sufficiently robustly to ensure that the community genuinely was in favour of xenotransplantation. If the requirement of community approval is indeed felt to be necessary, there are three main problems. First, how are we adequately to gauge the views of the public? Second, on what legal basis does their agreement or lack of it impact on the individual decision of a patient as to the risks he or she is prepared to undertake in the search for a cure? Third, of course, and most importantly, we must ask what is meant by society – or the public – for these purposes. Given fears that infections may spread following xenotransplantation, it is clear that 'community' cannot be conceived of as only including those within national boundaries. The entire population of the world is potentially threatened should infections follow xenotransplants, but if it is difficult to gauge the views of the immediate community, how much more difficult will it be to engage with the whole world?

In all, therefore, the consent issue looks to stand firmly in the way of proceeding to clinical trials at present; perhaps even in the foreseeable future. This, however, arguably only holds true in respect of those xenotransplants which were envisaged in the first definition of xenotransplantation and may be less relevant for those which would be added by the new definition. This could be argued because the new definition brings within the ambit of xenotransplantation procedures such as skin grafts using murine cell lines which have been carried out over a number of years, without apparent ill-effects. The fact that the new definition, if accepted, would mean that xenotransplantation has in fact already been being practised in the United Kingdom suggests that proportionately there is no need to impose draconian consent or surveillance/monitoring requirements in respect of these particular procedures, nor would there be cause to doubt the validity of a consent which otherwise satisfies the common law rules. However, the consent requirement also, we have argued, covers risks to third parties, and may yet prove problematic even for these apparently less risky xenotransplants.

---

1 *Select Committee on European Communities, Second Report*, Appendix, 'Biotechnology and the European Public Concerted Action Group', available at http://www.publications.parliament.uk/pa/ld/ldhome.htm.

2 Arundell, M.A. and McKenzie, I.F.C. (1997), 'The Acceptability of Pig Organ Xenografts to Patients Awaiting a Transplant', *Xenotransplantation*, **4**, pp. 62–66.

The Future of Xenotransplantation?

There would seem to be three main ways forward at a national level. The first would be to declare a moratorium, short or long term, on xenotransplantation research and/or clinical trials. The second would to be retain the status quo which could be described as a 'cautious, step by step approach',[3] and the third would be to proceed to clinical trials based on what we now know.

A Moratorium

The legal, ethical and scientific problems associated with xenotransplantation might make the notion of calling a halt appealing, either in the short term or indeed permanently. In fact a moratorium might permit an extensive analysis of the views of the public to be conducted in an atmosphere free from pressure and would presumably allow time for some of the ethical and legal problems to be at least moved towards resolution. Of course, a moratorium in the United Kingdom would have economic consequences in that the companies who are seeking to develop this technology would be discouraged from developing their techniques in the United Kingdom, choosing instead to base their research programmes in countries without strict regulations or in those prepared to support their research.[4] Despite this concern, it is clear that, although UKXIRA has done much laudable work, considerably more work remains to be done before clinical trials can be considered. This being so we contend that accepting applications before all the regulatory procedures are in their final (and not draft) form, and before sufficient information is available on xenotransplantation, suggests that we are closer to clinical trials than we really are. This predicament has the effect of enhancing the profile of animal to human transplantation and of preventing a thorough assessment of other technologies which may be able to perform the same tasks as xenotransplantation within a similar time-scale. In addition, there is a risk that if applications are accepted, the UK is a step closer to allowing trials without the necessary knowledge or regulations to support them.

The imposition of a moratorium (as recently advised in Australia) obviously remains possible only until the first application for a solid organ transplant clinical trial is accepted. At present, although we have has argued that the ethical, legal and scientific concerns in this area have been inadequately resolved, it would technically be possible for UKXIRA (a non-statutory body) to make the decision to proceed, even if these conclusions are correct. For this reason, the imposition of a moratorium, at least on solid organ transplants, has much to commend it. Although a role would remain for UKXIRA were a moratorium to be imposed, it would be a more appropriate role; that is, acting as a UK base for monitoring worldwide initiatives and feeding back relevant information to other nations and international organizations.

---

3 Hansard, 10 November 1999: Column 652.

4 This would be eminently possible given the variety of approaches to the regulation of xenotransplantation. For further discussion, see chapter 4.

The Status Quo

It will be evident from this critique that the option of retaining the status quo is not acceptable. Not only have we commented on the lack of adequate ethical and legal review preceding the acceptance of applications by UKXIRA (even although these applications were not authorized to proceed or were withdrawn), it has also been noted that the nature of UKXIRA itself is such that it rests on challengeable principles, has no direct ethical remit and lacks teeth. In some senses, then, the current UK position is the worst rather than the best of all possible options.

Proceed to Clinical Trials

It must be doubted whether anyone, having considered the ethical and legal issues in xenotransplantation, would seriously suggest moving to clinical trials at the present time. Additionally, many of the issues that have been raised in this book are extraordinarily difficult to resolve and this difficulty should act as a powerful disincentive to any such move unless and until they can be resolved. This caveat applies primarily to solid organ xenotransplantation, although the risks of cellular therapies are not finally known, nor have they yet been shown to produce significant benefits.

Regulation

Irrespective of which of the above options commends itself, the UK cannot revert to a situation of effective *laissez faire* in this area. No matter the approach adopted in the United Kingdom, xenotransplantation research is a global venture and the UK must be in a position to act and react to influence what happens next. To a large extent, therefore, the main question is how this should be done.

The National Standing Committee

Both the Nuffield Report and the Kennedy Report recommended the establishment of a National Standing Committee, which was satisfied with the creation of UKXIRA. Interestingly, the Kennedy Report recommended that this advisory body should eventually have a statutory basis,[5] something which has not yet come to pass more than six years after its creation. The new body was specifically to take account of the framework established by the Kennedy Report, which can broadly be described as follows:

- that primates not be used as source animals;
- that limitations be placed on the extent to which xenotransplantation can be developed in terms of the genetic modification of animals and that the types of tissue that can be used be monitored;

[5] Kennedy Report (Report of the Advisory Group on the Ethics of Xenotransplantation) (1997), *Animal Tissue into Humans*, HMSO: London, p. 141, para. 9.2.

- that more evidence be obtained on the risks posed by xenotransplantation to individuals and the wider community; including research in areas like physiology, immunology and infection;
- that measures to minimize risk to transplant recipients and the wider community be put in place. This should incorporate the manner in which source animals are kept, the monitoring the animals would undergo and the methods used to remove tissue. It is necessary to introduce measures to ensure that these are observed;
- that animal welfare be protected as far as possible;
- that systems be designed to collect tissue samples from source animals and human patients;
- that there be no sequential removal of tissue from source animals;
- that attention be afforded to other therapies that could meet the needs of patients.

Whilst worthy, it seems clear that these objectives, and therefore UKXIRA's ethical framework, leave a great deal to be desired. The range of ethical and legal issues which is of concern is considerably wider than this 'ethical' framework acknowledges, and forms a vital part of UKXIRA's current and future role. For the Kennedy Report, the critical role of the Standing Committee would be the creating and enforcing of standards. The standards which are specifically required, and for which UKXIRA would have 'responsibility', according to the Kennedy Report were:

1. Advising on the research which needs to be carried out on infection risks, immunology and physiology; assessing the results of research with a view to determining whether further conditions should be stipulated or existing ones modified or withdrawn. It would decide, on the basis of scientific evidence submitted to it, whether conditions had been met so as to permit clinical trials in xenotransplantation and, if appropriate, the introduction of a therapeutic programme.
2. Defining measures to minimise the risk of infection to the human recipient and to the wider population; the conditions in which the animals should be kept, the methods used to remove tissue and transport it to the clinical site, and infection control procedures at the clinical site. These measures will affect animal welfare.
3. Setting the standards under which source animals and the herds providing these animals should be kept with regard to the welfare of the animals. In doing so, liaising with the Home Office and other interested organisations as appropriate.
4. Ensuring that there were arrangements for long term surveillance and follow up of xenotransplantation recipients and advising on the analysis of the surveillance results as they became available. This would include the development of 'stopping rules' and their enforcement at the stage of clinical trials if necessary. Thereafter, there must be a mechanism to discontinue any therapeutic programme, if necessary.
5. Working with appropriate professional groups to take forward such matters as the complementary roles of these professionals. Training and professional registration for animal technicians and veterinary nurses.[6]

[6] Pp. 141–142, para. 9.3.

For the Kennedy Committee, the enforcement of UKXIRA's standards was also critical, and included the right of UKXIRA to inspect premises, approve animal facilities, approve those intending to undertake xenotransplantation procedures and approve applications for clinical trials with human subjects.[7] The Report proposed that these should be done under a licensing system, similar to that undertaken by the Human Fertilisation and Embryology Authority.[8]

In addition, the Report envisaged that the national standing body would give advice to Ministers, keep national and international developments under review, advise on developments which might give rise to public concern and on matters about consent, confidentiality and selection of patients,[9] all of which have already been shown to be highly problematic. Finally, UKXIRA would have what the Report called 'executive functions',[10] which would include maintaining a database of information about tissue recipients and of samples from source animals and recipients, and inspecting clinical sites.[11]

These are awesome responsibilities, yet they are arguably only one part of what is needed from the national body. The concerns identified in this review are of immense significance and UKXIRA is currently the sole body with the responsibility for addressing them. From the perspective presented here it seems evident that the role of UKXIRA will be significantly hampered unless statutory backing is provided. In this respect, therefore, the Kennedy Report would appear to be correct. In any event if UKXIRA is to act as a formal ethics committee for xenografting proposals, EU Directive 2001/20/EC[12] may require a re-evaluation of its status, at least in that aspect of its functions. The suitability of UKXIRA to perform these roles is in any event in doubt, adding further impetus to the call for a moratorium on clinical trials and research in this area.

The Kennedy Report was also concerned that membership of the committee – which should be independent, although funded by Government – must 'command the respect of the public', and 'therefore reflect an appropriate range of expertise and interests'.[13] This book has shown the firm view that the membership of UKXIRA should be realigned to reflect the complexity of the legal and ethical issues as well as the complexity of the science, and to ensure that the committee is kept abreast of developments in other initiatives in respect of organ transplantation. Indeed, as we were writing, UKXIRA had no permanent chairperson, no legal representation in its membership, and only one ethicist.[14]

---

7 Pp. 142–143, para. 9.3.

8 Established by the Human Fertilisation and Embryology Act 1990.

9 Kennedy Report, p. 144, para. 9.3.

10 P. 144, para. 9.4.

11 Ibid.

12 European Parliament and Council, 4 April 2001.

13 Kennedy Report, p. 146, para. 9.11.

14 In a press release dated September 2003 UKXIRA stated that it had made several changes to its membership. See http://www.advisorybodies.doh.gov.uk/ukxira/pressrelease_newmembers.PDF. However, it is understood from personal communication with the UKXIRA Secretariat that since this press release the interim chair has had to stand down, leaving UKXIRA without a chair, and also that UKXIRA currently has no-one with legal expertise amongst its membership.

Additionally, we have has hypothesized that the differences in the types of xenotransplantation which are carried out may mean that the requirements, for example of surveillance and life-long monitoring, may not be necessary in some areas. For the moment, UKXIRA has indicated that no evidence exists to support claims that extra-corporeal or cellular treatments are any safer than the use of whole organs, and has restated its concerns about xenotransplantation safety. UKXIRA is right to be cautious, but it also has a vital role to play in discovering whether or not its current position is evidence-based.

Summary

This book has highlighted a number of issues which have generated both interest in, and concern about, xenotransplantation. These are summarized below for convenience.

There remains a significant shortage of organs for transplantation into humans which is unlikely to be removed by recourse to any alternative schemes, such as presumed consent. Even were all of the options discussed in chapter 1 adopted simultaneously, there might still be a shortfall between supply and demand. Xenotransplantation, therefore, might still be considered as a legitimate or viable source of organs. None of the proposed alternatives to the current system is without legal and ethical problems, which would need to be resolved, just as they would with xenotransplantation. However, the ethical and legal concerns raised by xenotransplantation are considerably more significant than those associated with the alternatives. In any event, it seems likely that xenotransplantation may not be the technique to hold the most promise. The potential of stem cell research may in fact overtake xenotransplantation as a treatment of choice for the future. The report of the Government's Chief Medical Officer on stem cell research evaluated its potential as follows:

> In the long term there could be considerable potential for the use of tissues derived from stem cells in the treatment of a wide range of disorders by replacing cells that have become damaged or diseased ... In addition to this potential to develop tissue for use in the repair of failing organs, or for replacement of diseased or damaged tissues, the technique of cell nuclear replacement might be applied to treat some rare but serious inherited disorders.[15]

There are, of course, ethical concerns surrounding stem cell research, but assuming the potential to be there, developments in the use of cord blood and recent reports of success with adult stem cells suggests that these difficulties may be overcome. Stem cell therapy may then have the potential both to assist in the prevention of disorders which may lead to organ failure and to provide the means to treat these conditions. Stem cells may also offer assistance in the kinds of conditions to which cellular xenotransplantation addresses itself.

---

[15] Department of Health (2000), *Stem Cell Research: Medical Progress with Responsibility, Report of the CMO's Expert Group*, HMSO: London.

The legal and ethical problems in xenotransplantation are even more substantial than those inherent in other systems. The primary concerns about the use of animals can be addressed by ethical review, but cannot be resolved by it. In addition insufficient attempts have been made to gauge the public's response to animal to human transplantation.

The legal questions surrounding important matters such as consent are enormously complex and have been paid insufficient attention. This book contends that the treatment of these matters by the Nuffield and Kennedy Reports is inadequately robust and much more work is needed to inform the public of the possible risks of xenotransplantation, as well as seeking to gauge its attitudes to it. In addition, UKXIRA has not focused sufficiently on this issue. It will be recalled that the report of the Surveillance Steering Group stated that a detailed consideration of this issue was beyond its remit. However, it did not indicate what the correct forum to conduct a detailed assessment of consent and other ethico-legal issues might be.

Ethical assessment of xenotransplantation must be viewed as 'work in progress' as this is the only way in which scientific developments can be subject to rigorous ethical assessment. In light of the shortcomings identified with the work of the Kennedy Report and UKXIRA's remit, such iterative ethical work is dependent on some form of dynamic ethical framework being developed, along with ways to implement it.

It is recommended that ethical analyses of xenotransplantation should draw on a wide range of disciplines. If this is to be achieved, the regulatory agency with responsibility for ethically assessing xenotransplantation must encompass the views, not only of those with an interest in xenotransplantation, but also of those working in other areas of transplantation and of those seeking to overcome the shortage of organs in other ways. The ethical acceptability of animal to human transplantation is heavily dependent on this wider picture.

If xenotransplantation is to proceed to clinical trials and even beyond, the legal and ethical implications of surveillance programmes require a far more in-depth consideration than they have been given to date. All attempts to address this question have arguably taken insufficient account of the legal complexities, and have seemed content to assume that people will co-operate. This is a major, and highly speculative, assumption which cannot be sufficient to mandate the practical application of potentially high risk technologies.

Currently, attempts to develop a clinically viable cardiac assist device suggest that continued ethical work on cardiac xenotransplantation is highly problematic. This issue must be subject to urgent scientific and ethical review to determine whether public policy can legitimately allow research on this form of animal to human transplantation to continue. This assertion is reinforced by the fact that the UK Government is funding trials of cardiac assist devices to start in 2005.[16] While this technology may not be suitable for all cardiac patients, it does suggest that artificial organ technology is currently more advanced in some areas than cardiac xenogeneic research. Given the greater costs associated with the less successful

[16] The UK Government recently announced that it will begin trials of artificial heart pumps in 2005, *Sunday Times*, 23 May 2004, p. 11.

xenogeneic research, it is questionable whether it should be permitted to continue without a wide-ranging review of all other potential therapies.

Significant doubts remain about the capacity of individuals to agree to participation in clinical trials of xenotransplantation. Additionally, the critical role of third parties in the decision-making process is, at best, legally unusual and appears to conflict with existing rules about consent to treatment. Further, doubts also remain about whether or not sufficient consideration has been given to the selection of patients for xenotransplantation clinical trials.

Nation states must take seriously their responsibility for global safety, as required by international law. They must also be alert to the possibility of liability devolving on them for harm caused elsewhere, for example by the spread into the world's population of hitherto unknown infections resulting from xenotransplantation. They must take seriously their obligations under international humanitarian and human rights law, as well as their commitments to future generations. Xenotransplantation could be an enormously expensive procedure for the health service, especially for as long as it is market driven, and matters of the just allocation of health resources must be given attention both at the macro and the micro level.

Conclusions

If the United Kingdom comes to formally accept the definition of xenotransplantation which is now used in the United States, it will be the case that xenotransplants will have been taking place in the UK and elsewhere for some time. This has occurred without scrutiny and without the public agreement which many commentators believe to be necessary. That no apparent harm has resulted is to be welcomed, but the fact that xenotransplants have occurred without regulation also shows the way in which scientific advance can become clinical reality without the ethical and legal concerns being adequately explored. These concerns are clearly more acute in solid organ xenotransplantation, but all xenografting 'crosses a species barrier that has evolved over millions of years' and requires 'an approach different from that usually taken in the evaluation of new medical technologies'.[17]

Given the issues this book has discussed, it seems clear that appropriate regulation, with a clear ethical and legal remit is necessary in order to develop that 'different approach'. At present, that regulation is absent in the UK. Although UKXIRA has done much good work, there are legitimate grounds for criticism also. Certainly, accepting applications without having developed an intellectually coherent ethical or legal regime gives the wrong signals to would-be researchers, and suggests that the UK is nearer to accepting the move to clinical trials than it probably is. An overarching regulatory body such as UKXIRA needs to devise targets for how much research is enough to progress to trials. These targets need broad scientific and ethical agreement. If it appears that these targets cannot be reached in a timescale similar to other options, then we believe that xenogeneic

[17] Bach, F.H. et al. (1998), 'Uncertainty in Xenotransplantation: Individual Benefit Versus Collective Risk', *Nature Medicine*, **4**, pp. 141–144, at p. 141.

research on animals should stop. Moreover, the ethical analysis of xenotransplantation is insufficiently robust if based firmly on a cost-benefit analysis which has no way of accurately measuring costs, particularly costs to animals. UKXIRA can only operate within the framework it has been given; if it is to meet our concerns, that remit needs to be revised and extended.

It is also surprising that the ethical review on which UKXIRA was based (the Kennedy Report) has not been updated in more than eight years. Review of ethical and legal issues must be iterative if it is to be useful. Moreover, public engagement is critical and must also be iterative and up to date,[18] and should expose the public not simply to the science but also to the ethical and legal dilemmas with which the regulatory body is engaged. Indeed, Article 30 of the Council of Europe's 2003 Recommendation states:

> In accordance with the principles stated in Article 28 of the Convention on Human Rights and Biomedicine, member states should take active steps to ensure that the fundamental questions raised by xenotransplantation are the subject of appropriate public discussion particularly in light of relevant medical, psychological, cultural, ethical, legal, social and economic implications.[19]

Statutory backing for the regulatory body is imperative. Not only does it give the regulator 'teeth', but a statutory remit would build into the system the safeguards which come from the compatibility requirement with the Human Rights Act 1998. The regulatory framework must be designed 'to assure the respect for the fundamental rights of the people that undergo this kind of treatment'.[20] This requires that ethical and legal analysis are firmly built into the design of the regulator, as has occurred, for example, in Sweden.

Caution in simply following science to its logical conclusion is not unique to xenotransplantation, but it is of vital importance. As Incorvati says:

> Xenotransplantation involves decision making in a medical and scientific context with many uncertainties at all stages of the process. Here, the problems relating to risks are more important than in other fields not simply because they involve both human and animal life, but because they are not limited to the present and extend to future generations. It is no longer the individual or society that may be at risk but the human species itself.[21]

Interestingly, it is arguments about the risk to future generations which have proved persuasive in outlawing germline gene therapy, arguably a considerably less risky scientific possibility than xenotransplantation.

Additionally, there is risk to the welfare of the animals upon whom research and genetic modification will be undertaken. That welfare is not limited to physical harm, and the need to consider other matters is enshrined in the European

---

18 At the time of writing, UKXIRA's website still had a press release from 2003 as 'latest news'.

19 Council of Europe (2003) 10 of the Committee of Ministers to member states on xenotransplantation (adopted 19 June 2003).

20 Melo, H., Brandao, C., Rego, G. and Nunes, R. (2001), 'Ethical and Legal Issues in Xenotransplantation', *Bioethics*, **15** (5/6), at p. 441.

21 Incorvati, G. (2003), 'Xenotransplantation, Public Responsibility and Law', *European Journal of Health Law*, **10** (295), at pp. 299–300.

Convention for the Protection of Vertebrate Animals Used for Experimental and Other Scientific Purposes, which declares that:

> Any restriction on the extent to which an animal can satisfy its physiological and ethological needs shall be limited as far as practicable.[22]

Moreover, the same Convention states that '[a] procedure shall not be performed ... if another scientifically satisfactory method, not entailing the use of an animal, is reasonably and practicably available'.[23]

This latter requirement leads to a brief, but necessary, diversion from the subject of xenotransplantation. It has already been noted that the Kennedy Report proposed that, were alternatives available, xenotransplantation should not be contemplated, given the range of ethical, legal and welfare issues raised by it. At present, it is not possible to say with certainty that such an alternative does exist, but (and this is a further reason for adopting the recommended iterative approach) there is considerable reason to believe that an alternative is on the scientific horizon, namely stem cell research. Campbell, for example, says, '[f]ew could doubt the amazing potential for human benefit in this line of research, if the predictions of the scientists are correct'.[24] However, insufficient attention has been paid to the risks of xenotransplantation. He also cautions that:

> We need to carry out the moral groundwork very carefully, and especially we need to continue to find ways of allocating appropriate moral values to the complexity of our origins as humans.[25]

An evaluation of the potential of stem cells in the future is clearly outwith the scope of this book. However, its possibilities should be borne in mind when considering the ethics of pursuing and investing in xenotransplantation.

Given this analysis of the ethics and law surrounding xenotransplantation, it seems clear that there are few, if any, reasons to contemplate proceeding to clinical trials, at least in solid organ xenografting, and good reasons to require adequate regulation of cellular xenotransplantation. Although the need for a regulatory body remains, currently a moratorium on clinical trials is desirable and in the future a moratorium may also be required on some or all xenotransplantation research. Until we can adequately address the benefits and disbenefits of xenotransplantation, the state's obligation is 'the protection of the general public's health and safety'.[26] While 'it would surely be negligent to deny human beings the benefits and protections of new technology one moment longer than is necessary',[27] that moment is not now.

---

22 Strasbourg, 18.III.1986, ETS:123.

23 Ibid., article 6.1.

24 Campbell, A.V. (2000), 'Ethical Issues in Therapeutic Cloning', in The European Group in Science and New Technologies to the European Commission, *Opinion No 15, Adoption of an Opinion on Ethical Aspects of Human Stem Cell Research and Use*, European Commission: Paris, 14 November (revised edition, September 2002), at p. 130.

25 Ibid.

26 Malich, G., Braun, M., Panayotis, L. and Winder, C. (1998), 'Comparison of Regulations Concerning Hazardous Substances from an International Perspective', *Journal of Hazardous Materials*, **62** (143), at p. 144.

27 Harris, J. (1994), 'The Ethics of National Ethics Committees', *Journal of the Royal College of Physicians of London*, **28** (323), at p. 324.

Index

For Product Safety Concerns and Information please contact our EU representative GPSR@taylorandfrancis.com
Taylor & Francis Verlag GmbH, Kaufingerstraße 24, 80331 München, Germany

www.ingramcontent.com/pod-product-compliance
Ingram Content Group UK Ltd.
Pitfield, Milton Keynes, MK11 3LW, UK
UKHW010956180926
475701UK00004B/401

* 9 7 8 1 1 3 8 3 5 8 6 5 2 *